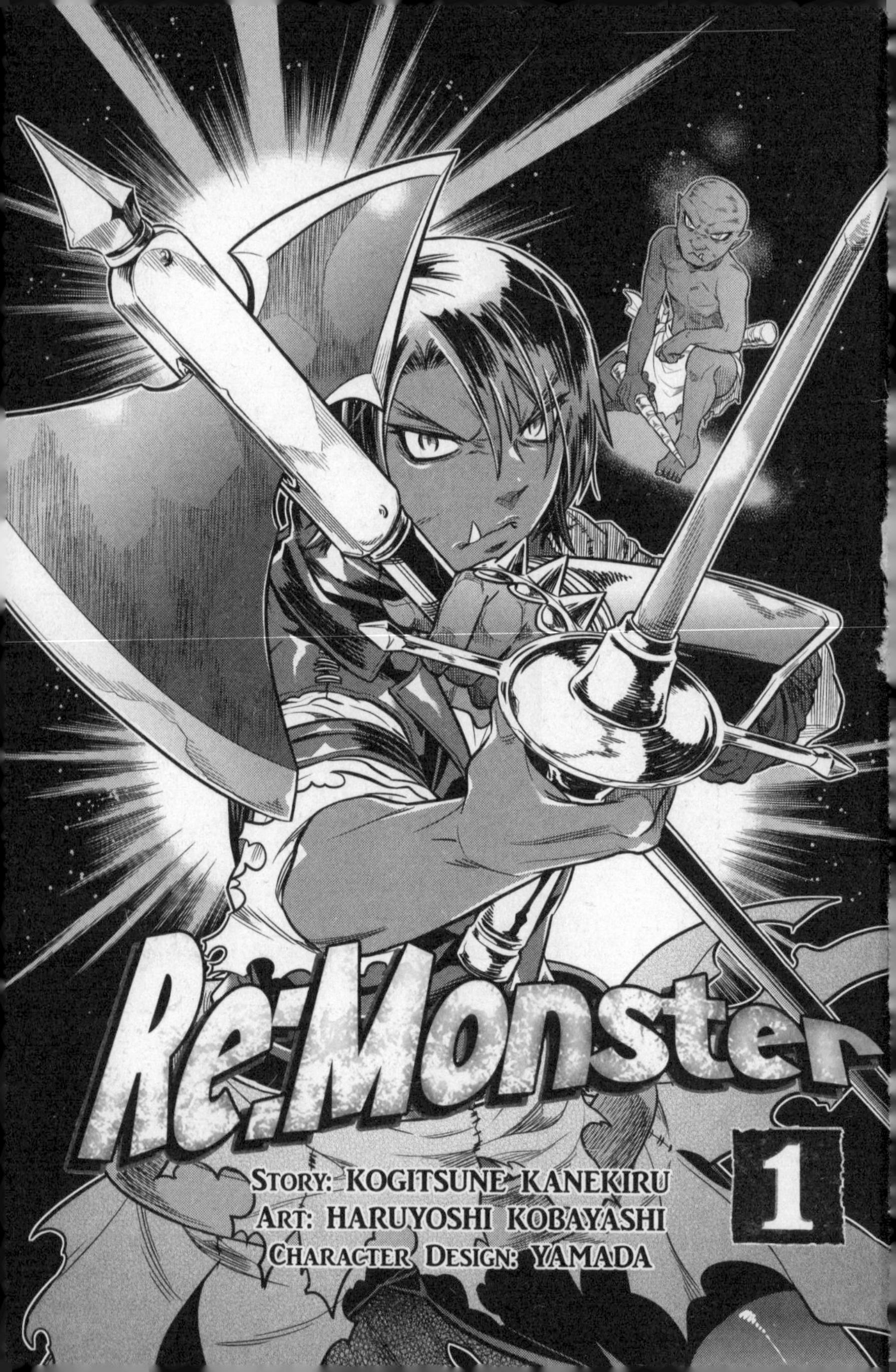

Re:Monster
1
STORY: KOGITSUNE KANEKIRU
ART: HARUYOSHI KOBAYASHI
CHARACTER DESIGN: YAMADA

Re:Monster

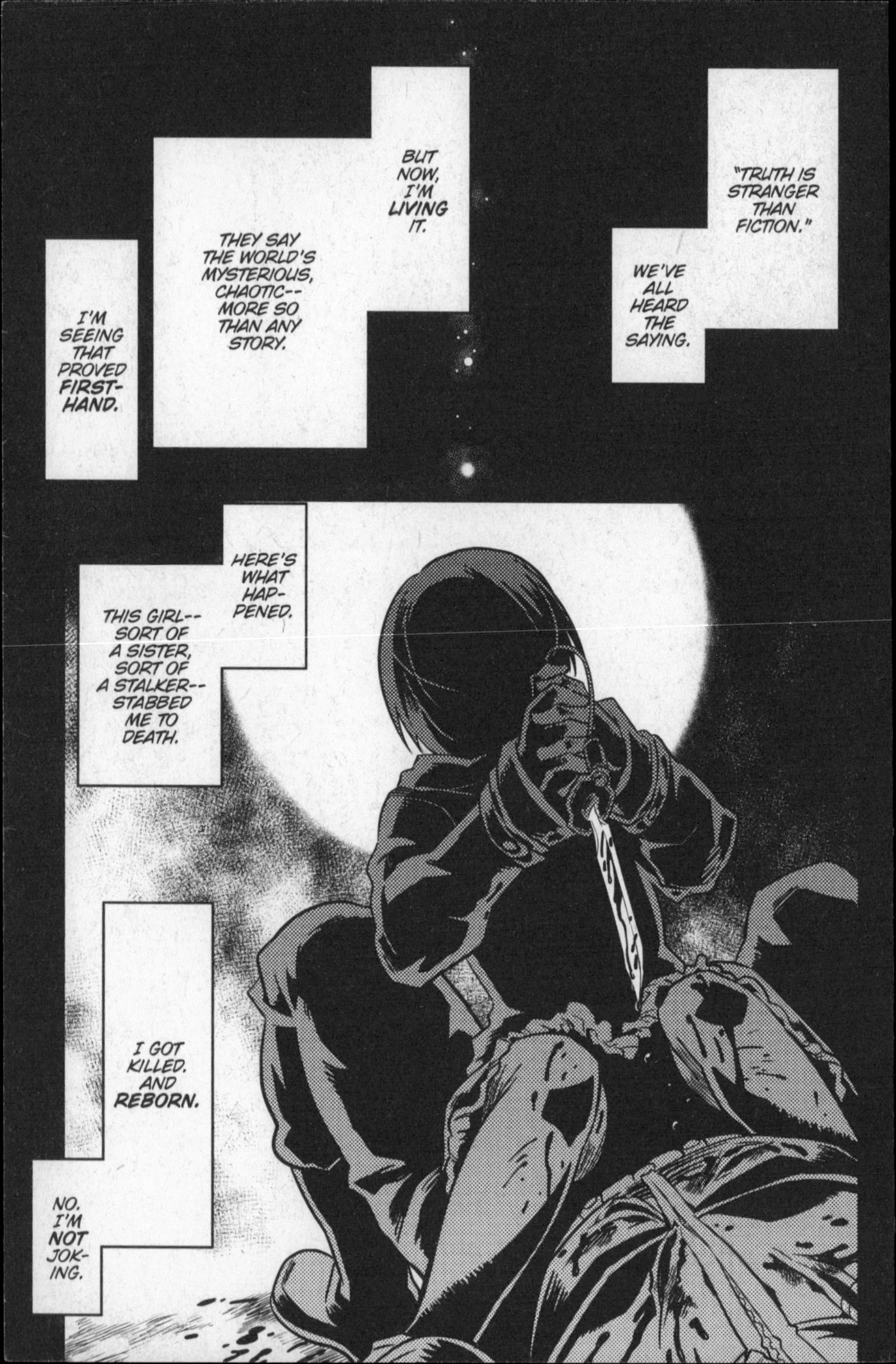
"TRUTH IS STRANGER THAN FICTION."
WE'VE ALL HEARD THE SAYING.
BUT NOW, I'M LIVING IT.
THEY SAY THE WORLD'S MYSTERIOUS, CHAOTIC-- MORE SO THAN ANY STORY.
I'M SEEING THAT PROVED FIRST-HAND.
HERE'S WHAT HAP-PENED.
THIS GIRL-- SORT OF A SISTER, SORT OF A STALKER-- STABBED ME TO DEATH.
I GOT KILLED. AND REBORN.
NO. I'M NOT JOK-ING.

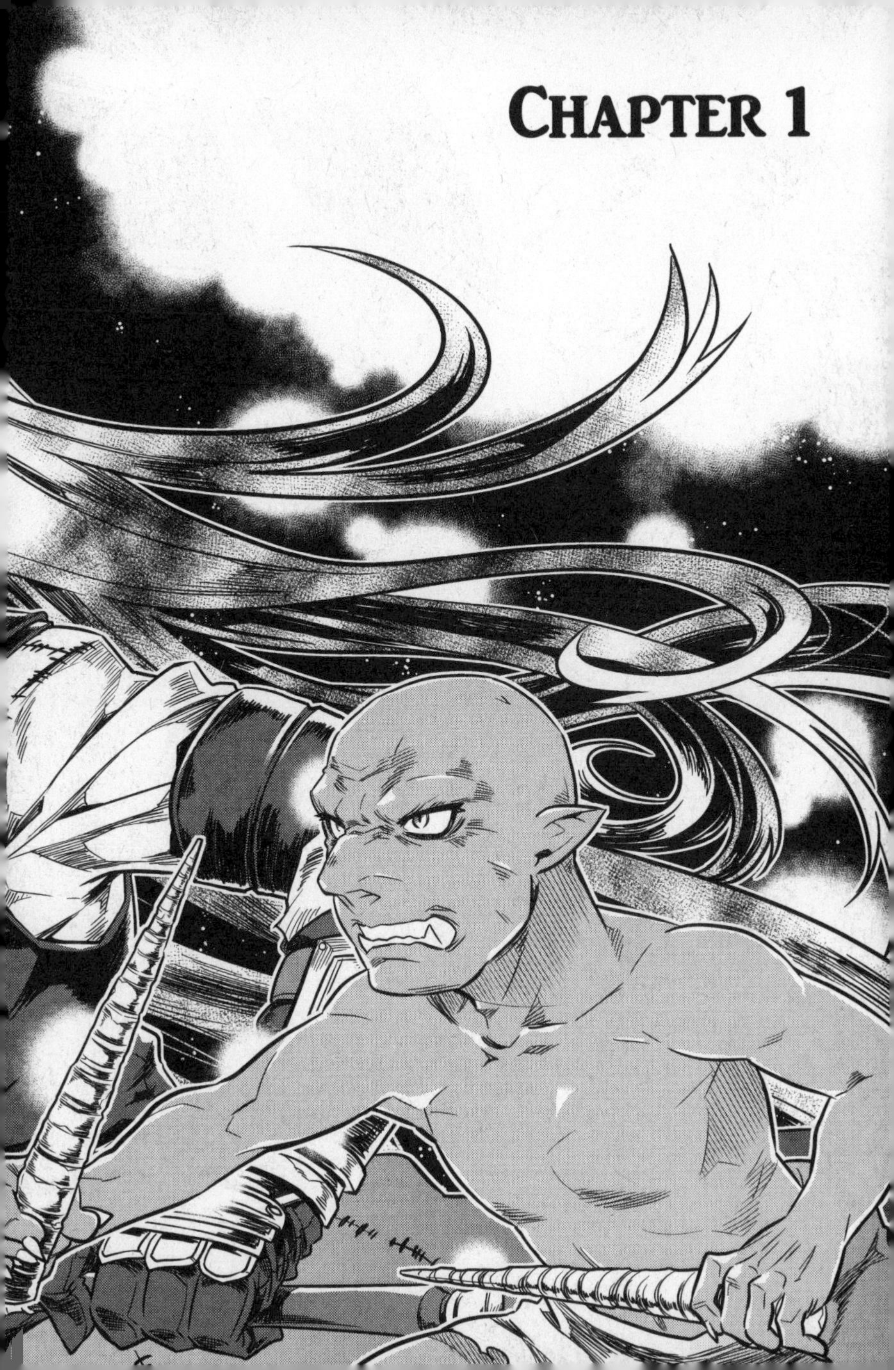
CHAPTER 1

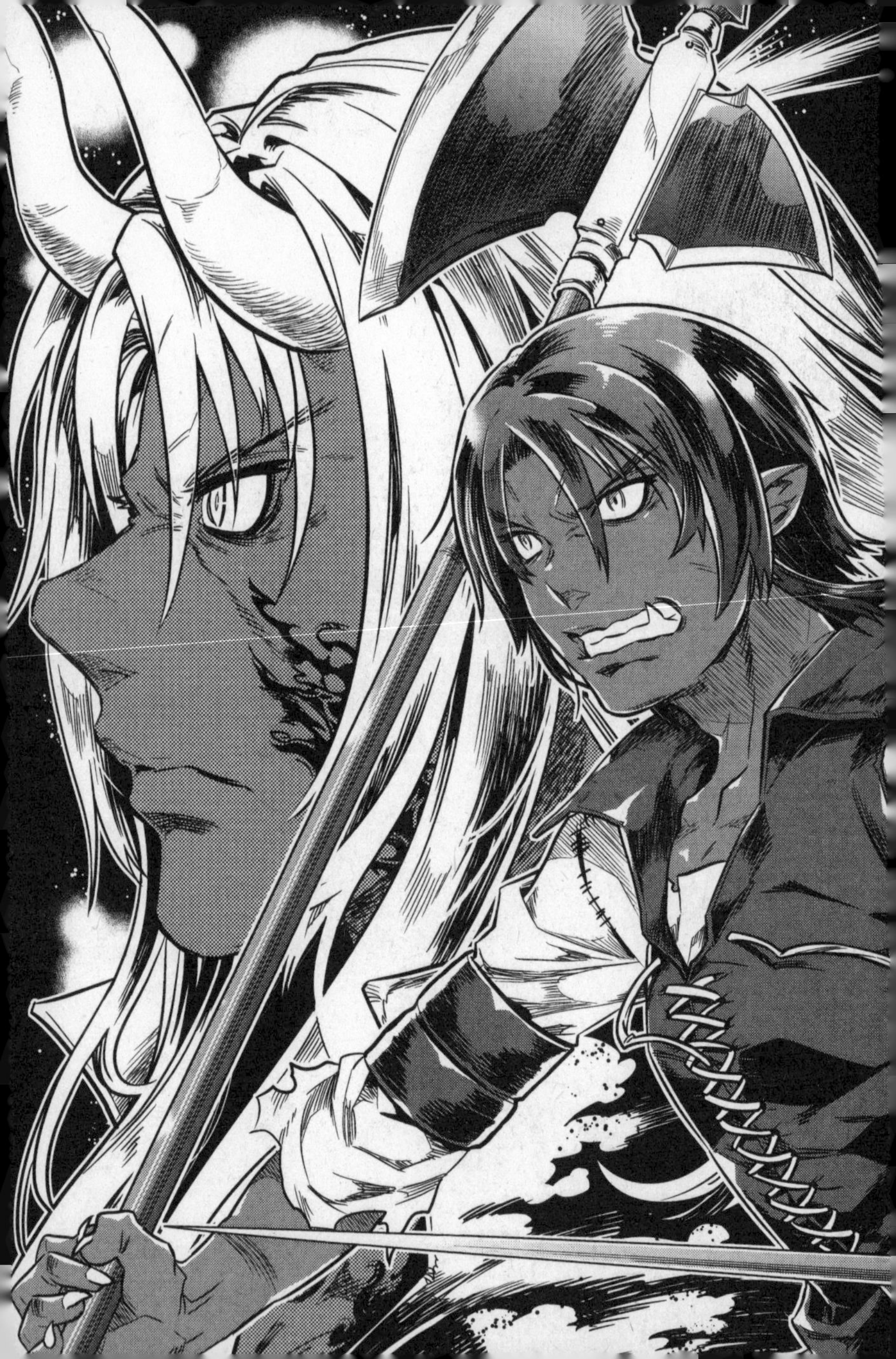

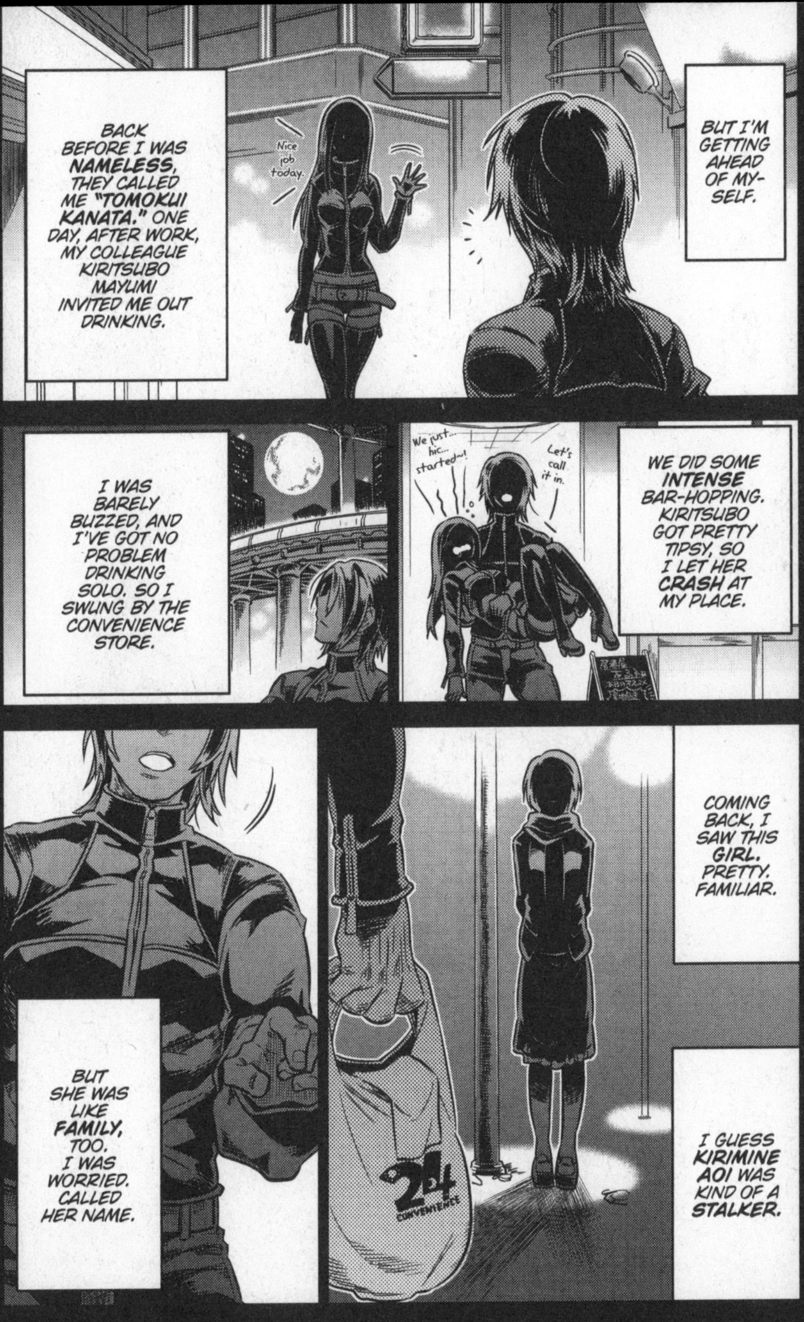
BUT I'M GETTING AHEAD OF MYSELF.
BACK BEFORE I WAS NAMELESS, THEY CALLED ME "TOMOKUI KANATA." ONE DAY, AFTER WORK, MY COLLEAGUE KIRITSUBO MAYUMI INVITED ME OUT DRINKING.
Nice job today.
WE DID SOME INTENSE BAR-HOPPING. KIRITSUBO GOT PRETTY TIPSY, SO I LET HER CRASH AT MY PLACE.
Let's call it in.
We just... hic... started~!
I WAS BARELY BUZZED, AND I'VE GOT NO PROBLEM DRINKING SOLO. SO I SWUNG BY THE CONVENIENCE STORE.
COMING BACK, I SAW THIS GIRL. PRETTY. FAMILIAR.
I GUESS KIRIMINE AOI WAS KIND OF A STALKER.
24 CONVENIENCE
BUT SHE WAS LIKE FAMILY, TOO. I WAS WORRIED. CALLED HER NAME.

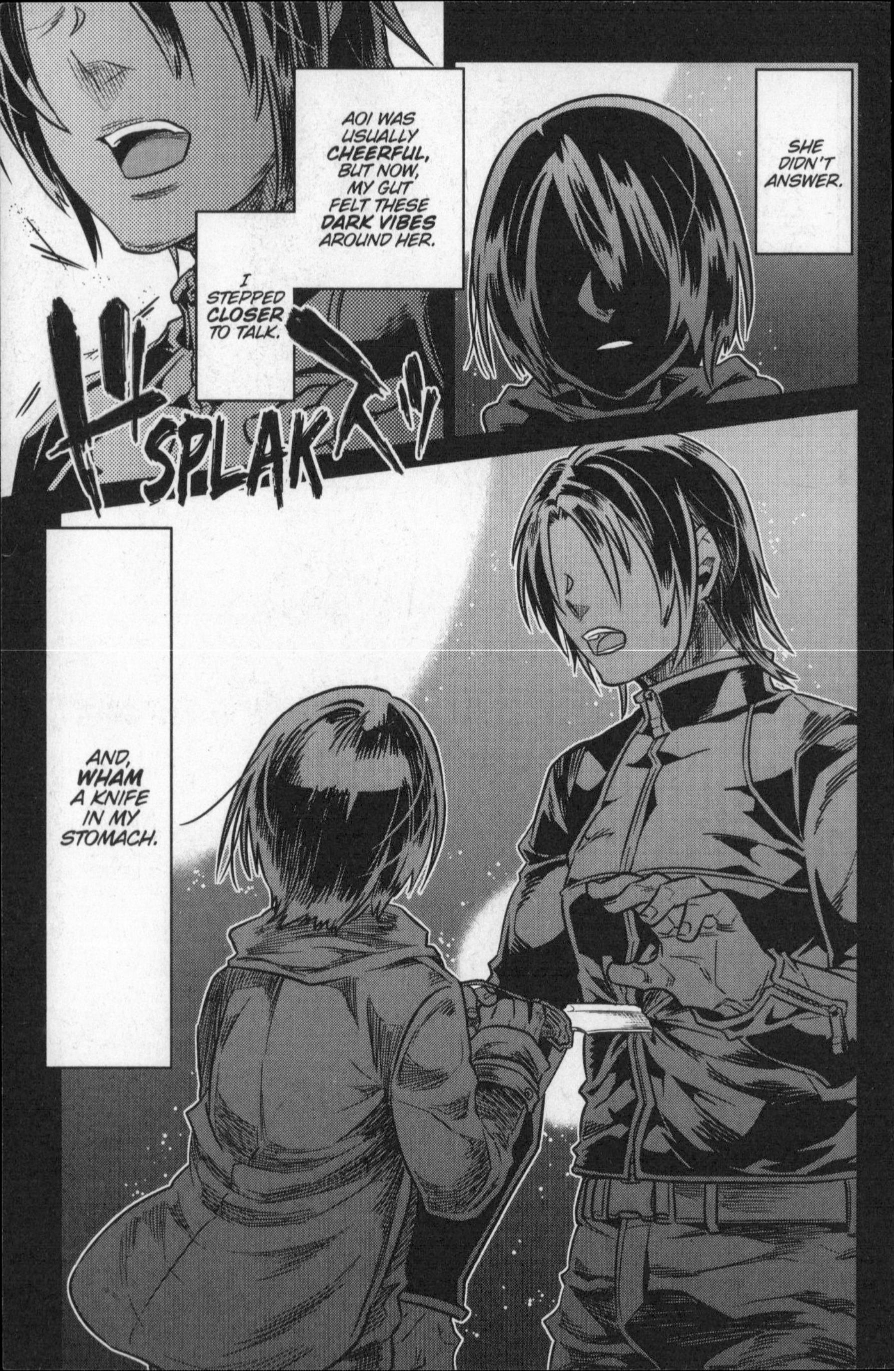
SHE DIDN'T ANSWER.
AOI WAS USUALLY CHEERFUL, BUT NOW, MY GUT FELT THESE DARK VIBES AROUND HER.
I STEPPED CLOSER TO TALK.
SPLAK
AND, WHAM A KNIFE IN MY STOMACH.

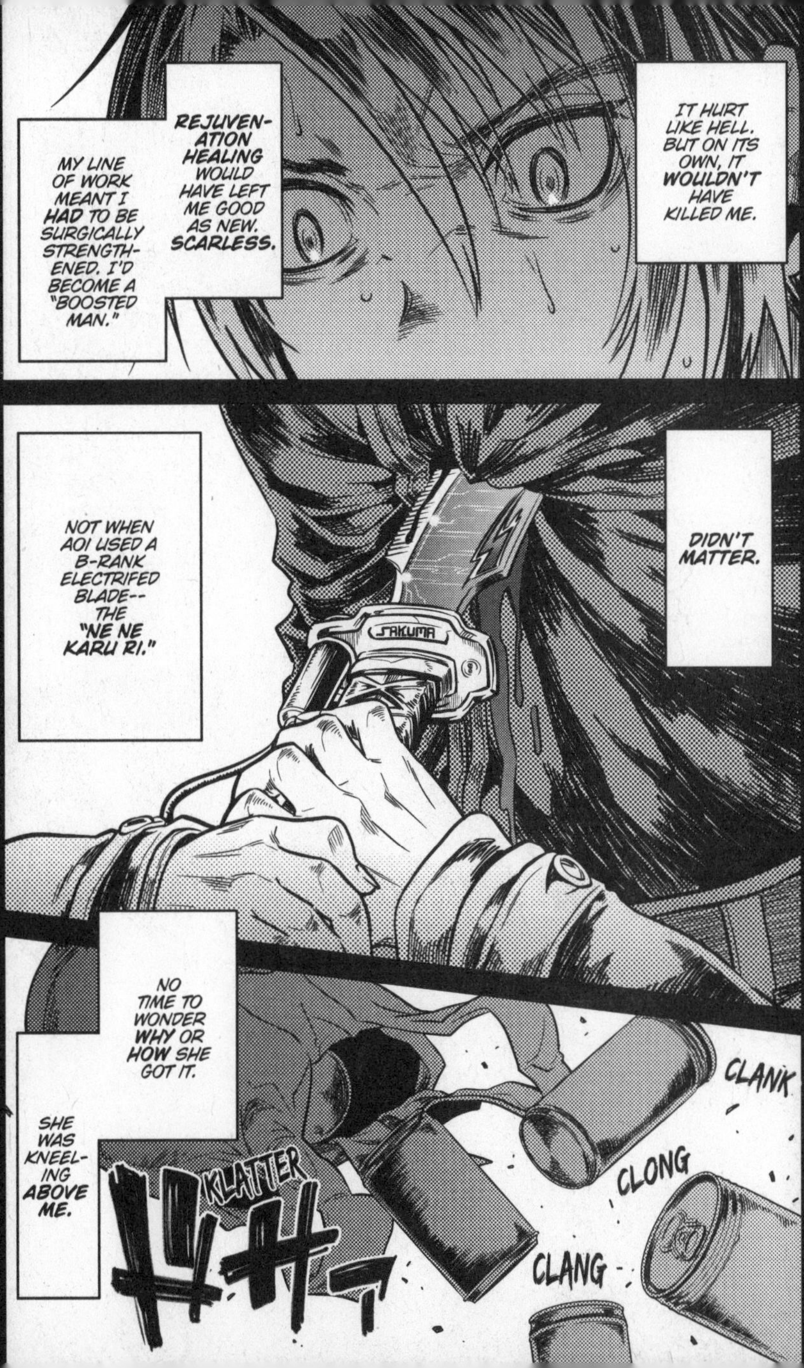

IT HURT LIKE HELL. BUT ON ITS OWN, IT WOULDN'T HAVE KILLED ME.
REJUVEN-ATION HEALING WOULD HAVE LEFT ME GOOD AS NEW. SCARLESS.
MY LINE OF WORK MEANT I HAD TO BE SURGICALLY STRENGTH-ENED. I'D BECOME A "BOOSTED MAN."
DIDN'T MATTER.
NOT WHEN AOI USED A B-RANK ELECTRIFED BLADE-- THE "NE NE KARU RI."
SAKUMA
NO TIME TO WONDER WHY OR HOW SHE GOT IT.
CLANK
CLONG
CLANG
KLATTER
SHE WAS KNEEL-ING ABOVE ME.

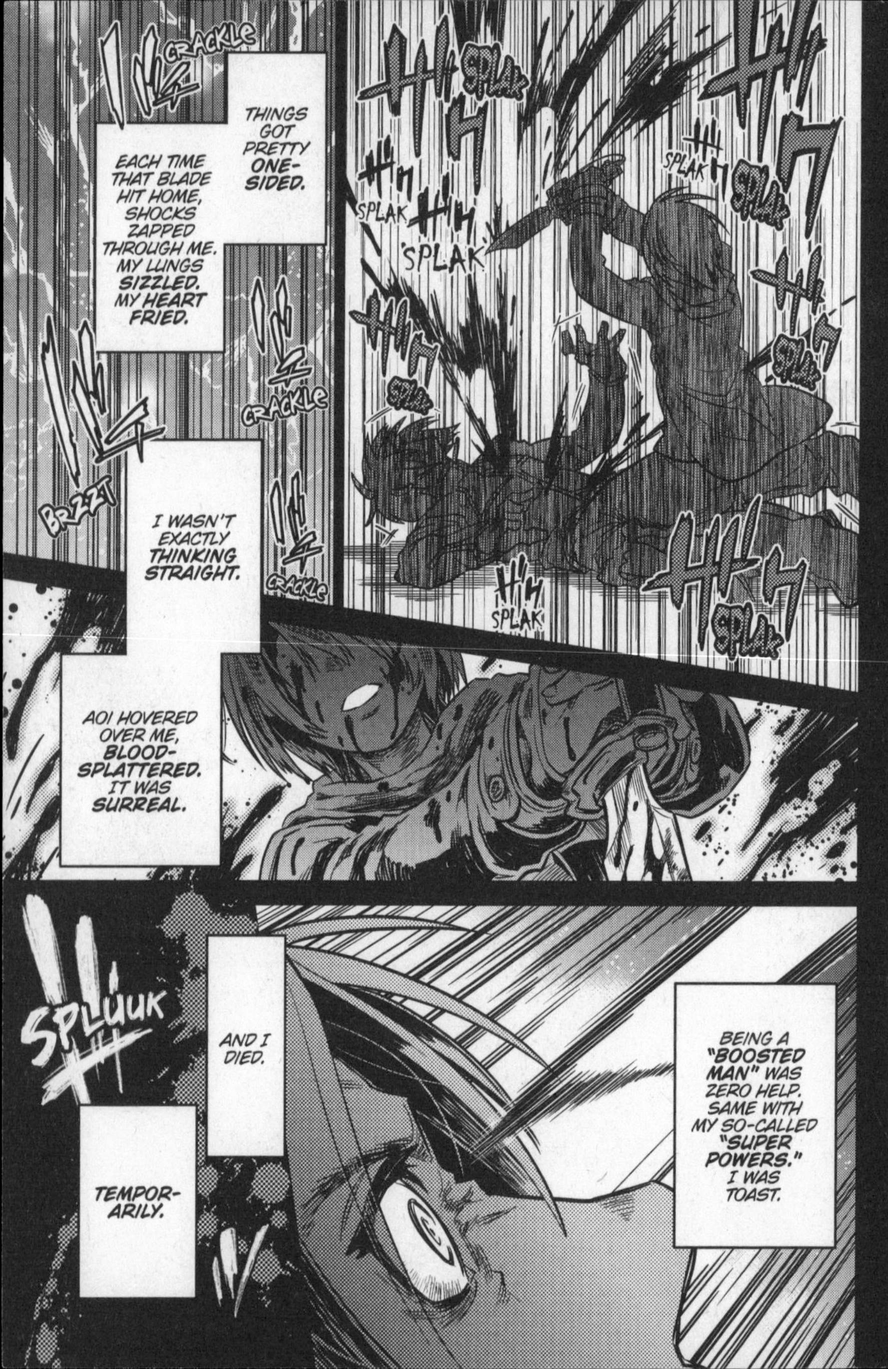
SPLAK
SPLAK
SPLAK
SPLAK
SPLAK
SPLAK
SPLAK
SPLAK
CRACKLE
THINGS GOT PRETTY ONE-SIDED.
EACH TIME THAT BLADE HIT HOME, SHOCKS ZAPPED THROUGH ME. MY LUNGS SIZZLED. MY HEART FRIED.
CRACKLE
BRZZT
I WASN'T EXACTLY THINKING STRAIGHT.
CRACKLE
AOI HOVERED OVER ME, BLOOD-SPLATTERED. IT WAS SURREAL.
BEING A "BOOSTED MAN" WAS ZERO HELP. SAME WITH MY SO-CALLED "SUPER POWERS." I WAS TOAST.
AND I DIED.
TEMPORARILY.
SPLUUK

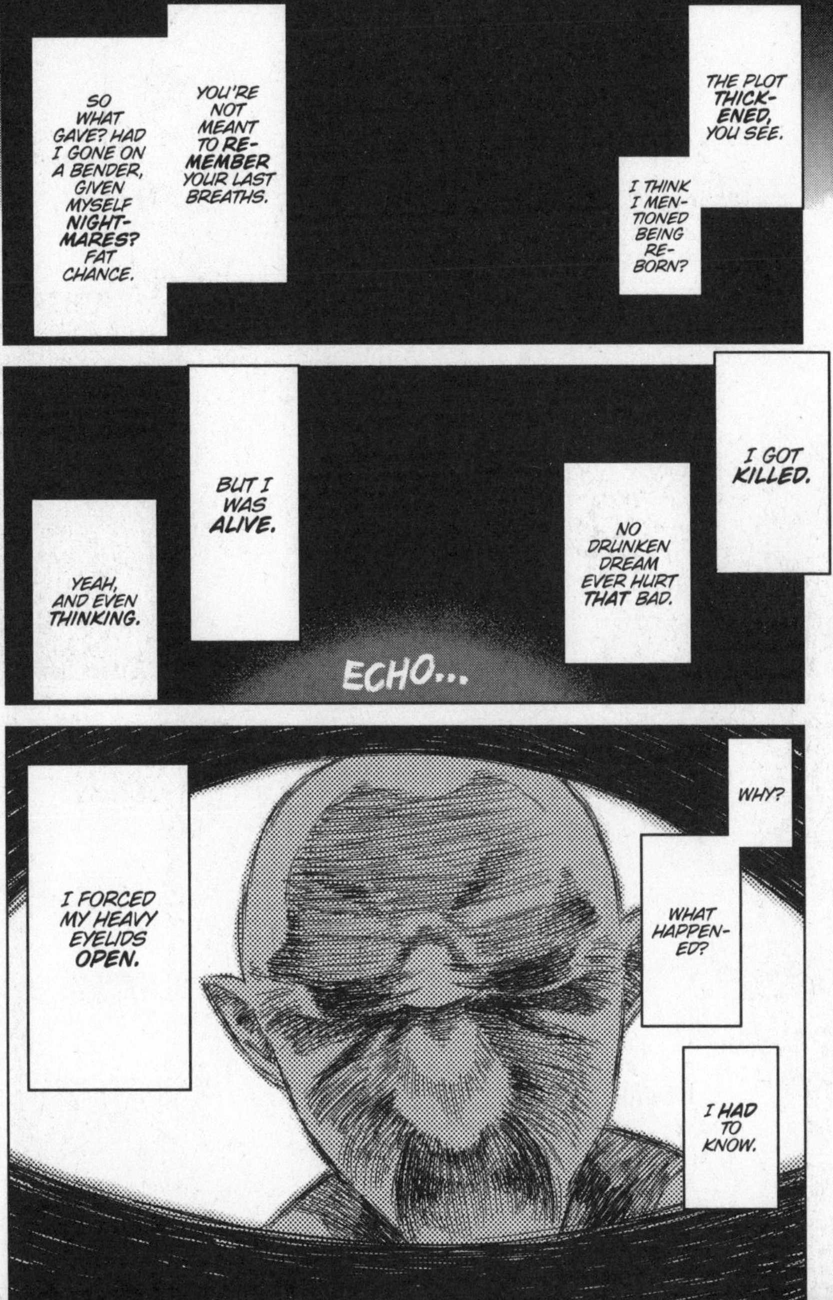
THE PLOT THICKENED, YOU SEE.
I THINK I MENTIONED BEING REBORN?
YOU'RE NOT MEANT TO REMEMBER YOUR LAST BREATHS.
SO WHAT GAVE? HAD I GONE ON A BENDER, GIVEN MYSELF NIGHTMARES? FAT CHANCE.
I GOT KILLED.
NO DRUNKEN DREAM EVER HURT THAT BAD.
ECHO...
BUT I WAS ALIVE.
YEAH, AND EVEN THINKING.
WHY?
WHAT HAPPENED?
I HAD TO KNOW.
I FORCED MY HEAVY EYELIDS OPEN.

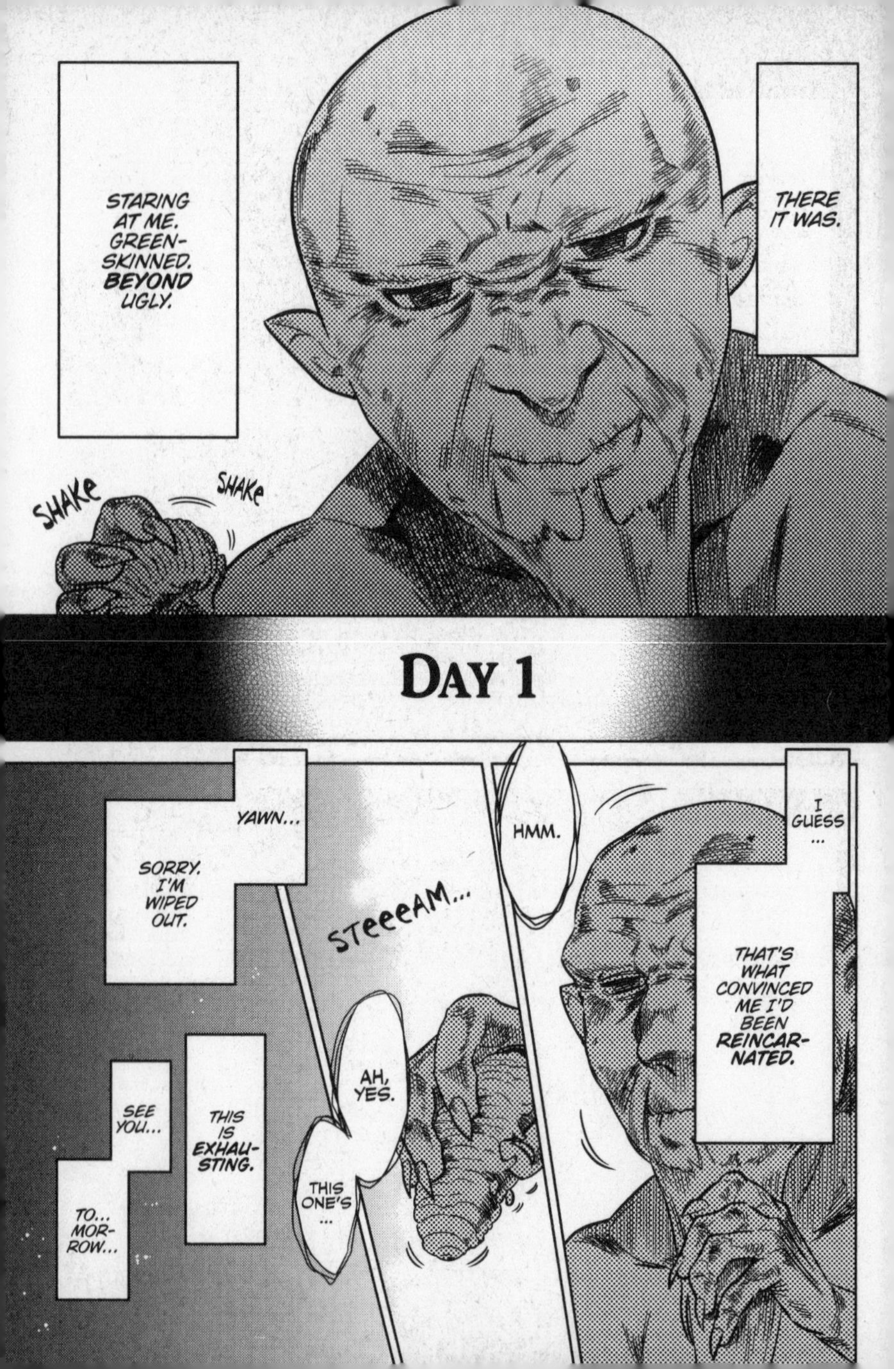
THERE IT WAS.
STARING AT ME. GREEN-SKINNED. BEYOND UGLY.
SHAKE
SHAKE
DAY 1
I GUESS...
THAT'S WHAT CONVINCED ME I'D BEEN REINCARNATED.
HMM.
AH, YES.
THIS ONE'S...
STEEEAM...
YAWN...
SORRY. I'M WIPED OUT.
THIS IS EXHAUSTING.
SEE YOU...
TO... MORROW...

DAY 2

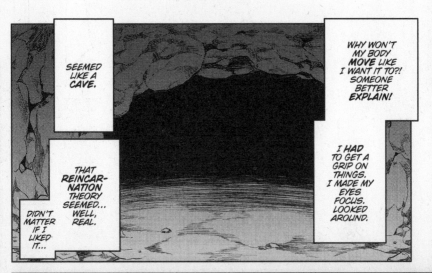

WHY WON'T MY BODY MOVE LIKE I WANT IT TO?! SOMEONE BETTER EXPLAIN!
I HAD TO GET A GRIP ON THINGS. I MADE MY EYES FOCUS. LOOKED AROUND.
SEEMED LIKE A CAVE.
THAT REINCARNATION THEORY SEEMED... WELL, REAL.
DIDN'T MATTER IF I LIKED IT...
I HAD A FUTURE TO ATTEND TO.
GURGLE
GAH
GOO GAH!
WAH
I WAS SURROUNDED BY ABOUT THREE THOUSAND UGLY GREEN RUNTS. ALL FAST ASLEEP.
YOU COULDN'T CALL THEM ANYTHING BUT GOBLINS.

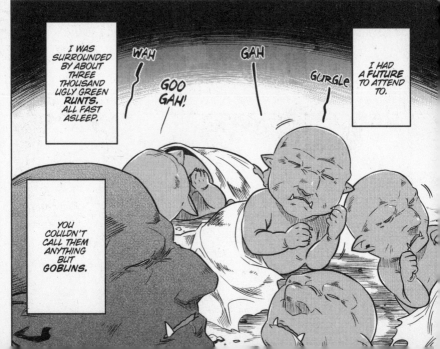

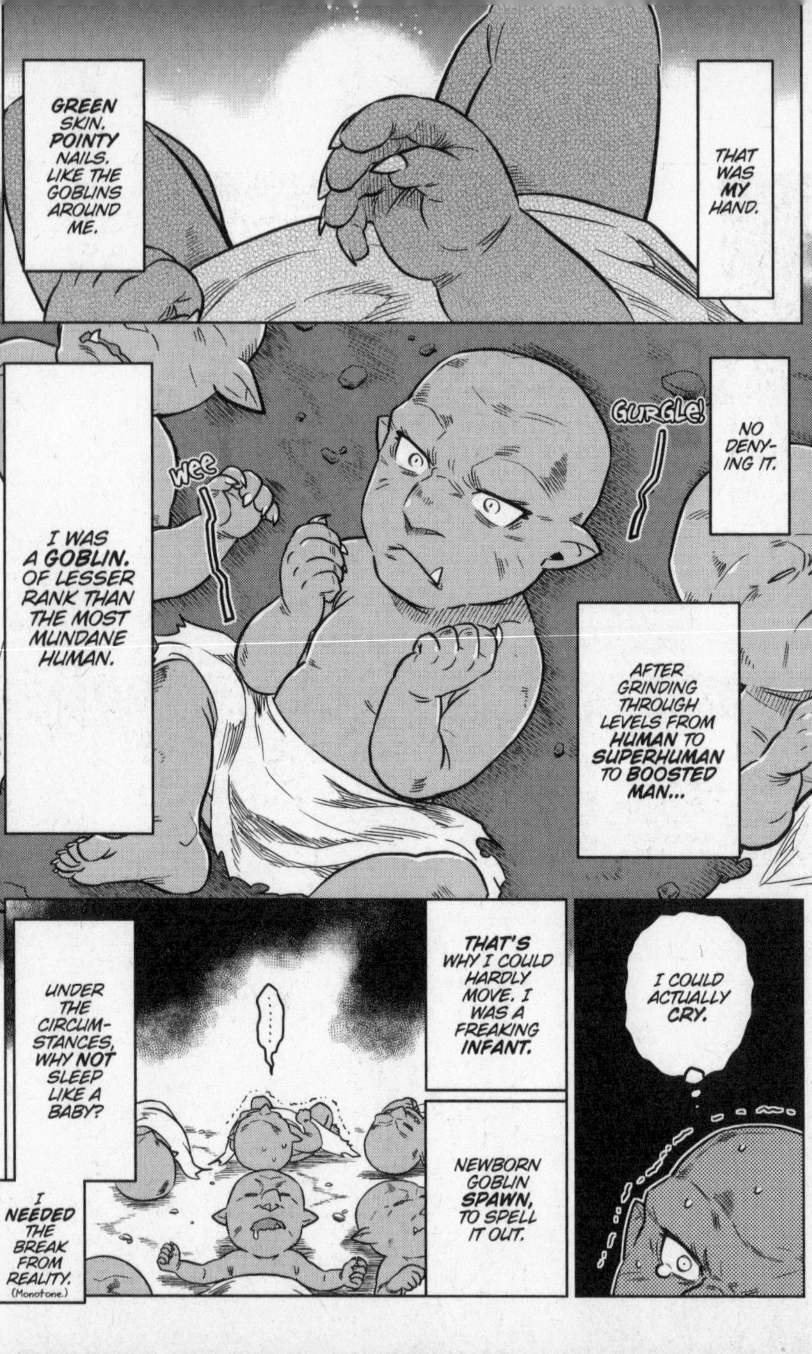
THAT WAS MY HAND.
GREEN SKIN. POINTY NAILS. LIKE THE GOBLINS AROUND ME.
NO DENYING IT.
GURGLE!
AFTER GRINDING THROUGH LEVELS FROM HUMAN TO SUPERHUMAN TO BOOSTED MAN...
wee
I WAS A GOBLIN. OF LESSER RANK THAN THE MOST MUNDANE HUMAN.
I COULD ACTUALLY CRY.
THAT'S WHY I COULD HARDLY MOVE. I WAS A FREAKING INFANT.
NEWBORN GOBLIN SPAWN, TO SPELL IT OUT.
UNDER THE CIRCUM-STANCES, WHY NOT SLEEP LIKE A BABY?
......
I NEEDED THE BREAK FROM REALITY.
(Monotone.)

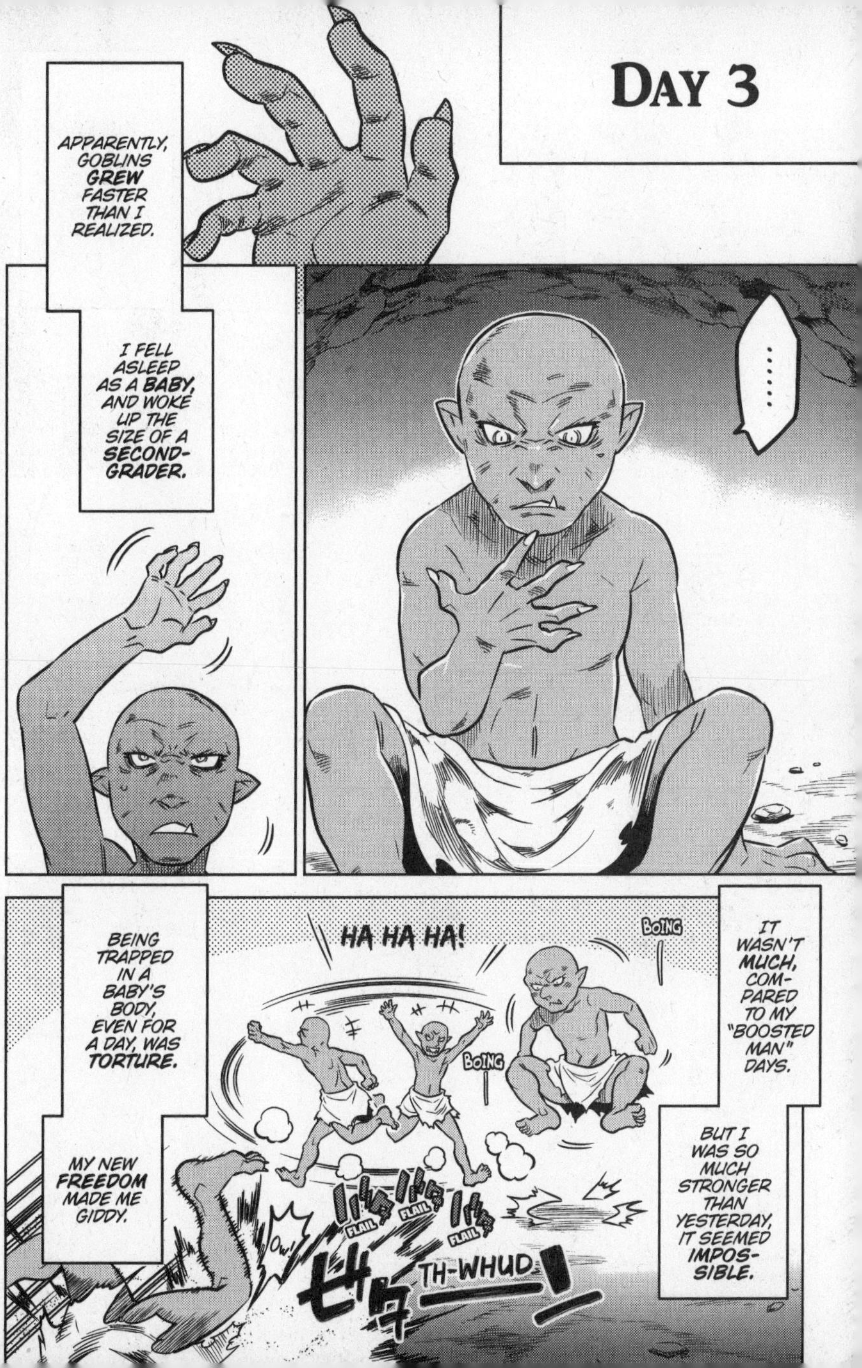
DAY 3
APPARENTLY, GOBLINS GREW FASTER THAN I REALIZED.
......
I FELL ASLEEP AS A BABY, AND WOKE UP THE SIZE OF A SECOND-GRADER.
IT WASN'T MUCH, COMPARED TO MY "BOOSTED MAN" DAYS.
BOING
HA HA HA!
BEING TRAPPED IN A BABY'S BODY, EVEN FOR A DAY, WAS TORTURE.
BUT I WAS SO MUCH STRONGER THAN YESTERDAY, IT SEEMED IMPOSSIBLE.
BOING
FLAIL
FLAIL
FLAIL
TH-WHUD
OW!
MY NEW FREEDOM MADE ME GIDDY.

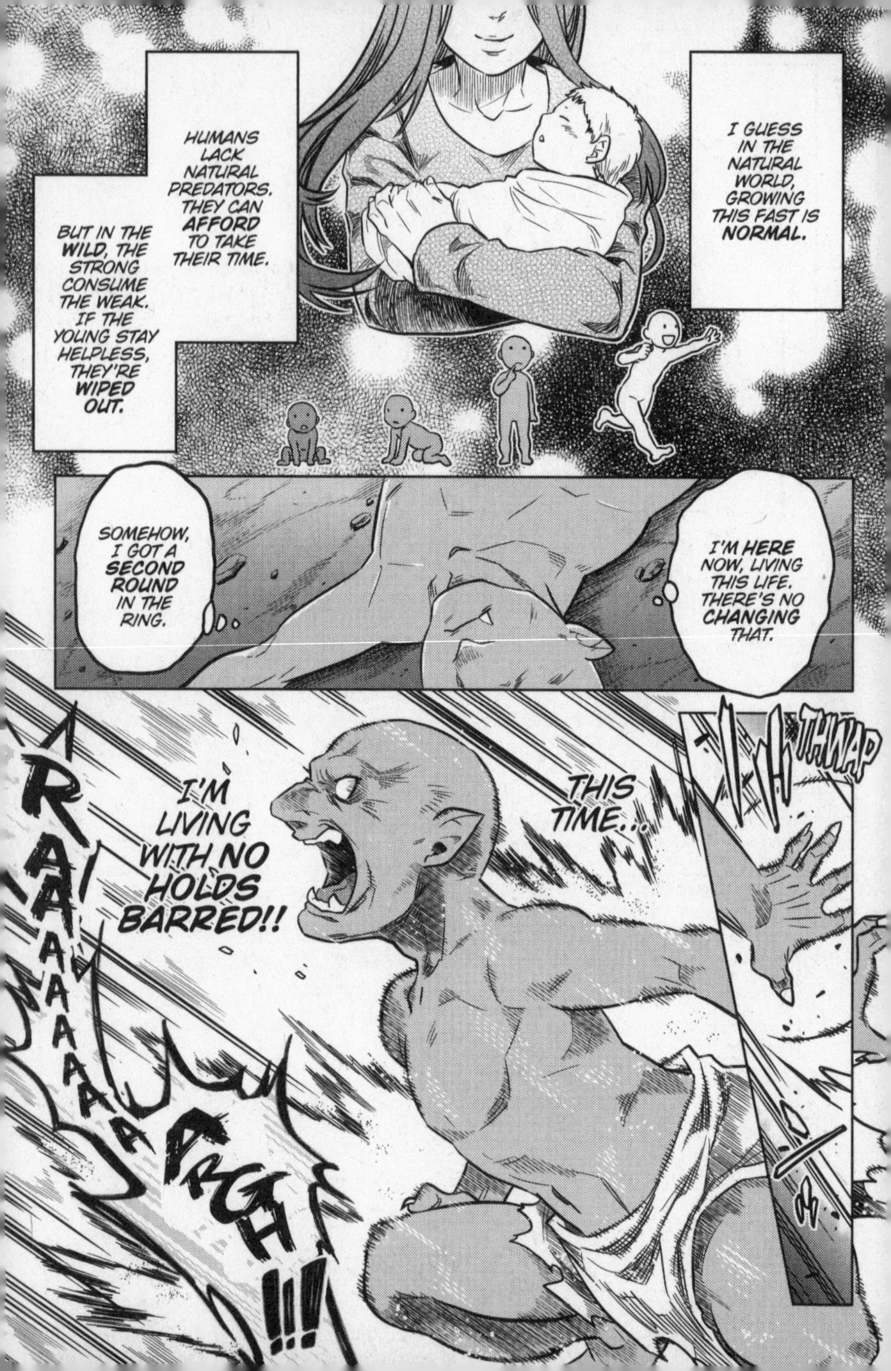
I GUESS IN THE NATURAL WORLD, GROWING THIS FAST IS NORMAL.
HUMANS LACK NATURAL PREDATORS. THEY CAN AFFORD TO TAKE THEIR TIME.
BUT IN THE WILD, THE STRONG CONSUME THE WEAK. IF THE YOUNG STAY HELPLESS, THEY'RE WIPED OUT.
I'M HERE NOW, LIVING THIS LIFE. THERE'S NO CHANGING THAT.
SOMEHOW, I GOT A SECOND ROUND IN THE RING.
THWAP
THIS TIME...
I'M LIVING WITH NO HOLDS BARRED!!
RAAAAAAAAAAARGH!!!

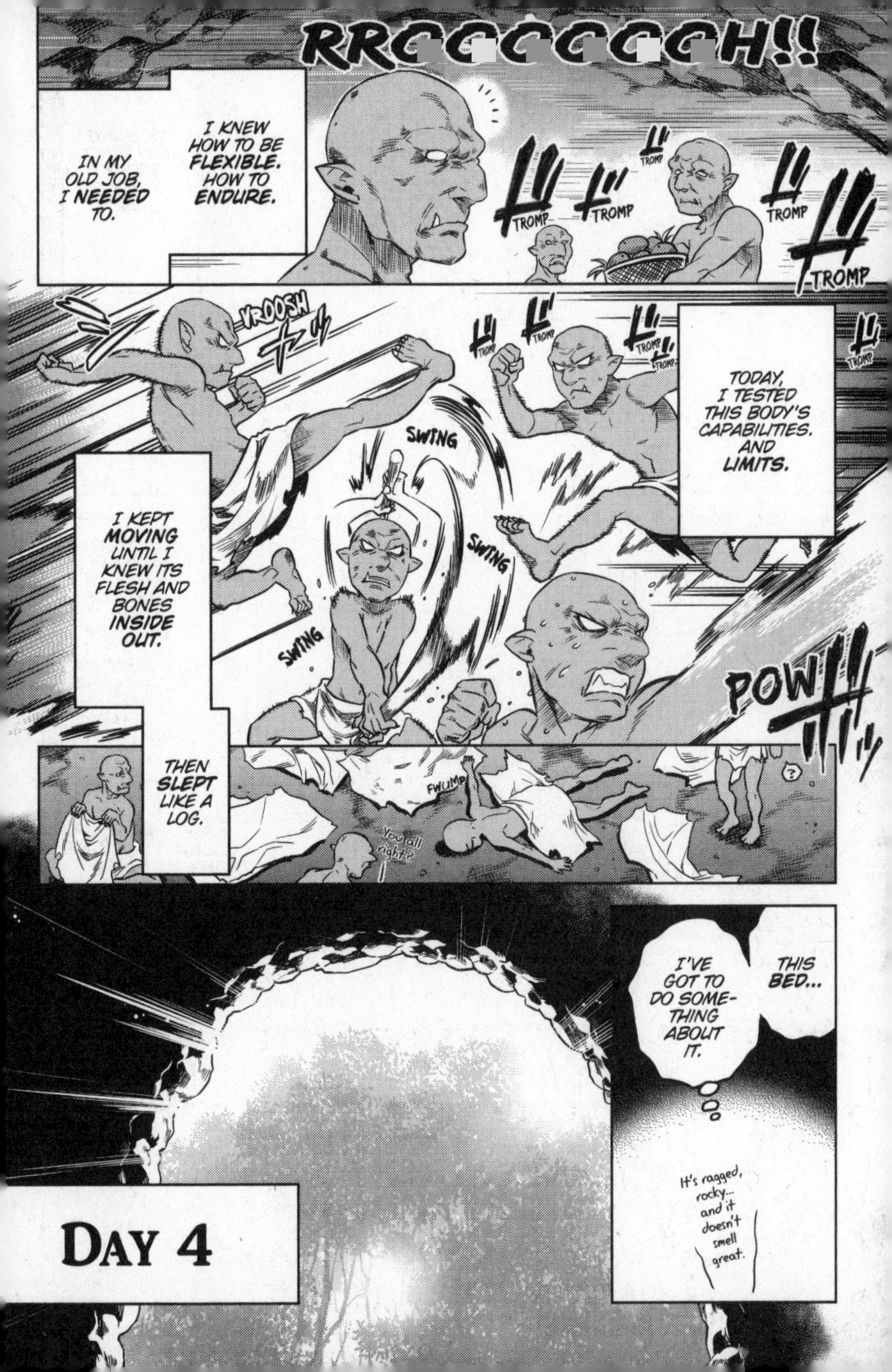
RROOOOOOOOGH!!
TROMP
TROMP
TROMP
TROMP
TROMP
I KNEW HOW TO BE FLEXIBLE. HOW TO ENDURE.
IN MY OLD JOB, I NEEDED TO.
TROMP
TROMP
TROMP
TROMP
TODAY, I TESTED THIS BODY'S CAPABILITIES. AND LIMITS.
TROMP
TROMP
VROOSH
SWING
SWING
SWING
I KEPT MOVING UNTIL I KNEW ITS FLESH AND BONES INSIDE OUT.
POW
?
FWUMP
You all right?
THEN SLEPT LIKE A LOG.
THIS BED...
I'VE GOT TO DO SOMETHING ABOUT IT.
It's ragged, rocky... and it doesn't smell great.
DAY 4

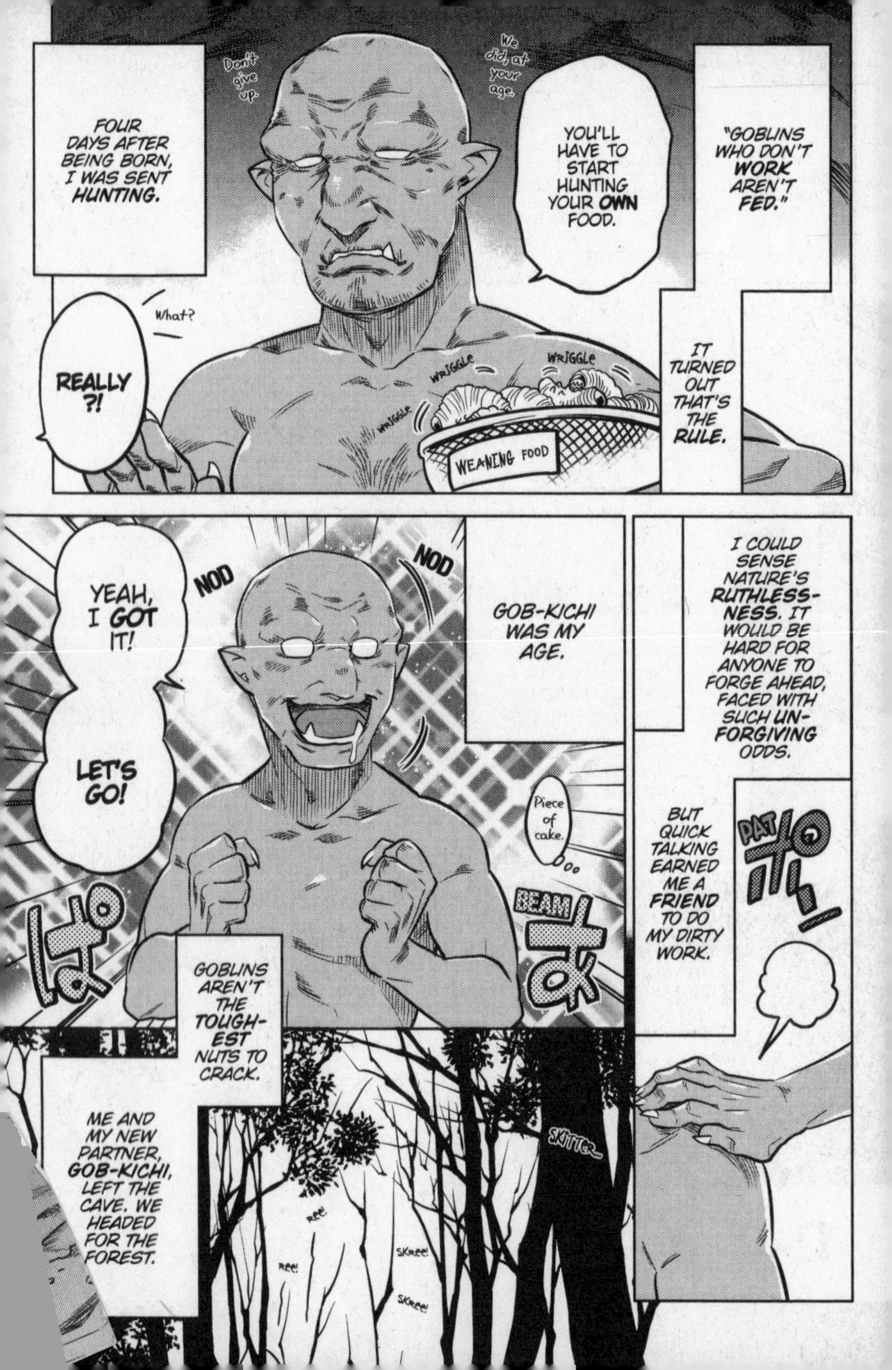

"GOBLINS WHO DON'T WORK AREN'T FED."
YOU'LL HAVE TO START HUNTING YOUR OWN FOOD.
We did, at your age.
Don't give up.
FOUR DAYS AFTER BEING BORN, I WAS SENT HUNTING.
IT TURNED OUT THAT'S THE RULE.
WRIGGLE
WRIGGLE
WRIGGLE
WEANING FOOD
What?
REALLY?!
I COULD SENSE NATURE'S RUTHLESS-NESS. IT WOULD BE HARD FOR ANYONE TO FORGE AHEAD, FACED WITH SUCH UN-FORGIVING ODDS.
GOB-KICHI WAS MY AGE.
NOD
NOD
YEAH, I GOT IT!
LET'S GO!
Piece of cake.
BEAM
BUT QUICK TALKING EARNED ME A FRIEND TO DO MY DIRTY WORK.
PAT
GOBLINS AREN'T THE TOUGH-EST NUTS TO CRACK.
ME AND MY NEW PARTNER, GOB-KICHI, LEFT THE CAVE. WE HEADED FOR THE FOREST.
SKITTER...
Ree!
SKree!
Ree!
SKree!

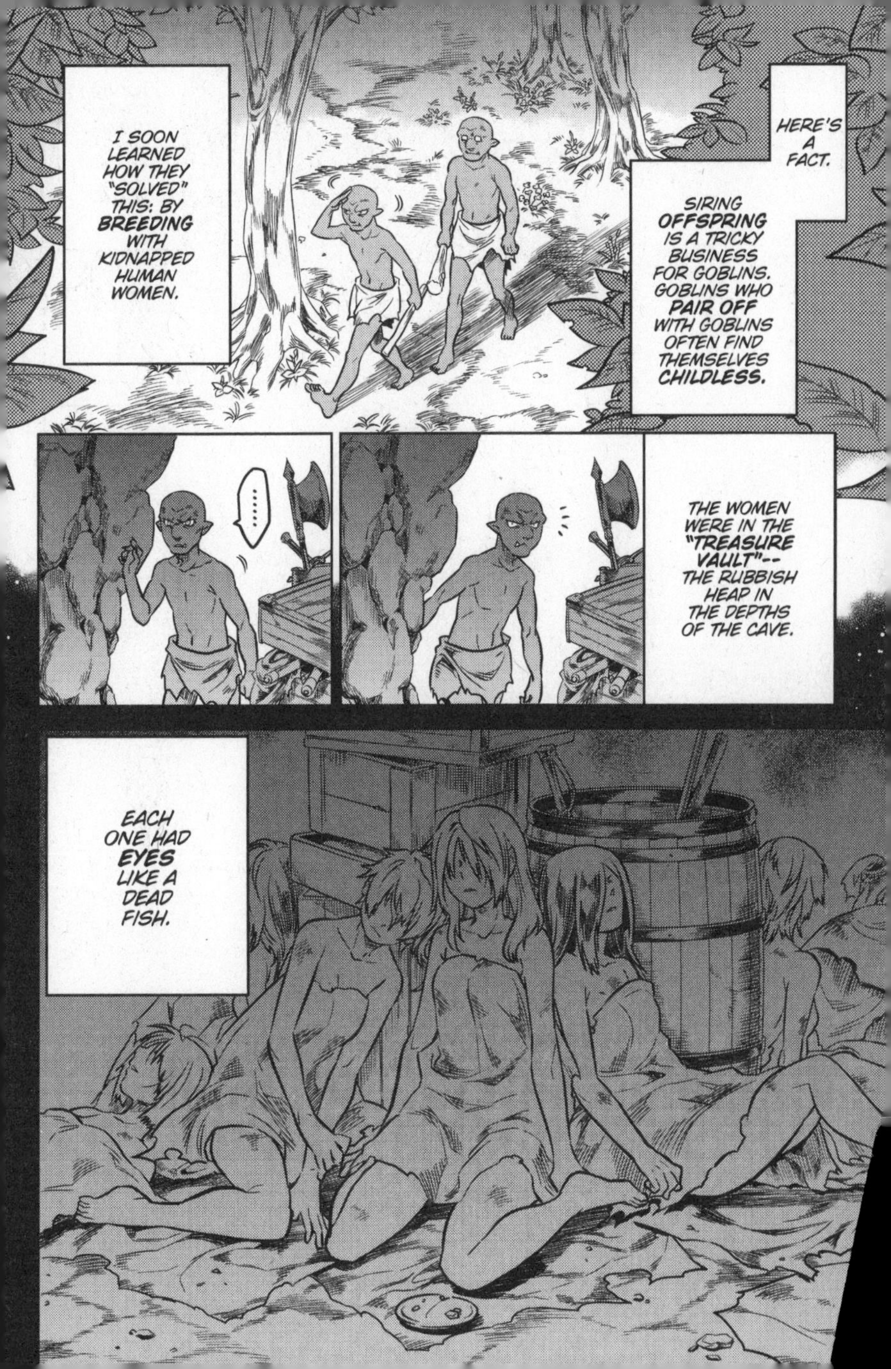
HERE'S A FACT.
SIRING OFFSPRING IS A TRICKY BUSINESS FOR GOBLINS. GOBLINS WHO PAIR OFF WITH GOBLINS OFTEN FIND THEMSELVES CHILDLESS.
I SOON LEARNED HOW THEY "SOLVED" THIS: BY BREEDING WITH KIDNAPPED HUMAN WOMEN.
THE WOMEN WERE IN THE "TREASURE VAULT"-- THE RUBBISH HEAP IN THE DEPTHS OF THE CAVE.
......
EACH ONE HAD EYES LIKE A DEAD FISH.

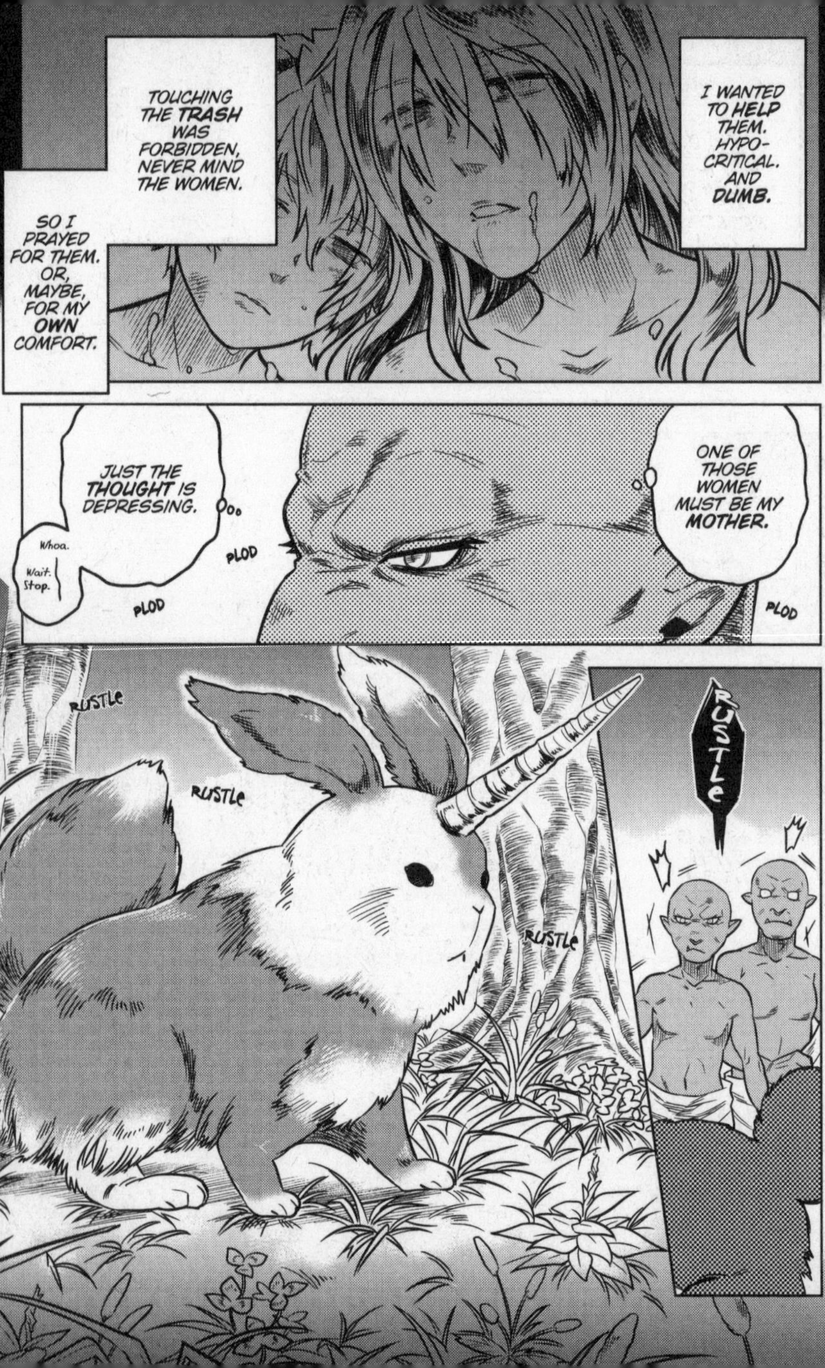
I WANTED TO HELP THEM. HYPO-CRITICAL. AND DUMB.
TOUCHING THE TRASH WAS FORBIDDEN, NEVER MIND THE WOMEN.
SO I PRAYED FOR THEM. OR, MAYBE, FOR MY OWN COMFORT.
ONE OF THOSE WOMEN MUST BE MY MOTHER.
PLOD
JUST THE THOUGHT IS DEPRESSING.
PLOD
Whoa. Wait. Stop.
PLOD
RUSTLE
RUSTLE
RUSTLE
RUSTLE

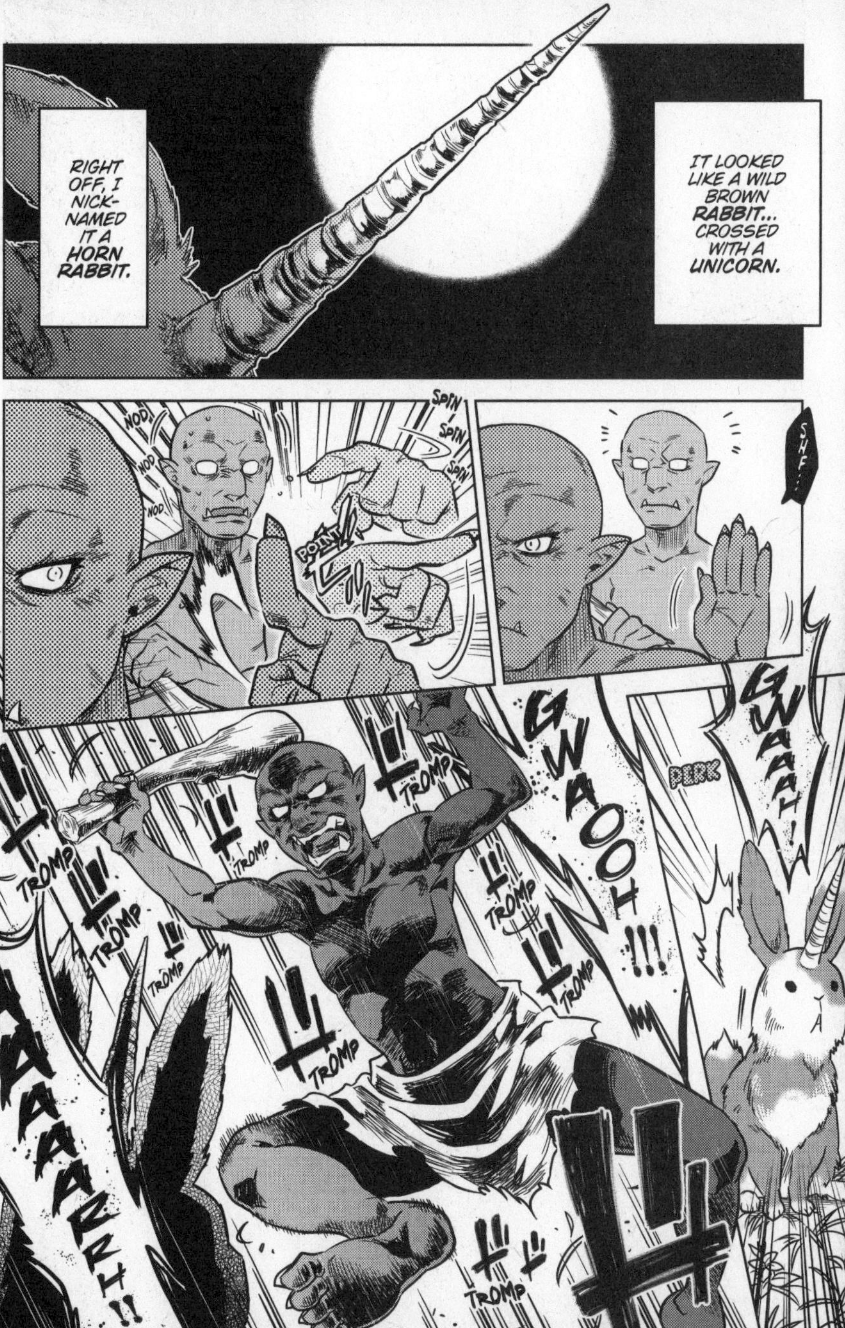
IT LOOKED LIKE A WILD BROWN RABBIT... CROSSED WITH A UNICORN.
RIGHT OFF, I NICK-NAMED IT A HORN RABBIT.
SHF...
SPIN SPIN SPIN
POINT
NOD NOD NOD
GWAAAH!
PERK
GWAOOOH!!!
TROMP TROMP TROMP TROMP TROMP TROMP TROMP TROMP TROMP TROMP
AAAAARH!!

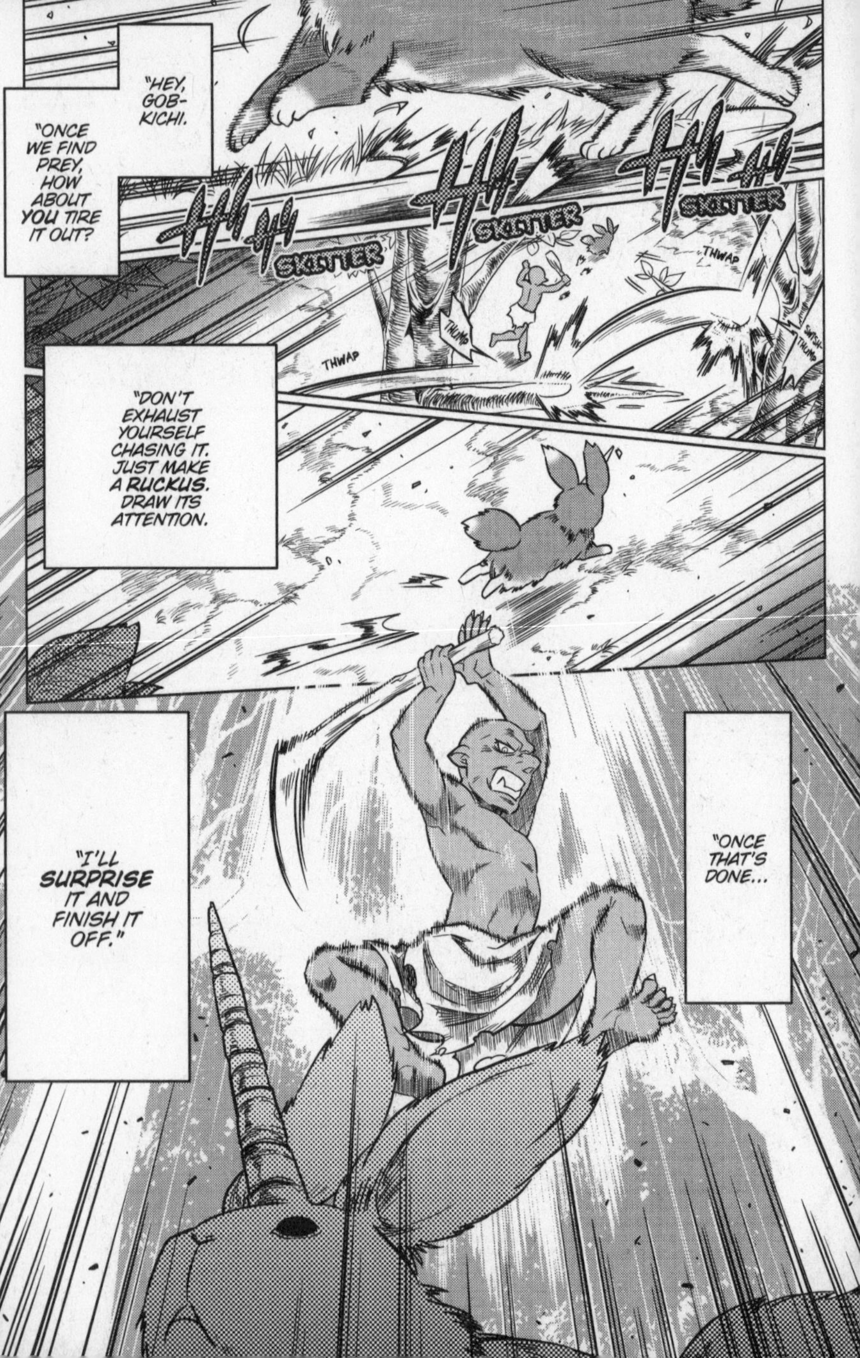
"HEY, GOB-KICHI.
"ONCE WE FIND PREY, HOW ABOUT YOU TIRE IT OUT?
SKITTER
SKITTER
SKITTER
THWAP
THUMP
SWISH-THUMP
THWAP
"DON'T EXHAUST YOURSELF CHASING IT. JUST MAKE A RUCKUS. DRAW ITS ATTENTION.
"ONCE THAT'S DONE...
"I'LL SURPRISE IT AND FINISH IT OFF."

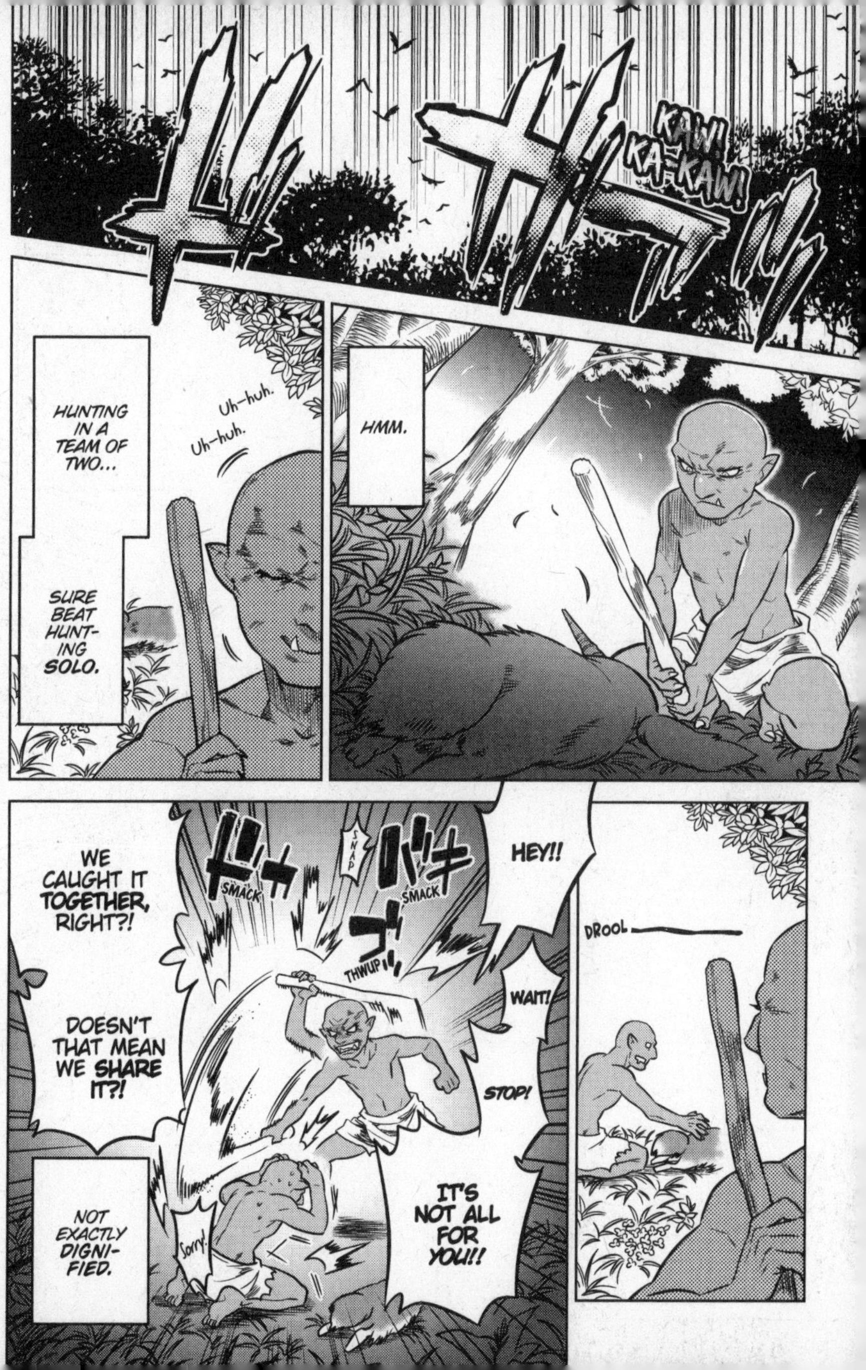
KAWI! KA-KAW!
HMM.
HUNTING IN A TEAM OF TWO...
Uh-huh. Uh-huh.
SURE BEAT HUNTING SOLO.
DROOL
HEY!!
SNAP
SMACK
SMACK
THWUP
WAIT!
STOP!
IT'S NOT ALL FOR YOU!!
WE CAUGHT IT TOGETHER, RIGHT?!
DOESN'T THAT MEAN WE SHARE IT?!
Sorry!
NOT EXACTLY DIGNIFIED.

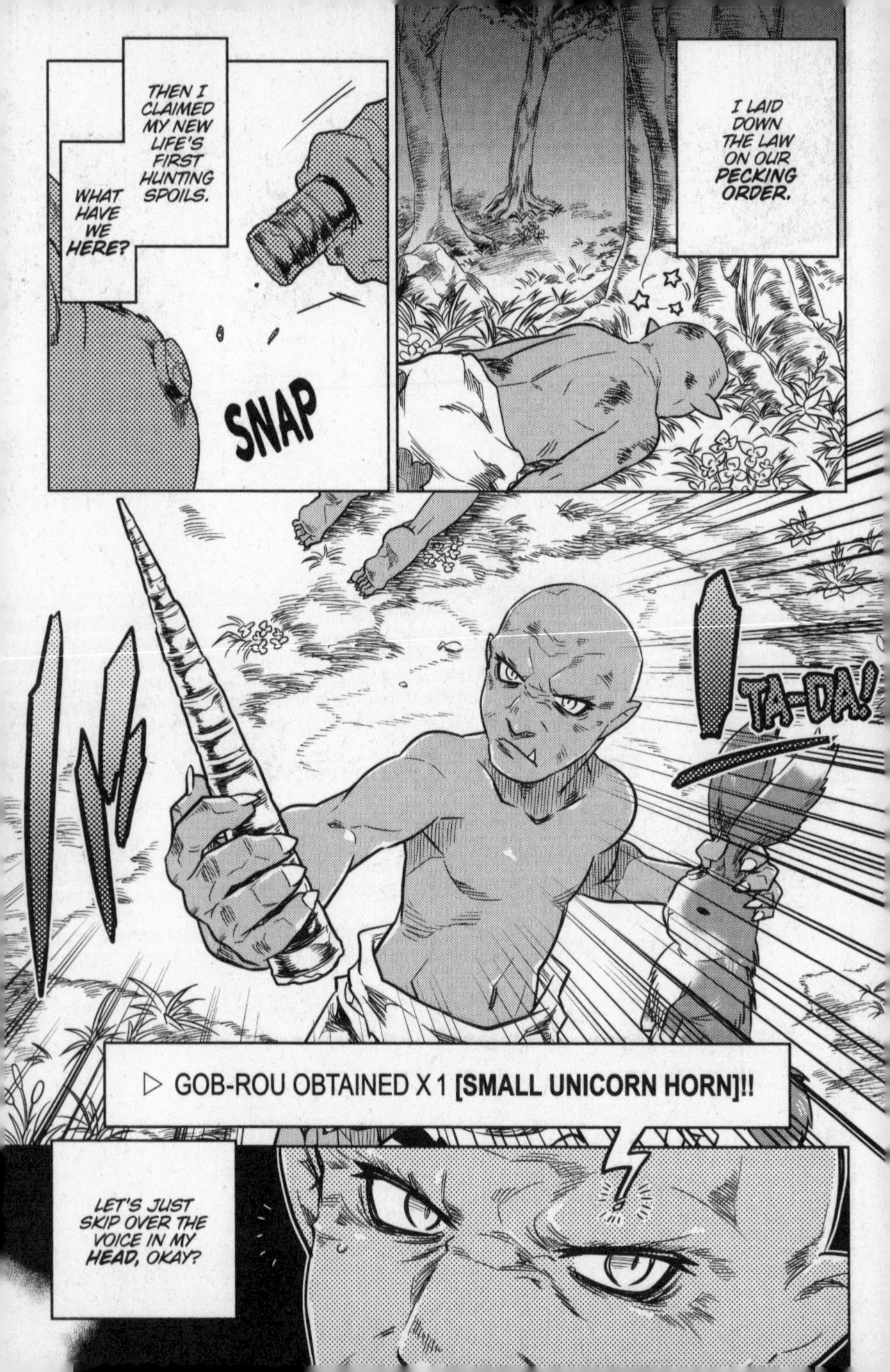
I LAID DOWN THE LAW ON OUR PECKING ORDER.
THEN I CLAIMED MY NEW LIFE'S FIRST HUNTING SPOILS.
WHAT HAVE WE HERE?
SNAP
TA-DA!
▷ GOB-ROU OBTAINED X 1 [SMALL UNICORN HORN]!!
LET'S JUST SKIP OVER THE VOICE IN MY HEAD, OKAY?

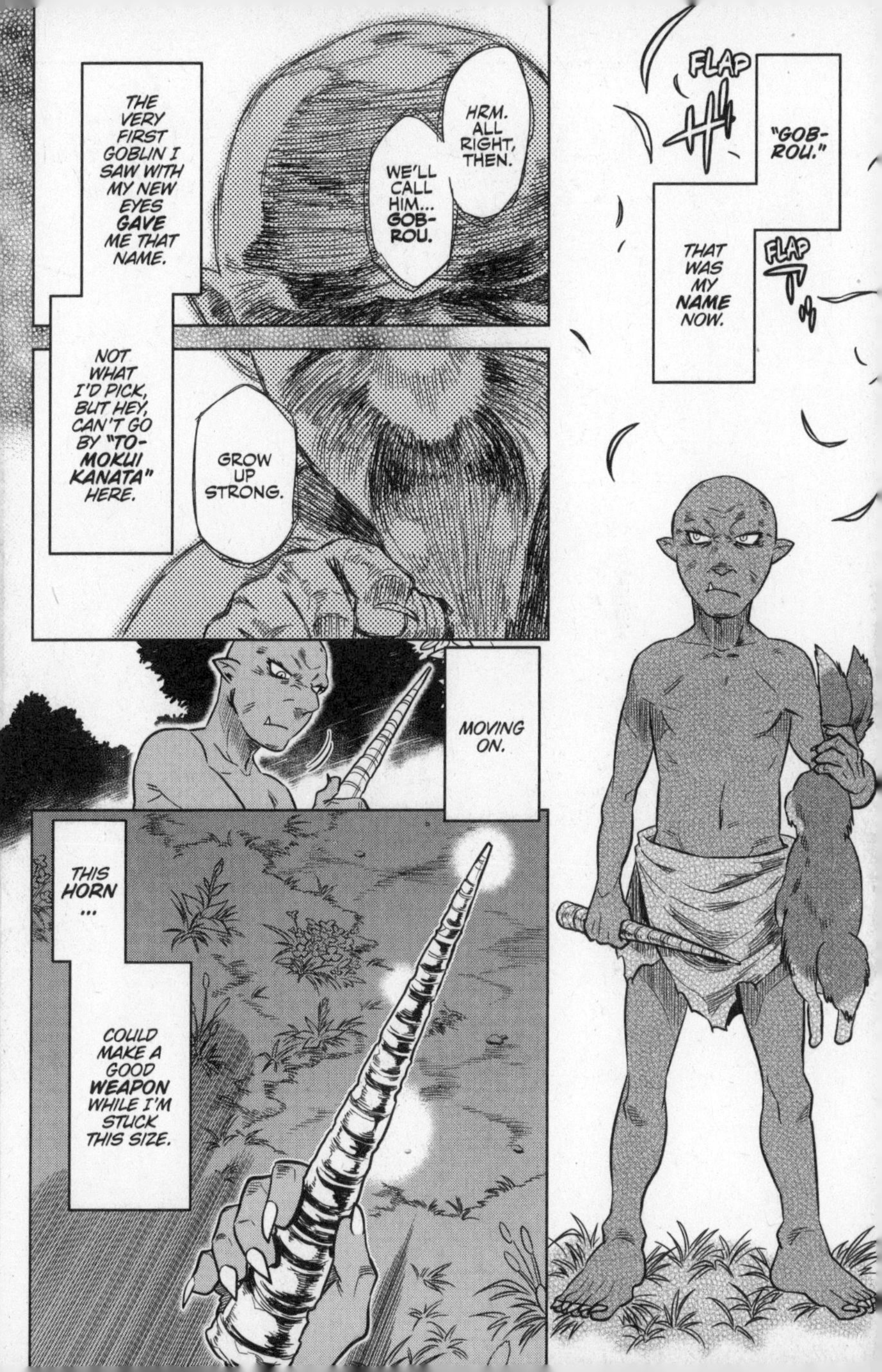
FLAP
"GOB-ROU."
THAT WAS MY NAME NOW.
FLAP
HRM. ALL RIGHT, THEN.
WE'LL CALL HIM... GOB-ROU.
THE VERY FIRST GOBLIN I SAW WITH MY NEW EYES GAVE ME THAT NAME.
GROW UP STRONG.
NOT WHAT I'D PICK, BUT HEY, CAN'T GO BY "TO-MOKUI KANATA" HERE.
MOVING ON.
THIS HORN...
COULD MAKE A GOOD WEAPON WHILE I'M STUCK THIS SIZE.

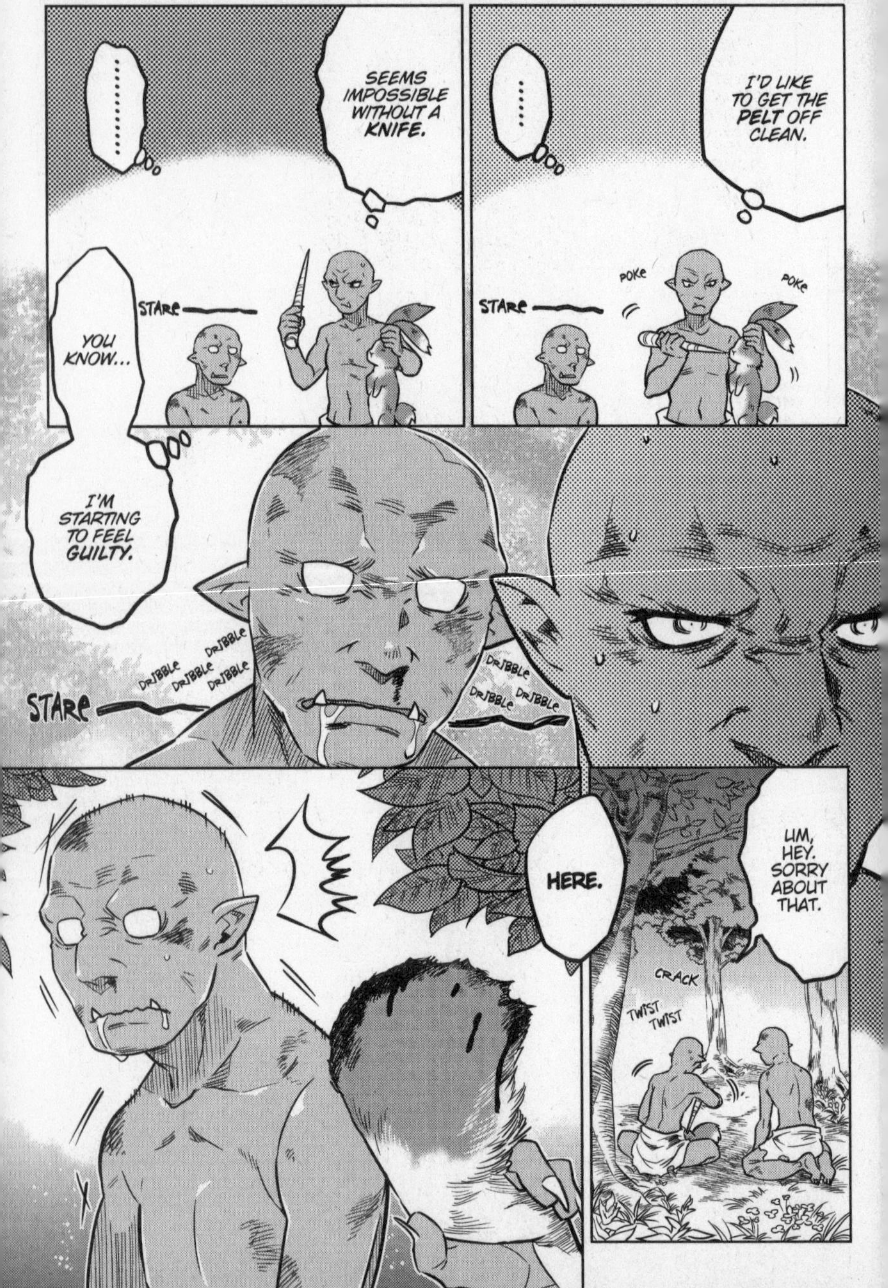
I'D LIKE TO GET THE PELT OFF CLEAN.
......
STARE
POKE
POKE
SEEMS IMPOSSIBLE WITHOUT A KNIFE.
....
STARE
YOU KNOW...
I'M STARTING TO FEEL GUILTY.
DRIBBLE
DRIBBLE
DRIBBLE
DRIBBLE
DRIBBLE
DRIBBLE
DRIBBLE
STARE
UM, HEY. SORRY ABOUT THAT.
CRACK
TWIST TWIST
HERE.

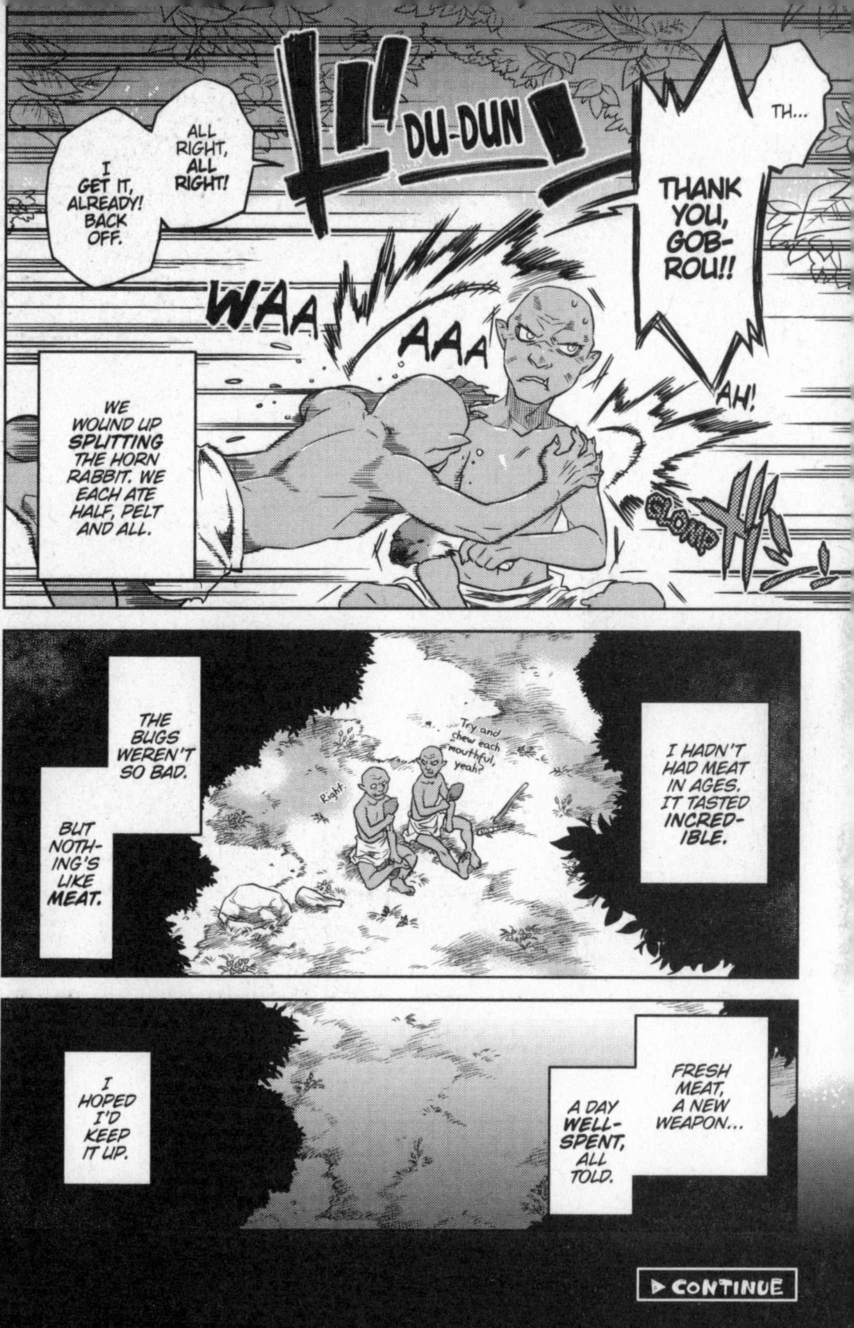
TH...
THANK YOU, GOB-ROU!!
DU-DUN
ALL RIGHT, ALL RIGHT!
I GET IT, ALREADY! BACK OFF.
AH!
WAAAAA
GLOMP
WE WOUND UP SPLITTING THE HORN RABBIT. WE EACH ATE HALF, PELT AND ALL.
I HADN'T HAD MEAT IN AGES. IT TASTED INCREDIBLE.
Try and chew each mouthful, yeah?
Right.
THE BUGS WEREN'T SO BAD.
BUT NOTHING'S LIKE MEAT.
FRESH MEAT, A NEW WEAPON...
A DAY WELL-SPENT, ALL TOLD.
I HOPED I'D KEEP IT UP.
CONTINUE

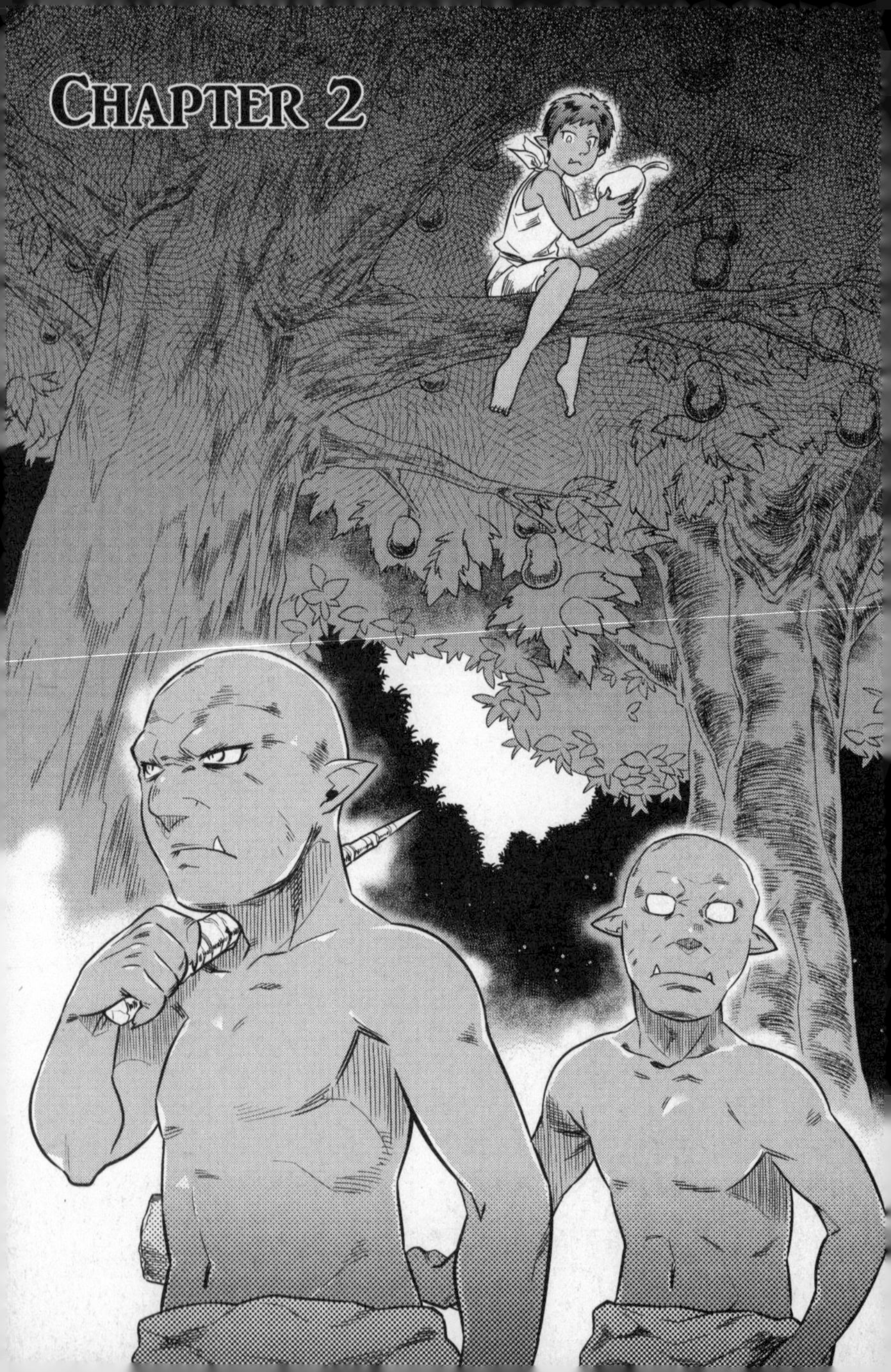
CHAPTER 2

DAY 5

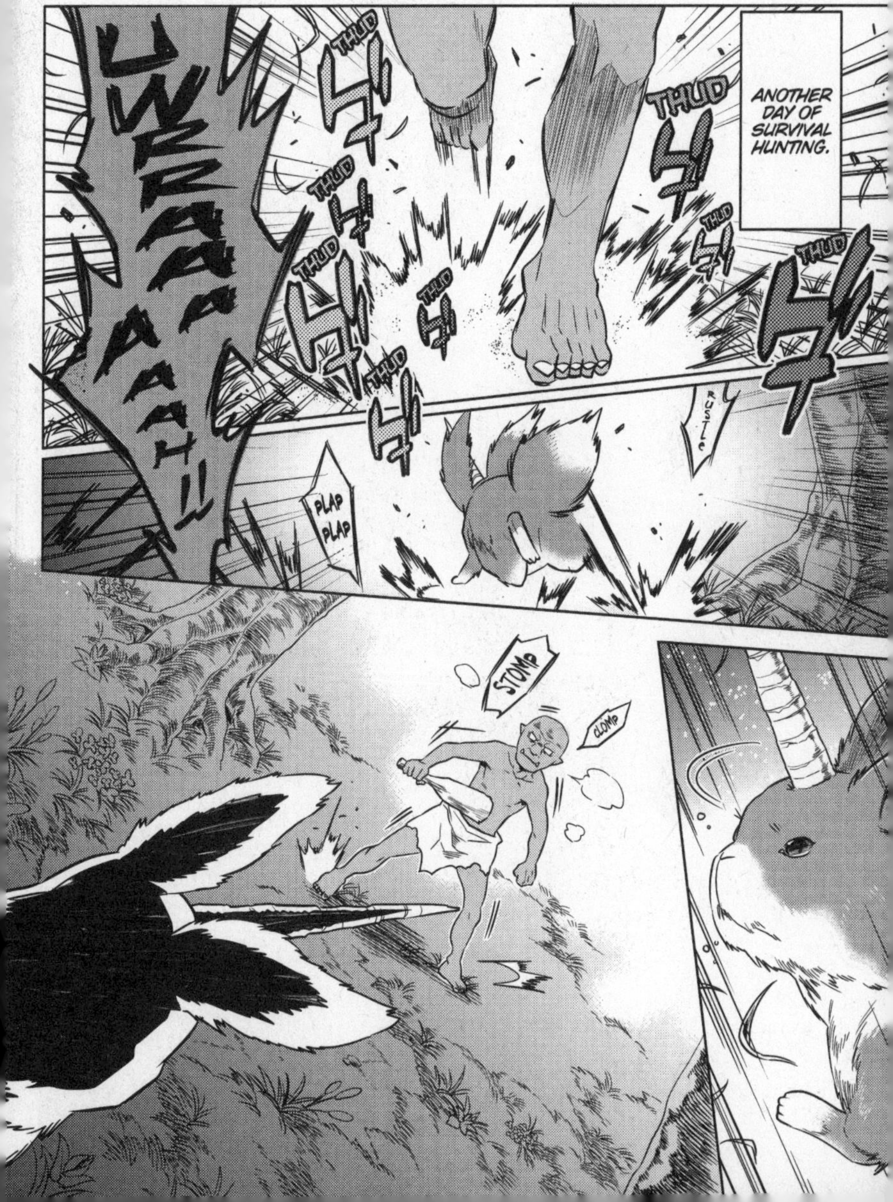

ANOTHER DAY OF SURVIVAL HUNTING.
THUD
THUD
THUD
THUD
THUD
THUD
THUD
UWRRAAAAAAH!!
RUSTLE
PLAP PLAP
STOMP
CLOMP

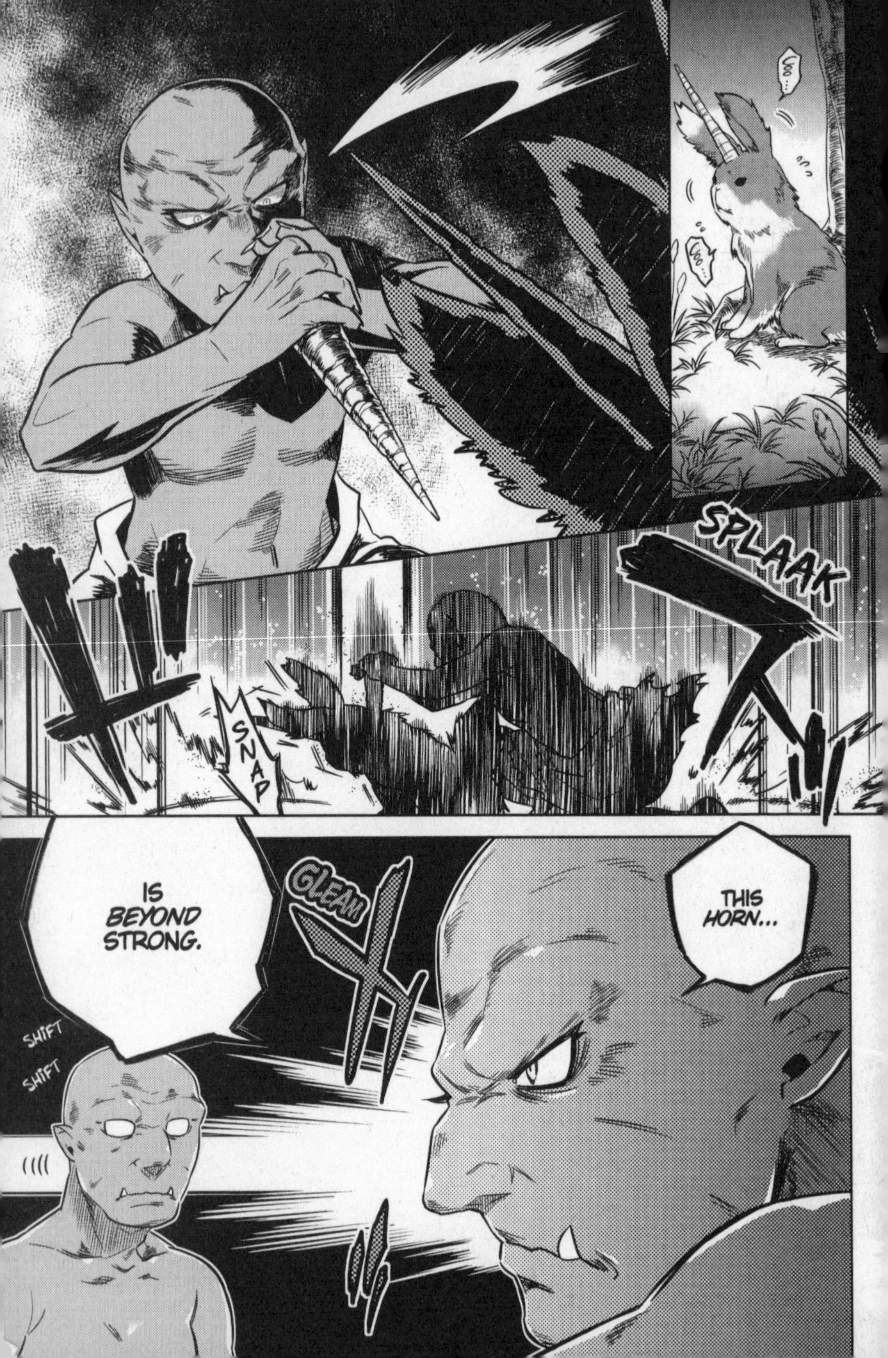
Goo...
Goo...
SPLAAK
SNAP
THIS HORN...
GLEAM
IS BEYOND STRONG.
SHIFT
SHIFT

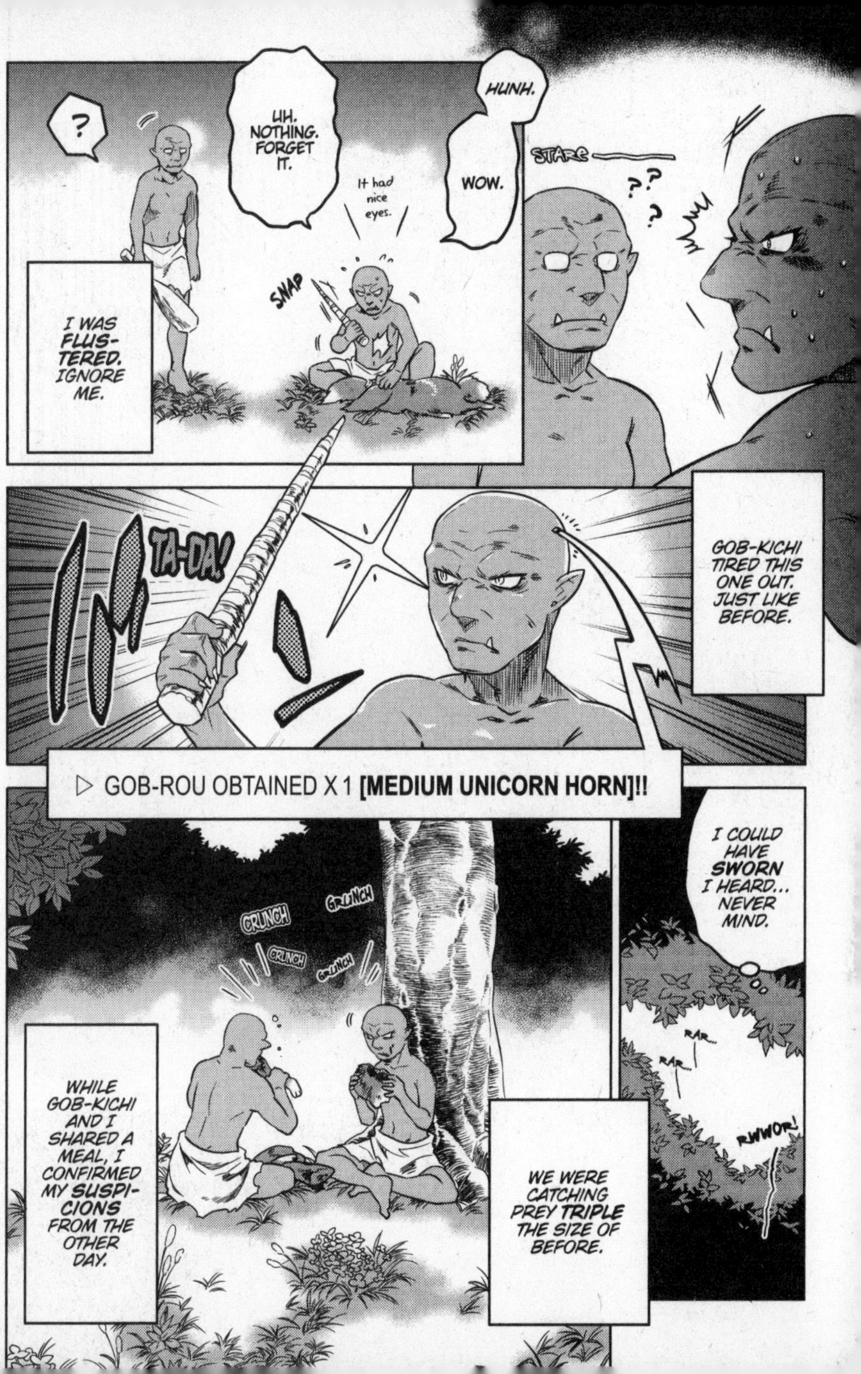
HUNH.
WOW.
STARE
??
?
UH. NOTHING. FORGET IT.
It had nice eyes.
?
SNAP
I WAS FLUSTERED. IGNORE ME.
GOB-KICHI TIRED THIS ONE OUT. JUST LIKE BEFORE.
TA-DA!
▷ GOB-ROU OBTAINED X 1 [MEDIUM UNICORN HORN]!!
I COULD HAVE SWORN I HEARD... NEVER MIND.
RAR...
RAR...
RWWOR!
WE WERE CATCHING PREY TRIPLE THE SIZE OF BEFORE.
GRUNCH
CRUNCH
GRUNCH
CRUNCH
WHILE GOB-KICHI AND I SHARED A MEAL, I CONFIRMED MY SUSPICIONS FROM THE OTHER DAY.

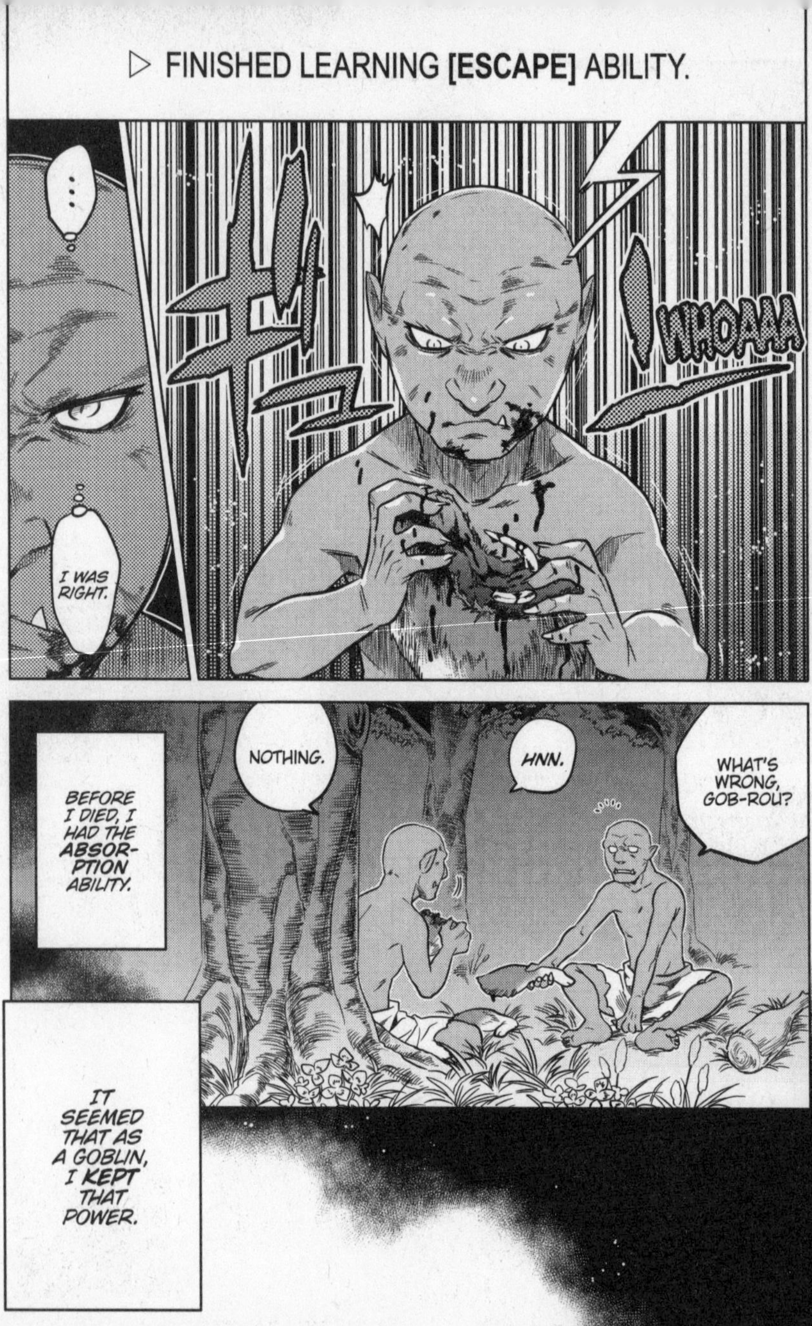

▷ FINISHED LEARNING [ESCAPE] ABILITY.
WHOAAA
...
I WAS RIGHT.
WHAT'S WRONG, GOB-ROU?
HNN.
NOTHING.
BEFORE I DIED, I HAD THE ABSORPTION ABILITY.
IT SEEMED THAT AS A GOBLIN, I KEPT THAT POWER.

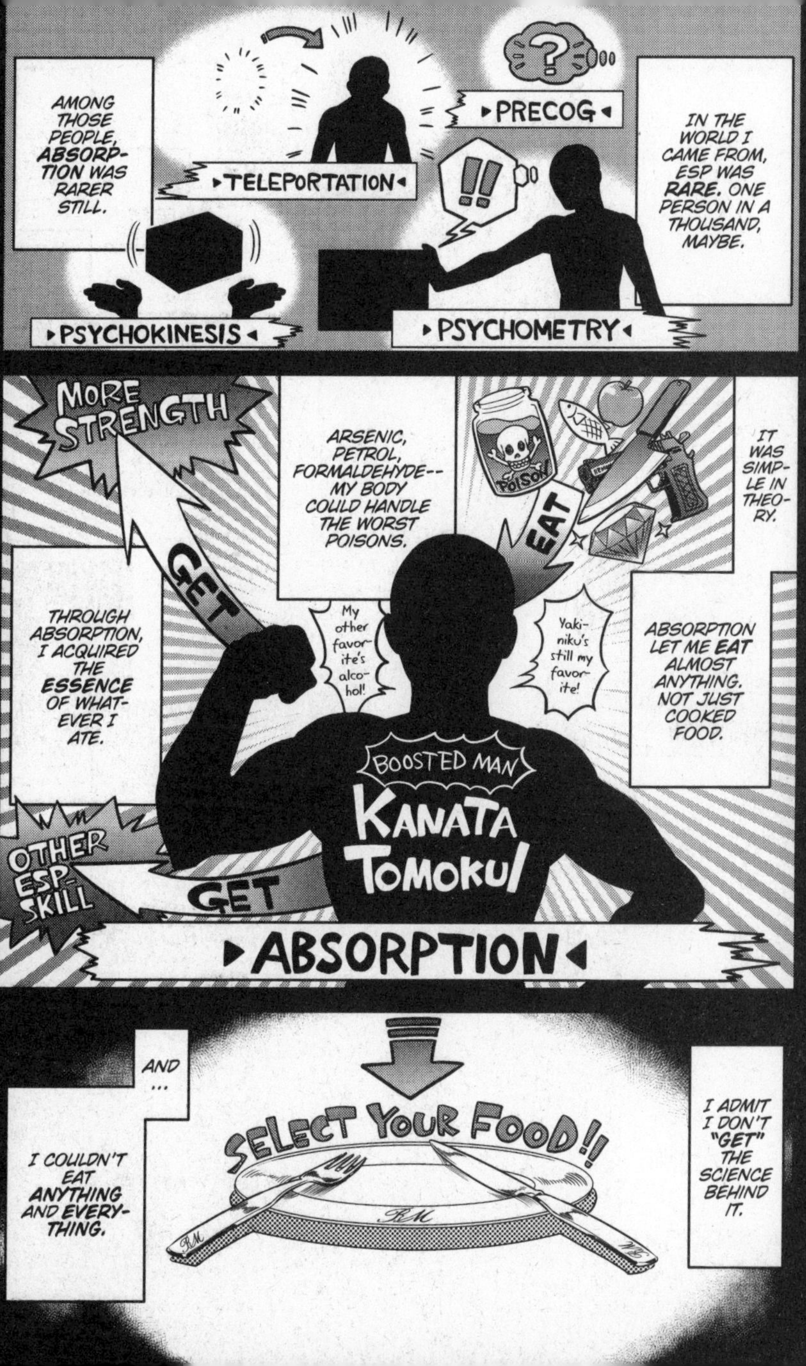
IN THE WORLD I CAME FROM, ESP WAS RARE. ONE PERSON IN A THOUSAND, MAYBE.
PRECOG
TELEPORTATION
PSYCHOMETRY
PSYCHOKINESIS
AMONG THOSE PEOPLE, ABSORPTION WAS RARER STILL.
IT WAS SIMPLE IN THEORY.
ARSENIC, PETROL, FORMALDEHYDE-- MY BODY COULD HANDLE THE WORST POISONS.
POISON
EAT
ABSORPTION LET ME EAT ALMOST ANYTHING. NOT JUST COOKED FOOD.
Yakiniku's still my favorite!
My other favorite's alcohol!
MORE STRENGTH
GET
THROUGH ABSORPTION, I ACQUIRED THE ESSENCE OF WHATEVER I ATE.
BOOSTED MAN
KANATA TOMOKUI
OTHER ESP-SKILL
GET
ABSORPTION
I ADMIT I DON'T "GET" THE SCIENCE BEHIND IT.
SELECT YOUR FOOD!!
AND...
I COULDN'T EAT ANYTHING AND EVERYTHING.

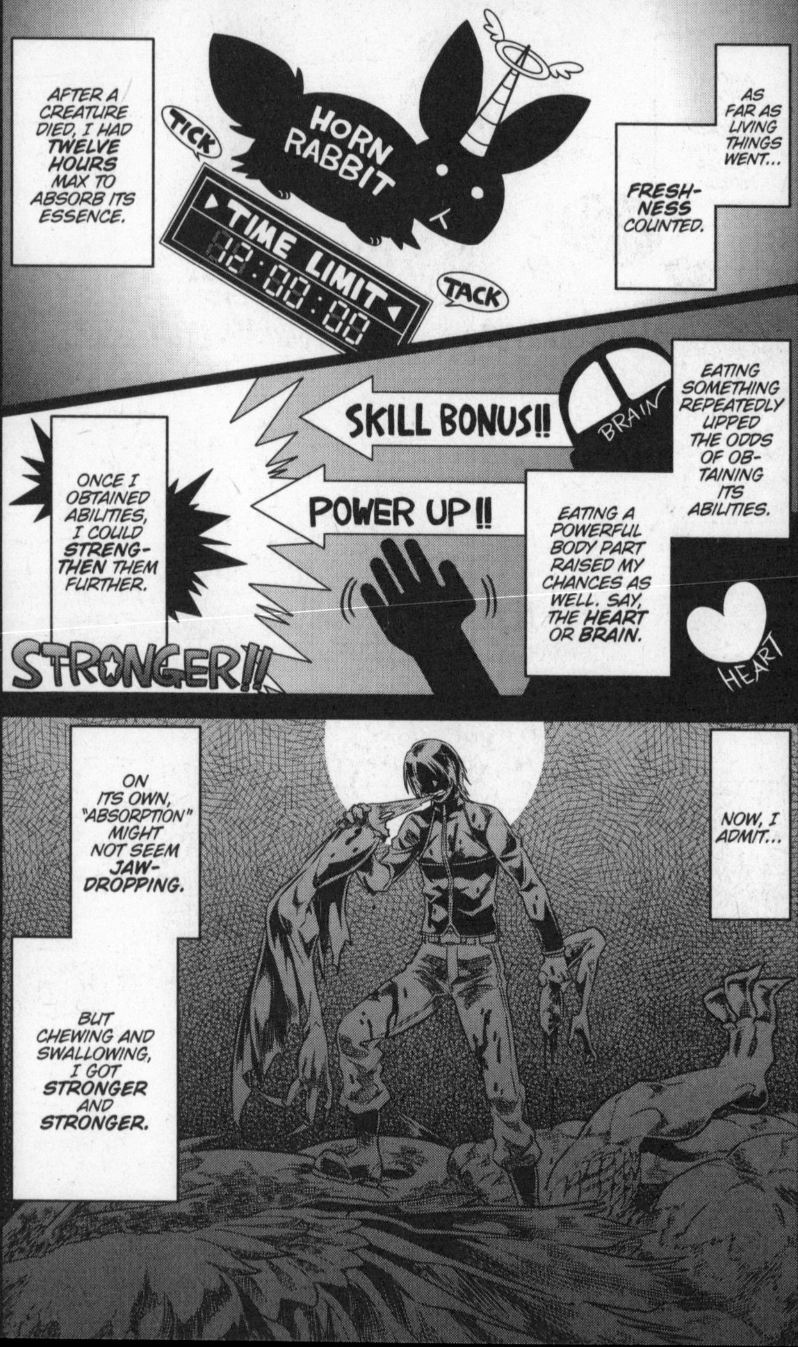
AS FAR AS LIVING THINGS WENT...
FRESHNESS COUNTED.
HORN RABBIT
TICK
TIME LIMIT
TACK
AFTER A CREATURE DIED, I HAD TWELVE HOURS MAX TO ABSORB ITS ESSENCE.
EATING SOMETHING REPEATEDLY UPPED THE ODDS OF OBTAINING ITS ABILITIES.
BRAIN
SKILL BONUS!!
EATING A POWERFUL BODY PART RAISED MY CHANCES AS WELL. SAY, THE HEART OR BRAIN.
HEART
POWER UP!!
ONCE I OBTAINED ABILITIES, I COULD STRENGTHEN THEM FURTHER.
STRONGER!!
NOW, I ADMIT...
ON ITS OWN, "ABSORPTION" MIGHT NOT SEEM JAW-DROPPING.
BUT CHEWING AND SWALLOWING, I GOT STRONGER AND STRONGER.

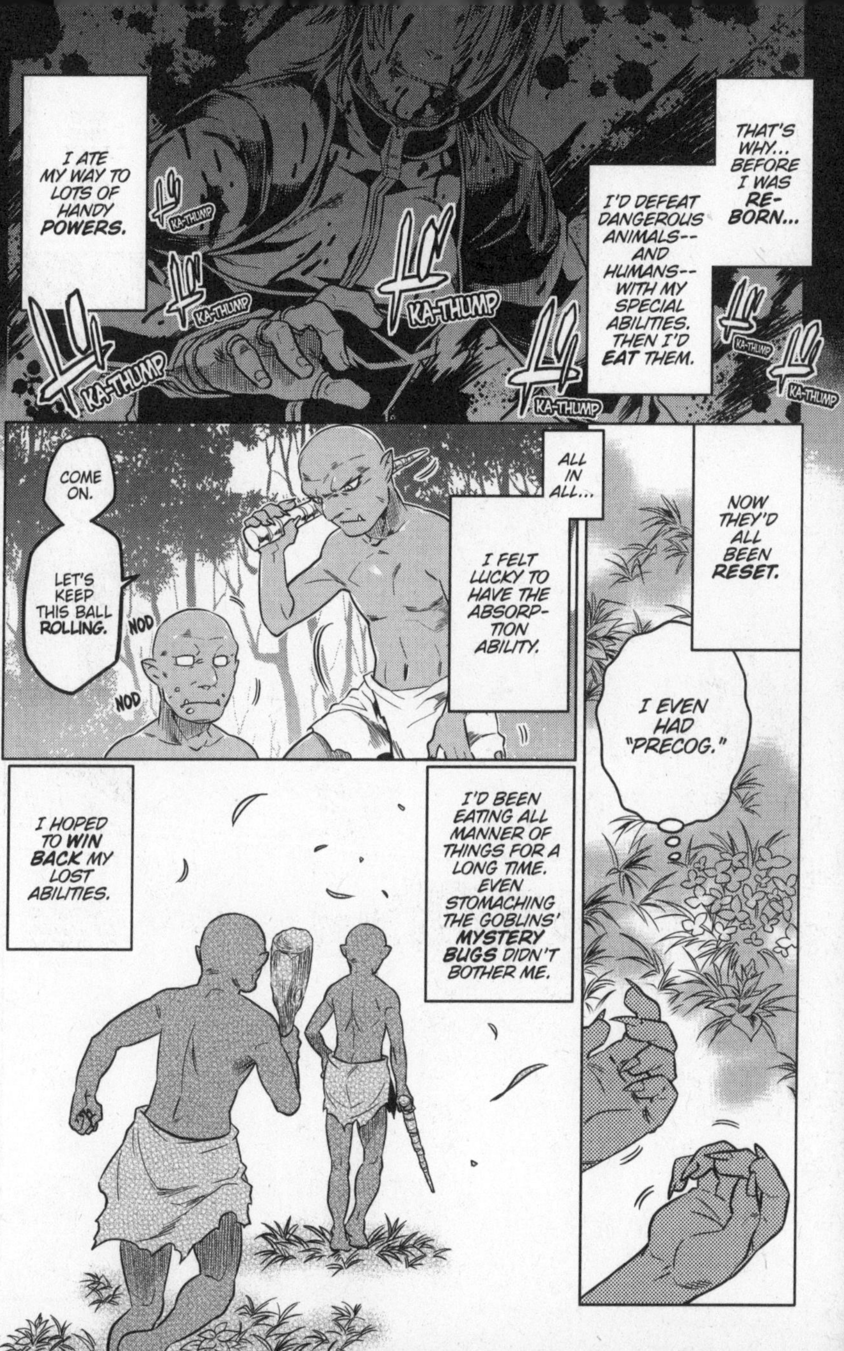
THAT'S WHY... BEFORE I WAS RE-BORN...
I'D DEFEAT DANGEROUS ANIMALS-- AND HUMANS-- WITH MY SPECIAL ABILITIES. THEN I'D EAT THEM.
KA-THUMP
KA-THUMP
KA-THUMP
KA-THUMP
I ATE MY WAY TO LOTS OF HANDY POWERS.
KA-THUMP
KA-THUMP
KA-THUMP
NOW THEY'D ALL BEEN RESET.
I EVEN HAD "PRECOG."
ALL IN ALL...
I FELT LUCKY TO HAVE THE ABSORP-TION ABILITY.
COME ON.
LET'S KEEP THIS BALL ROLLING.
NOD
NOD
I'D BEEN EATING ALL MANNER OF THINGS FOR A LONG TIME. EVEN STOMACHING THE GOBLINS' MYSTERY BUGS DIDN'T BOTHER ME.
I HOPED TO WIN BACK MY LOST ABILITIES.

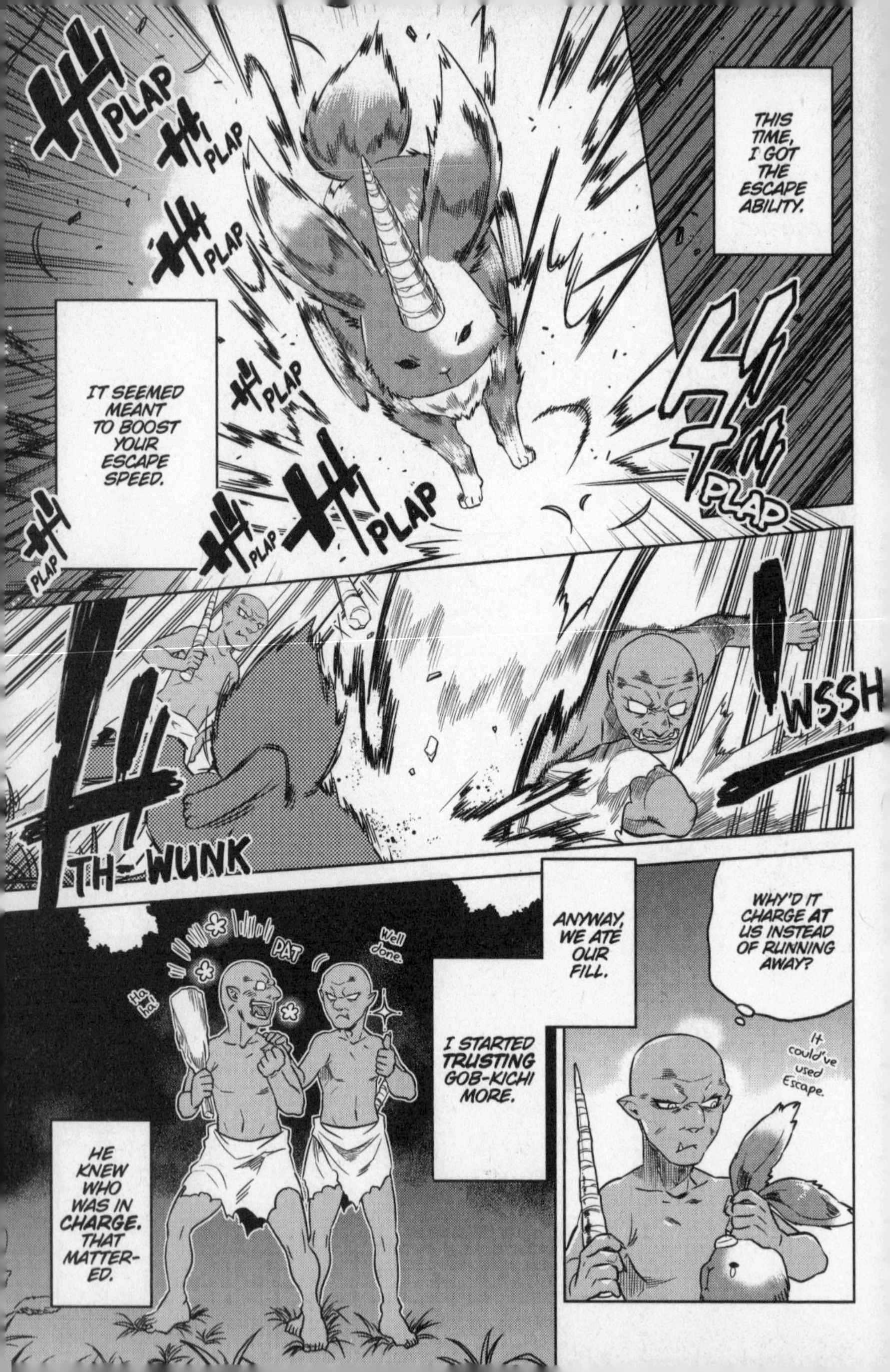
THIS TIME, I GOT THE ESCAPE ABILITY.
PLAP
PLAP
PLAP
PLAP
IT SEEMED MEANT TO BOOST YOUR ESCAPE SPEED.
PLAP
PLAP
PLAP
PLAP
WSSH
TH-WUNK
WHY'D IT CHARGE AT US INSTEAD OF RUNNING AWAY?
It could've used Escape.
ANYWAY, WE ATE OUR FILL.
I STARTED TRUSTING GOB-KICHI MORE.
Well done.
PAT
Ha ha!
HE KNEW WHO WAS IN CHARGE. THAT MATTER-ED.

Day 6

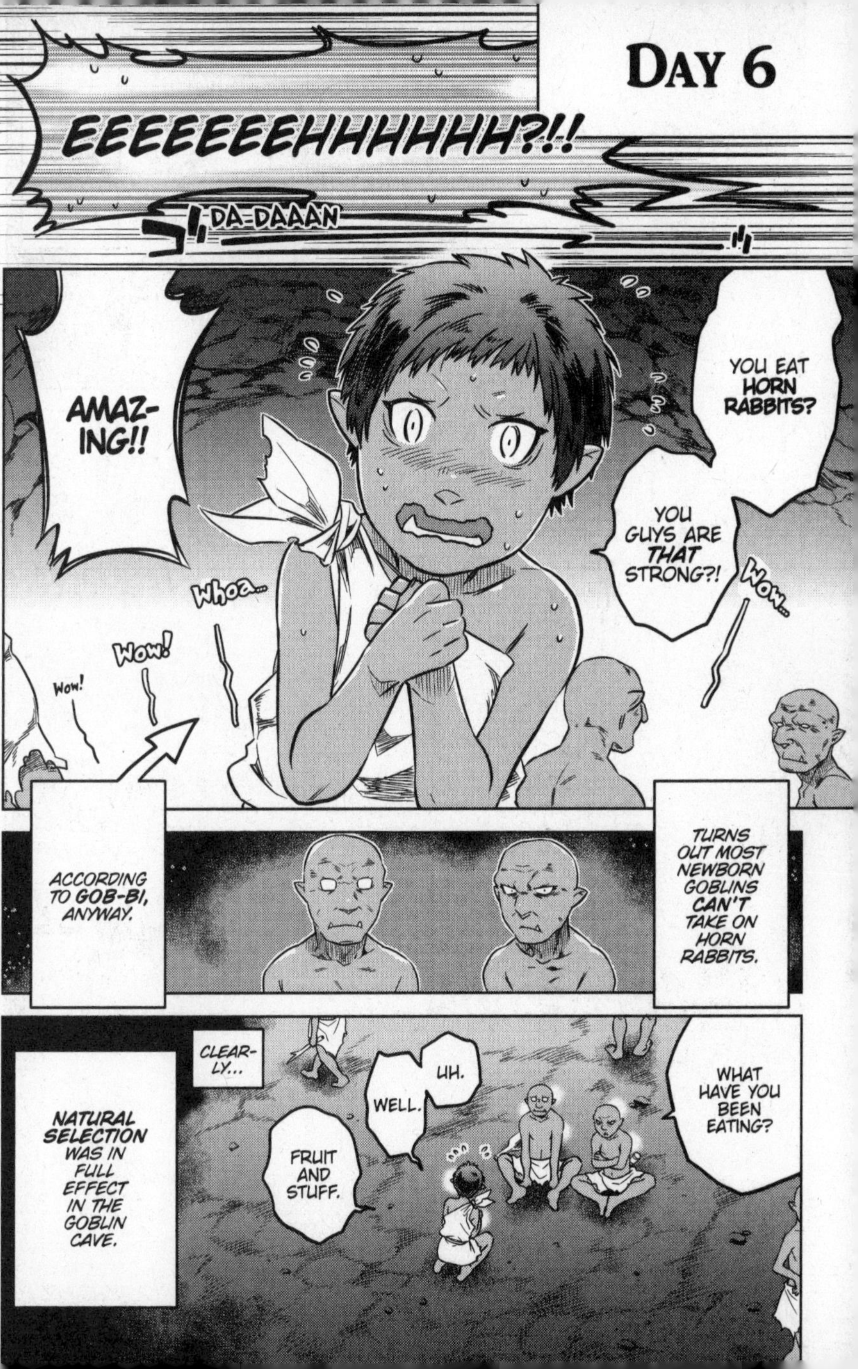
EEEEEEEEHHHHHHH?!!
DA-DAAAN
YOU EAT HORN RABBITS?
YOU GUYS ARE THAT STRONG?!
Wow...
Whoa...
Wow!
Wow!
AMAZ-ING!!
TURNS OUT MOST NEWBORN GOBLINS CAN'T TAKE ON HORN RABBITS.
ACCORDING TO GOB-BI, ANYWAY.
WHAT HAVE YOU BEEN EATING?
UH.
WELL.
FRUIT AND STUFF.
CLEAR-LY...
NATURAL SELECTION WAS IN FULL EFFECT IN THE GOBLIN CAVE.

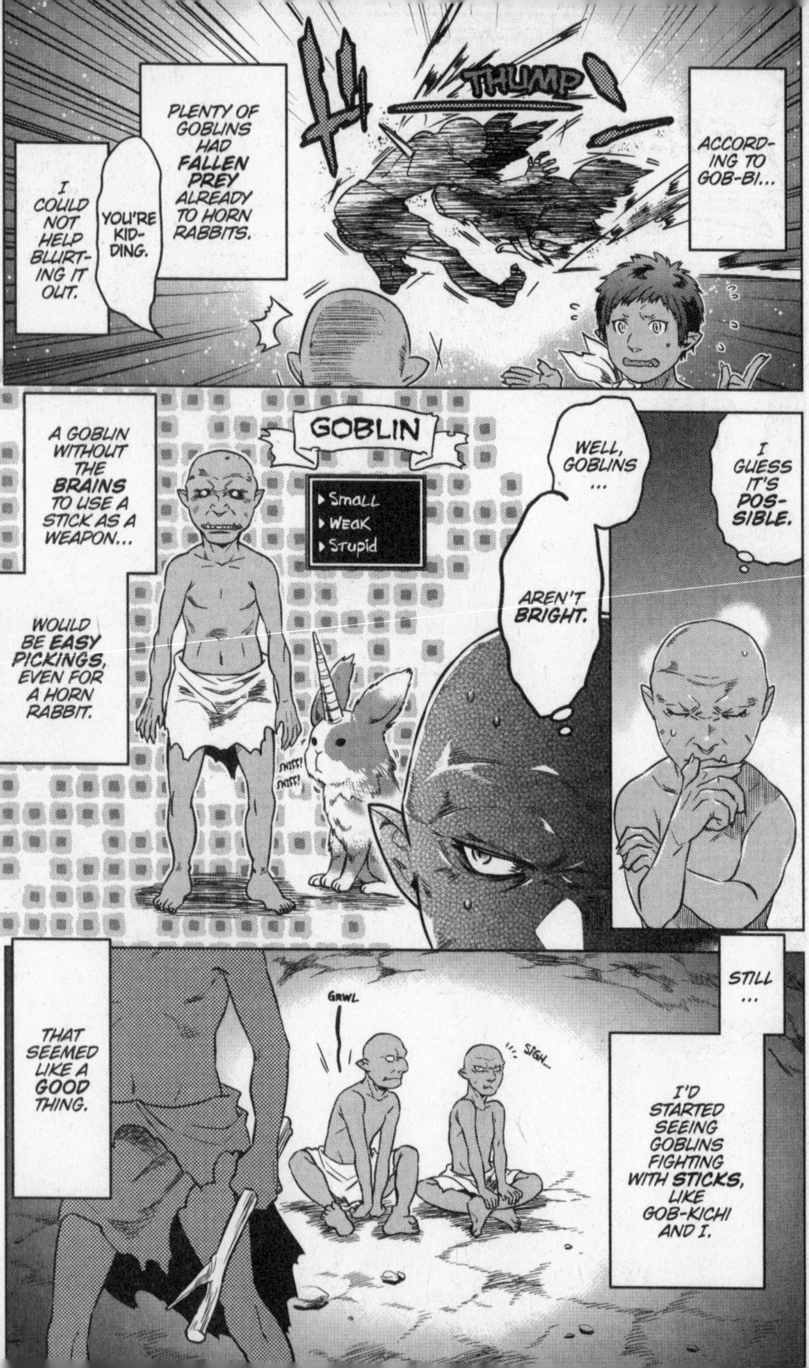
ACCORDING TO GOB-BI...
THUMP
PLENTY OF GOBLINS HAD FALLEN PREY ALREADY TO HORN RABBITS.
YOU'RE KIDDING.
I COULD NOT HELP BLURTING IT OUT.
I GUESS IT'S POSSIBLE.
WELL, GOBLINS ...
AREN'T BRIGHT.
GOBLIN
▸Small
▸Weak
▸Stupid
A GOBLIN WITHOUT THE BRAINS TO USE A STICK AS A WEAPON...
WOULD BE EASY PICKINGS, EVEN FOR A HORN RABBIT.
SNIFF! SNIFF!
STILL ...
I'D STARTED SEEING GOBLINS FIGHTING WITH STICKS, LIKE GOB-KICHI AND I.
SIGH...
GRWL
THAT SEEMED LIKE A GOOD THING.

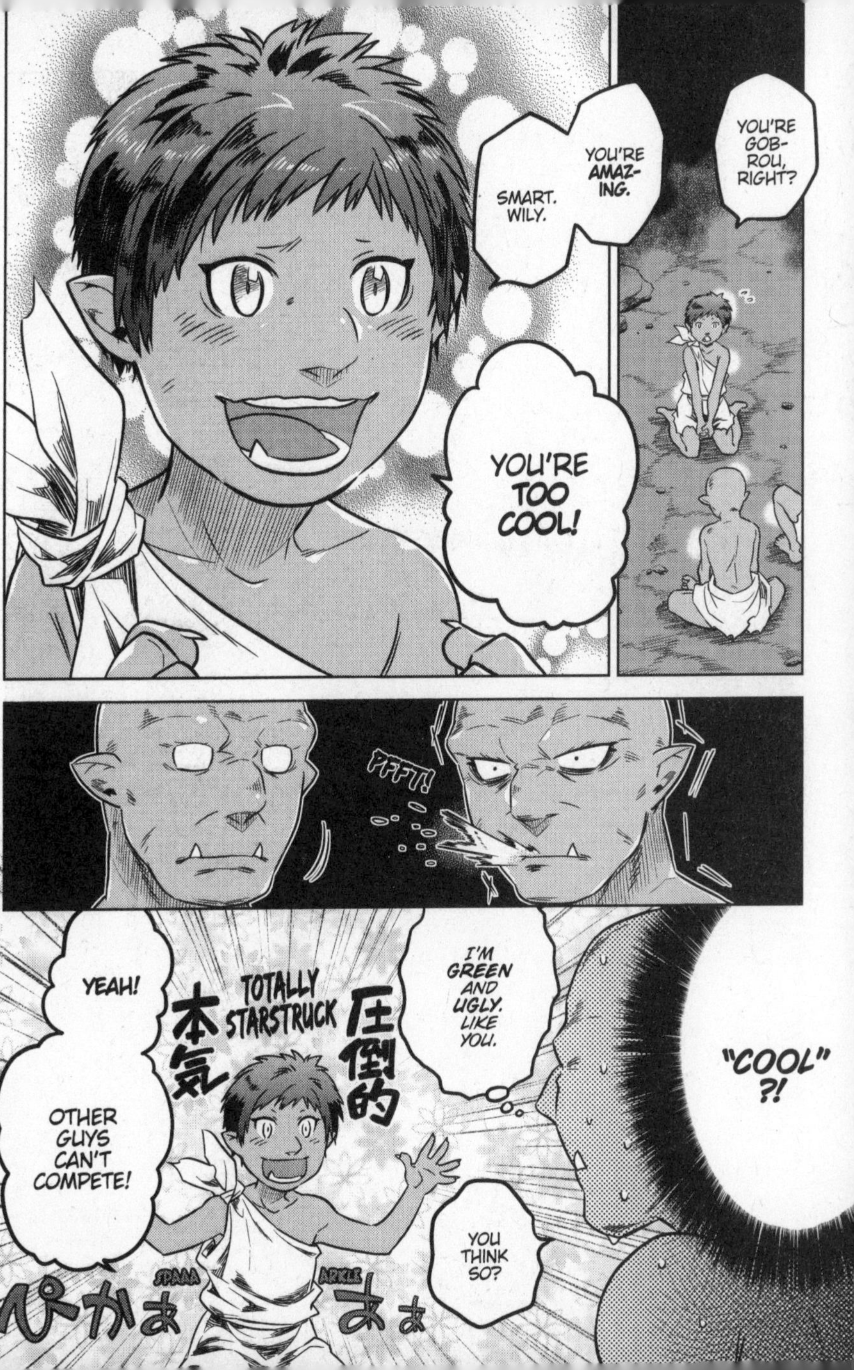
YOU'RE GOB-ROU, RIGHT?
YOU'RE AMAZ-ING.
SMART. WILY.
YOU'RE TOO COOL!
PFFFT!
"COOL" ?!
I'M GREEN AND UGLY. LIKE YOU.
YOU THINK SO?
YEAH!
TOTALLY STARSTRUCK
圧倒的本気
OTHER GUYS CAN'T COMPETE!
SPAAA ARKLE
ぴかぁ あぁ

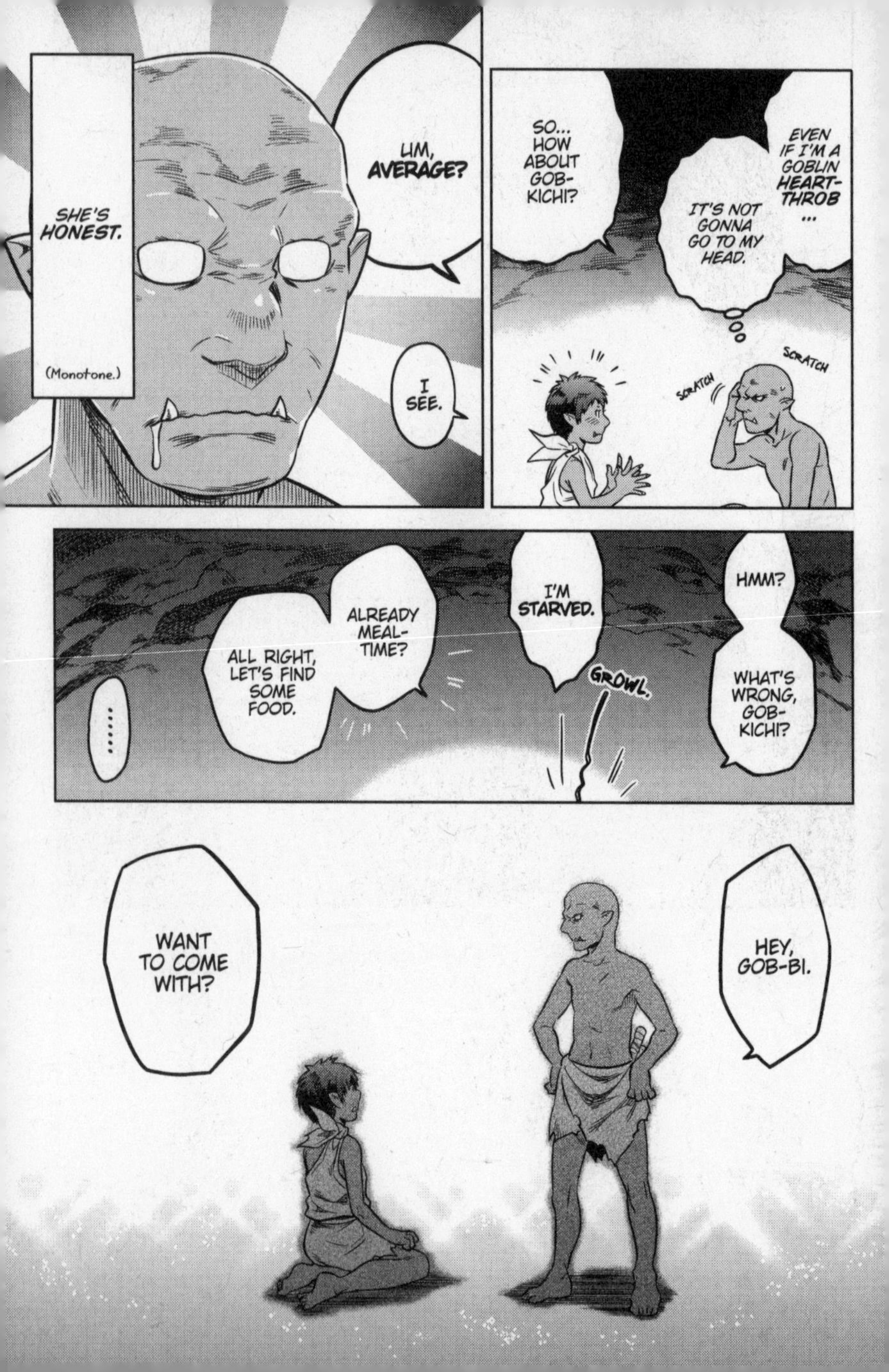
SO... HOW ABOUT GOB-KICHI?
EVEN IF I'M A GOBLIN HEART-THROB...
IT'S NOT GONNA GO TO MY HEAD.
SCRATCH
SCRATCH
UM, **AVERAGE?**
SHE'S **HONEST.**
I SEE.
(Monotone.)
HMM?
WHAT'S WRONG, GOB-KICHI?
GROWL.
I'M **STARVED.**
ALREADY MEAL-TIME?
ALL RIGHT, LET'S FIND SOME FOOD.
......
HEY, GOB-BI.
WANT TO COME WITH?

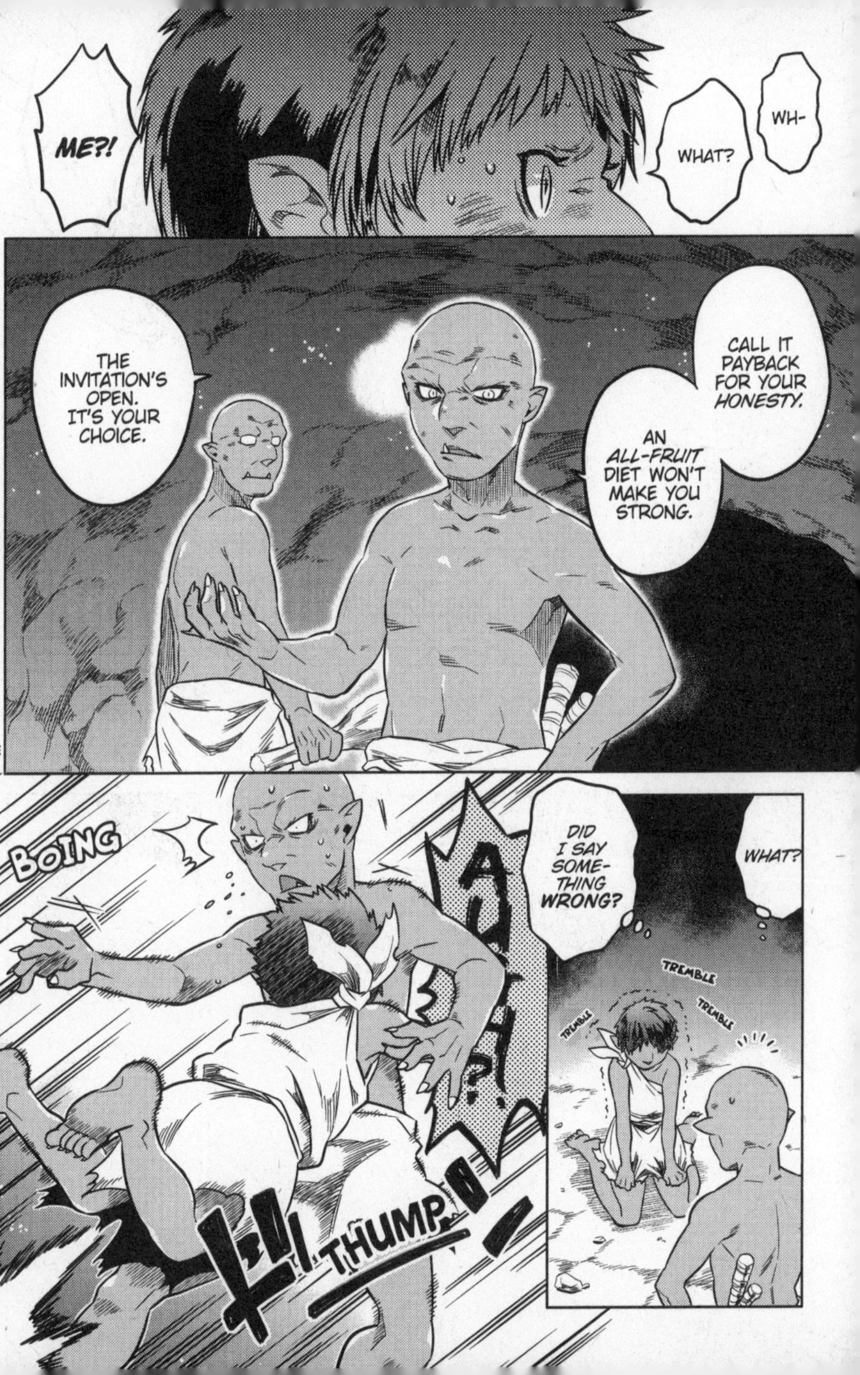
WH-
WHAT?
ME?!
CALL IT PAYBACK FOR YOUR *HONESTY.*
AN *ALL-FRUIT* DIET WON'T MAKE YOU STRONG.
THE INVITATION'S OPEN. IT'S YOUR CHOICE.
WHAT?
DID I SAY SOME-THING *WRONG?*
TREMBLE
TREMBLE
TREMBLE
AUGH?!
BOING
THUMP

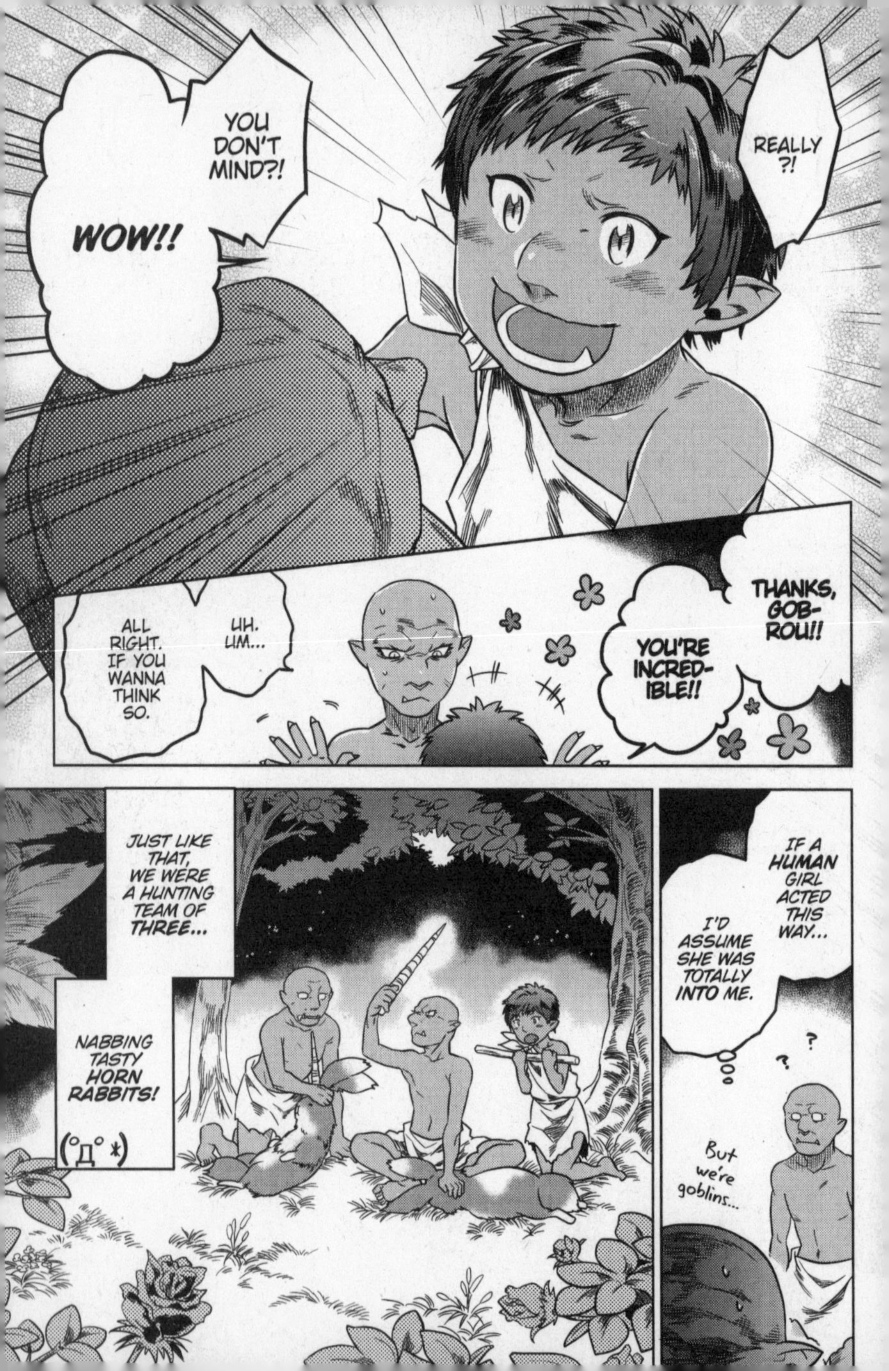
REALLY ?!
YOU DON'T MIND?!
WOW!!
THANKS, GOB-ROU!!
YOU'RE INCRED-IBLE!!
UH. UM...
ALL RIGHT. IF YOU WANNA THINK SO.
IF A HUMAN GIRL ACTED THIS WAY...
I'D ASSUME SHE WAS TOTALLY INTO ME.
? ?
But we're goblins...
JUST LIKE THAT, WE WERE A HUNTING TEAM OF THREE...
NABBING TASTY HORN RABBITS!
(°Д°*)

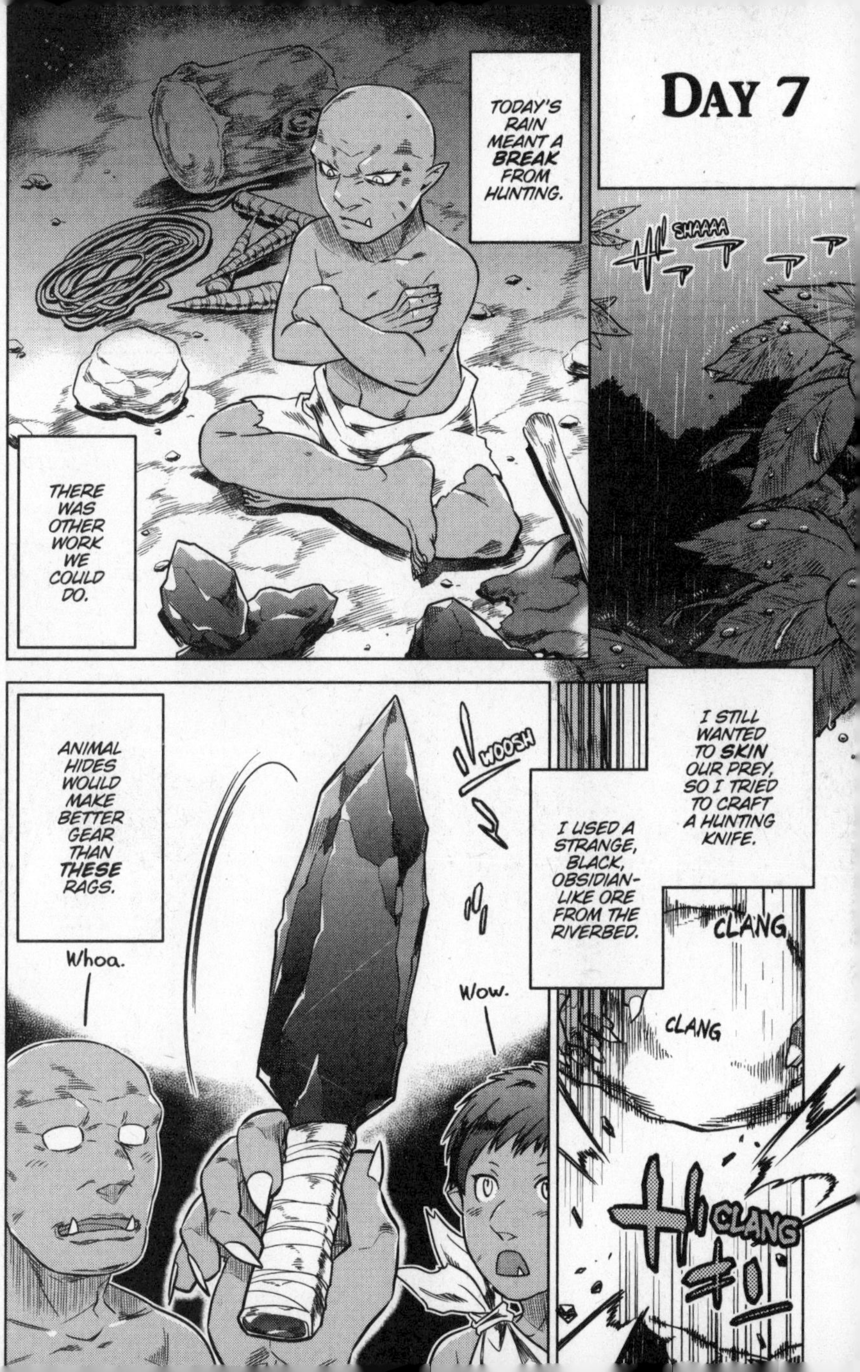
DAY 7
SHAAAA
TODAY'S RAIN MEANT A BREAK FROM HUNTING.
THERE WAS OTHER WORK WE COULD DO.
I STILL WANTED TO SKIN OUR PREY, SO I TRIED TO CRAFT A HUNTING KNIFE.
I USED A STRANGE, BLACK, OBSIDIAN-LIKE ORE FROM THE RIVERBED.
CLANG
CLANG
CLANG
WOOSH
ANIMAL HIDES WOULD MAKE BETTER GEAR THAN THESE RAGS.
Wow.
Whoa.

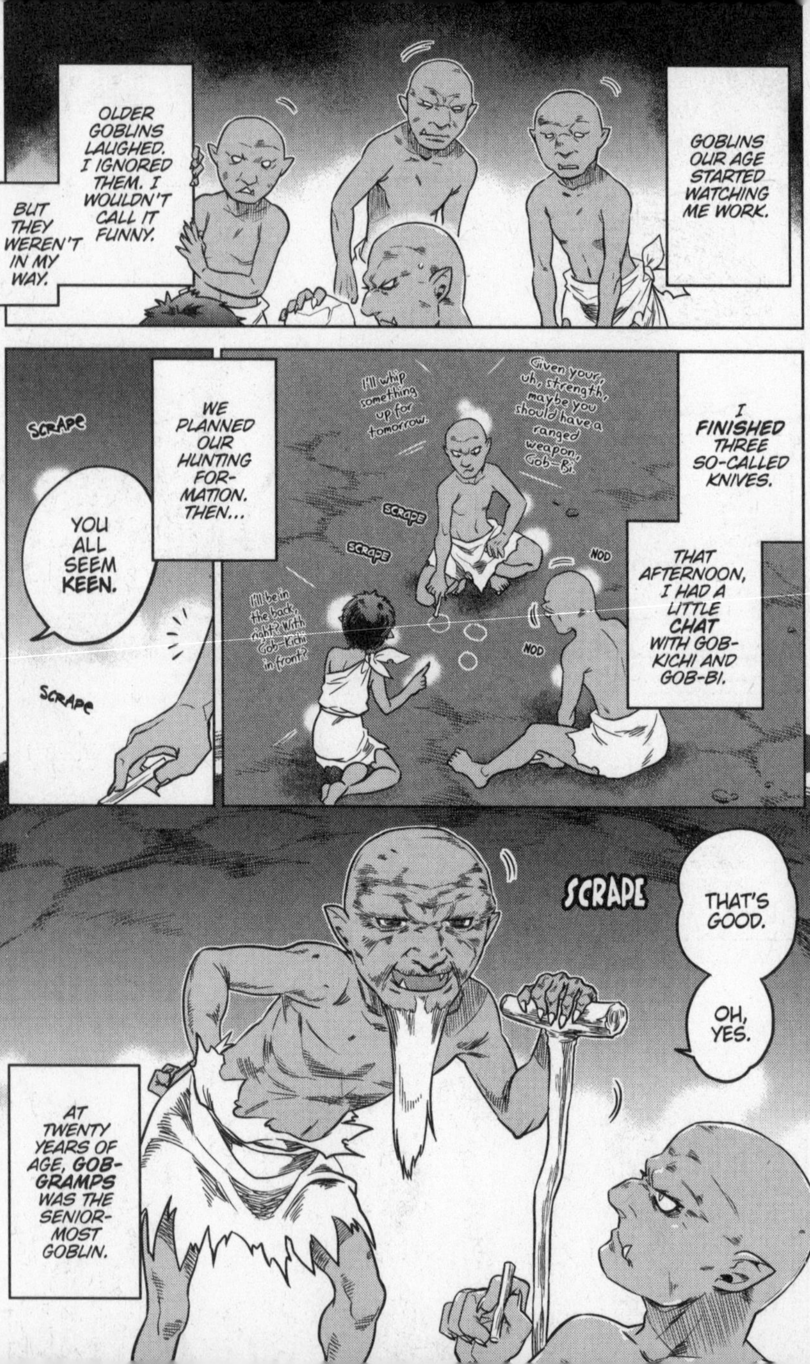
GOBLINS OUR AGE STARTED WATCHING ME WORK.
OLDER GOBLINS LAUGHED. I IGNORED THEM. I WOULDN'T CALL IT FUNNY.
BUT THEY WEREN'T IN MY WAY.
I FINISHED THREE SO-CALLED KNIVES.
THAT AFTERNOON, I HAD A LITTLE CHAT WITH GOB-KICHI AND GOB-BI.
Given your, uh, strength, maybe you should have a ranged weapon, Gob-Bi.
I'll whip something up for tomorrow.
NOD
NOD
I'll be in the back, right? With Gob-Kichi in front?
SCRAPE
SCRAPE
WE PLANNED OUR HUNTING FORMATION. THEN...
SCRAPE
YOU ALL SEEM KEEN.
SCRAPE
THAT'S GOOD.
OH, YES.
SCRAPE
AT TWENTY YEARS OF AGE, GOB-GRAMPS WAS THE SENIOR-MOST GOBLIN.

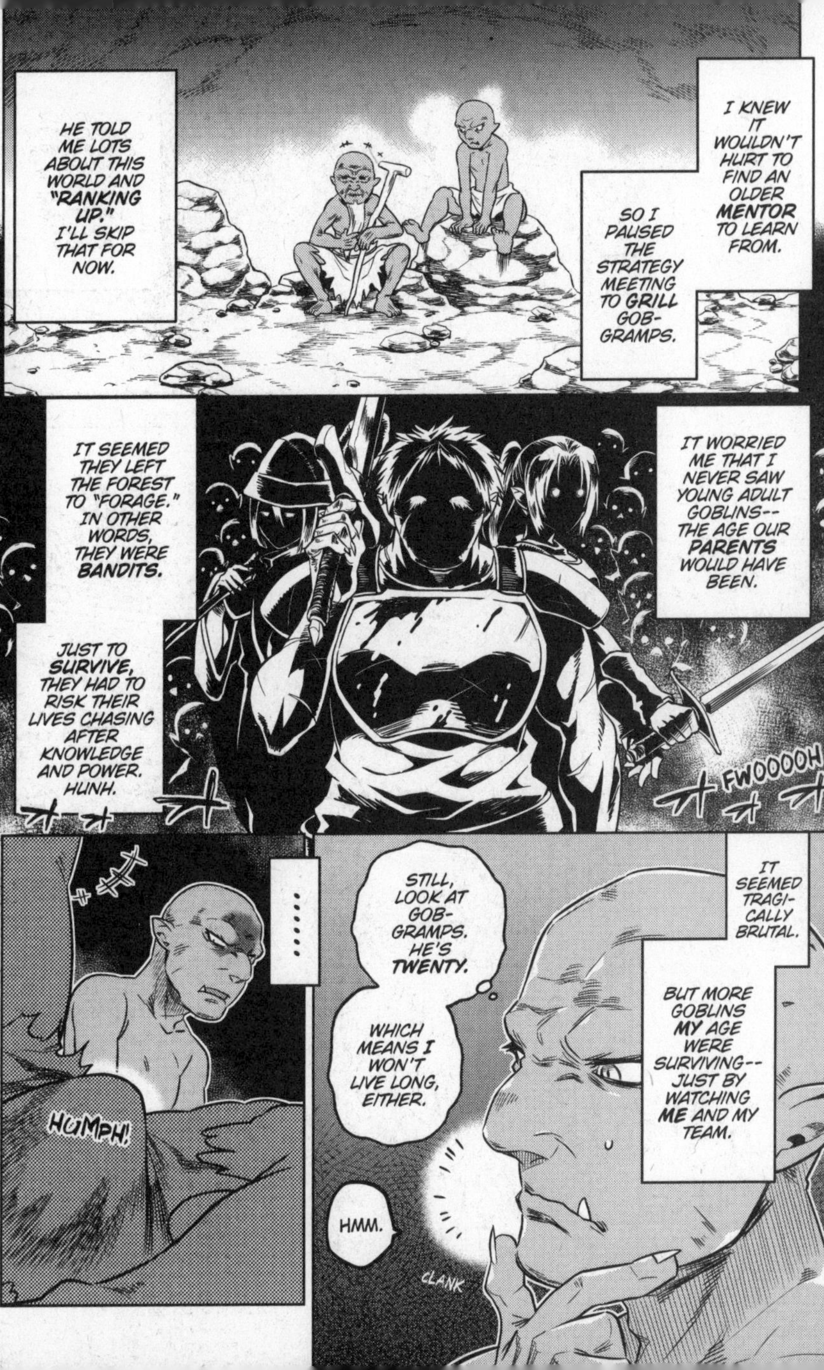
I KNEW IT WOULDN'T HURT TO FIND AN OLDER **MENTOR** TO LEARN FROM.
SO I PAUSED THE STRATEGY MEETING TO **GRILL** GOB-GRAMPS.
HE TOLD ME LOTS ABOUT THIS WORLD AND **"RANKING UP."** I'LL SKIP THAT FOR NOW.
IT WORRIED ME THAT I NEVER SAW YOUNG ADULT GOBLINS-- THE AGE OUR **PARENTS** WOULD HAVE BEEN.
IT SEEMED THEY LEFT THE FOREST TO "FORAGE." IN OTHER WORDS, THEY WERE **BANDITS.**
JUST TO **SURVIVE,** THEY HAD TO RISK THEIR LIVES CHASING AFTER KNOWLEDGE AND POWER. HUNH.
FWOOOOH
IT SEEMED TRAGI-CALLY BRUTAL.
BUT MORE GOBLINS **MY** AGE WERE SURVIVING-- JUST BY WATCHING **ME** AND MY TEAM.
STILL, LOOK AT GOB-GRAMPS. HE'S **TWENTY.**
WHICH MEANS I WON'T LIVE LONG, EITHER.
HMM.
CLANK
......
HUMPH!

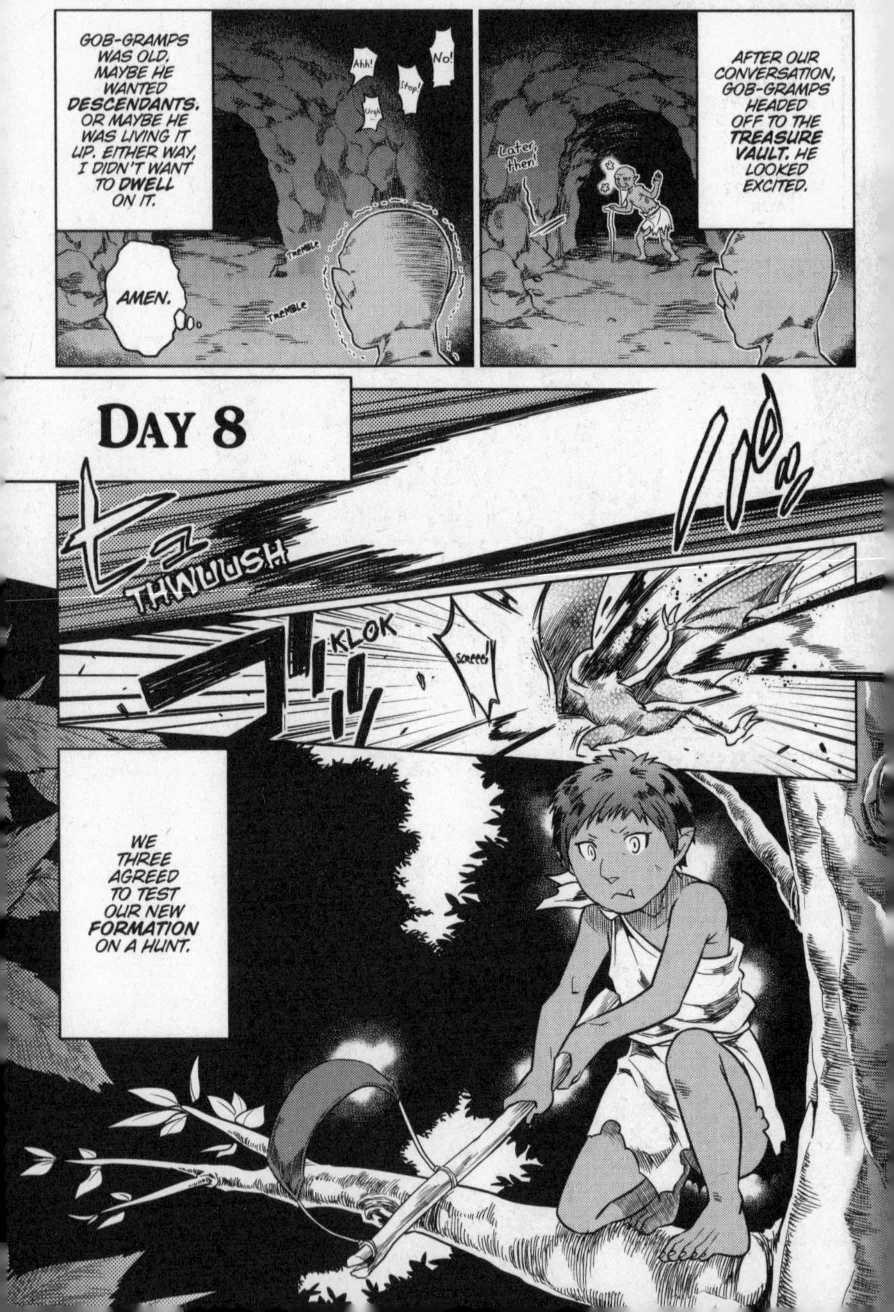
AFTER OUR CONVERSATION, GOB-GRAMPS HEADED OFF TO THE TREASURE VAULT. HE LOOKED EXCITED.
Later, then!
GOB-GRAMPS WAS OLD, MAYBE HE WANTED DESCENDANTS. OR MAYBE HE WAS LIVING IT UP. EITHER WAY, I DIDN'T WANT TO DWELL ON IT.
No!
Ahh!
Stop!
Urgh...
TREMBLE
TREMBLE
AMEN.
DAY 8
THWUUSH
KLOK
Screee!
WE THREE AGREED TO TEST OUR NEW FORMATION ON A HUNT.

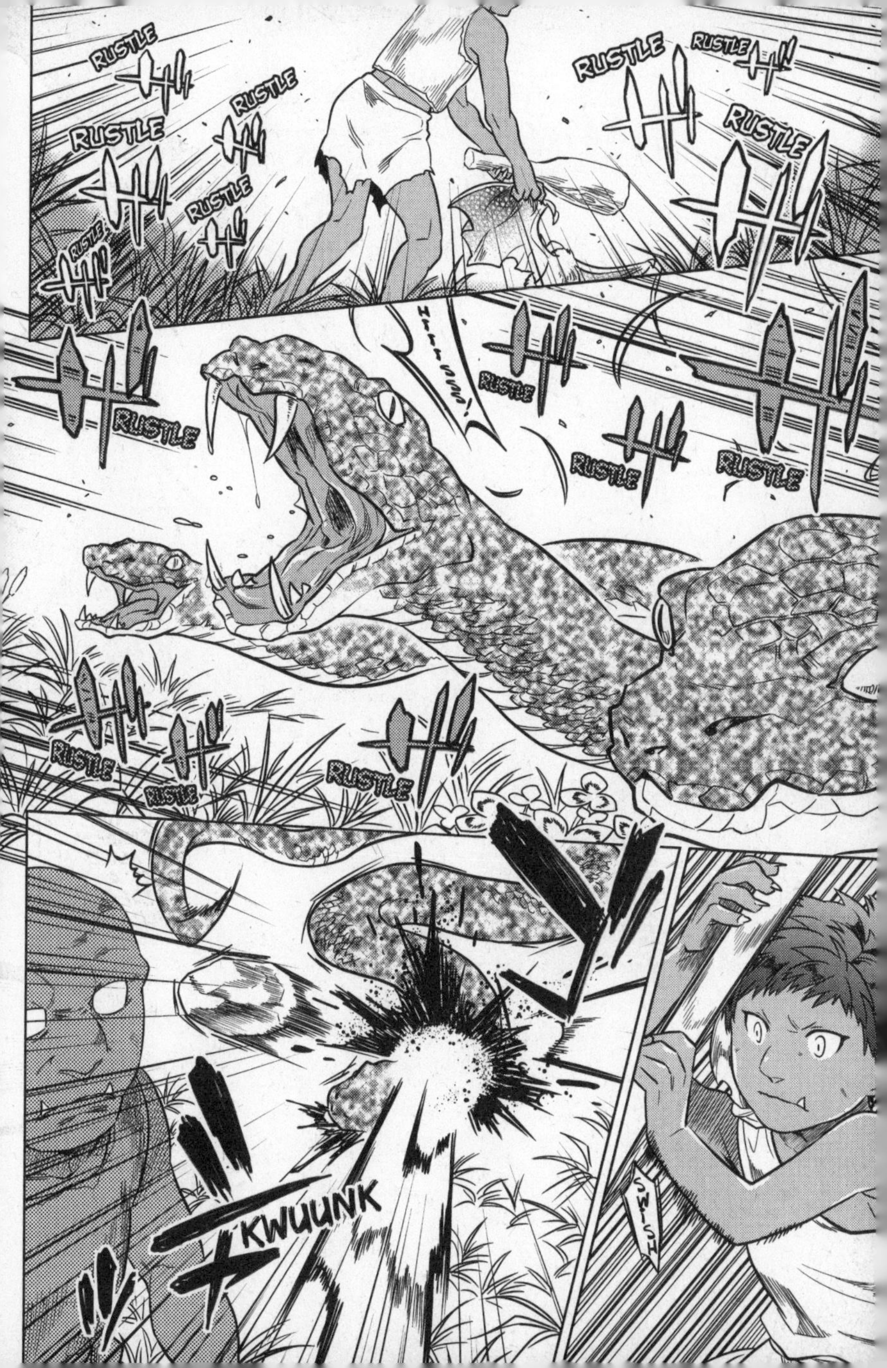

RUSTLE
RUSTLE
RUSTLE
RUSTLE
RUSTLE
RUSTLE
RUSTLE
RUSTLE
HIIIISSS!
RUSTLE
RUSTLE
RUSTLE
RUSTLE
RUSTLE
RUSTLE
RUSTLE
SWISH
KWUUNK

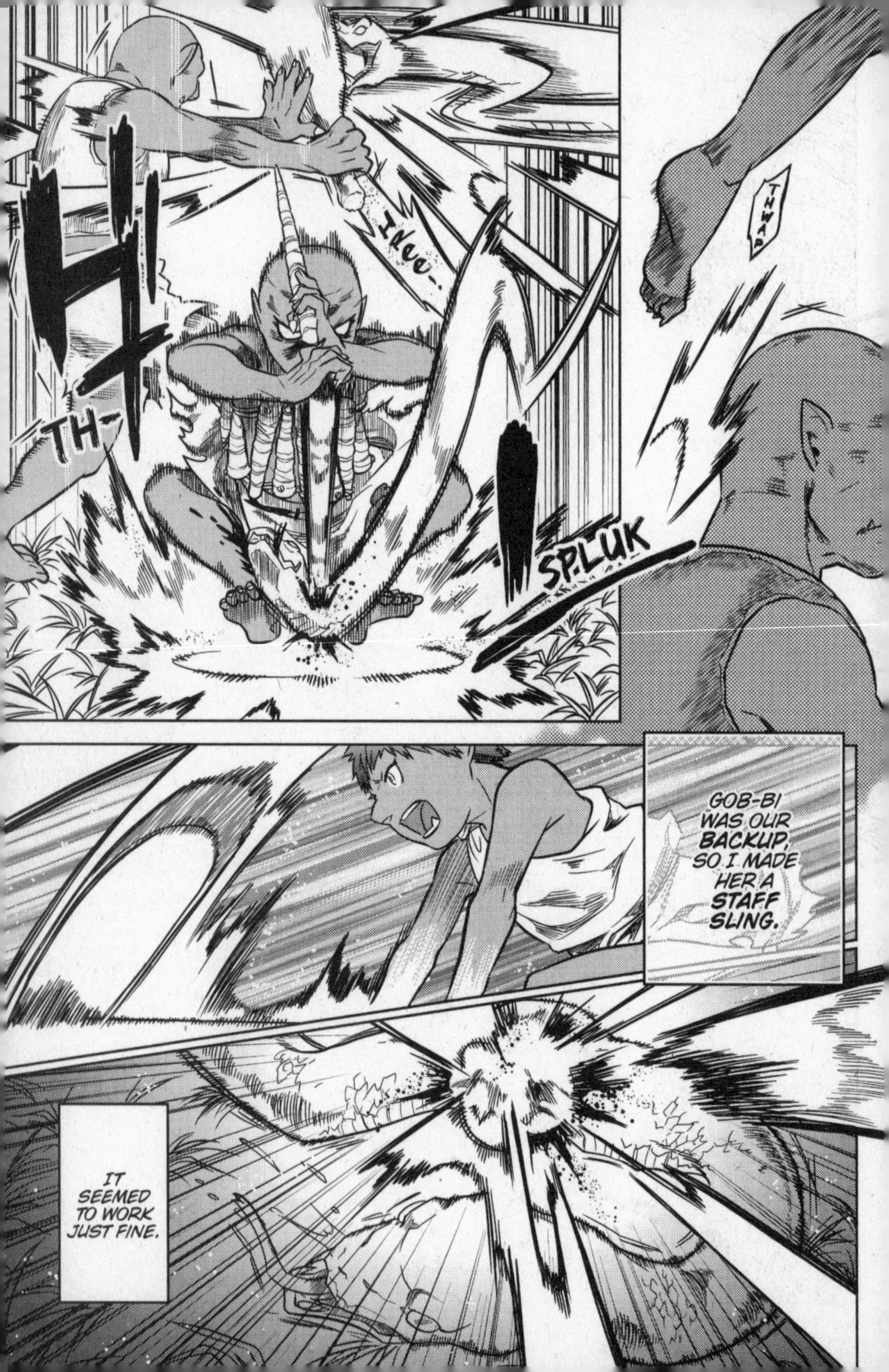
THWAP
Hnee...
SPLUK
TH-
GOB-BI WAS OUR BACKUP, SO I MADE HER A STAFF SLING.
IT SEEMED TO WORK JUST FINE.

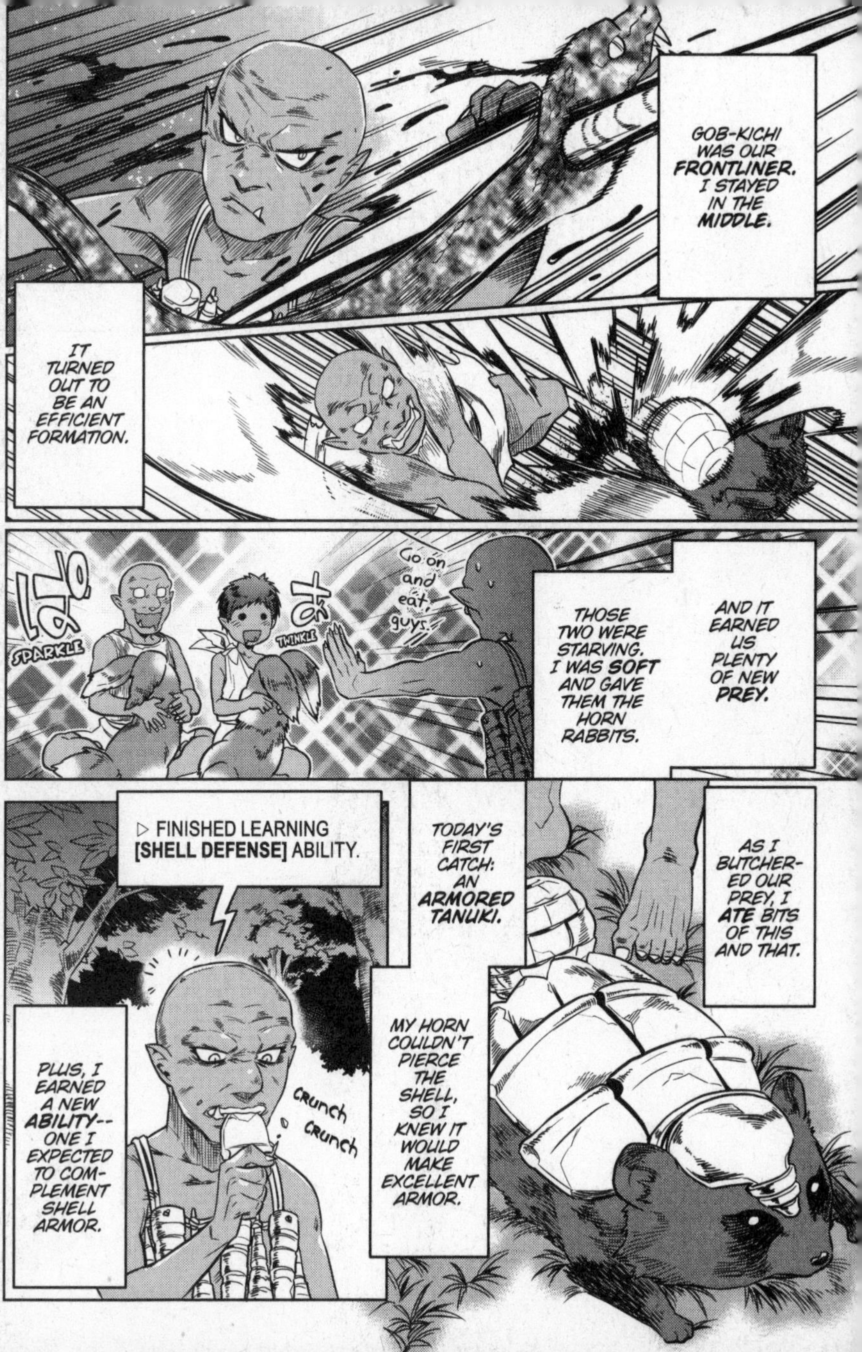
GOB-KICHI WAS OUR **FRONTLINER.** I STAYED IN THE **MIDDLE.**
IT TURNED OUT TO BE AN EFFICIENT FORMATION.
AND IT EARNED US PLENTY OF NEW **PREY.**
THOSE TWO WERE STARVING. I WAS **SOFT** AND GAVE THEM THE HORN RABBITS.
Go on and eat, guys.
TWINKLE
SPARKLE
AS I BUTCHERED OUR PREY, I **ATE** BITS OF THIS AND THAT.
TODAY'S FIRST CATCH: AN **ARMORED TANUKI.**
MY HORN COULDN'T PIERCE THE SHELL, SO I KNEW IT WOULD MAKE EXCELLENT ARMOR.
▷ FINISHED LEARNING **[SHELL DEFENSE]** ABILITY.
PLUS, I EARNED A NEW **ABILITY**-- ONE I EXPECTED TO COMPLEMENT SHELL ARMOR.
Crunch
Crunch

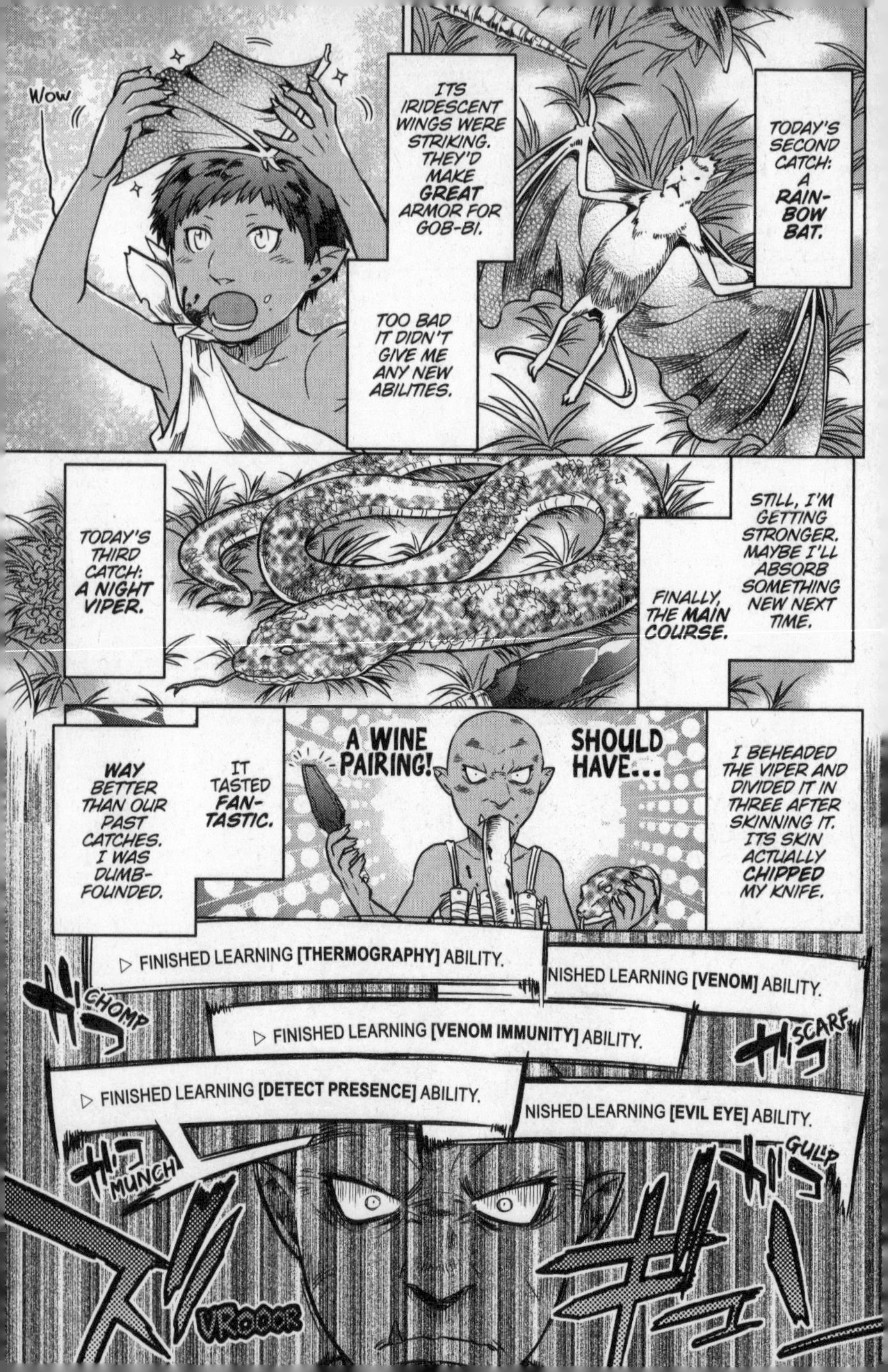

TODAY'S SECOND CATCH: A RAIN-BOW BAT.
ITS IRIDESCENT WINGS WERE STRIKING. THEY'D MAKE GREAT ARMOR FOR GOB-BI.
WOW
TOO BAD IT DIDN'T GIVE ME ANY NEW ABILITIES.
STILL, I'M GETTING STRONGER. MAYBE I'LL ABSORB SOMETHING NEW NEXT TIME.
FINALLY, THE MAIN COURSE.
TODAY'S THIRD CATCH: A NIGHT VIPER.
I BEHEADED THE VIPER AND DIVIDED IT IN THREE AFTER SKINNING IT. ITS SKIN ACTUALLY CHIPPED MY KNIFE.
SHOULD HAVE...
A WINE PAIRING!
IT TASTED FAN-TASTIC.
WAY BETTER THAN OUR PAST CATCHES. I WAS DUMB-FOUNDED.
SCARF
NISHED LEARNING [VENOM] ABILITY.
▷ FINISHED LEARNING [THERMOGRAPHY] ABILITY.
CHOMP
▷ FINISHED LEARNING [VENOM IMMUNITY] ABILITY.
NISHED LEARNING [EVIL EYE] ABILITY.
▷ FINISHED LEARNING [DETECT PRESENCE] ABILITY.
GULP
MUNCH

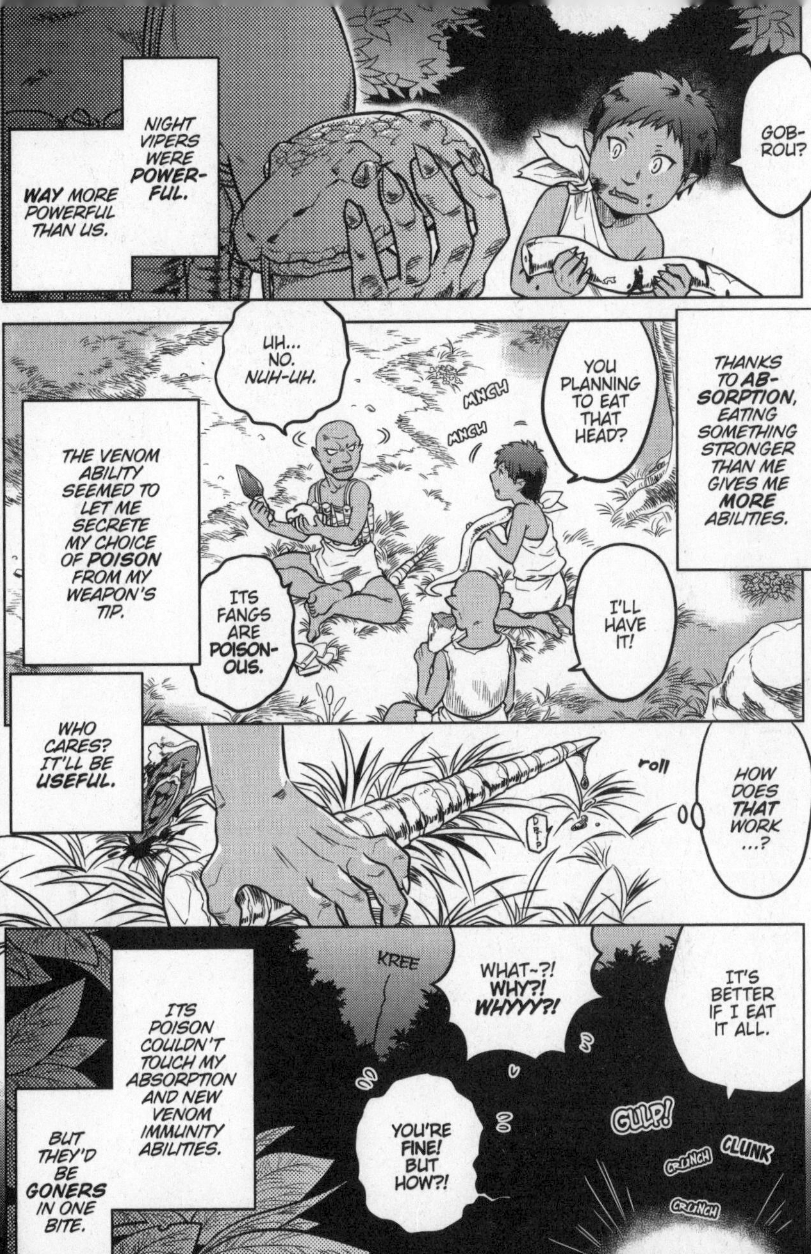
GOB-ROU?
NIGHT VIPERS WERE POWERFUL.
WAY MORE POWERFUL THAN US.
THANKS TO ABSORPTION, EATING SOMETHING STRONGER THAN ME GIVES ME MORE ABILITIES.
YOU PLANNING TO EAT THAT HEAD?
MNCH
MNCH
UH... NO. NUH-UH.
THE VENOM ABILITY SEEMED TO LET ME SECRETE MY CHOICE OF POISON FROM MY WEAPON'S TIP.
I'LL HAVE IT!
ITS FANGS ARE POISONOUS.
HOW DOES THAT WORK ...?
roll
DRIP
WHO CARES? IT'LL BE USEFUL.
IT'S BETTER IF I EAT IT ALL.
WHAT~?! WHY?! WHYYY?!
KREE
GULP!
CLUNK
CRUNCH
CRUNCH
YOU'RE FINE! BUT HOW?!
ITS POISON COULDN'T TOUCH MY ABSORPTION AND NEW VENOM IMMUNITY ABILITIES.
BUT THEY'D BE GONERS IN ONE BITE.

▶ CONTINUE

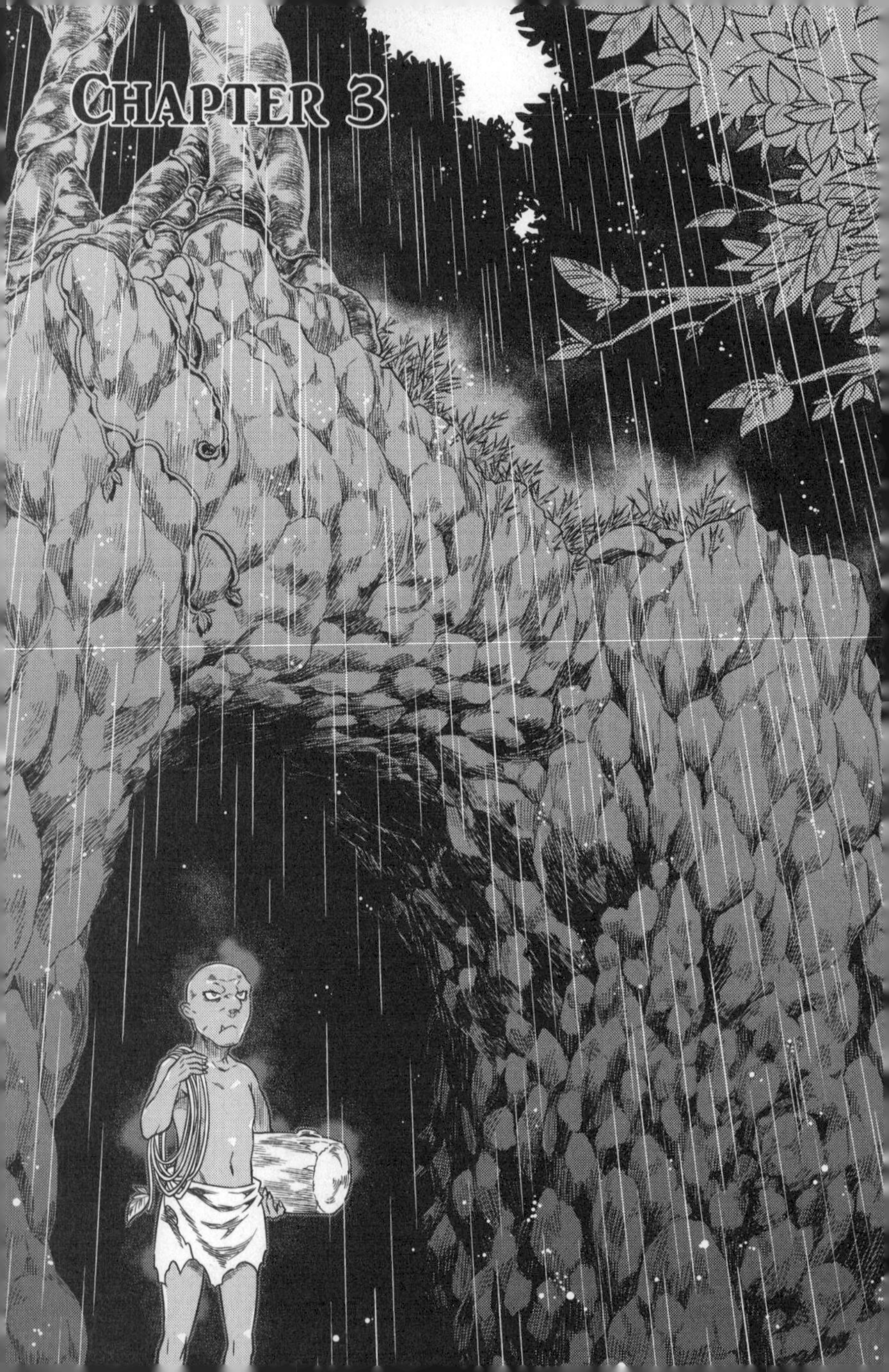
CHAPTER 3

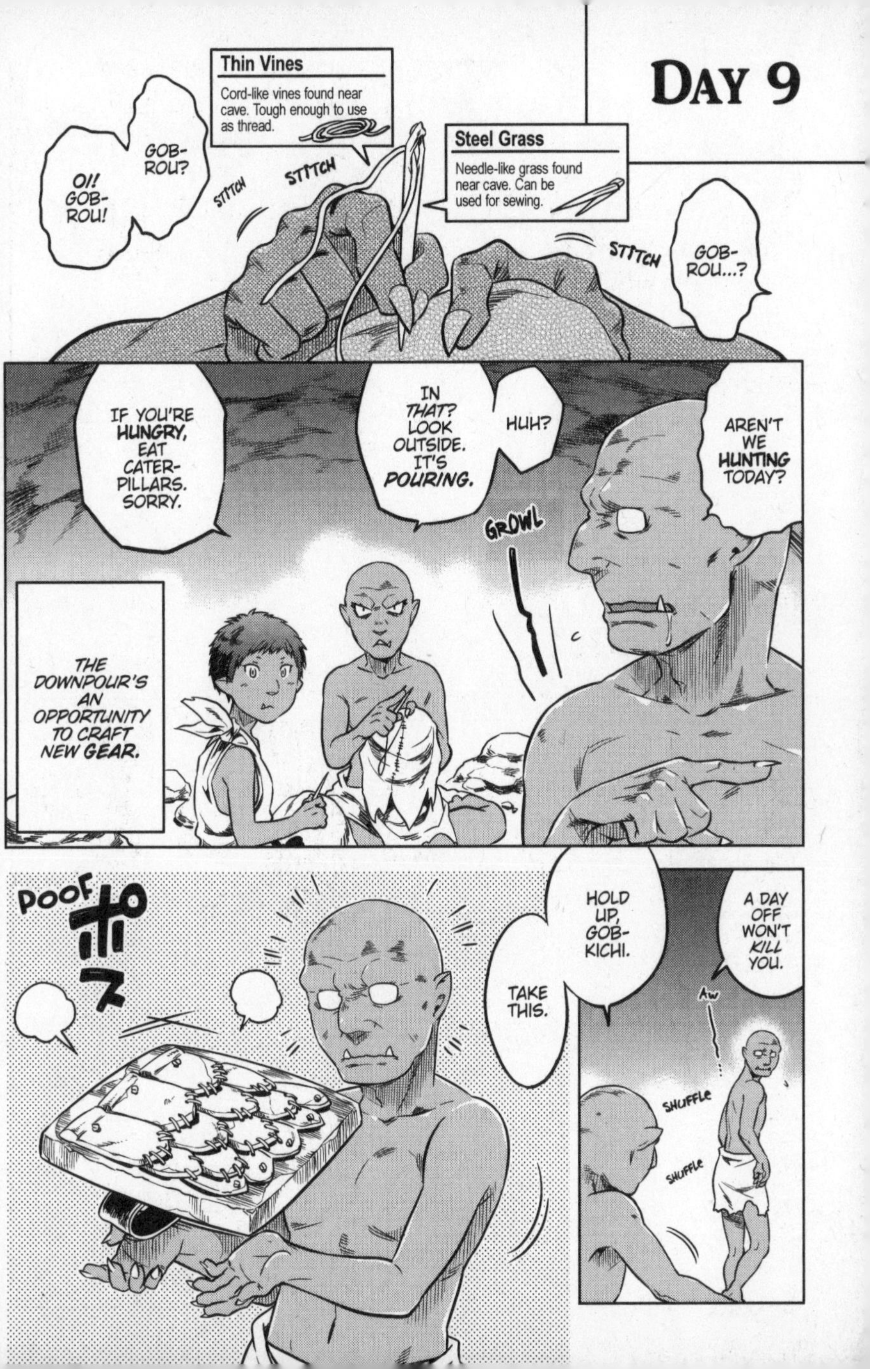

DAY 9
GOB-ROU...?
STITCH
Steel Grass
Needle-like grass found near cave. Can be used for sewing.
Thin Vines
Cord-like vines found near cave. Tough enough to use as thread.
STITCH
STITCH
GOB-ROU?
OI! GOB-ROU!
AREN'T WE HUNTING TODAY?
GROWL
HUH?
IN THAT? LOOK OUTSIDE. IT'S POURING.
IF YOU'RE HUNGRY, EAT CATER-PILLARS. SORRY.
THE DOWNPOUR'S AN OPPORTUNITY TO CRAFT NEW GEAR.
A DAY OFF WON'T KILL YOU.
AW...
SHUFFLE
SHUFFLE
HOLD UP, GOB-KICHI.
TAKE THIS.
POOF ポフ

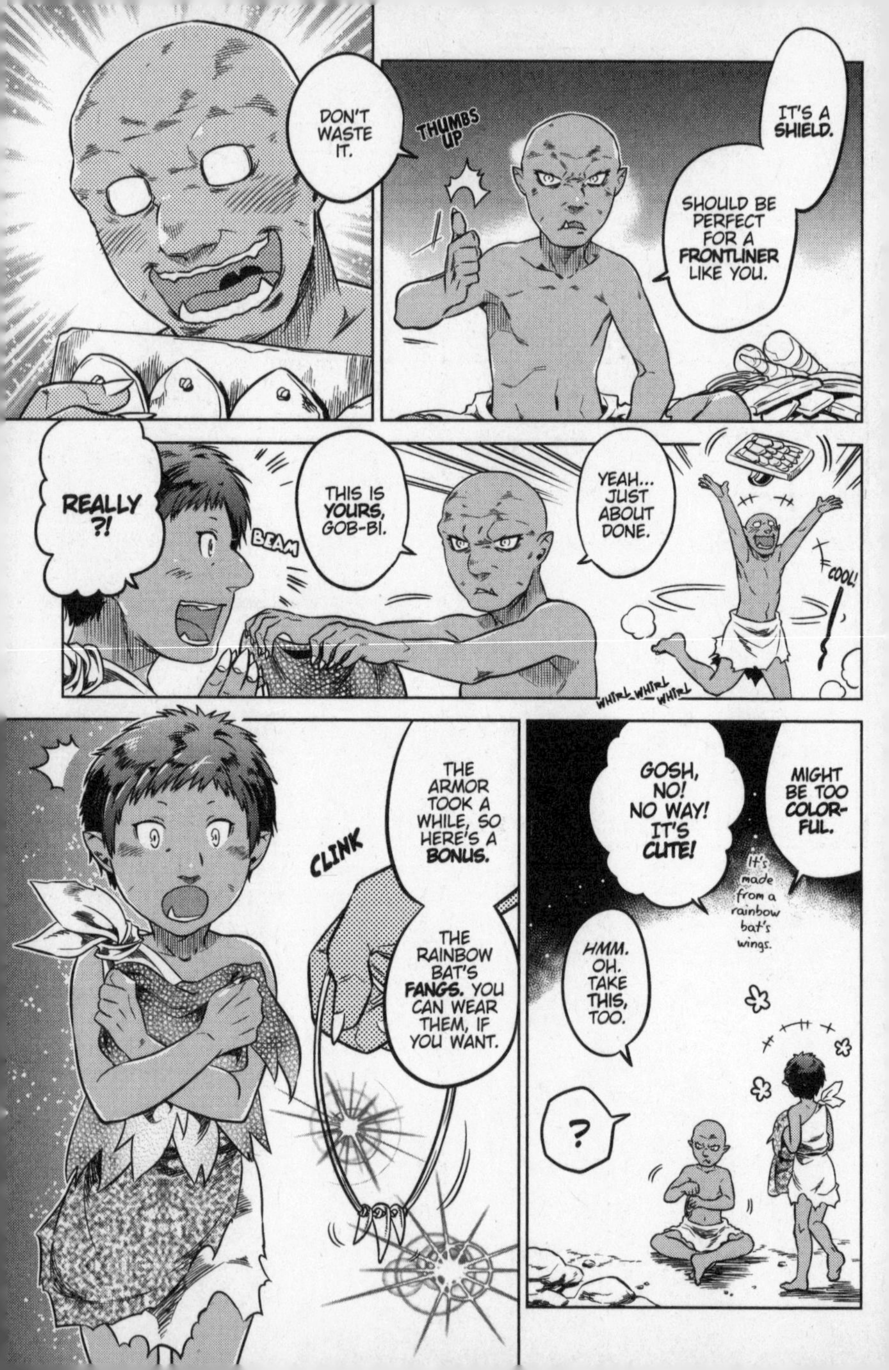
IT'S A SHIELD.
SHOULD BE PERFECT FOR A FRONTLINER LIKE YOU.
THUMBS UP
DON'T WASTE IT.
COOL!
YEAH... JUST ABOUT DONE.
THIS IS YOURS, GOB-BI.
REALLY?!
BEAM
WHIRL WHIRL WHIRL
MIGHT BE TOO COLORFUL.
It's made from a rainbow bat's wings.
GOSH, NO! NO WAY! IT'S CUTE!
HMM. OH. TAKE THIS, TOO.
?
THE ARMOR TOOK A WHILE, SO HERE'S A BONUS.
CLINK
THE RAINBOW BAT'S FANGS. YOU CAN WEAR THEM, IF YOU WANT.

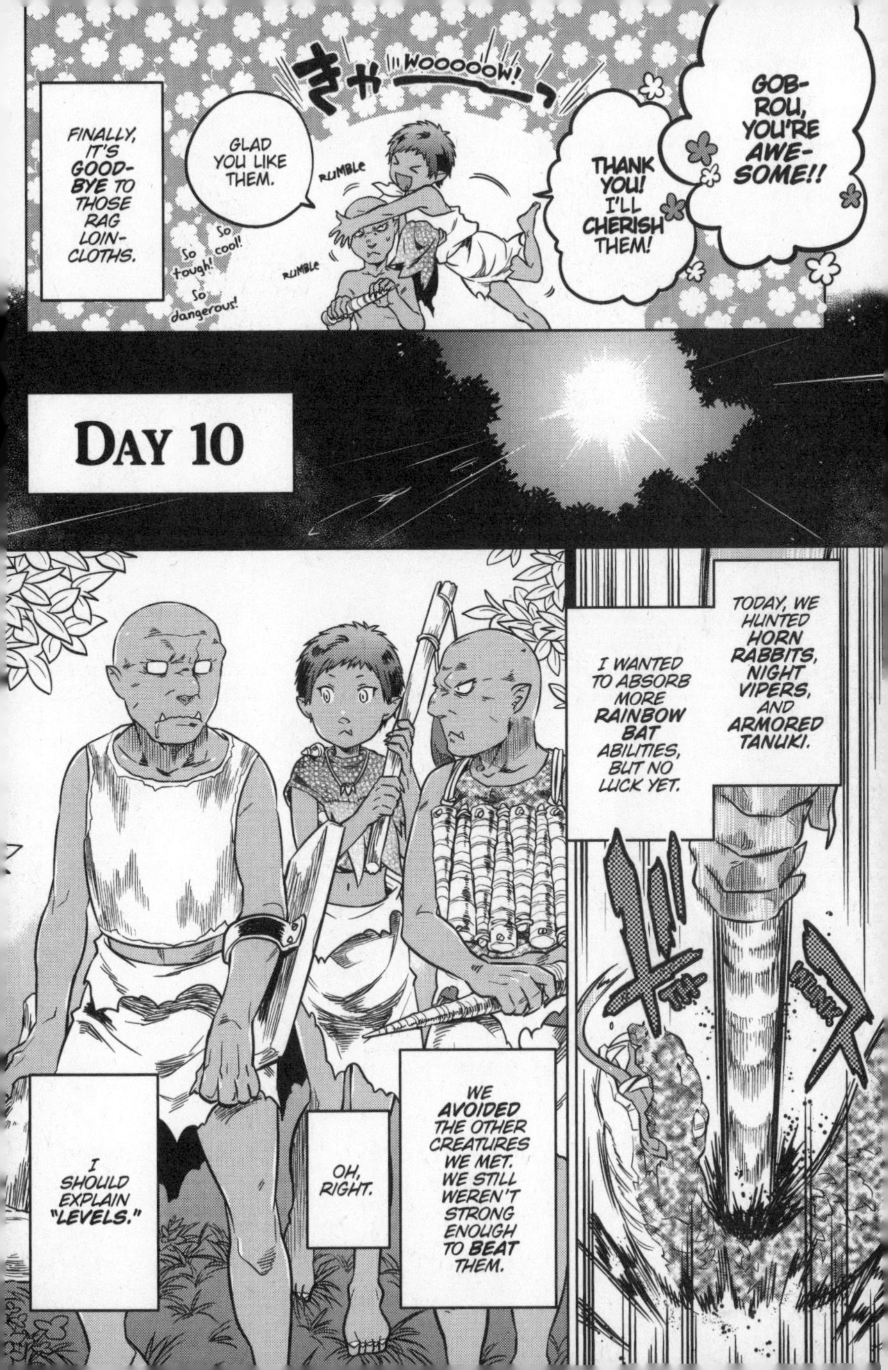

GOB-ROU, YOU'RE AWESOME!!
THANK YOU! I'LL CHERISH THEM!
きゃ— WOOOOOW!
RUMBLE
GLAD YOU LIKE THEM.
So cool!
So tough!
So dangerous!
RUMBLE
FINALLY, IT'S GOODBYE TO THOSE RAG LOINCLOTHS.
DAY 10
TODAY, WE HUNTED HORN RABBITS, NIGHT VIPERS, AND ARMORED TANUKI.
I WANTED TO ABSORB MORE RAINBOW BAT ABILITIES, BUT NO LUCK YET.
WE AVOIDED THE OTHER CREATURES WE MET. WE STILL WEREN'T STRONG ENOUGH TO BEAT THEM.
OH, RIGHT.
I SHOULD EXPLAIN "LEVELS."

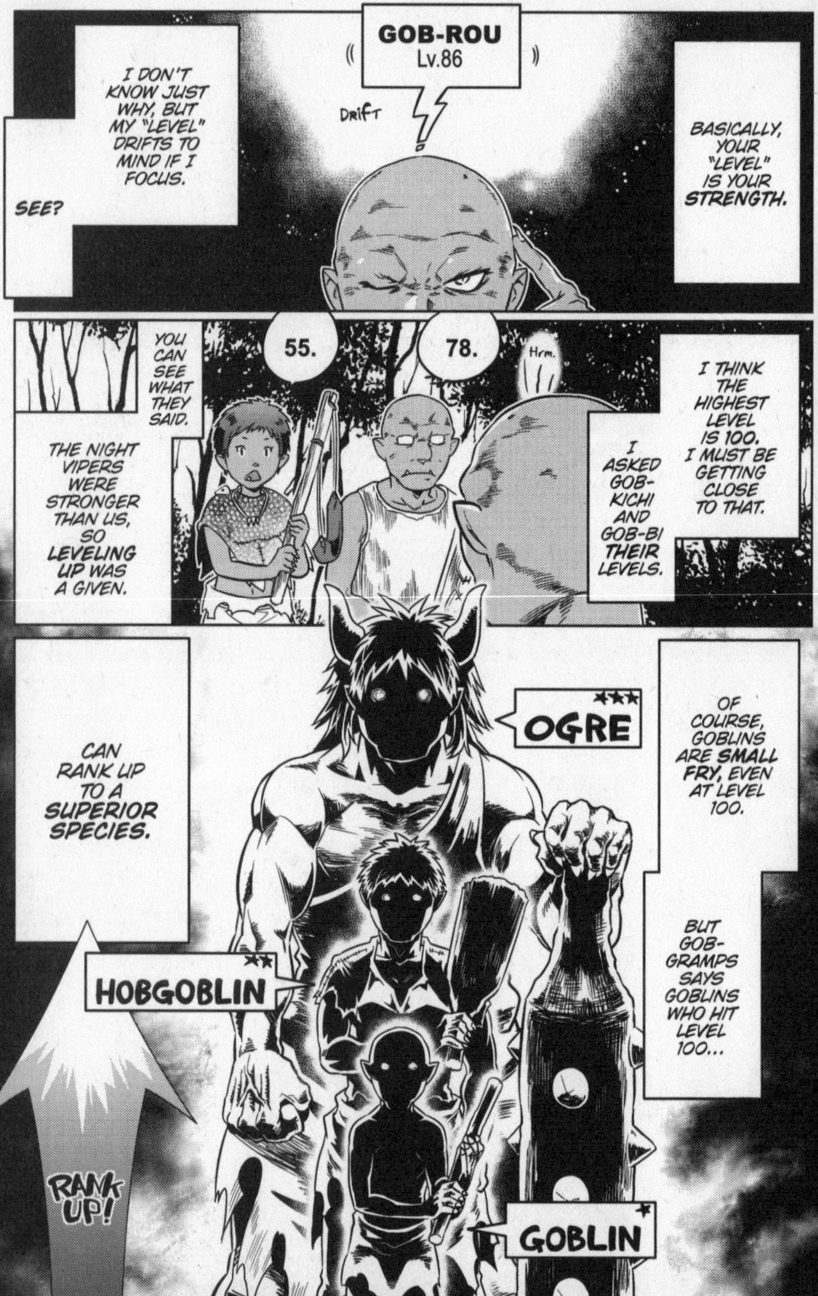

BASICALLY, YOUR "LEVEL" IS YOUR STRENGTH.
GOB-ROU Lv.86
DRIFT
I DON'T KNOW JUST WHY, BUT MY "LEVEL" DRIFTS TO MIND IF I FOCUS.
SEE?
I THINK THE HIGHEST LEVEL IS 100. I MUST BE GETTING CLOSE TO THAT.
I ASKED GOB-KICHI AND GOB-BI THEIR LEVELS.
Hrm.
78.
55.
YOU CAN SEE WHAT THEY SAID.
THE NIGHT VIPERS WERE STRONGER THAN US, SO LEVELING UP WAS A GIVEN.
OF COURSE, GOBLINS ARE SMALL FRY, EVEN AT LEVEL 100.
BUT GOB-GRAMPS SAYS GOBLINS WHO HIT LEVEL 100...
OGRE
CAN RANK UP TO A SUPERIOR SPECIES.
HOBGOBLIN
GOBLIN
RANK UP!

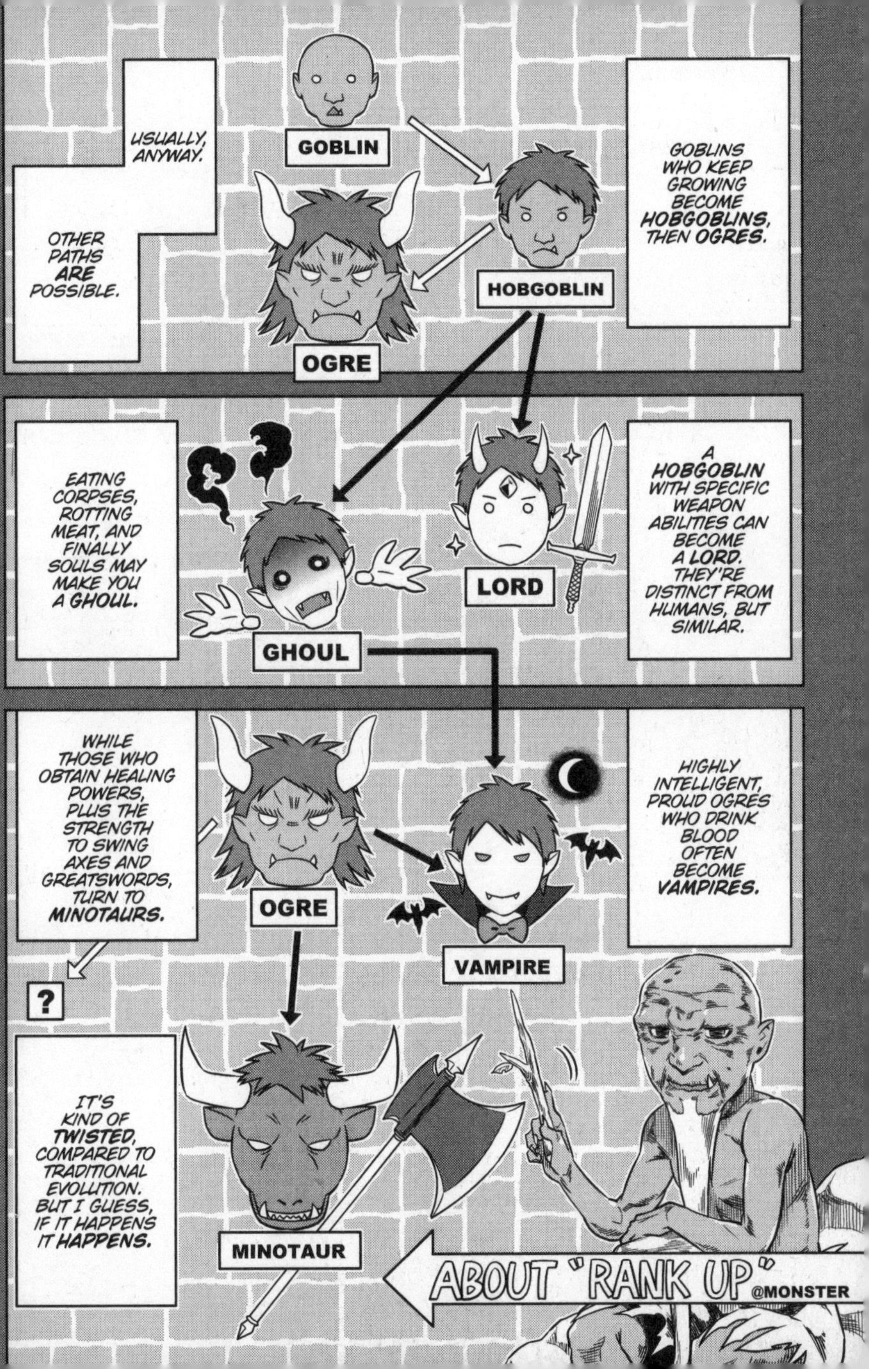
GOBLINS WHO KEEP GROWING BECOME HOBGOBLINS, THEN OGRES.
GOBLIN
HOBGOBLIN
OGRE
USUALLY, ANYWAY.
OTHER PATHS ARE POSSIBLE.
A HOBGOBLIN WITH SPECIFIC WEAPON ABILITIES CAN BECOME A LORD. THEY'RE DISTINCT FROM HUMANS, BUT SIMILAR.
LORD
GHOUL
EATING CORPSES, ROTTING MEAT, AND FINALLY SOULS MAY MAKE YOU A GHOUL.
HIGHLY INTELLIGENT, PROUD OGRES WHO DRINK BLOOD OFTEN BECOME VAMPIRES.
VAMPIRE
OGRE
WHILE THOSE WHO OBTAIN HEALING POWERS, PLUS THE STRENGTH TO SWING AXES AND GREATSWORDS, TURN TO MINOTAURS.
?
MINOTAUR
IT'S KIND OF TWISTED, COMPARED TO TRADITIONAL EVOLUTION. BUT I GUESS, IF IT HAPPENS IT HAPPENS.
ABOUT "RANK UP" @MONSTER

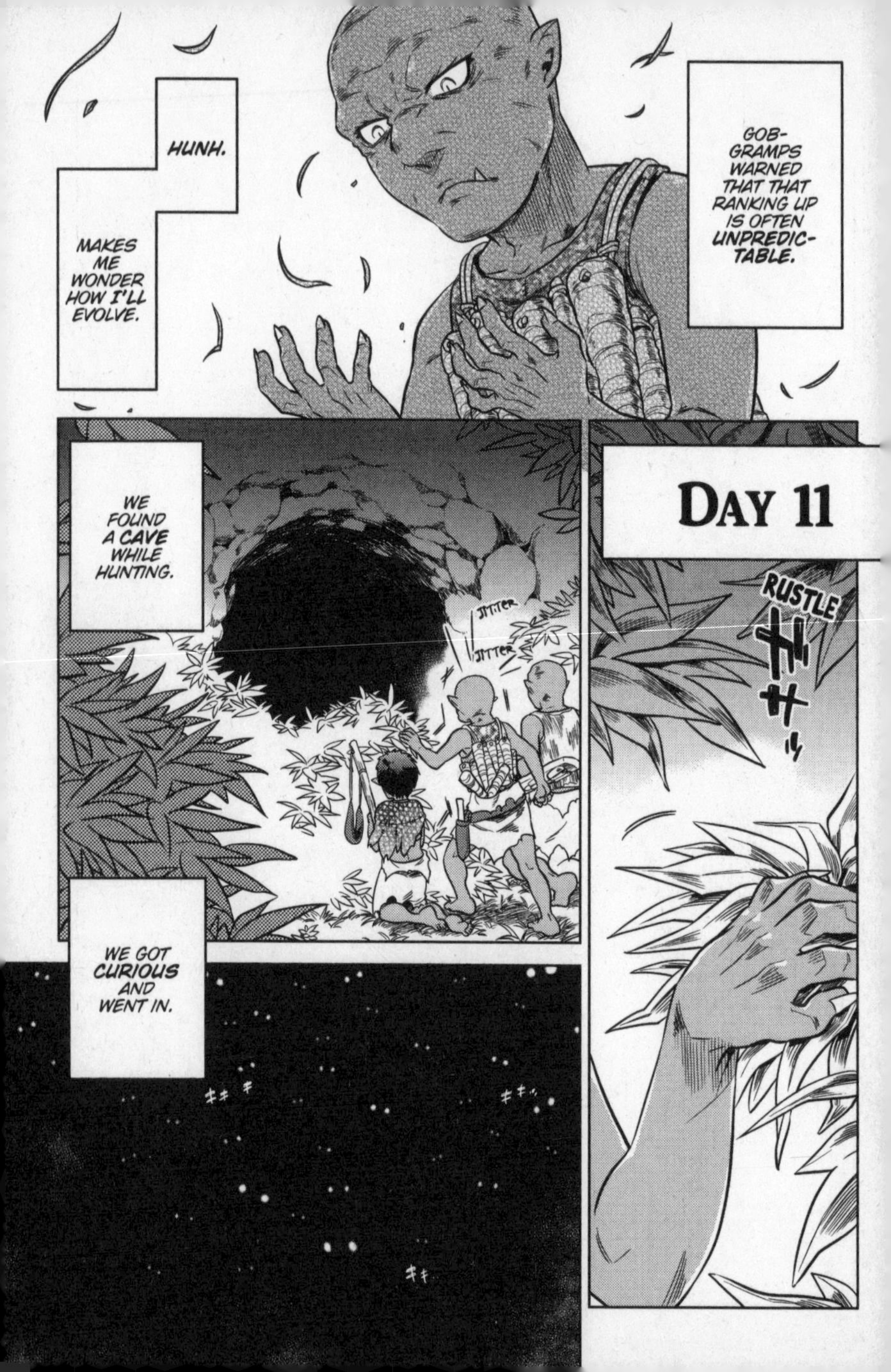
GOB-GRAMPS WARNED THAT THAT RANKING UP IS OFTEN UNPREDICTABLE.
HUNH.
MAKES ME WONDER HOW I'LL EVOLVE.
DAY 11
RUSTLE
WE FOUND A CAVE WHILE HUNTING.
JITTER
JITTER
WE GOT CURIOUS AND WENT IN.

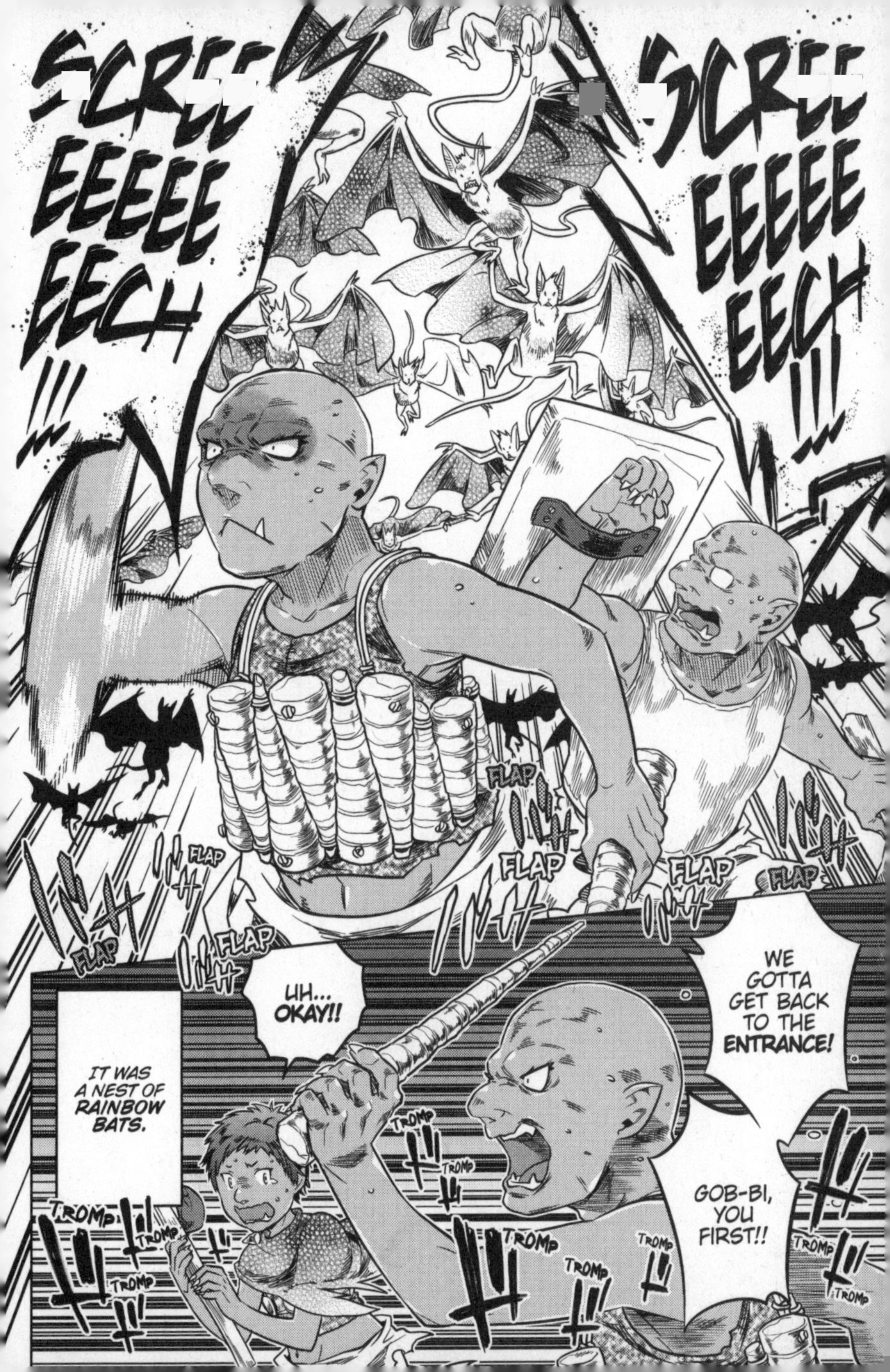
SCREEEEEEEEECH!!!
SCREEEEEEEEECH!!!
FLAP
FLAP
FLAP
FLAP
FLAP
FLAP
FLAP
WE GOTTA GET BACK TO THE **ENTRANCE!**
GOB-BI, YOU FIRST!!
UH... **OKAY!!**
IT WAS A NEST OF **RAINBOW** BATS.
TROMP
TROMP
TROMP
TROMP
TROMP
TROMP
TROMP
TROMP

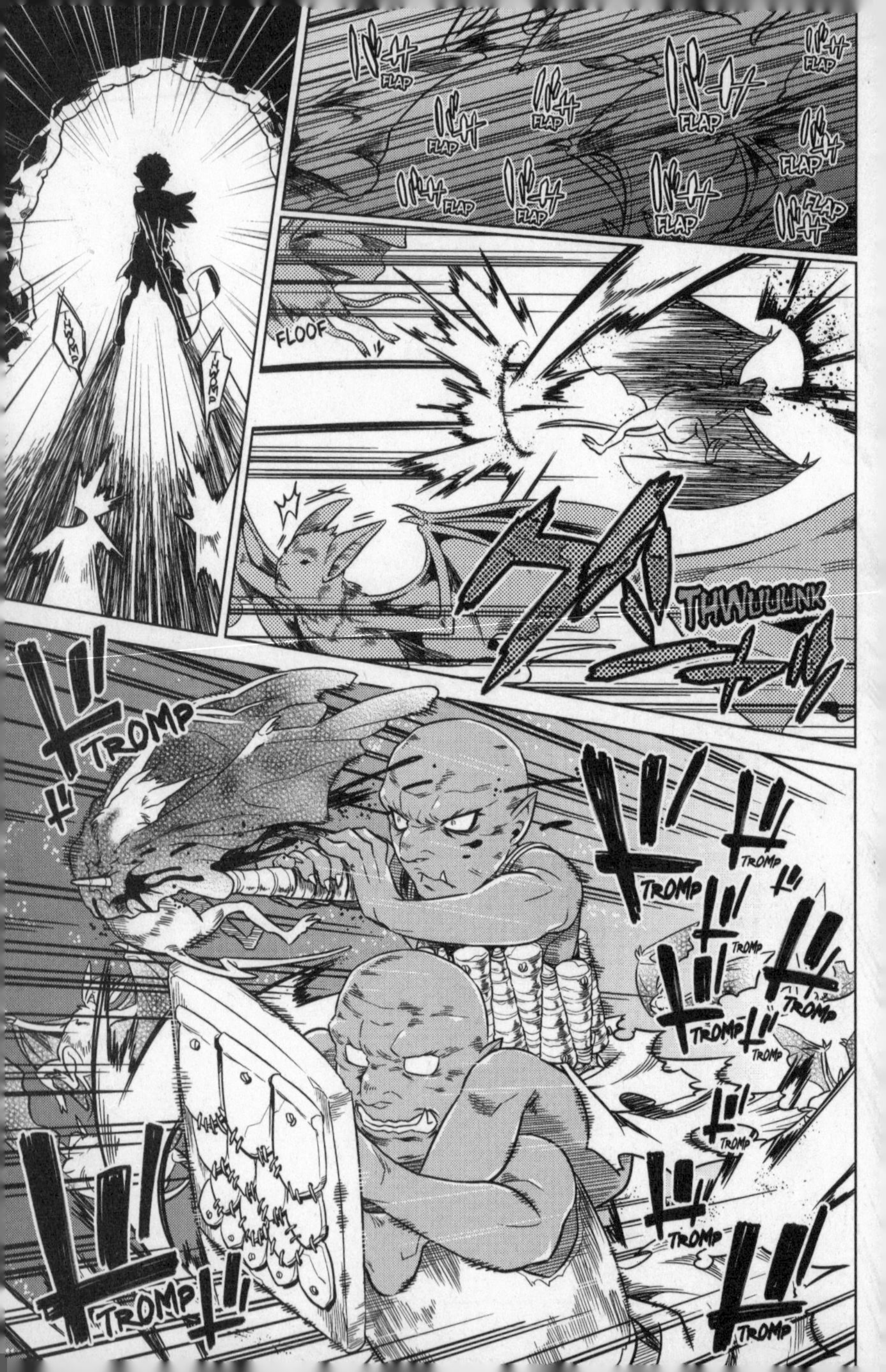
FLAP
FLAP
FLAP
FLAP
FLAP
FLAP
FLAP
FLAP
FLAP
FLAP
FLOOF
THWUUUNK
THWOMP
THWOMP
TROMP
TROMP
TROMP
TROMP
TROMP
TROMP
TROMP
TROMP
TROMP
TROMP
TROMP

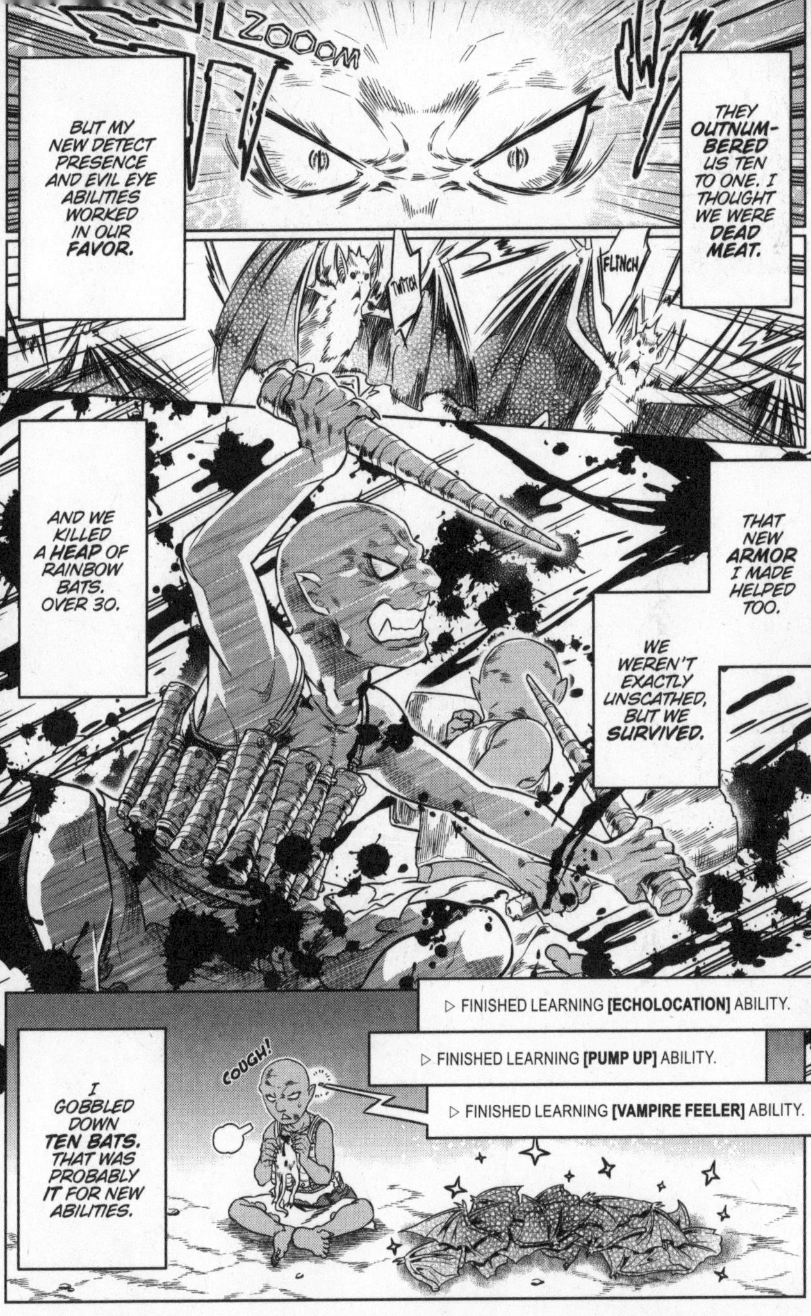

THEY OUTNUMBERED US TEN TO ONE. I THOUGHT WE WERE DEAD MEAT.
ZOOOM
BUT MY NEW DETECT PRESENCE AND EVIL EYE ABILITIES WORKED IN OUR FAVOR.
FLINCH
TWITCH
THAT NEW ARMOR I MADE HELPED TOO.
WE WEREN'T EXACTLY UNSCATHED, BUT WE SURVIVED.
AND WE KILLED A HEAP OF RAINBOW BATS. OVER 30.
▷ FINISHED LEARNING [ECHOLOCATION] ABILITY.
▷ FINISHED LEARNING [PUMP UP] ABILITY.
▷ FINISHED LEARNING [VAMPIRE FEELER] ABILITY.
COUGH!
I GOBBLED DOWN TEN BATS. THAT WAS PROBABLY IT FOR NEW ABILITIES.

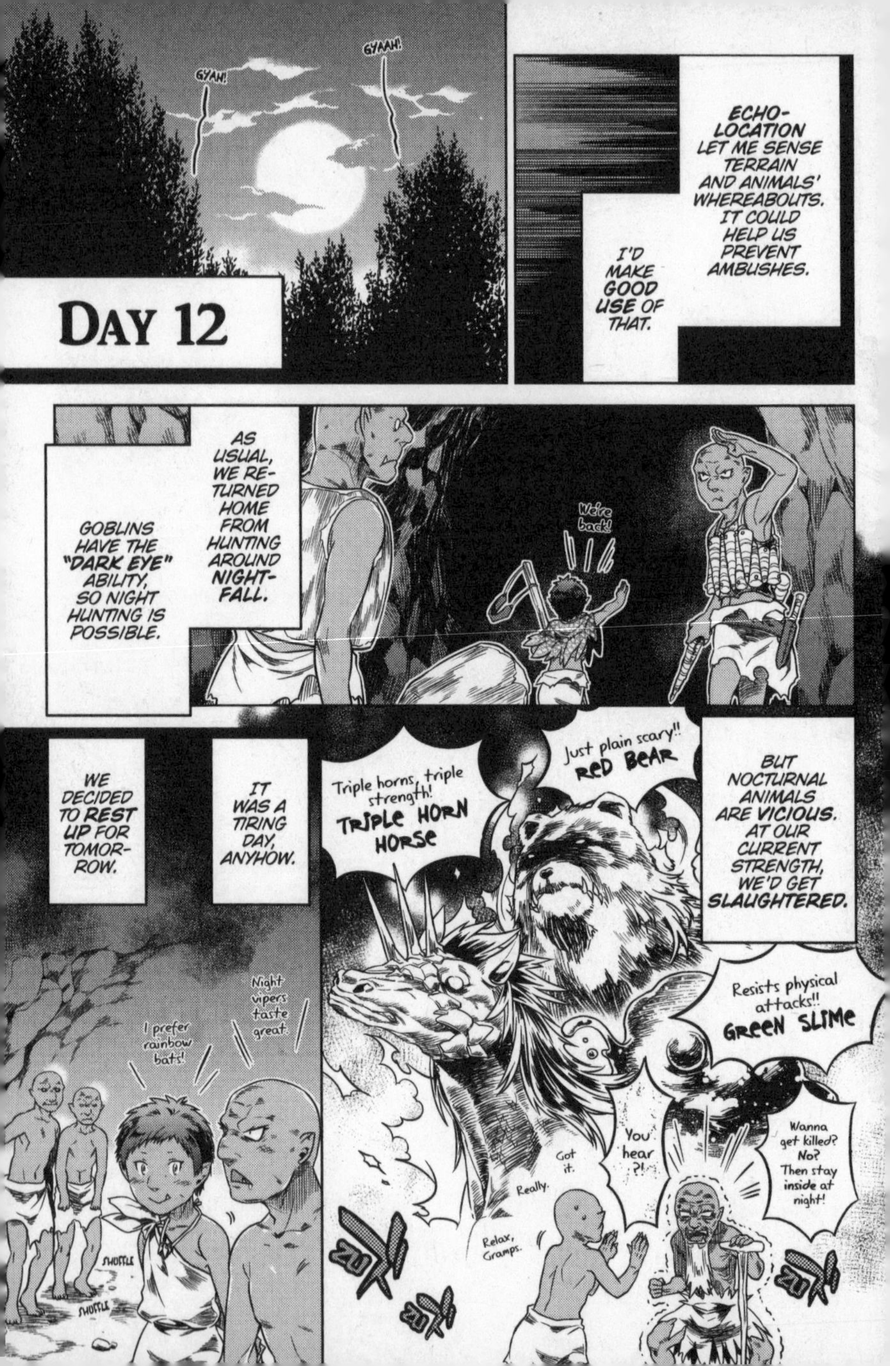
ECHO-LOCATION LET ME SENSE TERRAIN AND ANIMALS' WHEREABOUTS. IT COULD HELP US PREVENT AMBUSHES.
I'D MAKE GOOD USE OF THAT.
GYAAH!
GYAN!
DAY 12
AS USUAL, WE RETURNED HOME FROM HUNTING AROUND NIGHTFALL.
GOBLINS HAVE THE "DARK EYE" ABILITY, SO NIGHT HUNTING IS POSSIBLE.
We're back!
BUT NOCTURNAL ANIMALS ARE VICIOUS. AT OUR CURRENT STRENGTH, WE'D GET SLAUGHTERED.
Just plain scary!! RED BEAR
Triple horns, triple strength! TRIPLE HORN HORSE
Resists physical attacks!! GREEN SLIME
Wanna get killed? No? Then stay inside at night!
You hear?!
Got it.
Really.
Relax, Gramps.
ZU
ZU
ZU
IT WAS A TIRING DAY, ANYHOW.
WE DECIDED TO REST UP FOR TOMORROW.
Night vipers taste great.
I prefer rainbow bats!
SHUFFLE
SHUFFLE

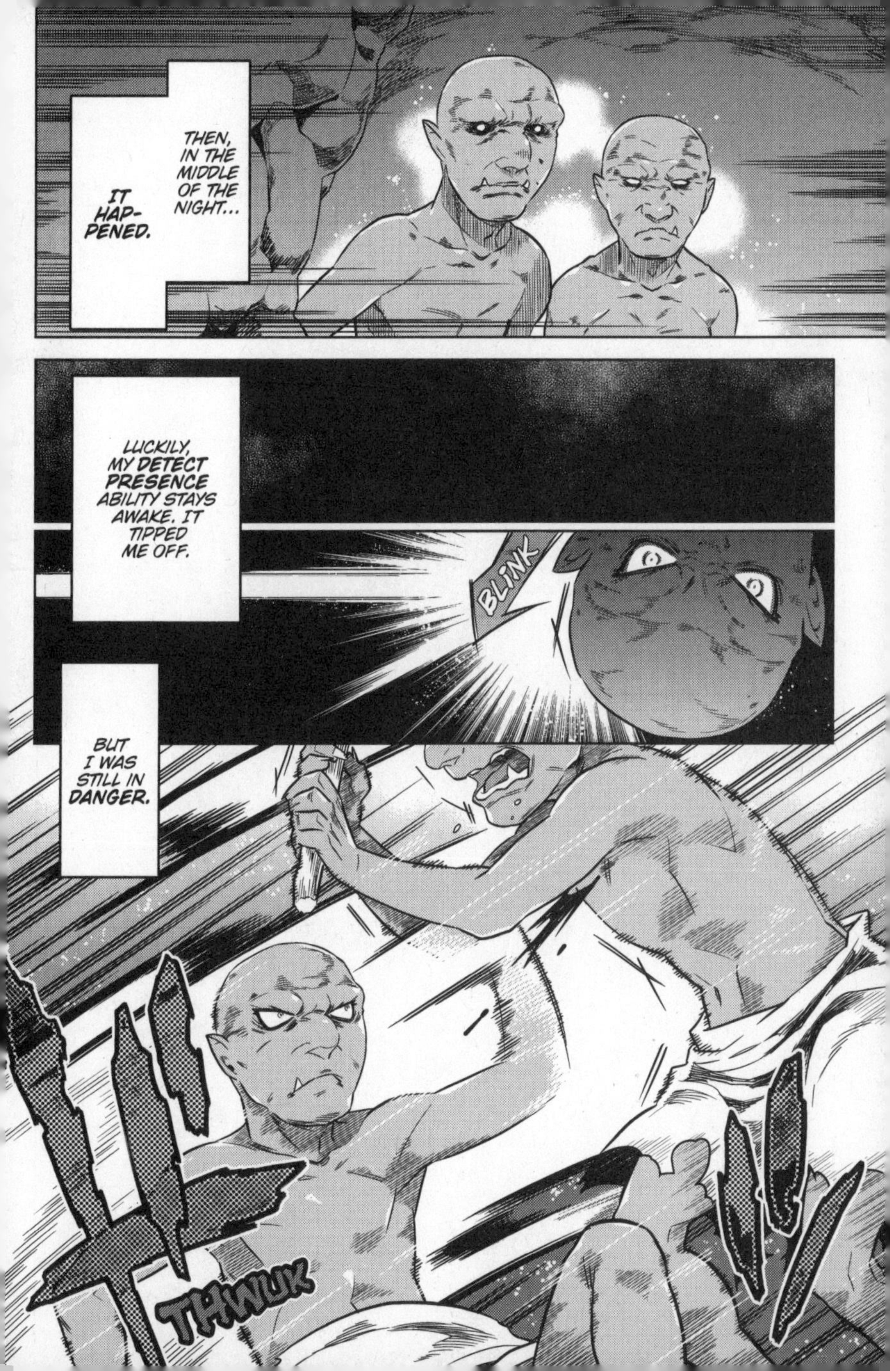
THEN, IN THE MIDDLE OF THE NIGHT...
IT HAP-PENED.
LUCKILY, MY DETECT PRESENCE ABILITY STAYS AWAKE. IT TIPPED ME OFF.
BLINK
BUT I WAS STILL IN DANGER.
THWUK

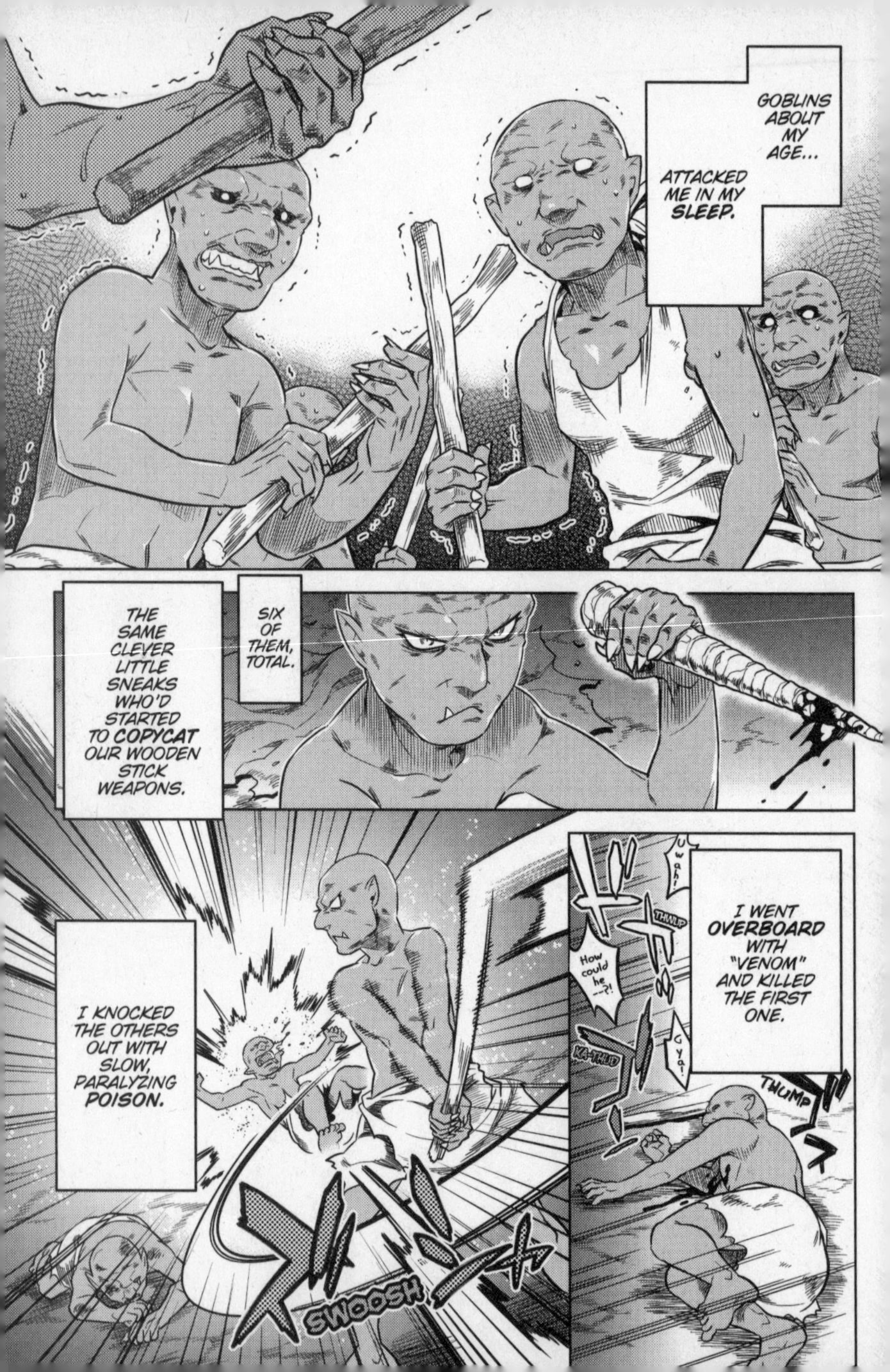
GOBLINS ABOUT MY AGE...
ATTACKED ME IN MY SLEEP.
SIX OF THEM, TOTAL.
THE SAME CLEVER LITTLE SNEAKS WHO'D STARTED TO COPYCAT OUR WOODEN STICK WEAPONS.
I WENT OVERBOARD WITH "VENOM" AND KILLED THE FIRST ONE.
Uwah!
THWUP
How could he--?!
Gya!
KA-THUD
THUMP
I KNOCKED THE OTHERS OUT WITH SLOW, PARALYZING POISON.
SWOOSH

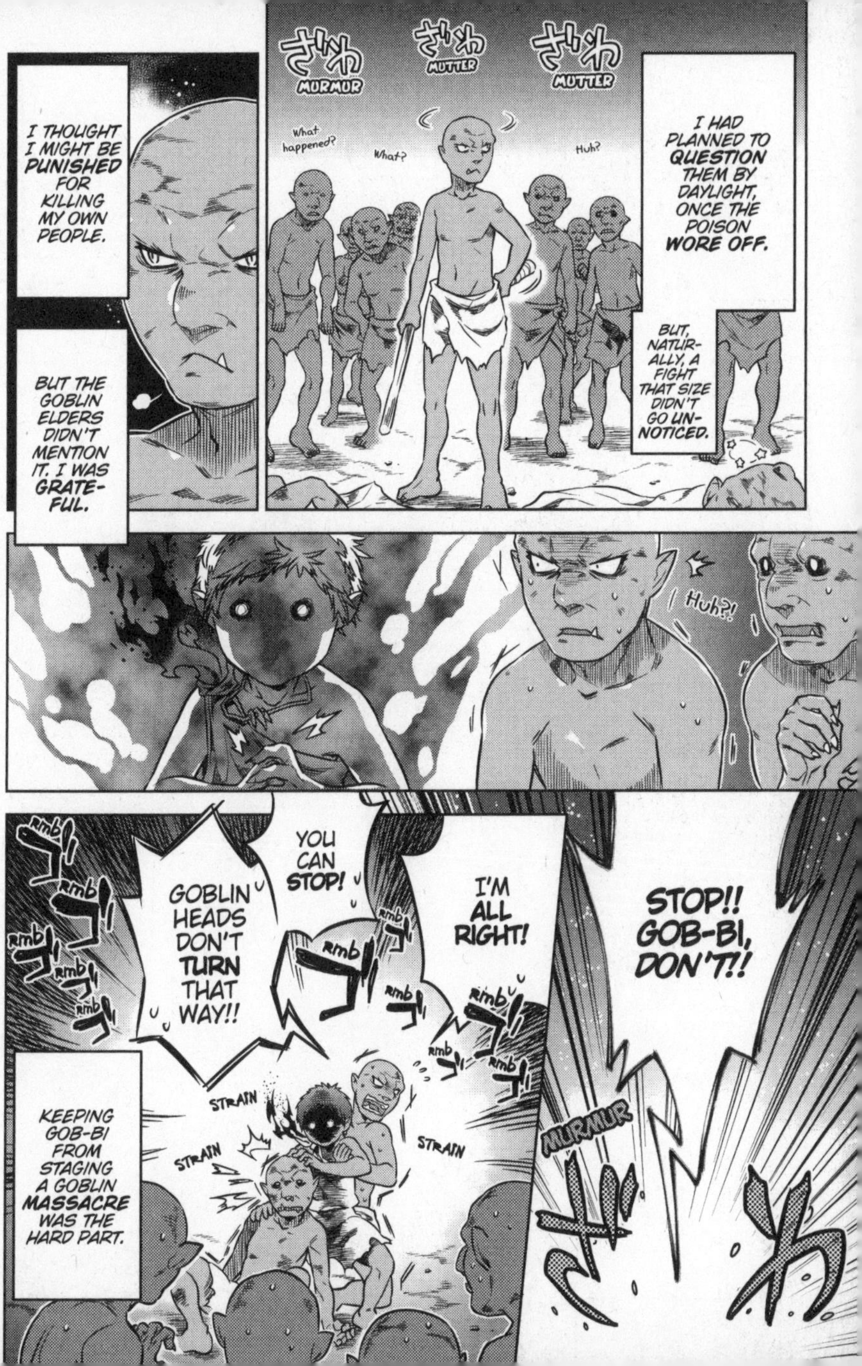

ざわ MUTTER
ざわ MUTTER
ざわ MURMUR
I HAD PLANNED TO QUESTION THEM BY DAYLIGHT, ONCE THE POISON WORE OFF.
Huh?
What?
What happened?
BUT, NATURALLY, A FIGHT THAT SIZE DIDN'T GO UNNOTICED.
I THOUGHT I MIGHT BE PUNISHED FOR KILLING MY OWN PEOPLE.
BUT THE GOBLIN ELDERS DIDN'T MENTION IT. I WAS GRATEFUL.
Huh?!
STOP!! GOB-BI, DON'T!!
ざわ MURMUR
I'M ALL RIGHT!
YOU CAN STOP!
GOBLIN HEADS DON'T TURN THAT WAY!!
ゴ rmb ゴ rmb ゴ rmb ゴ rmb
STRAIN STRAIN STRAIN
ゴ rmb ゴ rmb ゴ rmb ゴ rmb ゴ rmb
KEEPING GOB-BI FROM STAGING A GOBLIN MASSACRE WAS THE HARD PART.

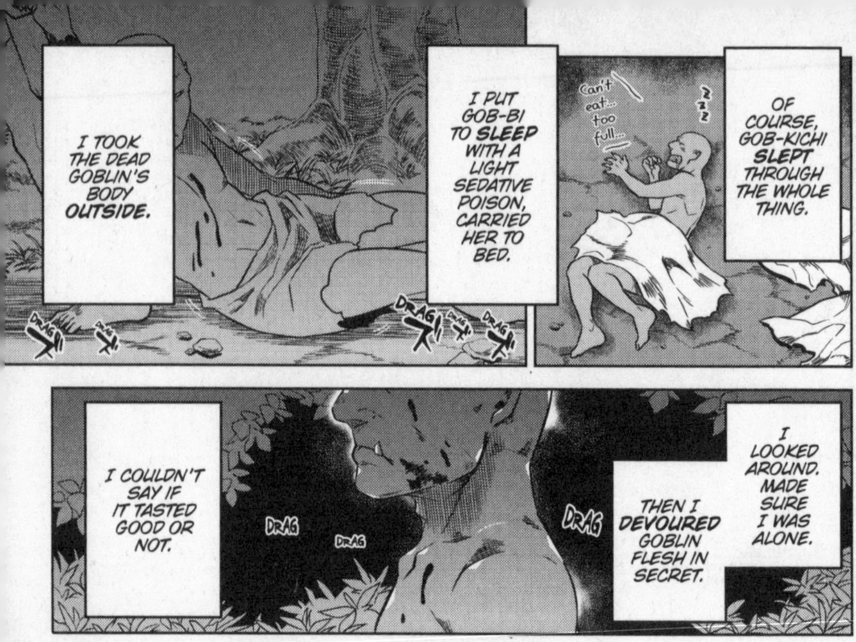
OF COURSE, GOB-KICHI SLEPT THROUGH THE WHOLE THING.
Z Z Z
Can't eat... too full...
I PUT GOB-BI TO SLEEP WITH A LIGHT SEDATIVE POISON, CARRIED HER TO BED.
DRAG
DRAG
DRAG
I TOOK THE DEAD GOBLIN'S BODY OUTSIDE.
I LOOKED AROUND. MADE SURE I WAS ALONE.
THEN I DEVOURED GOBLIN FLESH IN SECRET.
DRAG
DRAG
DRAG
I COULDN'T SAY IF IT TASTED GOOD OR NOT.

DAY 13

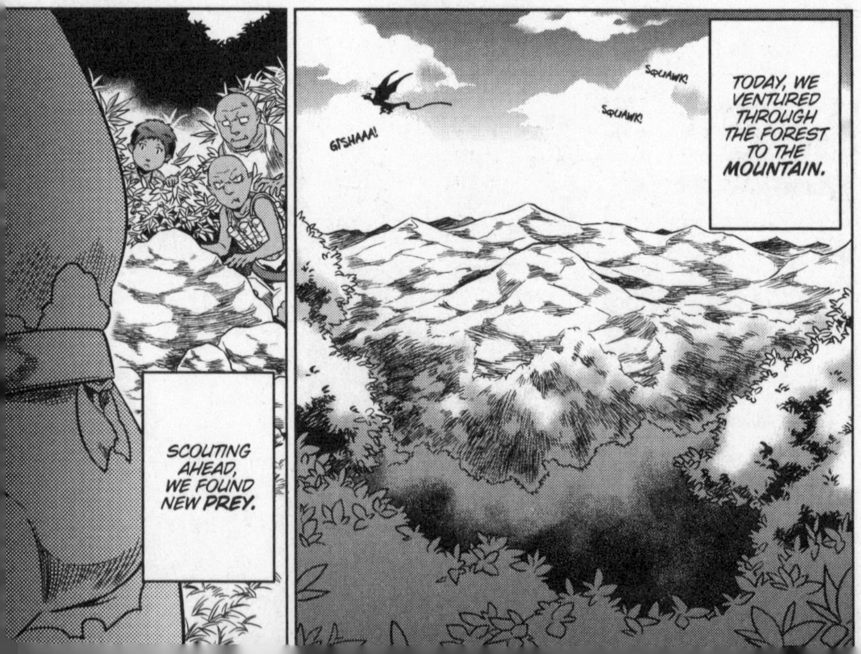
TODAY, WE VENTURED THROUGH THE FOREST TO THE MOUNTAIN.
SQUAWK!
SQUAWK!
GISHAAA!
SCOUTING AHEAD, WE FOUND NEW PREY.

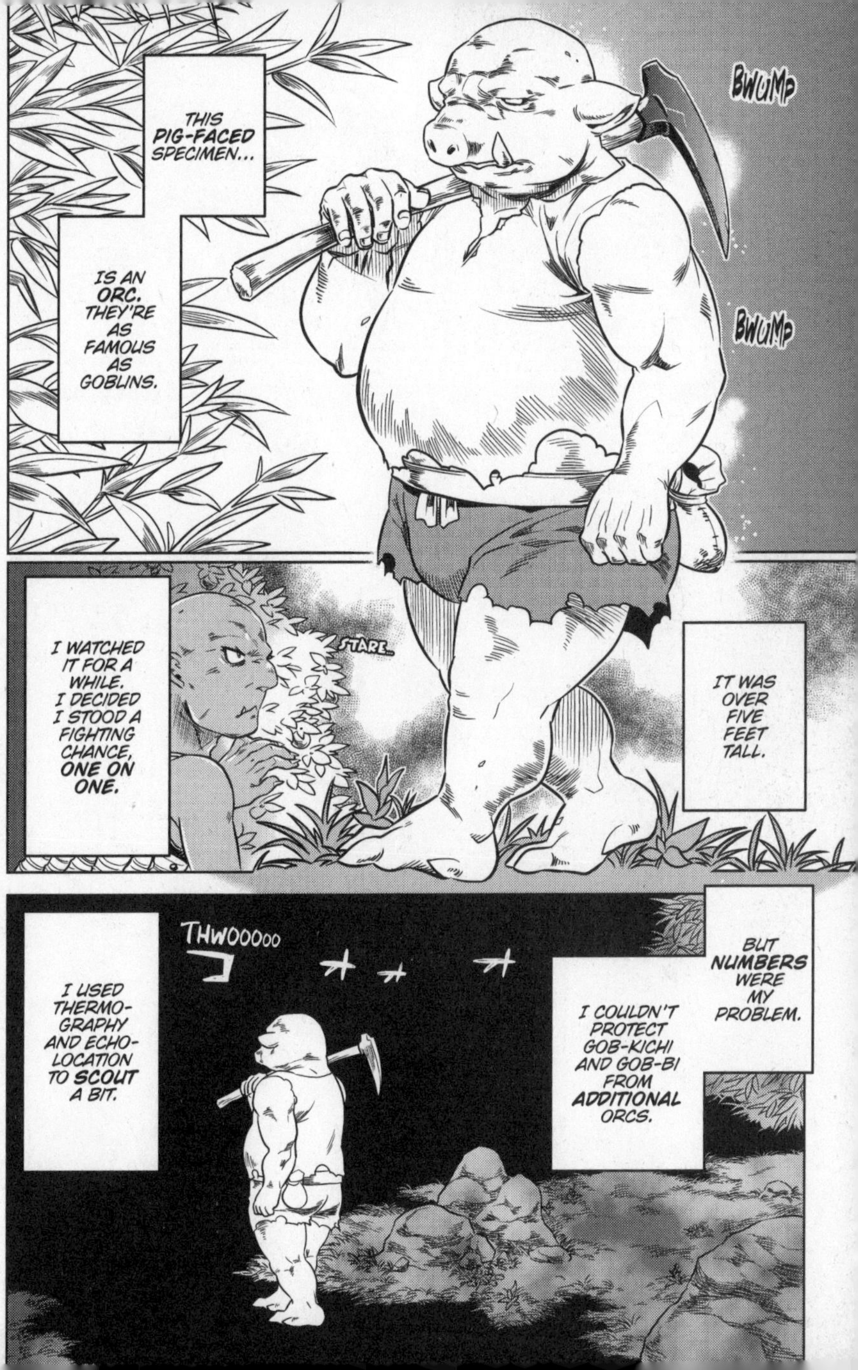

BWUMP
THIS PIG-FACED SPECIMEN...
BWUMP
IS AN ORC. THEY'RE AS FAMOUS AS GOBLINS.
IT WAS OVER FIVE FEET TALL.
STARE...
I WATCHED IT FOR A WHILE. I DECIDED I STOOD A FIGHTING CHANCE, ONE ON ONE.
BUT NUMBERS WERE MY PROBLEM.
I COULDN'T PROTECT GOB-KICHI AND GOB-BI FROM ADDITIONAL ORCS.
THWOOOOO
I USED THERMO-GRAPHY AND ECHO-LOCATION TO SCOUT A BIT.

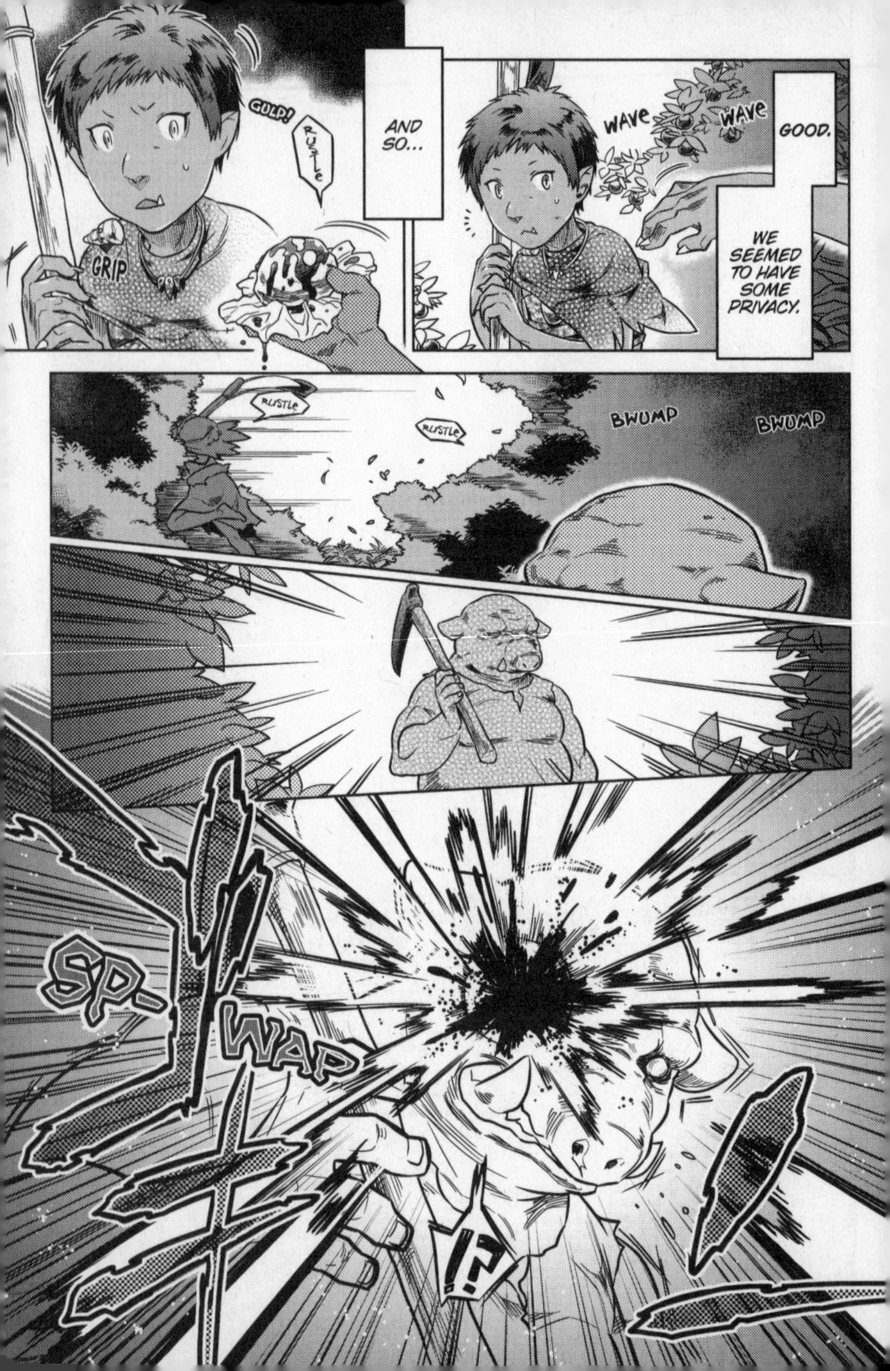
GOOD.
WAVE
WAVE
AND SO...
WE SEEMED TO HAVE SOME PRIVACY.
RUSTLE
GULP!
GRIP
BWUMP
BWUMP
RUSTLE
RUSTLE
!?
SP-
WAP

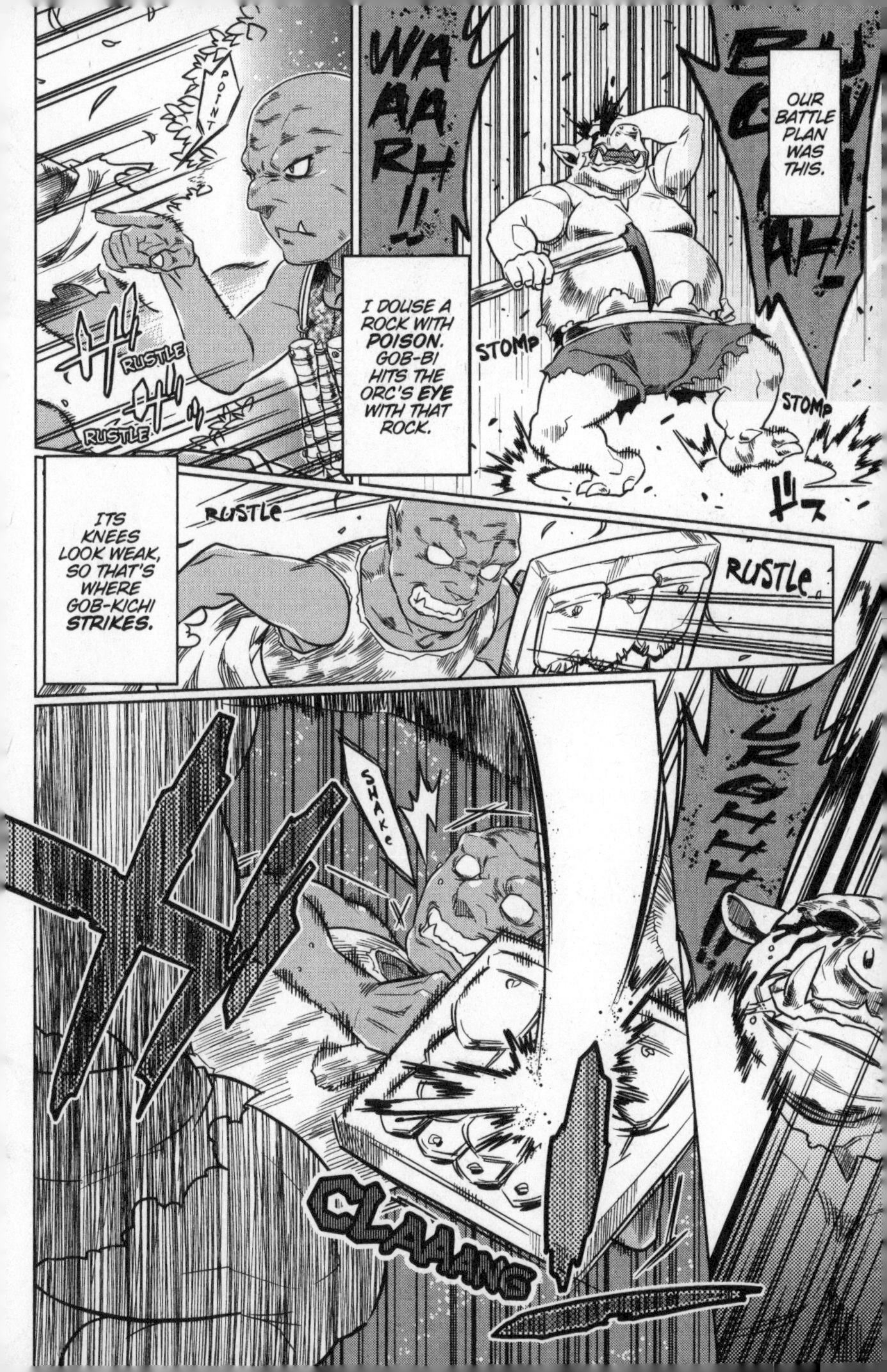
OUR BATTLE PLAN WAS THIS.
WAAARH!!
STOMP
STOMP
ドス
I DOUSE A ROCK WITH POISON. GOB-BI HITS THE ORC'S EYE WITH THAT ROCK.
POINT
RUSTLE
RUSTLE
RUSTLE
RUSTLE
ITS KNEES LOOK WEAK, SO THAT'S WHERE GOB-KICHI STRIKES.
URGHHH!
SHAKE
CLAAANG

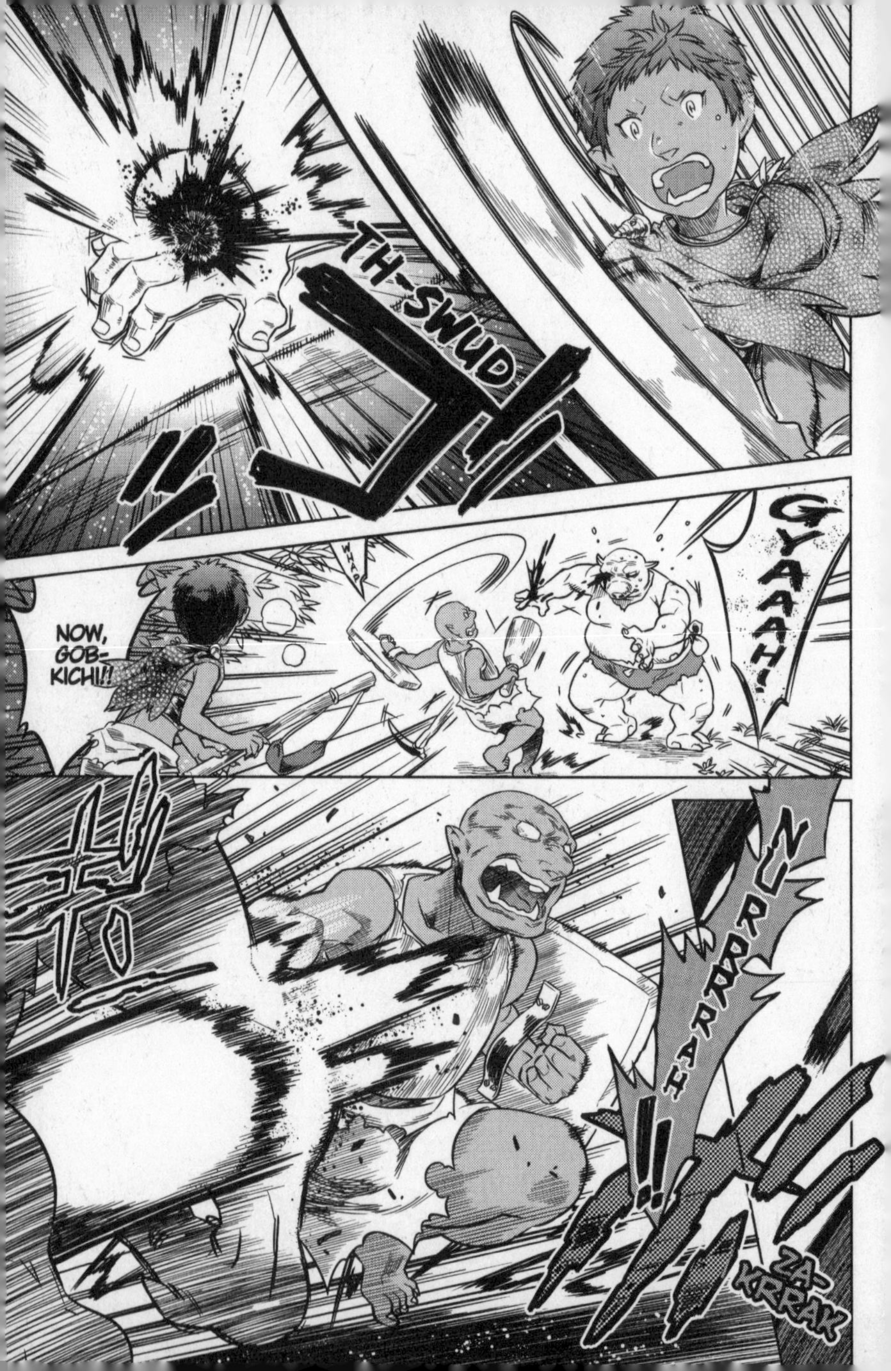
TH-SWUD
GYAAAAH!
WHAP
NOW, GOB-KICHI!!
NURRRRRAH!!
ZA-KRRAK

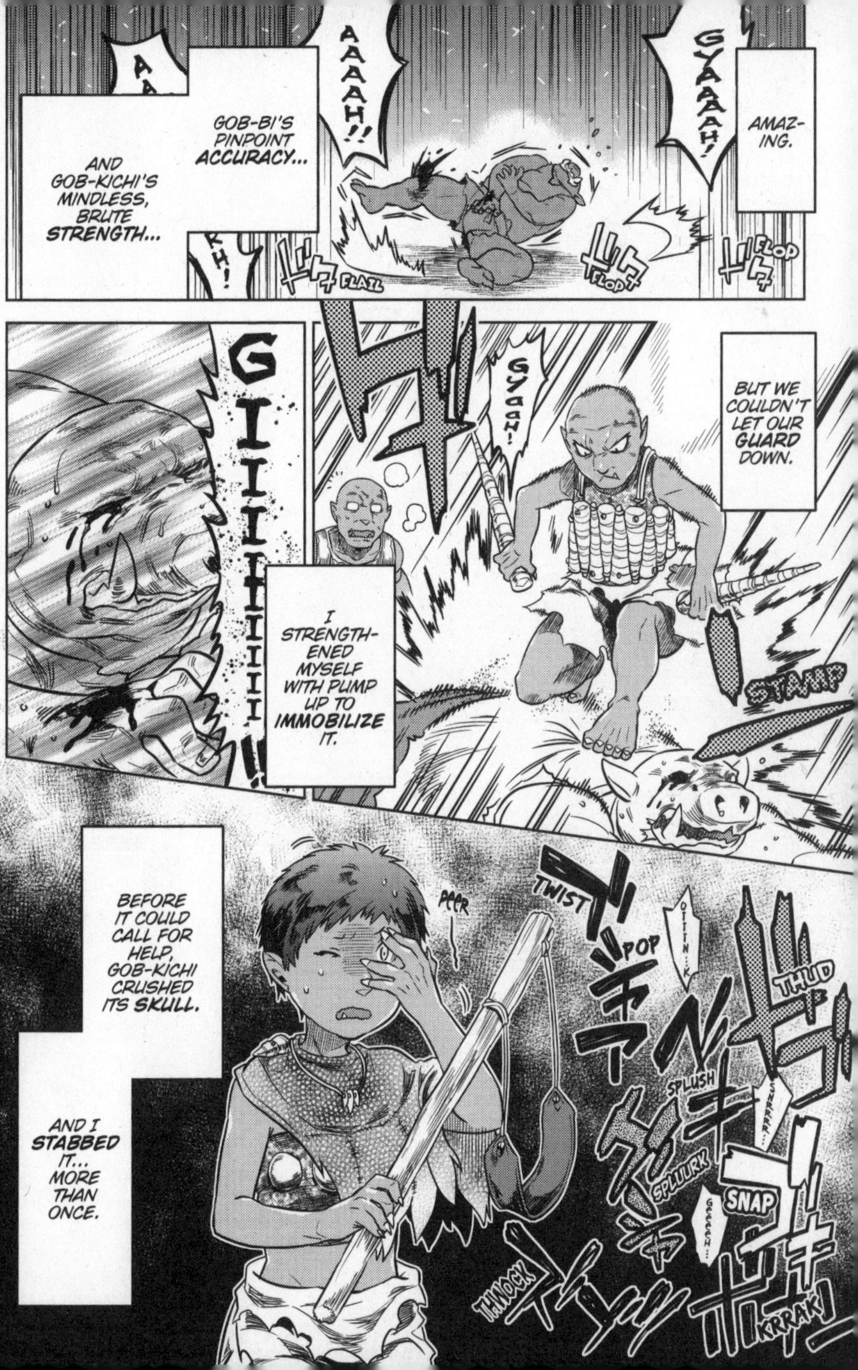
AMAZ-ING.
GYAAAAAH!
FLOP
FLOP
AAAAAH!!
GOB-BI'S PINPOINT ACCURACY...
AND GOB-KICHI'S MINDLESS, BRUTE STRENGTH...
FLAIL
BUT WE COULDN'T LET OUR GUARD DOWN.
Gyaaah!
STAMP
I STRENGTH-ENED MYSELF WITH PUMP UP TO IMMOBILIZE IT.
GIIIIIIIII!!
BEFORE IT COULD CALL FOR HELP, GOB-KICHI CRUSHED ITS SKULL.
PEER
TWIST
POP
THUD
SPLUSH
SPLUURK
SNAP
AND I STABBED IT... MORE THAN ONCE.
THWOCK
KRRAK

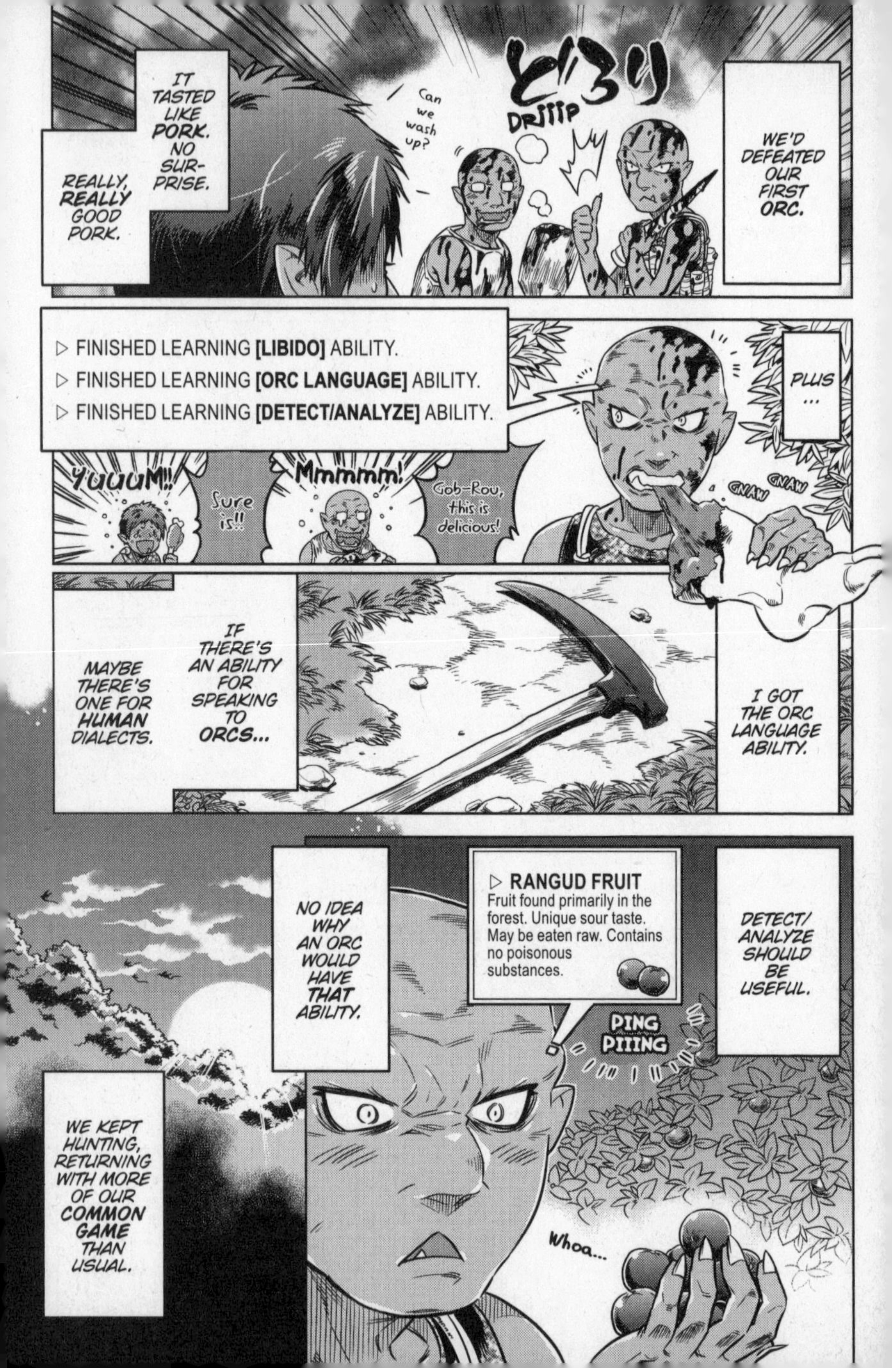
WE'D DEFEATED OUR FIRST ORC.
とろり
DRIIIP
Can we wash up?
IT TASTED LIKE PORK. NO SURPRISE.
REALLY, REALLY GOOD PORK.
PLUS...
▷ FINISHED LEARNING [LIBIDO] ABILITY.
▷ FINISHED LEARNING [ORC LANGUAGE] ABILITY.
▷ FINISHED LEARNING [DETECT/ANALYZE] ABILITY.
GNAW GNAW
Gob-Rou, this is delicious!
Mmmmm!
Sure is!!
YUUUM!!
I GOT THE ORC LANGUAGE ABILITY.
IF THERE'S AN ABILITY FOR SPEAKING TO ORCS...
MAYBE THERE'S ONE FOR HUMAN DIALECTS.
DETECT/ANALYZE SHOULD BE USEFUL.
▷ RANGUD FRUIT
Fruit found primarily in the forest. Unique sour taste. May be eaten raw. Contains no poisonous substances.
PING PIIING
NO IDEA WHY AN ORC WOULD HAVE THAT ABILITY.
Whoa...
WE KEPT HUNTING, RETURNING WITH MORE OF OUR COMMON GAME THAN USUAL.

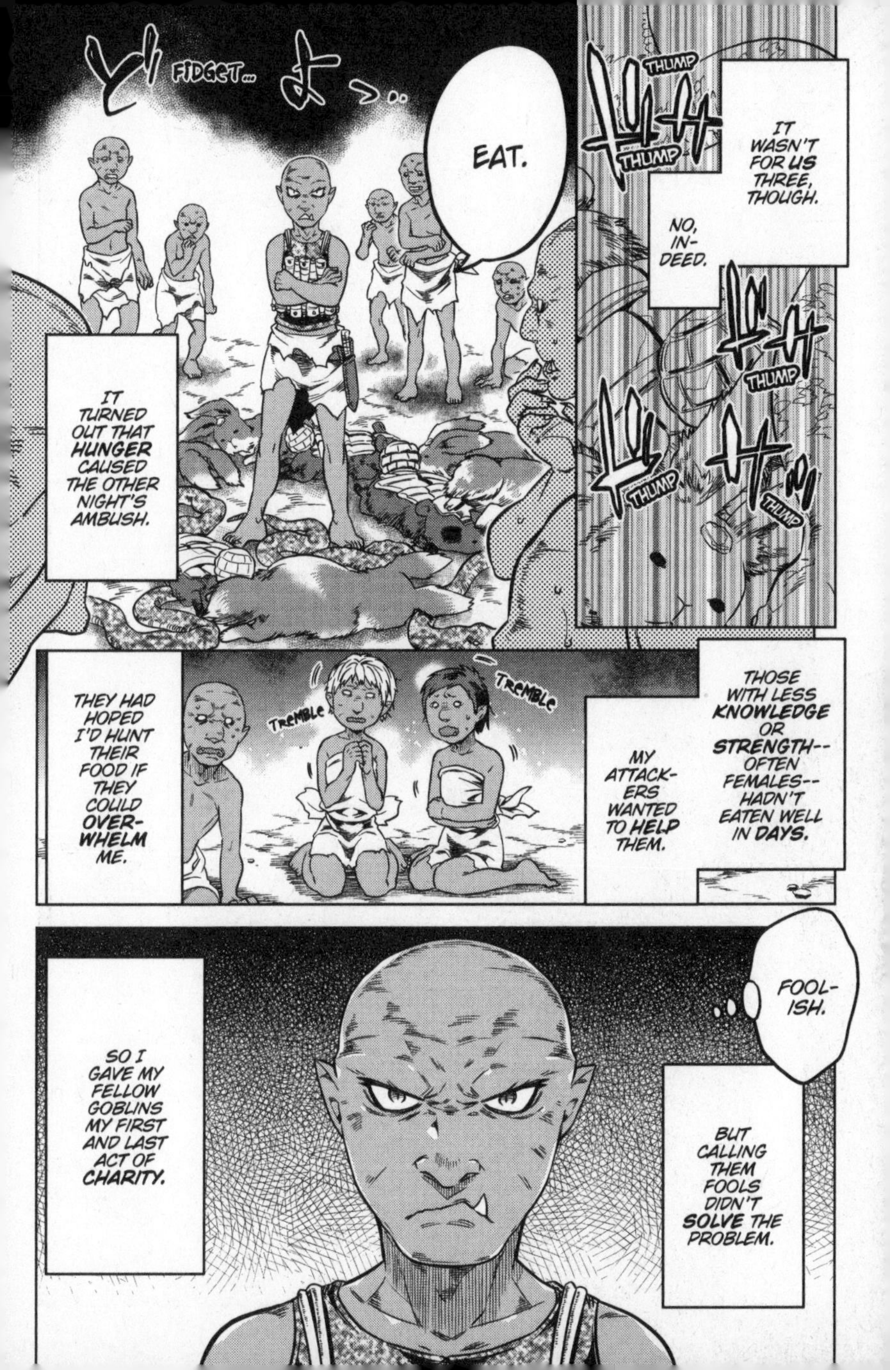
THUMP
THUMP
IT WASN'T FOR US THREE, THOUGH.
NO, IN-DEED.
THUMP
THUMP
THUMP
FIDGET...
EAT.
IT TURNED OUT THAT HUNGER CAUSED THE OTHER NIGHT'S AMBUSH.
THOSE WITH LESS KNOWLEDGE OR STRENGTH-- OFTEN FEMALES-- HADN'T EATEN WELL IN DAYS.
MY ATTACK-ERS WANTED TO HELP THEM.
TREMBLE
TREMBLE
THEY HAD HOPED I'D HUNT THEIR FOOD IF THEY COULD OVER-WHELM ME.
FOOL-ISH.
BUT CALLING THEM FOOLS DIDN'T SOLVE THE PROBLEM.
SO I GAVE MY FELLOW GOBLINS MY FIRST AND LAST ACT OF CHARITY.

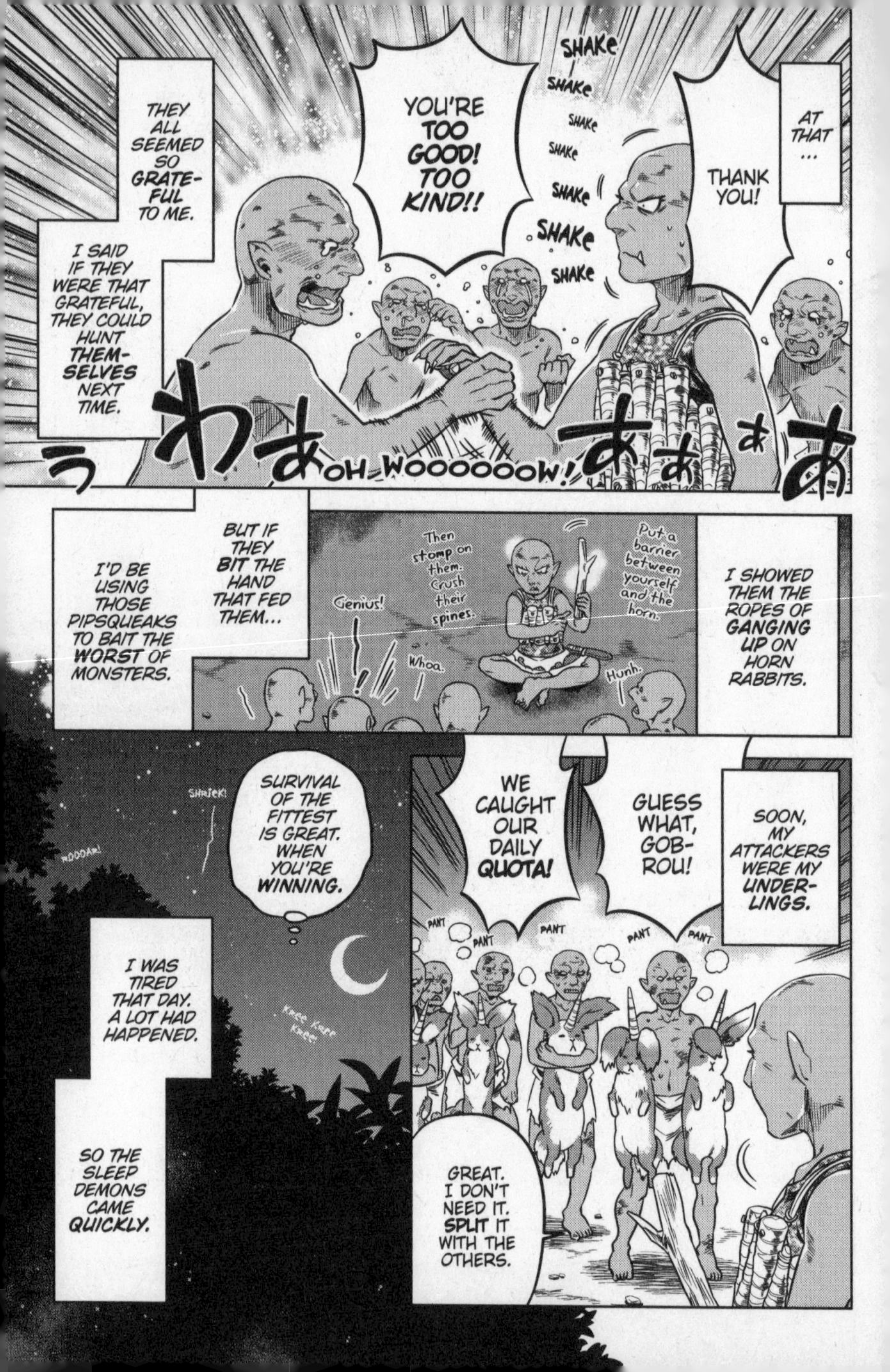
AT THAT...
THANK YOU!
SHAKE SHAKE SHAKE SHAKE SHAKE SHAKE SHAKE
YOU'RE TOO GOOD! TOO KIND!!
THEY ALL SEEMED SO GRATEFUL TO ME.
I SAID IF THEY WERE THAT GRATEFUL, THEY COULD HUNT THEMSELVES NEXT TIME.
うわぁあぁあ
OH WOOOOOOW!
I SHOWED THEM THE ROPES OF GANGING UP ON HORN RABBITS.
Put a barrier between yourself and the horn.
Then stomp on them. Crush their spines.
Genius!
Whoa.
Hunh.
BUT IF THEY BIT THE HAND THAT FED THEM...
I'D BE USING THOSE PIPSQUEAKS TO BAIT THE WORST OF MONSTERS.
SOON, MY ATTACKERS WERE MY UNDERLINGS.
GUESS WHAT, GOB-ROU!
WE CAUGHT OUR DAILY QUOTA!
PANT PANT PANT PANT PANT
GREAT. I DON'T NEED IT. SPLIT IT WITH THE OTHERS.
SURVIVAL OF THE FITTEST IS GREAT. WHEN YOU'RE WINNING.
SHRIEK!
ROOOAR!
Kree Kree Kree
I WAS TIRED THAT DAY. A LOT HAD HAPPENED.
SO THE SLEEP DEMONS CAME QUICKLY.

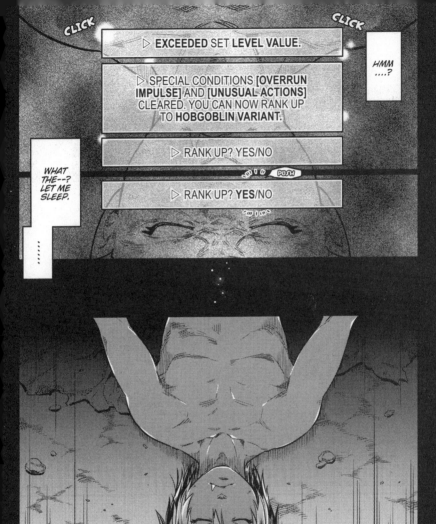

▷ EXCEEDED SET LEVEL VALUE.

▷ SPECIAL CONDITIONS [OVERRUN IMPULSE] AND [UNUSUAL ACTIONS] CLEARED. YOU CAN NOW RANK UP TO HOBGOBLIN VARIANT.

▷ RANK UP? YES/NO

▷ RANK UP? YES/NO

HMM ....?

WHAT THE--? LET ME SLEEP.

▷ GOB-ROU OBTAINED [DIVINE PROTECTION] FROM THE GOD OF ENDINGS AND ORIGINS.

▷ CONTINUE

DAY 14

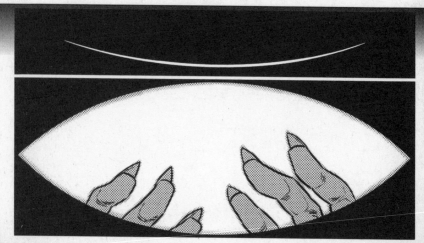

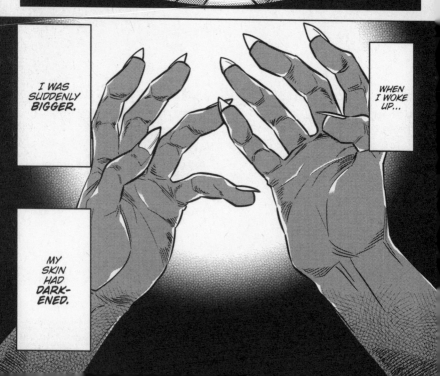

WHEN I WOKE UP...

I WAS SUDDENLY BIGGER.

MY SKIN HAD DARK-ENED.

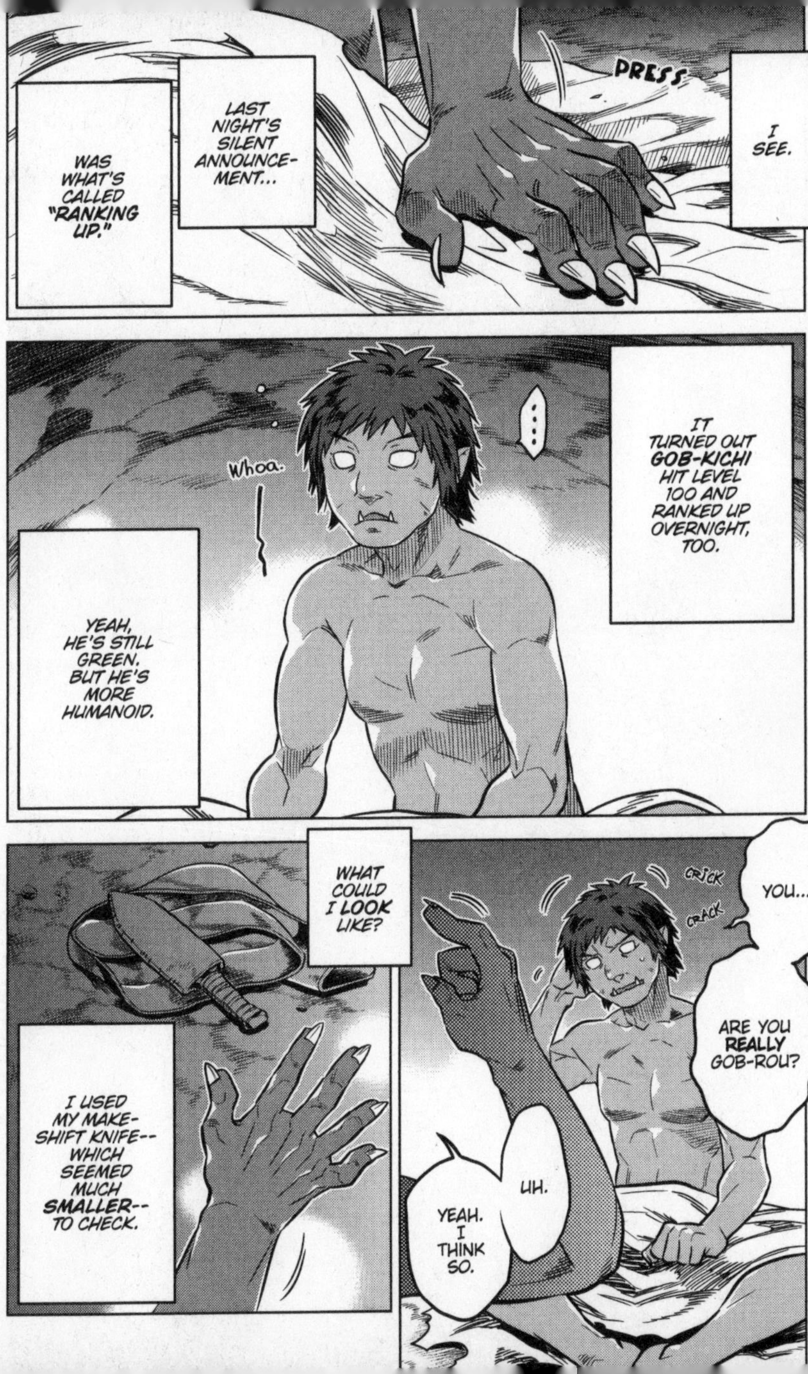
PRESS
I SEE.
LAST NIGHT'S SILENT ANNOUNCEMENT...
WAS WHAT'S CALLED "RANKING UP."
IT TURNED OUT GOB-KICHI HIT LEVEL 100 AND RANKED UP OVERNIGHT, TOO.
...!
Whoa.
YEAH, HE'S STILL GREEN. BUT HE'S MORE HUMANOID.
CRICK
CRACK
YOU...
ARE YOU REALLY GOB-ROU?
UH.
YEAH. I THINK SO.
WHAT COULD I LOOK LIKE?
I USED MY MAKE-SHIFT KNIFE--WHICH SEEMED MUCH SMALLER--TO CHECK.

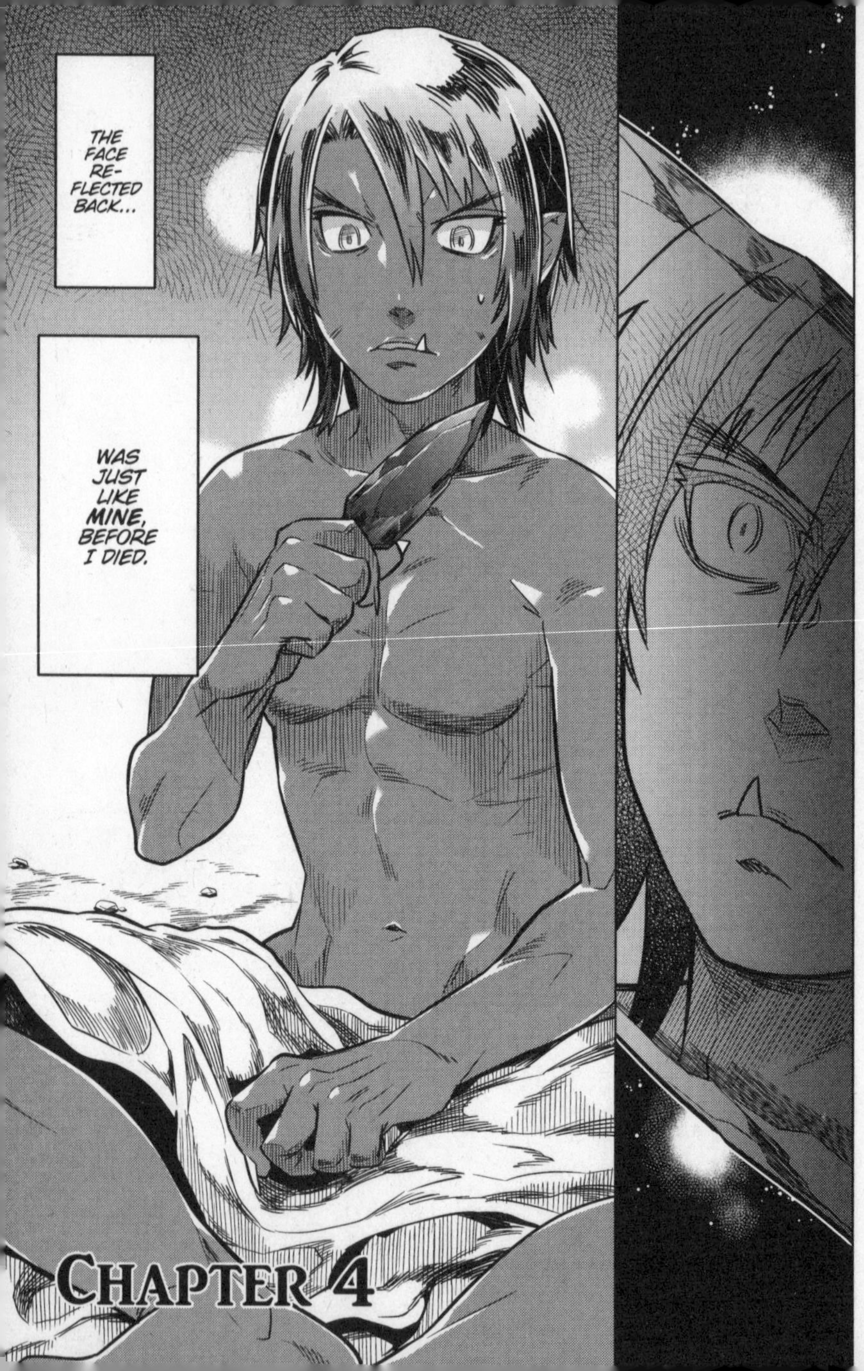
THE FACE RE-FLECTED BACK...
WAS JUST LIKE MINE, BEFORE I DIED.
CHAPTER 4

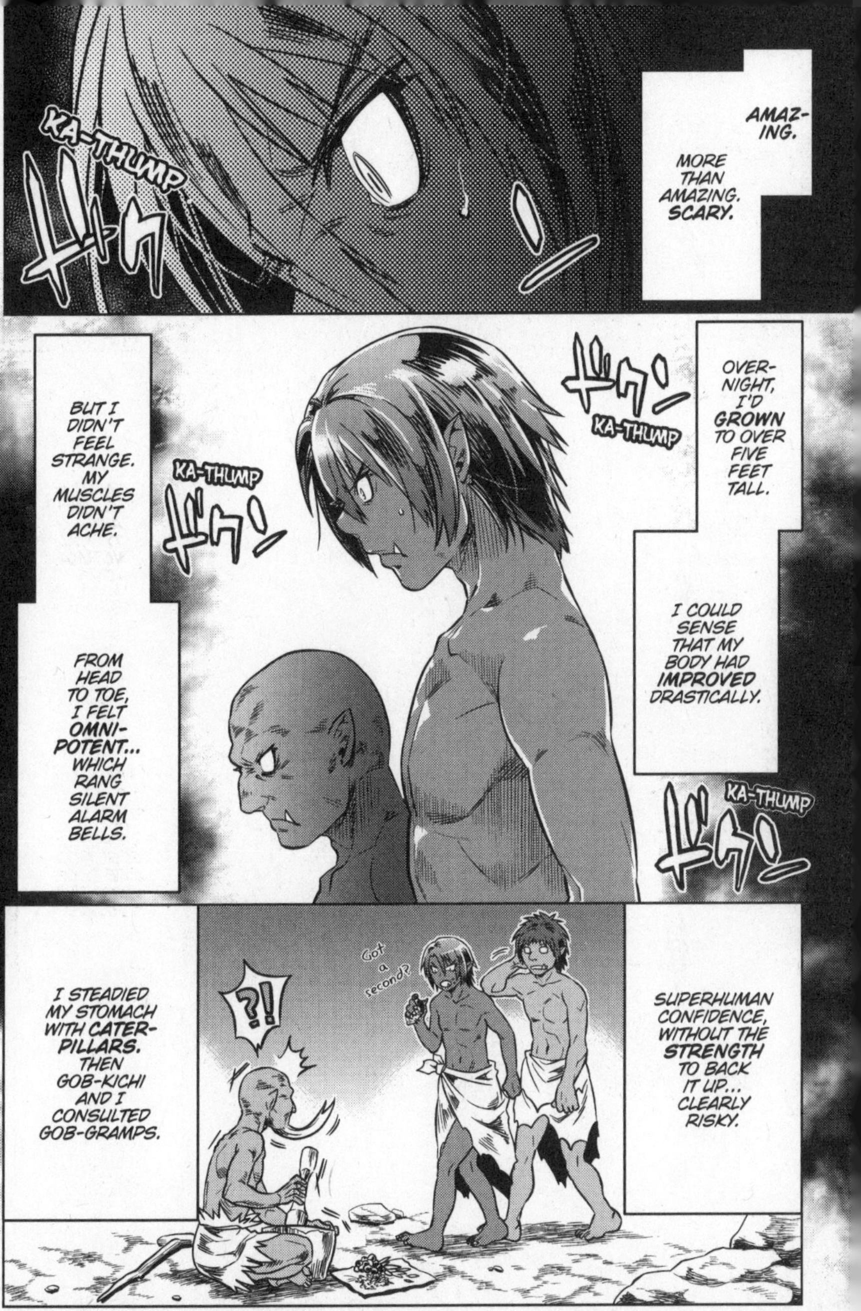
AMAZ-ING.
MORE THAN AMAZING. SCARY.
KA-THUMP
OVER-NIGHT, I'D GROWN TO OVER FIVE FEET TALL.
KA-THUMP
I COULD SENSE THAT MY BODY HAD IMPROVED DRASTICALLY.
KA-THUMP
BUT I DIDN'T FEEL STRANGE. MY MUSCLES DIDN'T ACHE.
KA-THUMP
FROM HEAD TO TOE, I FELT OMNI-POTENT... WHICH RANG SILENT ALARM BELLS.
SUPERHUMAN CONFIDENCE, WITHOUT THE STRENGTH TO BACK IT UP... CLEARLY RISKY.
Got a second?
?!
I STEADIED MY STOMACH WITH CATER-PILLARS. THEN GOB-KICHI AND I CONSULTED GOB-GRAMPS.

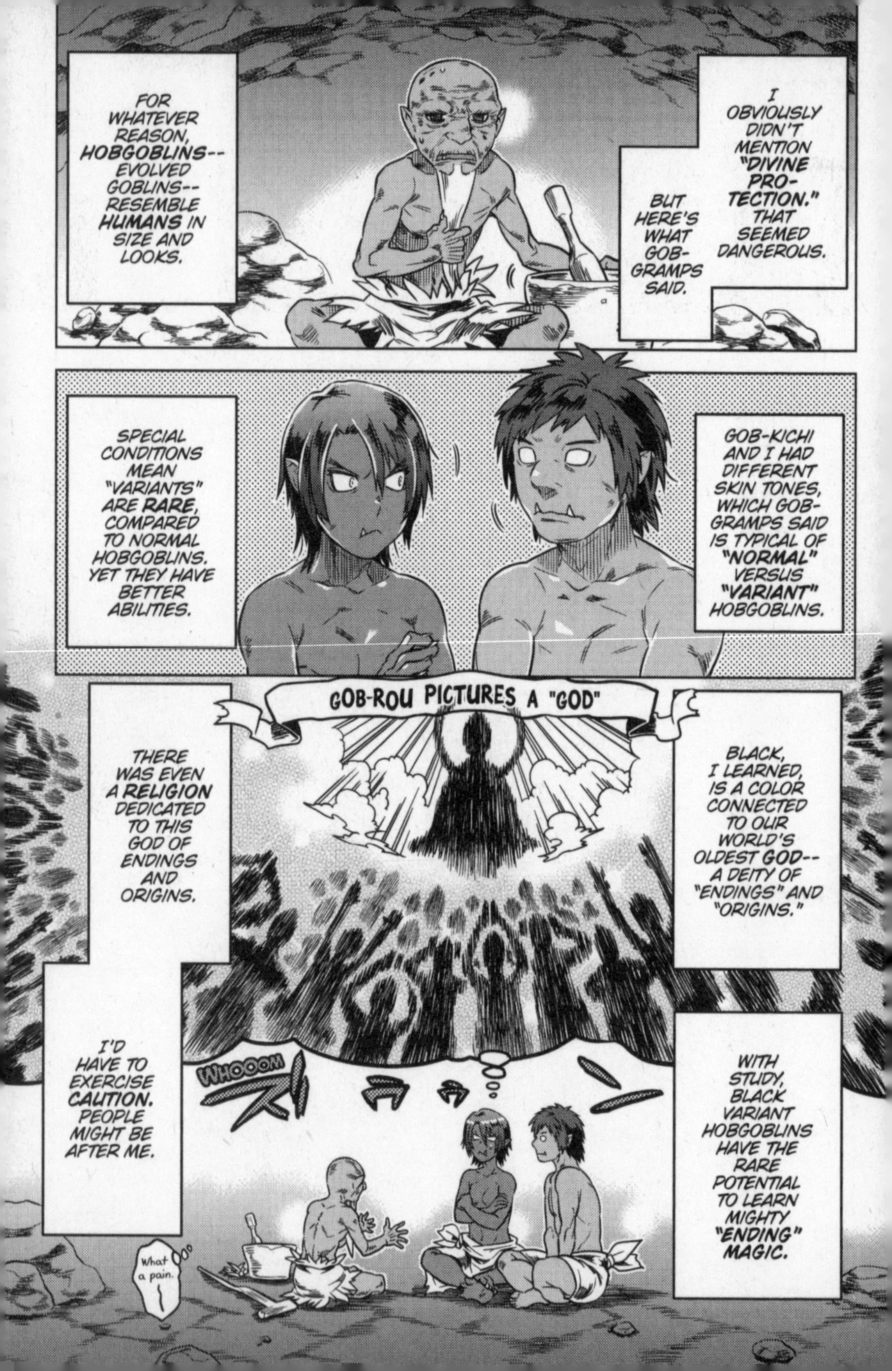
I OBVIOUSLY DIDN'T MENTION "DIVINE PROTECTION." THAT SEEMED DANGEROUS.
BUT HERE'S WHAT GOB-GRAMPS SAID.
FOR WHATEVER REASON, HOBGOBLINS-- EVOLVED GOBLINS-- RESEMBLE HUMANS IN SIZE AND LOOKS.
GOB-KICHI AND I HAD DIFFERENT SKIN TONES, WHICH GOB-GRAMPS SAID IS TYPICAL OF "NORMAL" VERSUS "VARIANT" HOBGOBLINS.
SPECIAL CONDITIONS MEAN "VARIANTS" ARE RARE, COMPARED TO NORMAL HOBGOBLINS. YET THEY HAVE BETTER ABILITIES.
GOB-ROU PICTURES A "GOD"
BLACK, I LEARNED, IS A COLOR CONNECTED TO OUR WORLD'S OLDEST GOD-- A DEITY OF "ENDINGS" AND "ORIGINS."
THERE WAS EVEN A RELIGION DEDICATED TO THIS GOD OF ENDINGS AND ORIGINS.
WITH STUDY, BLACK VARIANT HOBGOBLINS HAVE THE RARE POTENTIAL TO LEARN MIGHTY "ENDING" MAGIC.
I'D HAVE TO EXERCISE CAUTION. PEOPLE MIGHT BE AFTER ME.
WHOOOM
What a pain.

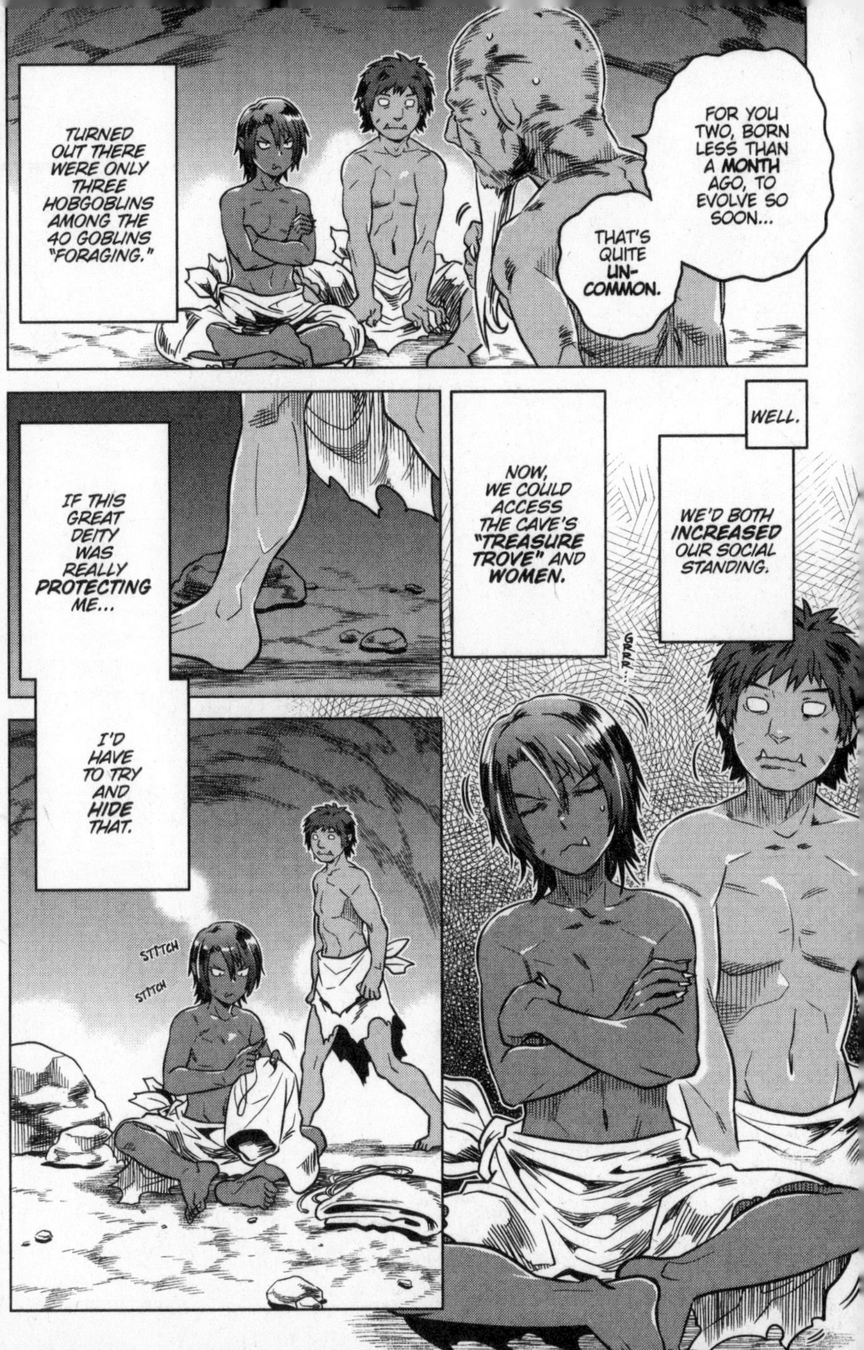

FOR YOU TWO, BORN LESS THAN A MONTH AGO, TO EVOLVE SO SOON...
THAT'S QUITE UN-COMMON.
TURNED OUT THERE WERE ONLY THREE HOBGOBLINS AMONG THE 40 GOBLINS "FORAGING."
WELL.
WE'D BOTH INCREASED OUR SOCIAL STANDING.
NOW, WE COULD ACCESS THE CAVE'S "TREASURE TROVE" AND WOMEN.
GRRR...
IF THIS GREAT DEITY WAS REALLY PROTECTING ME...
I'D HAVE TO TRY AND HIDE THAT.
STITCH
STITCH

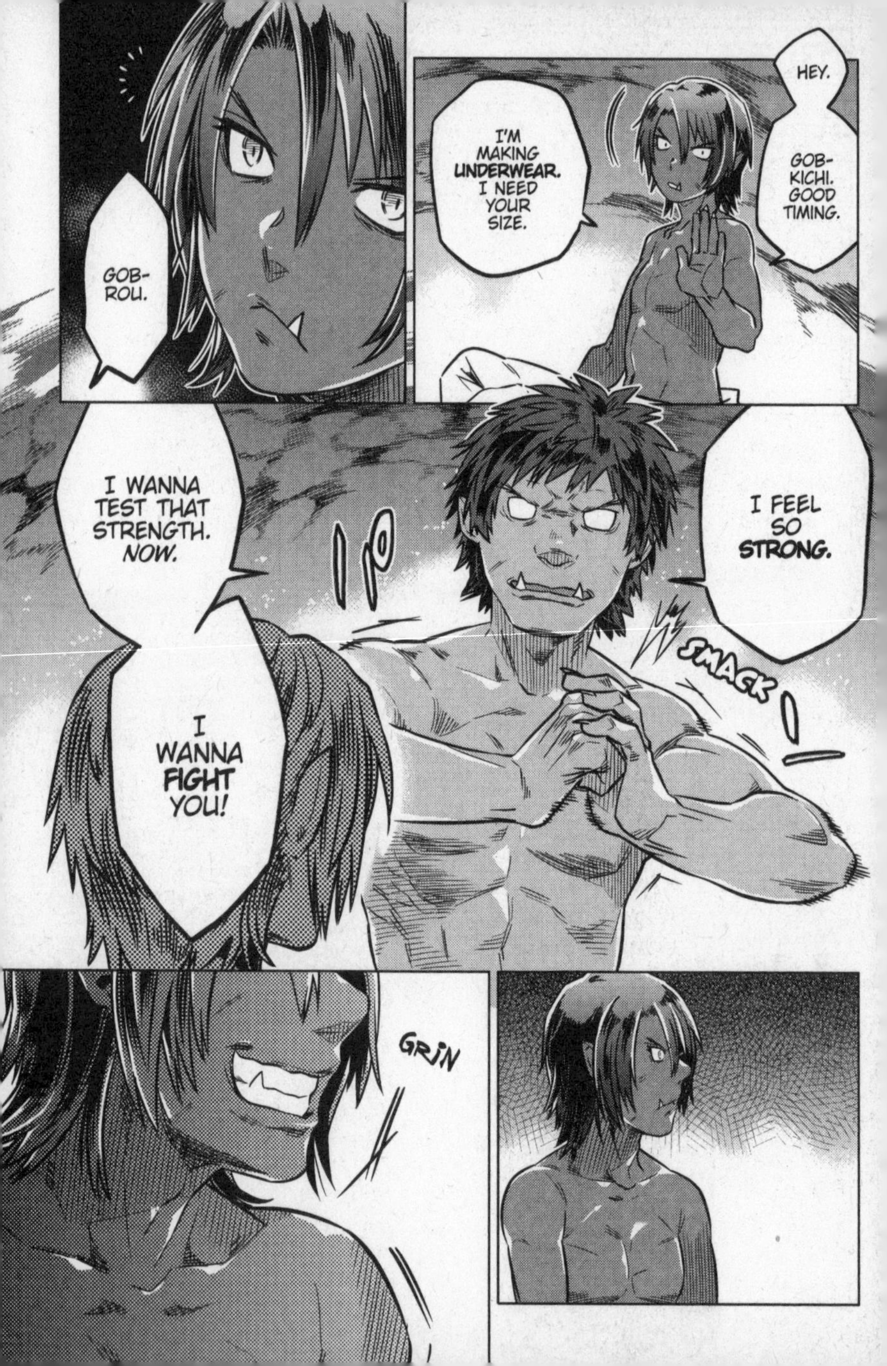
HEY.
GOB-KICHI. GOOD TIMING.
I'M MAKING UNDERWEAR. I NEED YOUR SIZE.
GOB-ROU.
I FEEL SO STRONG.
SMACK
I WANNA TEST THAT STRENGTH. NOW.
I WANNA FIGHT YOU!
GRIN

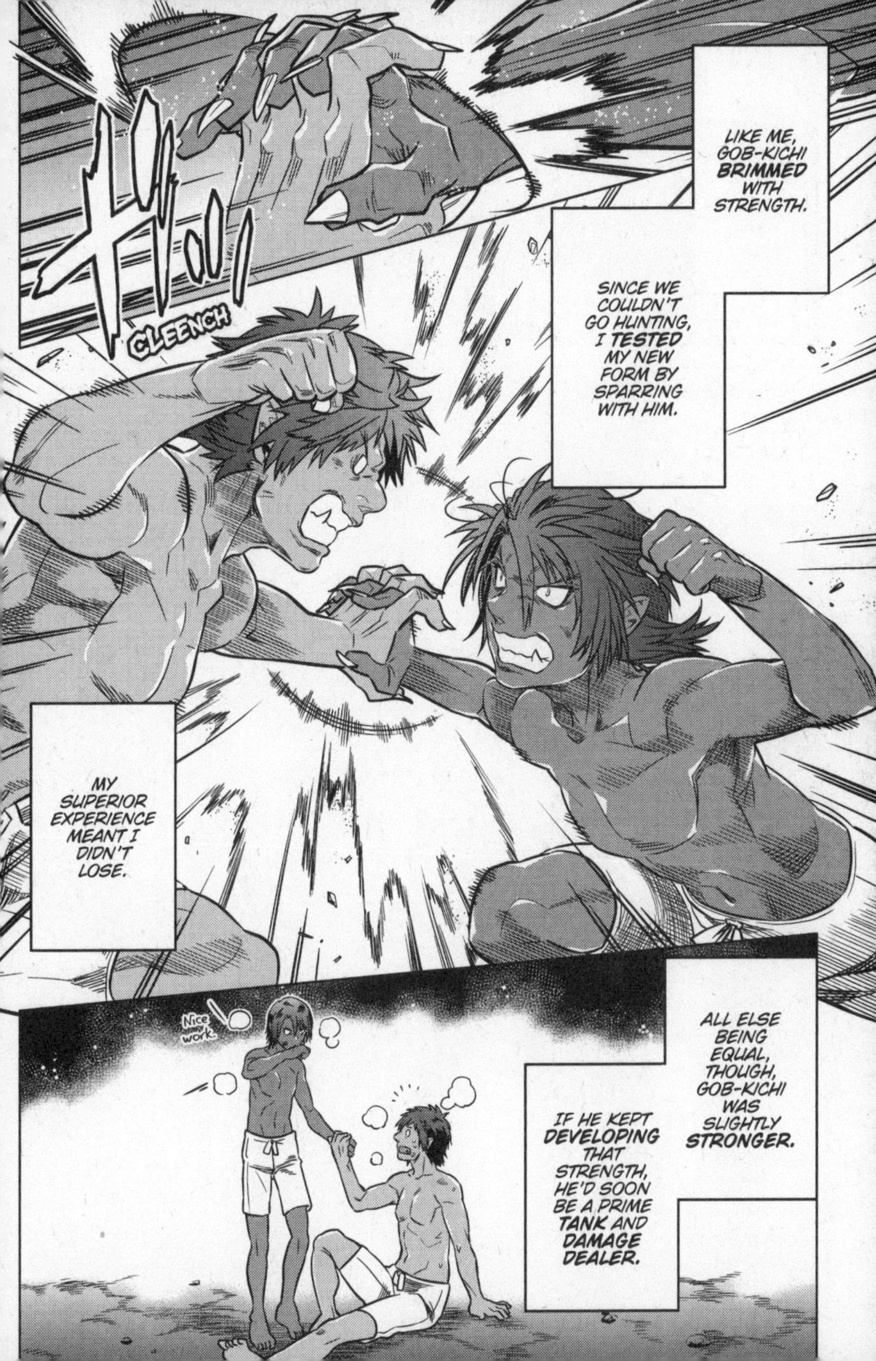
LIKE ME, GOB-KICHI BRIMMED WITH STRENGTH.
SINCE WE COULDN'T GO HUNTING, I TESTED MY NEW FORM BY SPARRING WITH HIM.
CLEENCH
MY SUPERIOR EXPERIENCE MEANT I DIDN'T LOSE.
ALL ELSE BEING EQUAL, THOUGH, GOB-KICHI WAS SLIGHTLY STRONGER.
IF HE KEPT DEVELOPING THAT STRENGTH, HE'D SOON BE A PRIME TANK AND DAMAGE DEALER.
Nice work.

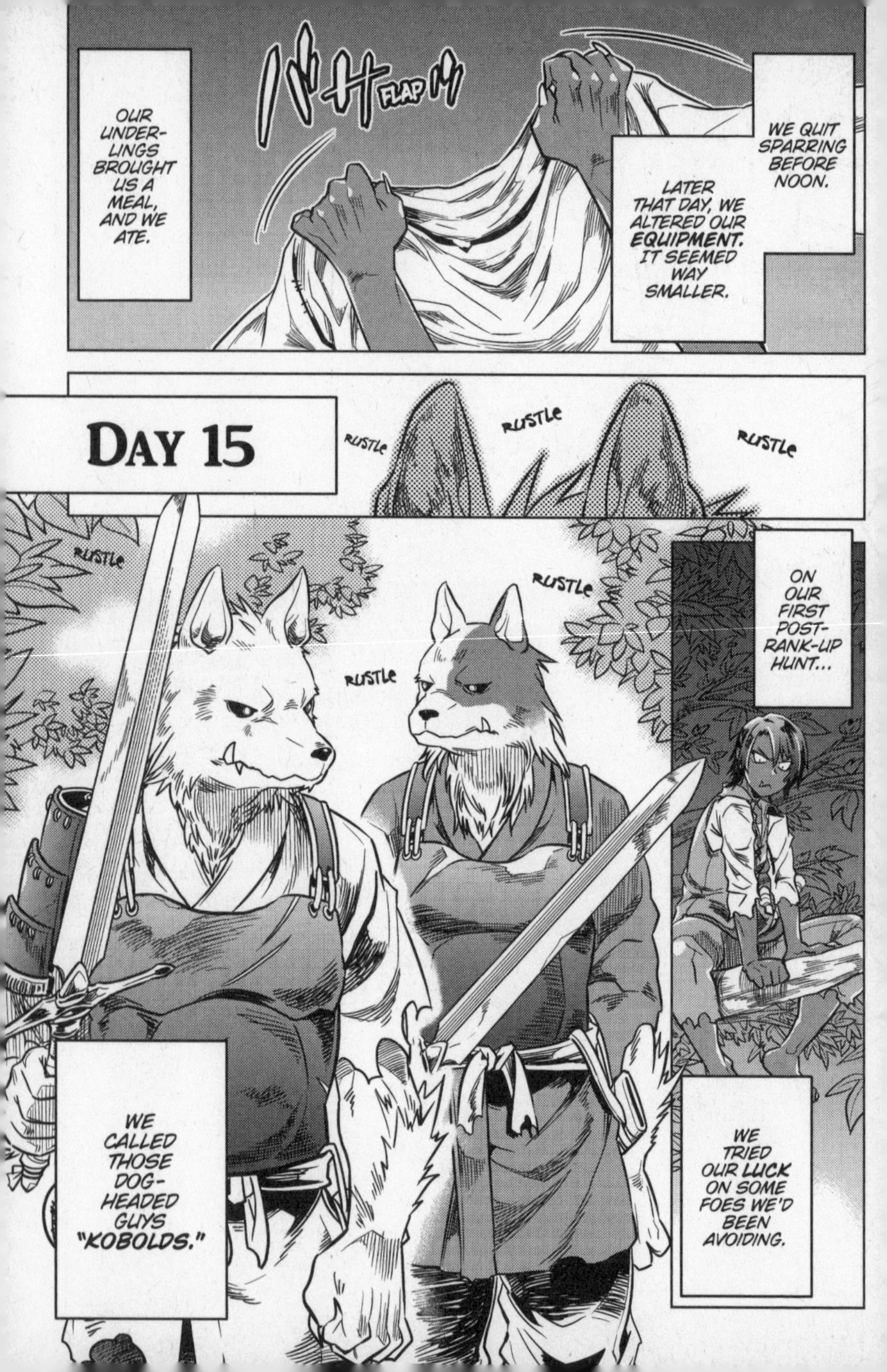
WE QUIT SPARRING BEFORE NOON.
LATER THAT DAY, WE ALTERED OUR EQUIPMENT. IT SEEMED WAY SMALLER.
FLAP
OUR UNDER-LINGS BROUGHT US A MEAL, AND WE ATE.
RUSTLE
RUSTLE
RUSTLE
DAY 15
ON OUR FIRST POST-RANK-UP HUNT...
WE TRIED OUR LUCK ON SOME FOES WE'D BEEN AVOIDING.
RUSTLE
RUSTLE
RUSTLE
WE CALLED THOSE DOG-HEADED GUYS "KOBOLDS."

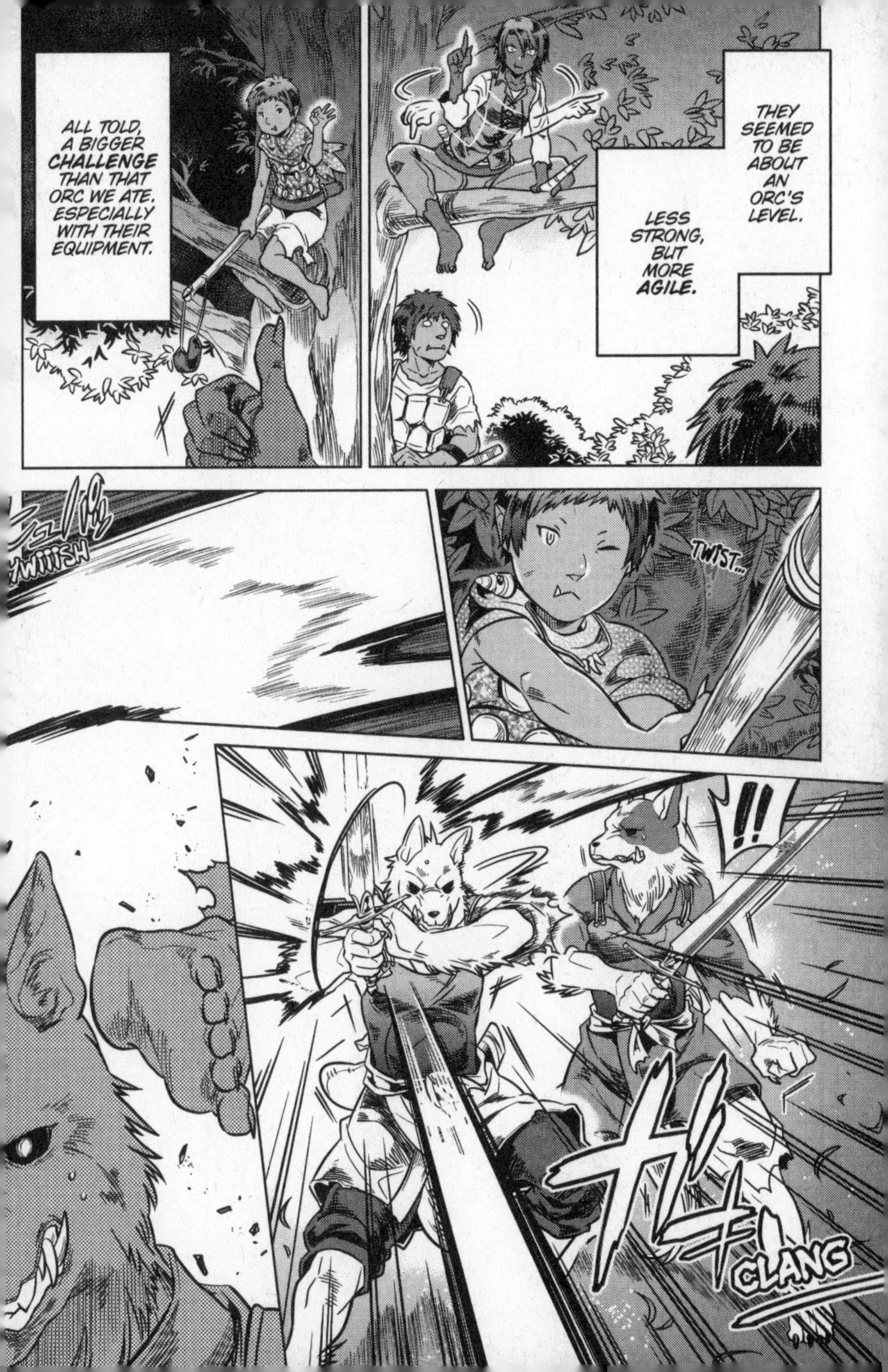
THEY SEEMED TO BE ABOUT AN ORC'S LEVEL.
LESS STRONG, BUT MORE AGILE.
ALL TOLD, A BIGGER CHALLENGE THAN THAT ORC WE ATE. ESPECIALLY WITH THEIR EQUIPMENT.
TWIST...
WIIIISH
!!
CLANG

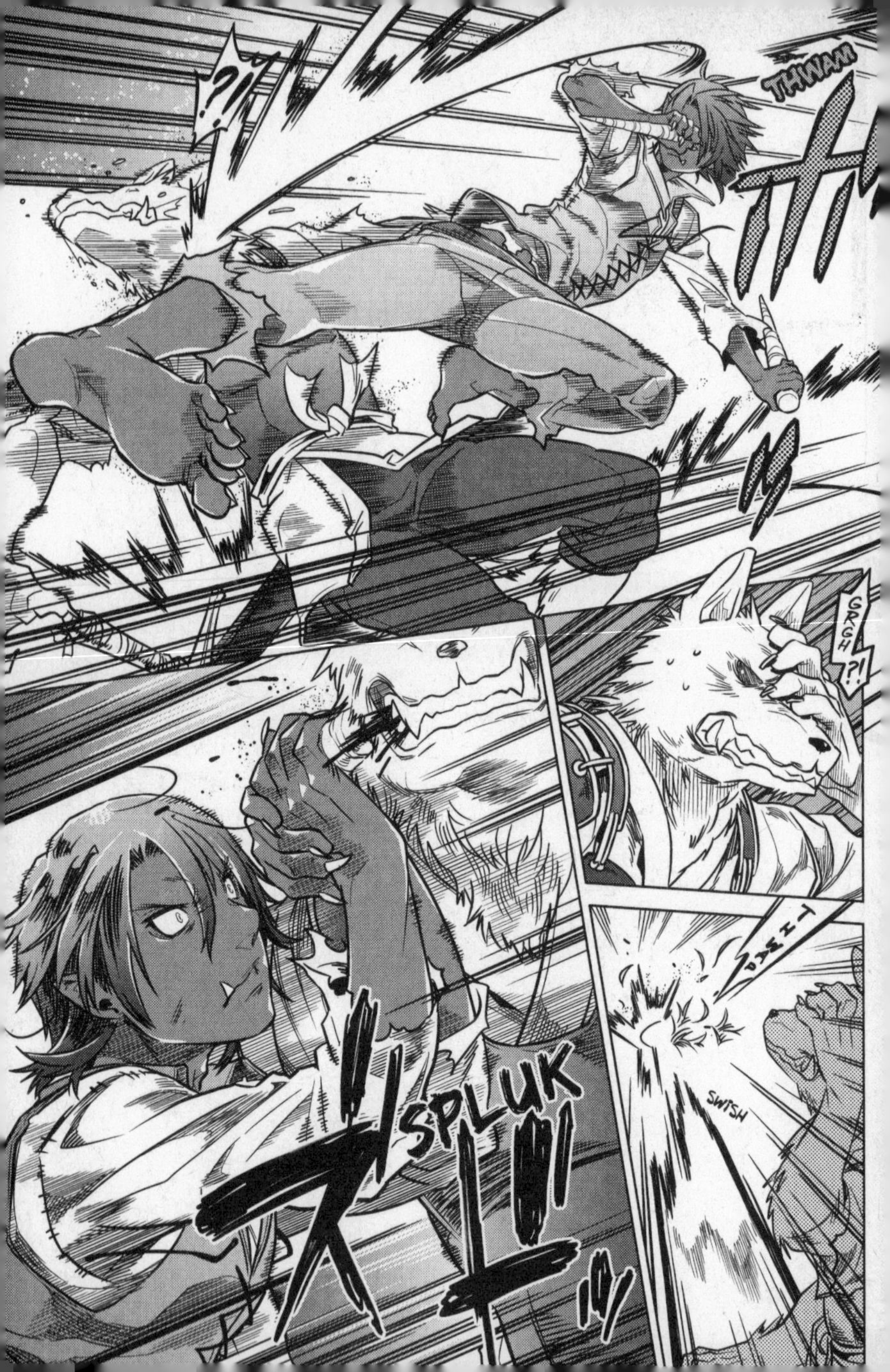
THWAM
?!
GRGH ?!
DAEIT
SWISH
SPLUK

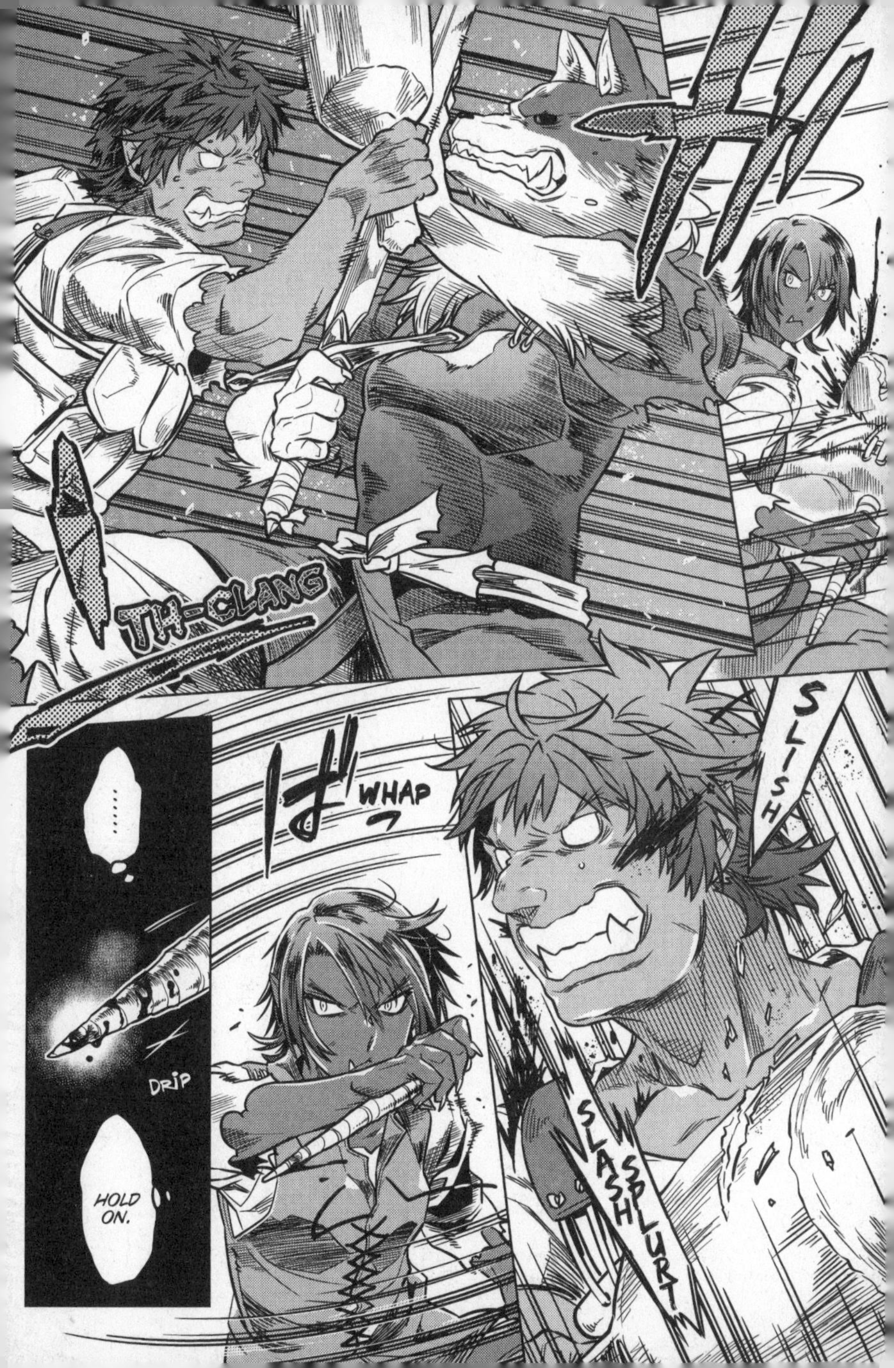
TH-CLANG
SLISH
SLASH
SPLURT
WHAP
......
DRIP
HOLD ON.

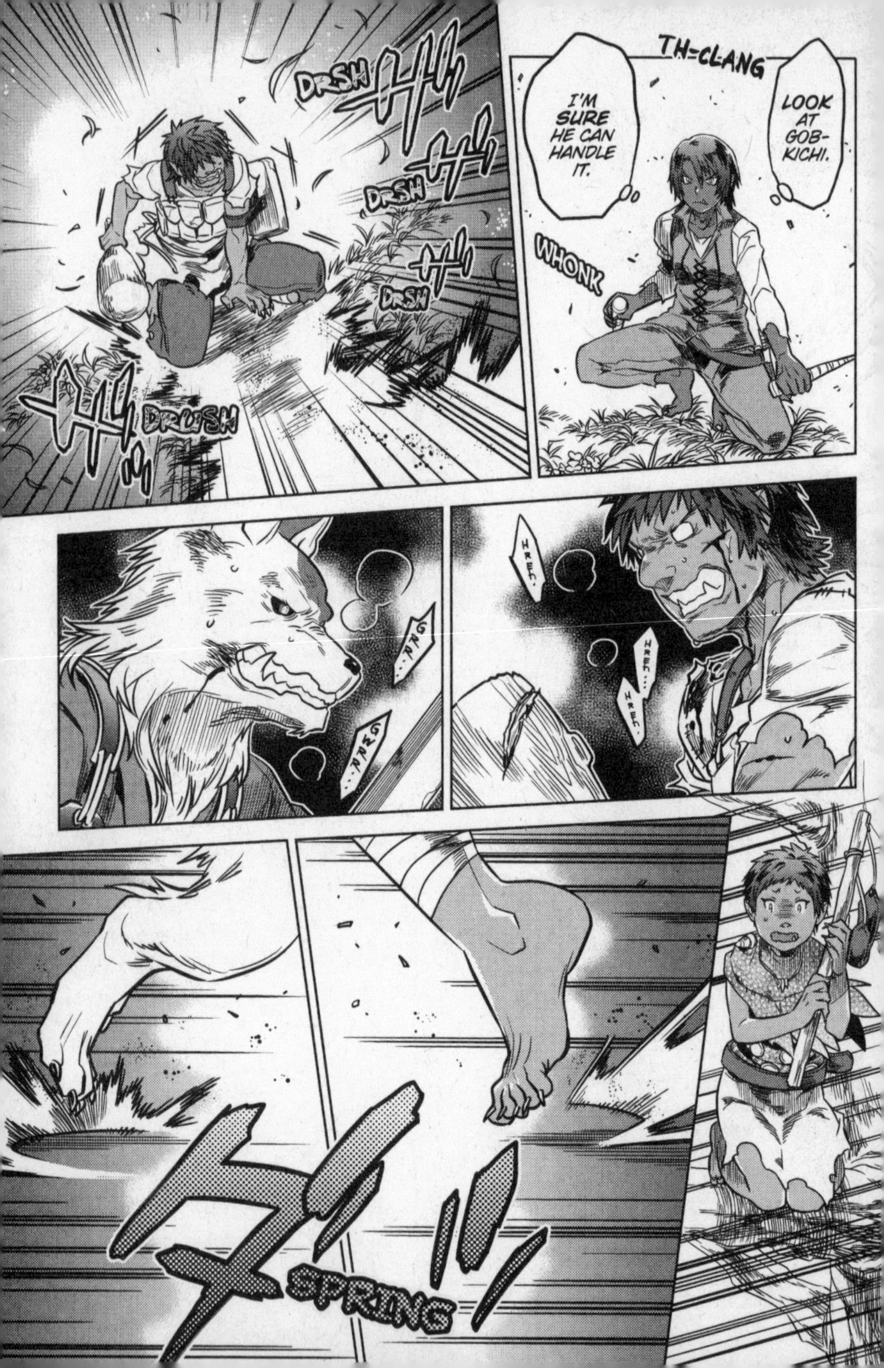
TH-CLANG
LOOK AT GOB-KICHI.
I'M SURE HE CAN HANDLE IT.
WHONK
DRSH
DRSH
DRSH
DRUSH
HREN.
HREN...
HREN.
GRR...
GRRRR...
SPRING

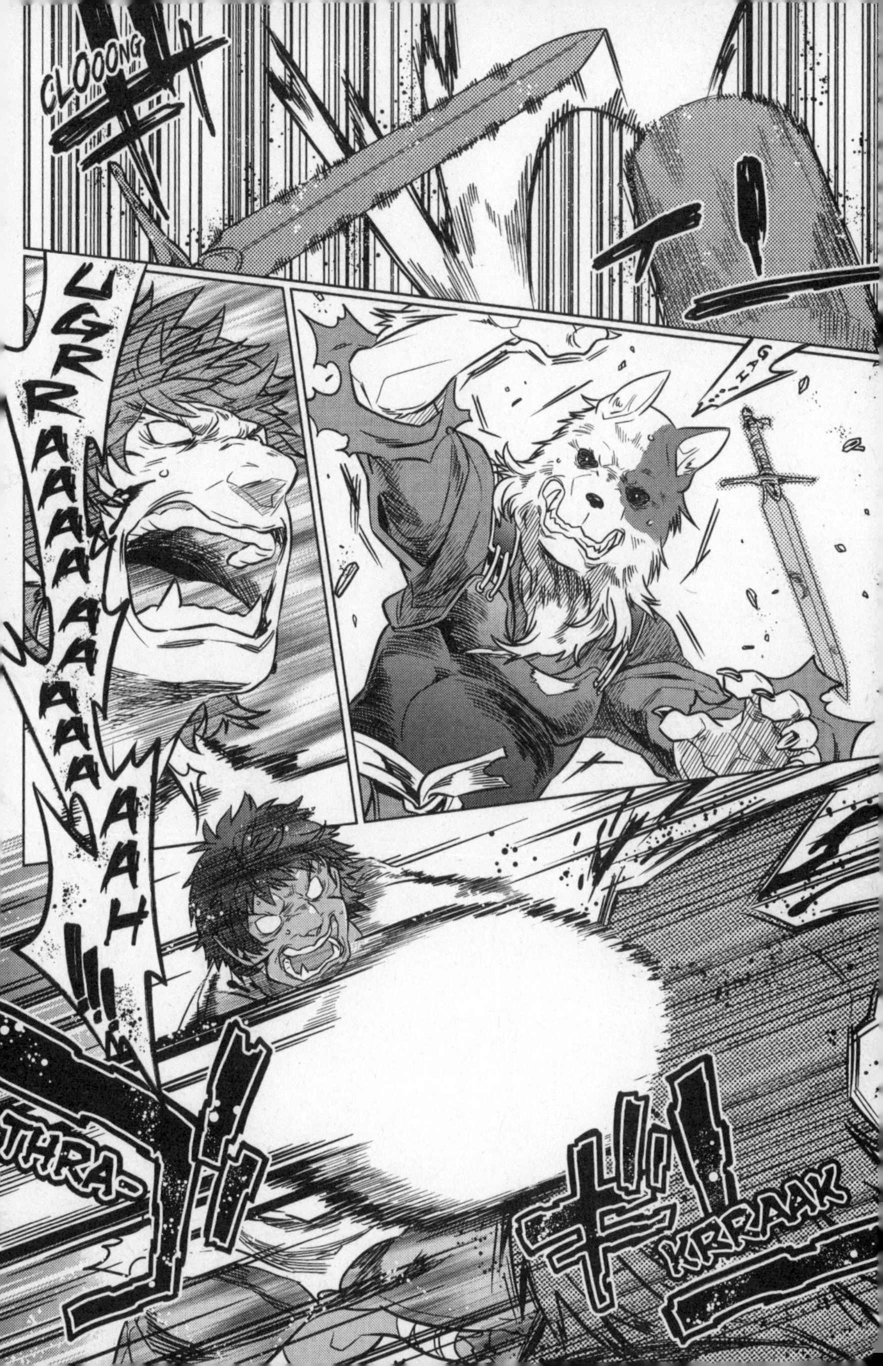
CLOOONG
GAI—...
UGRRAAAAAAAAAAAAAAAH!!!
THRA-
KRRAAK

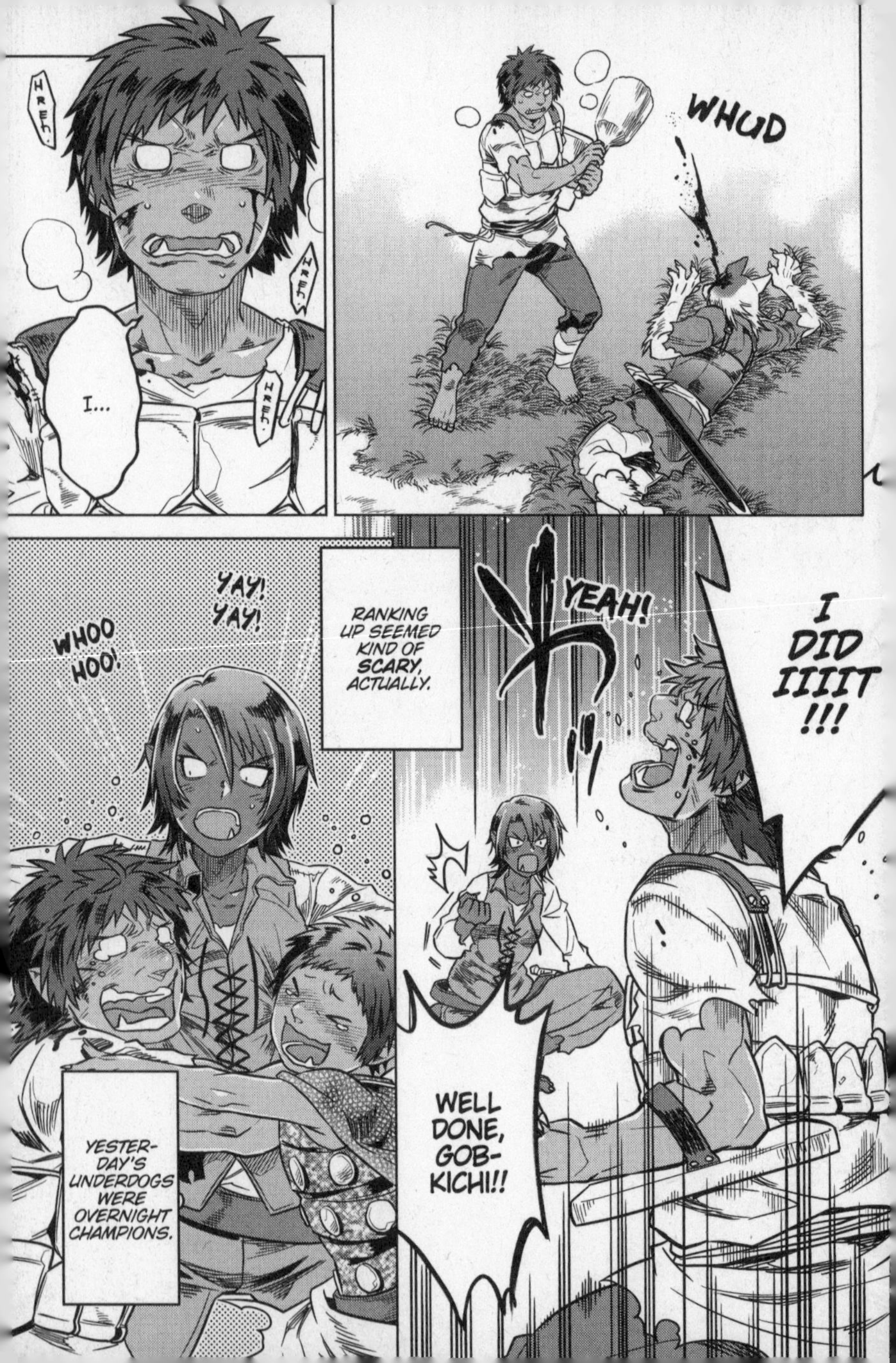
WHUD
HREH.
HREH.
HREH.
I...
YEAH!
I DID IIIIT!!!
WELL DONE, GOB-KICHI!!
RANKING UP SEEMED KIND OF SCARY, ACTUALLY.
YAY! YAY!
WHOO HOO!
YESTER-DAY'S UNDERDOGS WERE OVERNIGHT CHAMPIONS.

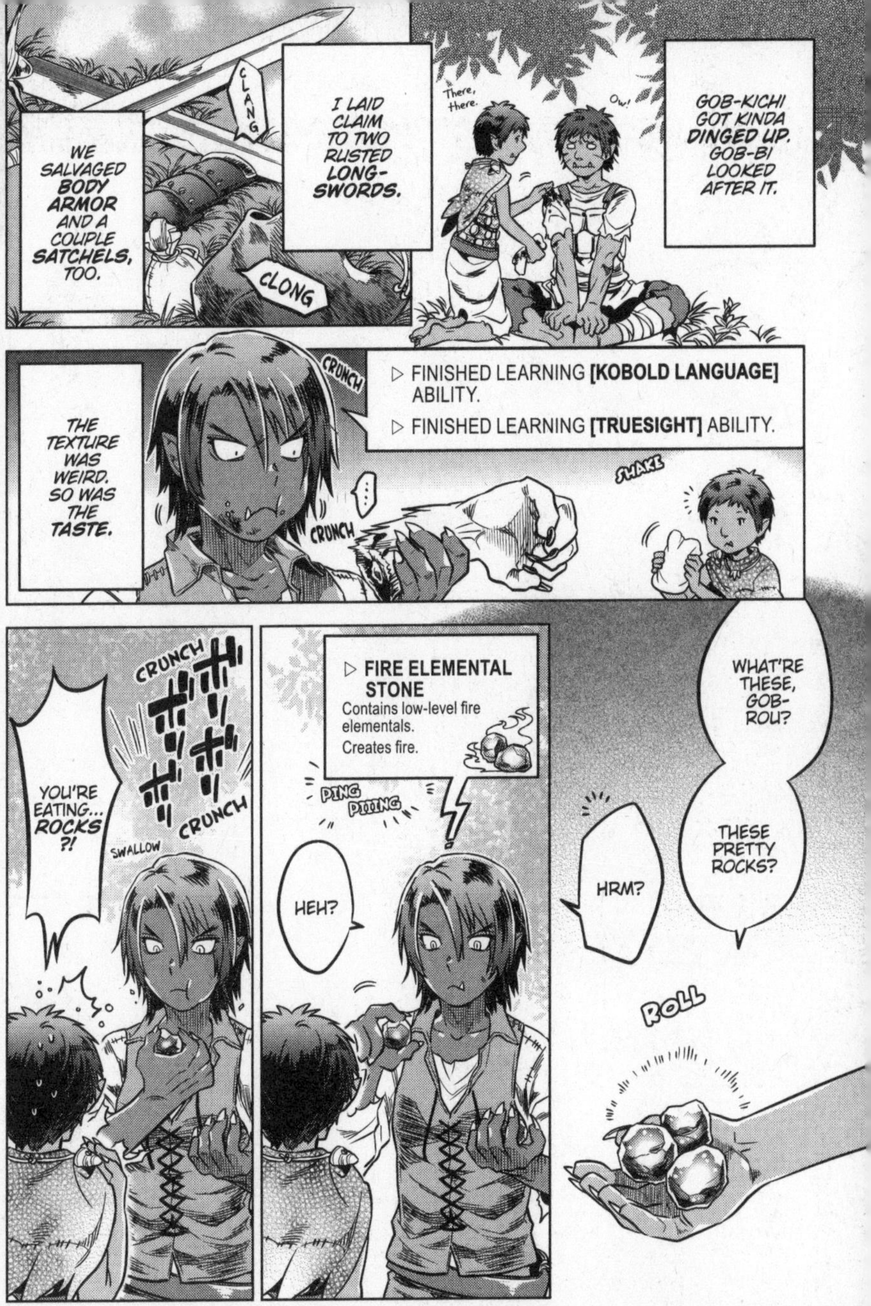
There, there.
Ow!
GOB-KICHI GOT KINDA DINGED UP. GOB-BI LOOKED AFTER IT.
I LAID CLAIM TO TWO RUSTED LONG-SWORDS.
CLANG
WE SALVAGED BODY ARMOR AND A COUPLE SATCHELS, TOO.
CLONG
▷ FINISHED LEARNING [KOBOLD LANGUAGE] ABILITY.
▷ FINISHED LEARNING [TRUESIGHT] ABILITY.
CRUNCH
SHAKE
...
CRUNCH
THE TEXTURE WAS WEIRD. SO WAS THE TASTE.
WHAT'RE THESE, GOB-ROU?
THESE PRETTY ROCKS?
HRM?
ROLL
▷ FIRE ELEMENTAL STONE
Contains low-level fire elementals.
Creates fire.
PING
PIIING
HEH?
CRUNCH
CRUNCH
YOU'RE EATING... ROCKS?!
SWALLOW

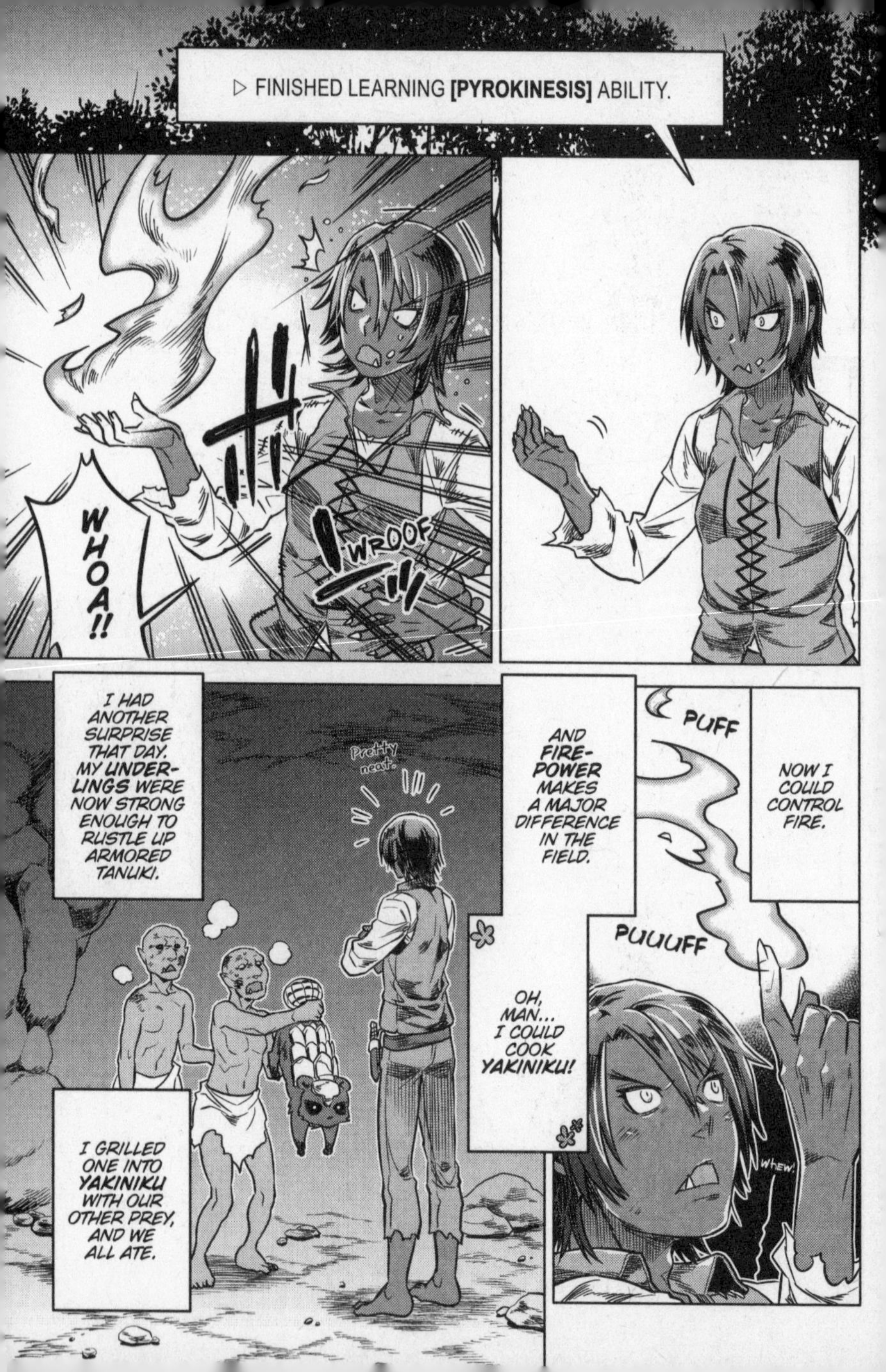
▷ FINISHED LEARNING [PYROKINESIS] ABILITY.
WHOA!!
WROOF
NOW I COULD CONTROL FIRE.
PUFF
PUUUFF
Whew!
AND FIREPOWER MAKES A MAJOR DIFFERENCE IN THE FIELD.
OH, MAN... I COULD COOK YAKINIKU!
I HAD ANOTHER SURPRISE THAT DAY. MY UNDERLINGS WERE NOW STRONG ENOUGH TO RUSTLE UP ARMORED TANUKI.
Pretty neat.
I GRILLED ONE INTO YAKINIKU WITH OUR OTHER PREY, AND WE ALL ATE.

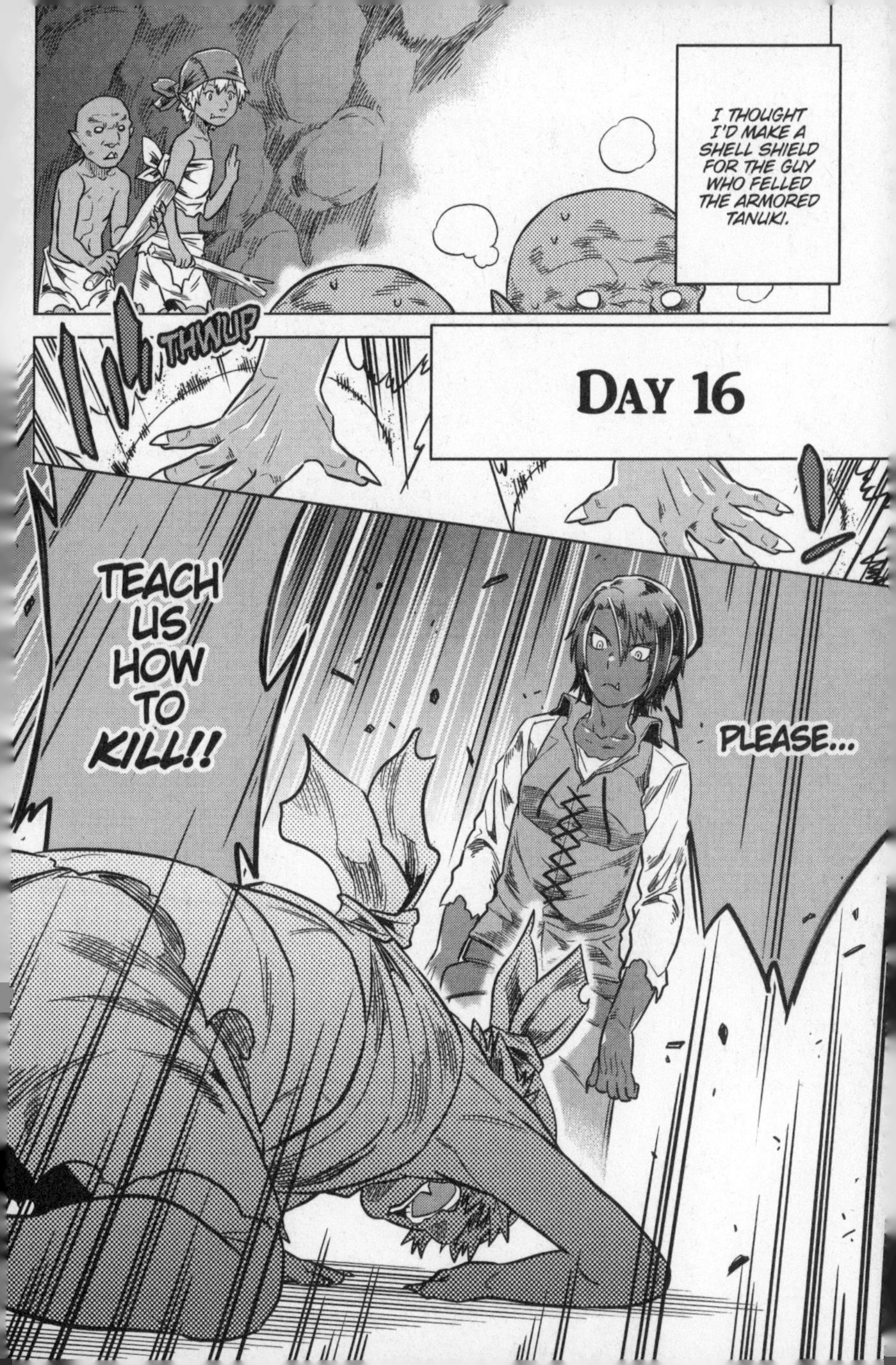
I THOUGHT I'D MAKE A SHELL SHIELD FOR THE GUY WHO FELLED THE ARMORED TANUKI.
DAY 16
THWUP
PLEASE...
TEACH US HOW TO KILL!!

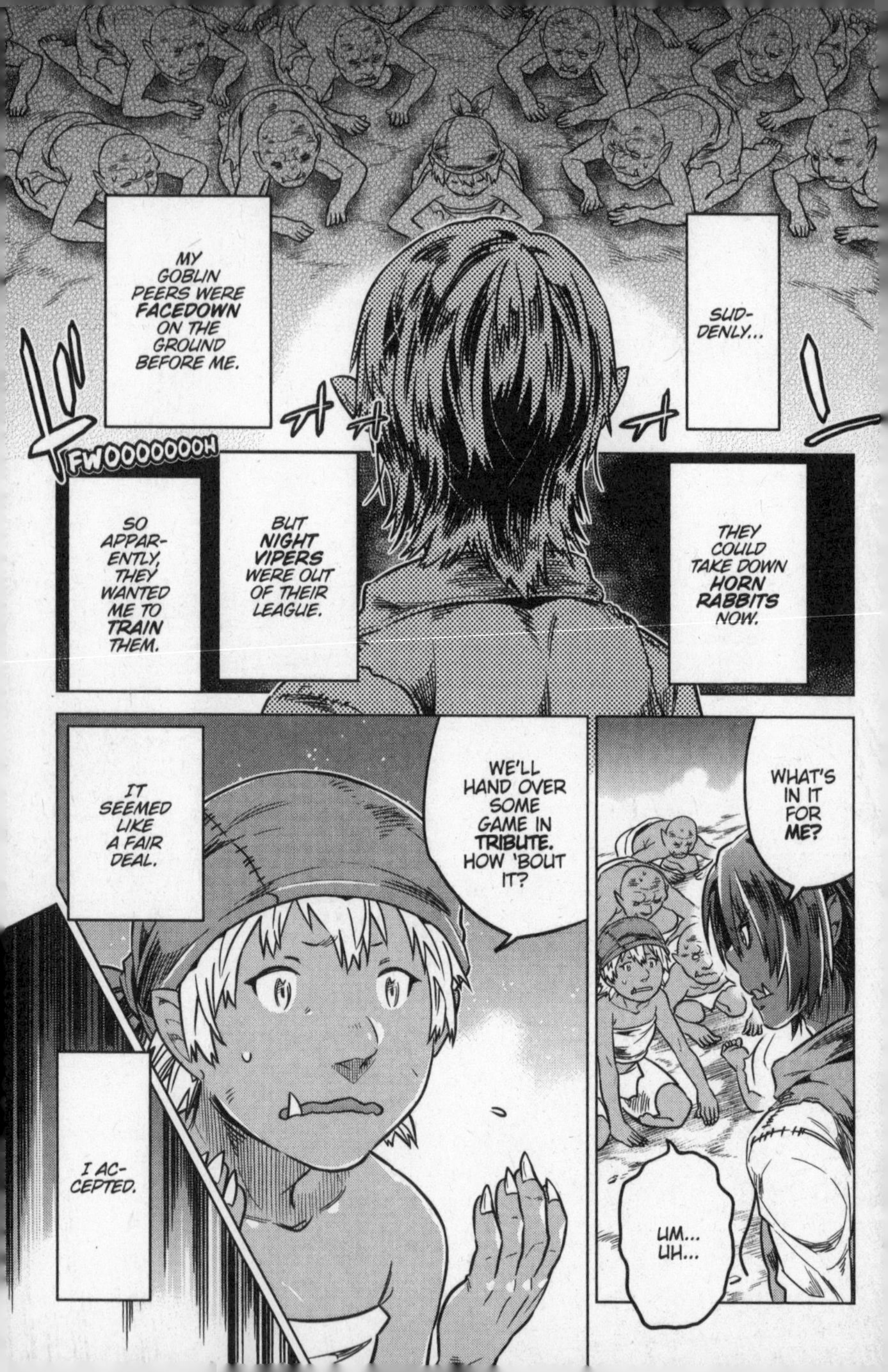
SUDDENLY...
MY GOBLIN PEERS WERE FACEDOWN ON THE GROUND BEFORE ME.
FWOOOOOOOH
THEY COULD TAKE DOWN HORN RABBITS NOW.
BUT NIGHT VIPERS WERE OUT OF THEIR LEAGUE.
SO APPARENTLY, THEY WANTED ME TO TRAIN THEM.
WHAT'S IN IT FOR ME?
UM... UH...
WE'LL HAND OVER SOME GAME IN TRIBUTE. HOW 'BOUT IT?
IT SEEMED LIKE A FAIR DEAL.
I ACCEPTED.

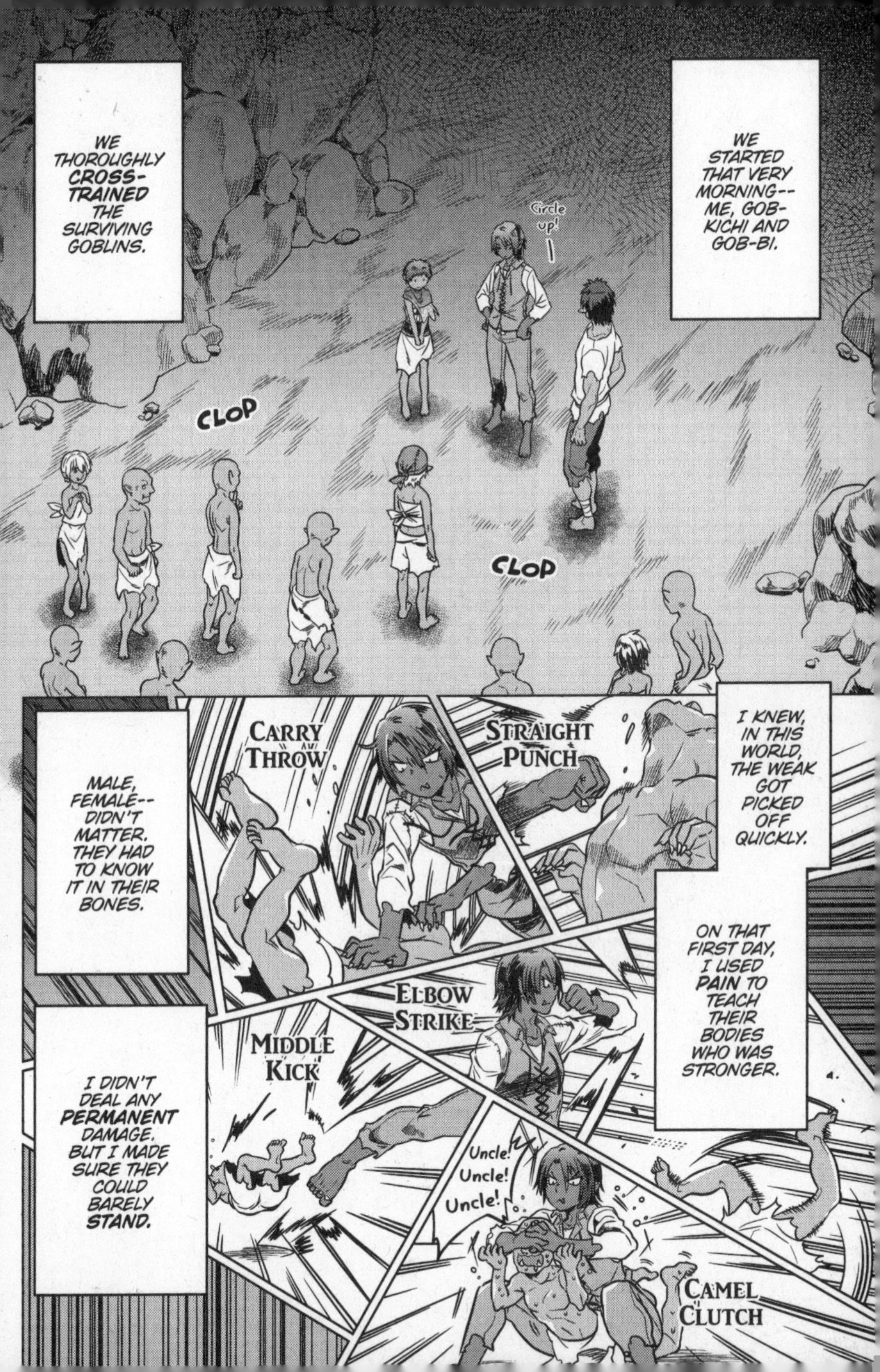
WE STARTED THAT VERY MORNING-- ME, GOB-KICHI AND GOB-BI.
Circle up!
WE THOROUGHLY CROSS-TRAINED THE SURVIVING GOBLINS.
CLOP
CLOP
I KNEW, IN THIS WORLD, THE WEAK GOT PICKED OFF QUICKLY.
STRAIGHT PUNCH
CARRY THROW
MALE, FEMALE-- DIDN'T MATTER. THEY HAD TO KNOW IT IN THEIR BONES.
ON THAT FIRST DAY, I USED PAIN TO TEACH THEIR BODIES WHO WAS STRONGER.
ELBOW STRIKE
MIDDLE KICK
I DIDN'T DEAL ANY PERMANENT DAMAGE. BUT I MADE SURE THEY COULD BARELY STAND.
Uncle!
Uncle!
Uncle!
CAMEL CLUTCH

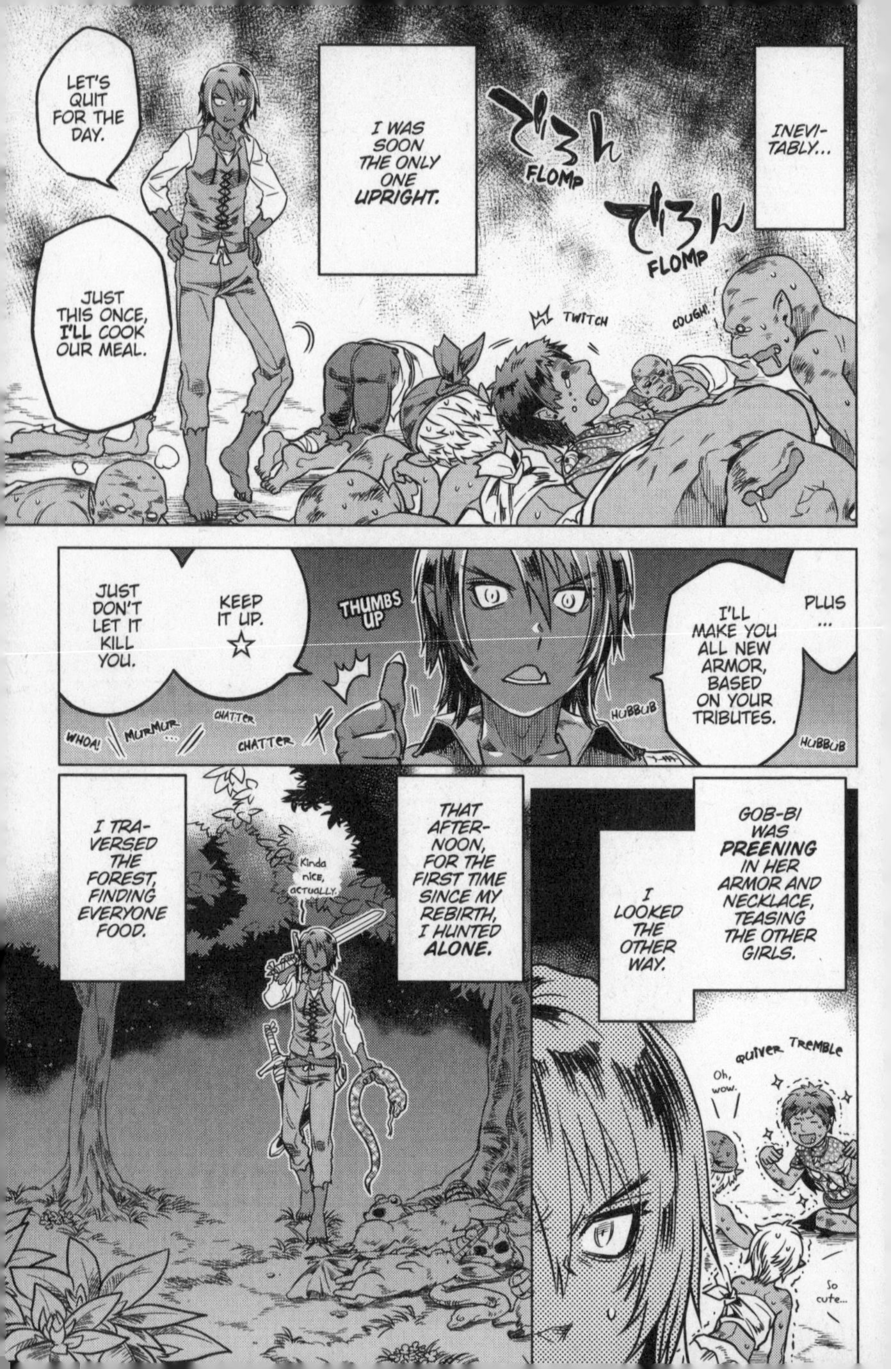

INEVI-TABLY...
でろん
FLOMP
I WAS SOON THE ONLY ONE UPRIGHT.
でろん
FLOMP
COUGH!
TWITCH
LET'S QUIT FOR THE DAY.
JUST THIS ONCE, I'LL COOK OUR MEAL.
PLUS...
I'LL MAKE YOU ALL NEW ARMOR, BASED ON YOUR TRIBUTES.
HUBBUB
HUBBUB
THUMBS UP
KEEP IT UP. ☆
JUST DON'T LET IT KILL YOU.
CHATTER
CHATTER
MURMUR...
WHOA!
GOB-BI WAS PREENING IN HER ARMOR AND NECKLACE, TEASING THE OTHER GIRLS.
I LOOKED THE OTHER WAY.
TREMBLE
QUIVER
Oh, wow.
So cute...
THAT AFTER-NOON, FOR THE FIRST TIME SINCE MY REBIRTH, I HUNTED ALONE.
I TRA-VERSED THE FOREST, FINDING EVERYONE FOOD.
Kinda nice, actually.

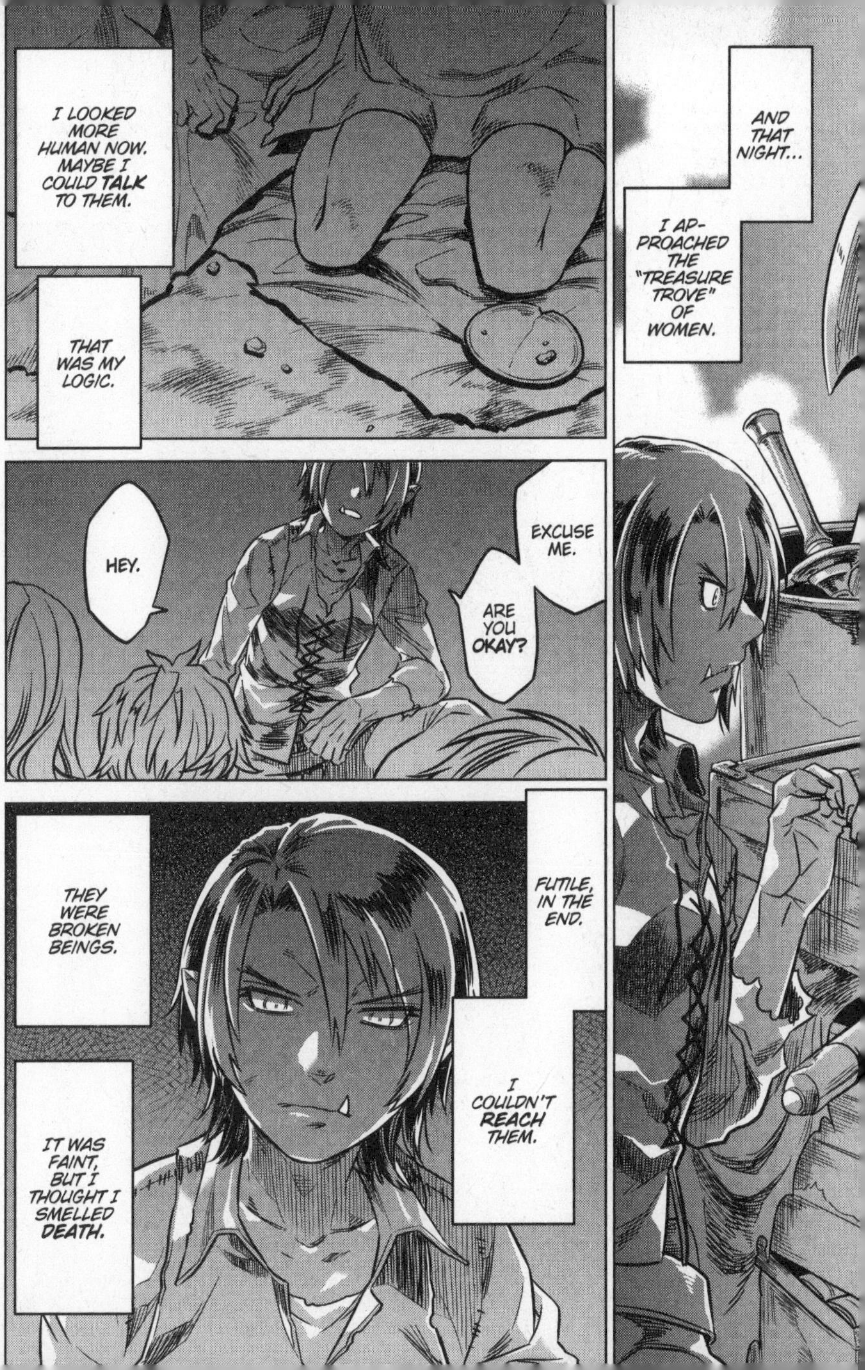
AND THAT NIGHT...
I APPROACHED THE "TREASURE TROVE" OF WOMEN.
I LOOKED MORE HUMAN NOW. MAYBE I COULD TALK TO THEM.
THAT WAS MY LOGIC.
EXCUSE ME.
ARE YOU OKAY?
HEY.
FUTILE, IN THE END.
THEY WERE BROKEN BEINGS.
I COULDN'T REACH THEM.
IT WAS FAINT, BUT I THOUGHT I SMELLED DEATH.

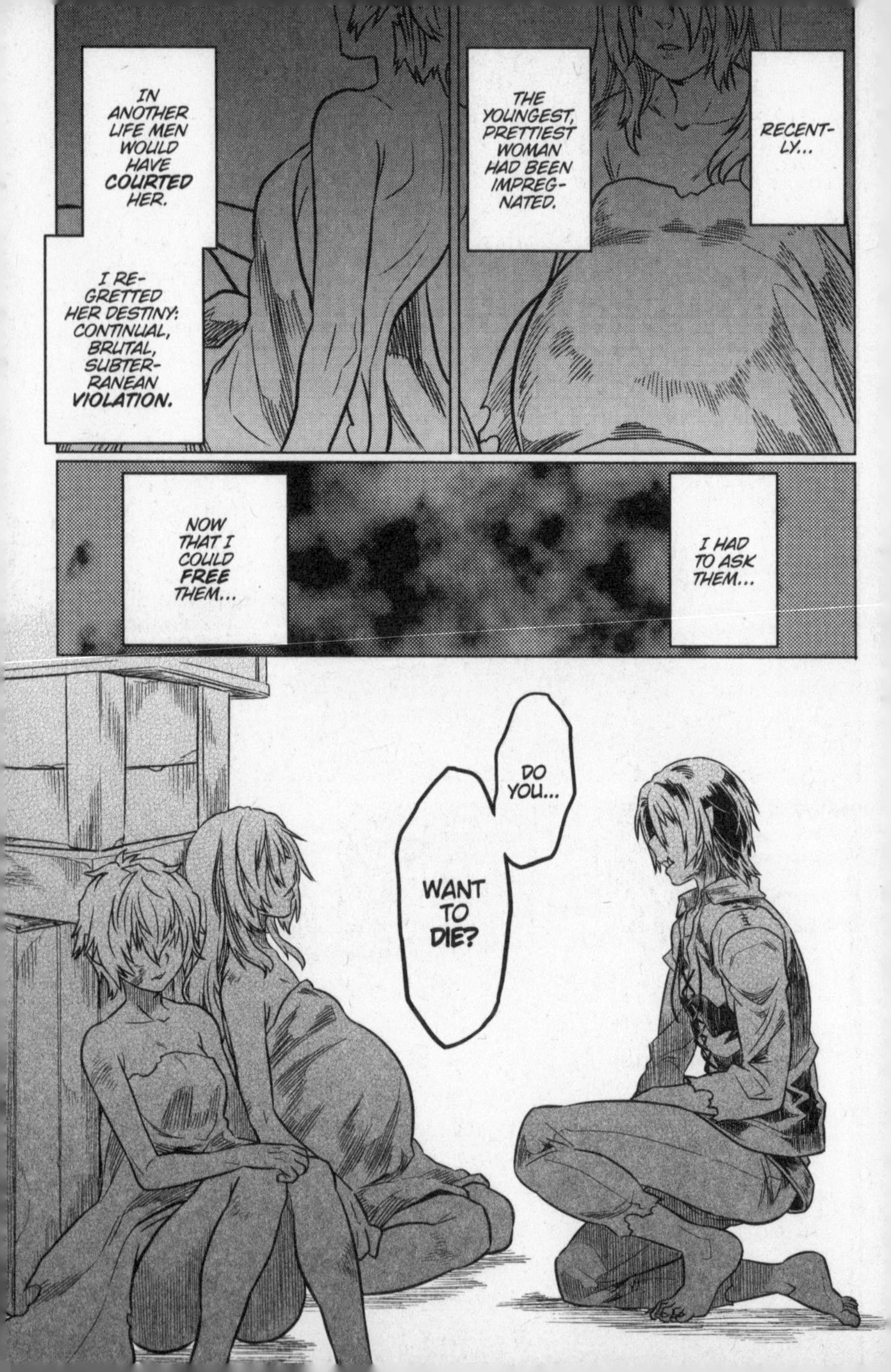
RECENT-LY...
THE YOUNGEST, PRETTIEST WOMAN HAD BEEN IMPREG-NATED.
IN ANOTHER LIFE MEN WOULD HAVE COURTED HER.
I RE-GRETTED HER DESTINY: CONTINUAL, BRUTAL, SUBTER-RANEAN VIOLATION.
I HAD TO ASK THEM...
NOW THAT I COULD FREE THEM...
DO YOU...
WANT TO DIE?

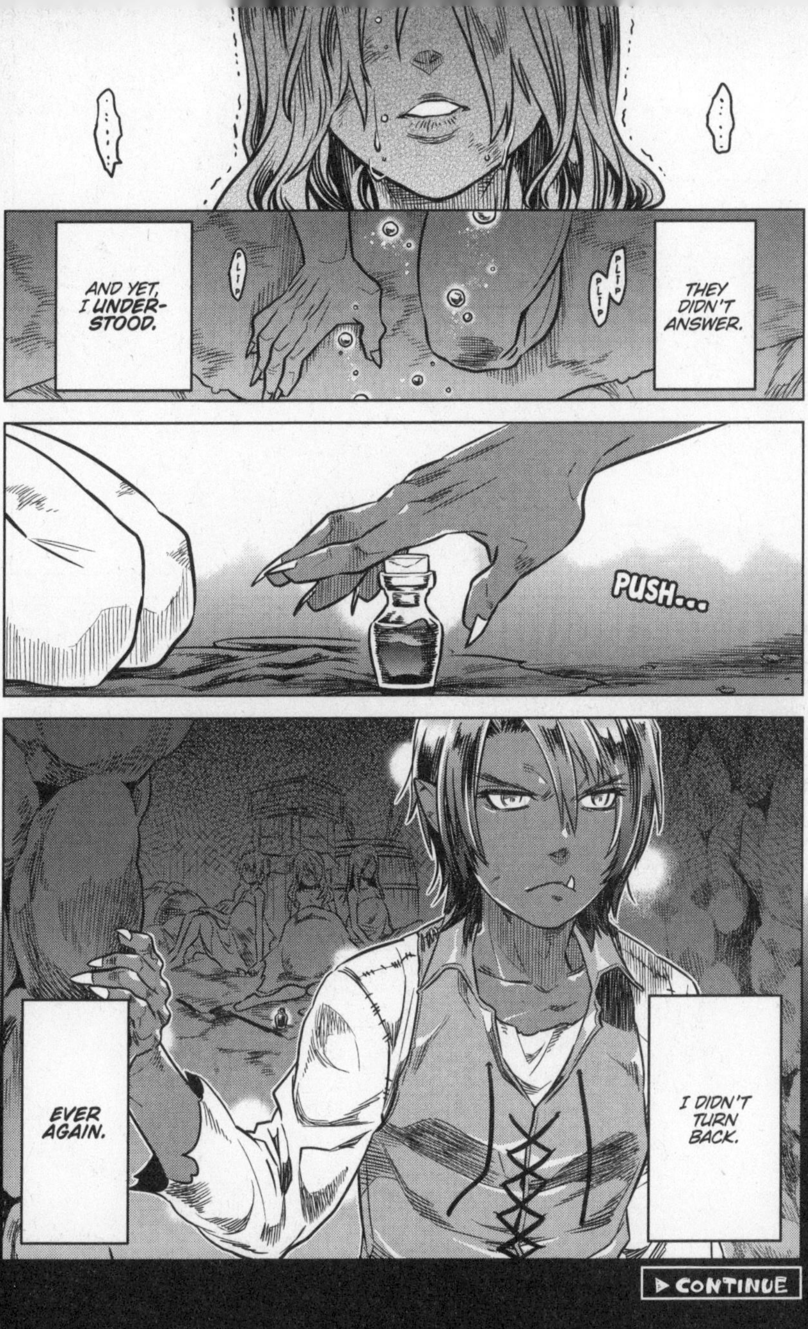
...
...
THEY DIDN'T ANSWER.
PLTP PLTP
PLTP
AND YET, I UNDER-STOOD.
PUSH...
I DIDN'T TURN BACK.
EVER AGAIN.
CONTINUE

DAY 17

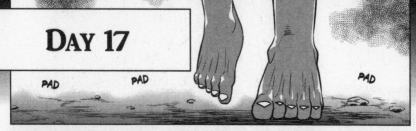

PAD · PAD · PAD

PAD · PAD · PAD · PAD

WAKE UP.

SHAKE · SHAKE

GOB-GRA-MPS.

SOMETHING AWFUL'S HAPPENED.

Heh heh heh.

Ho ho

CLUTCH

CLUTCH

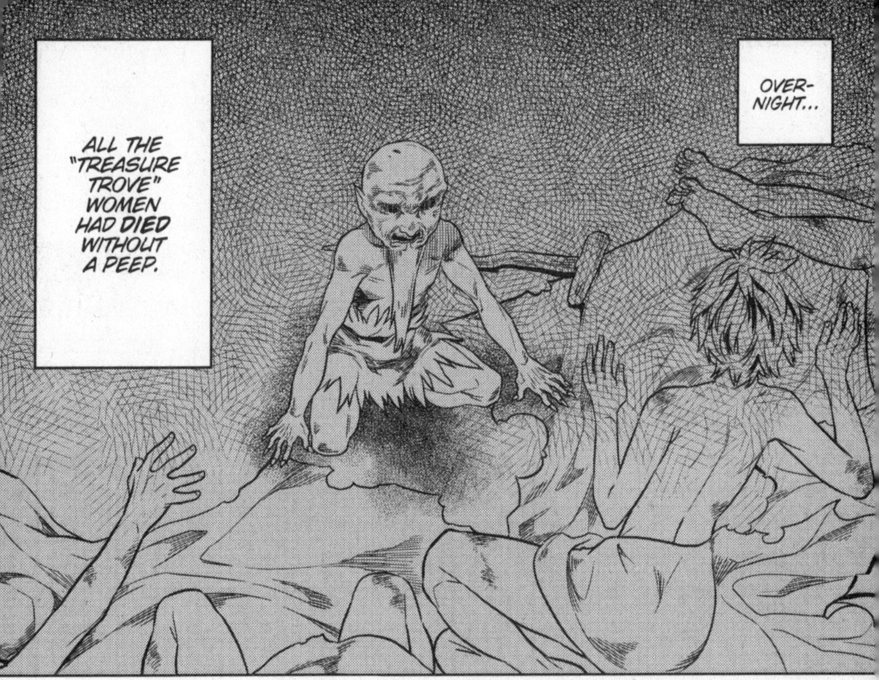
OVER-NIGHT...
ALL THE "TREASURE TROVE" WOMEN HAD DIED WITHOUT A PEEP.

CHAPTER 5

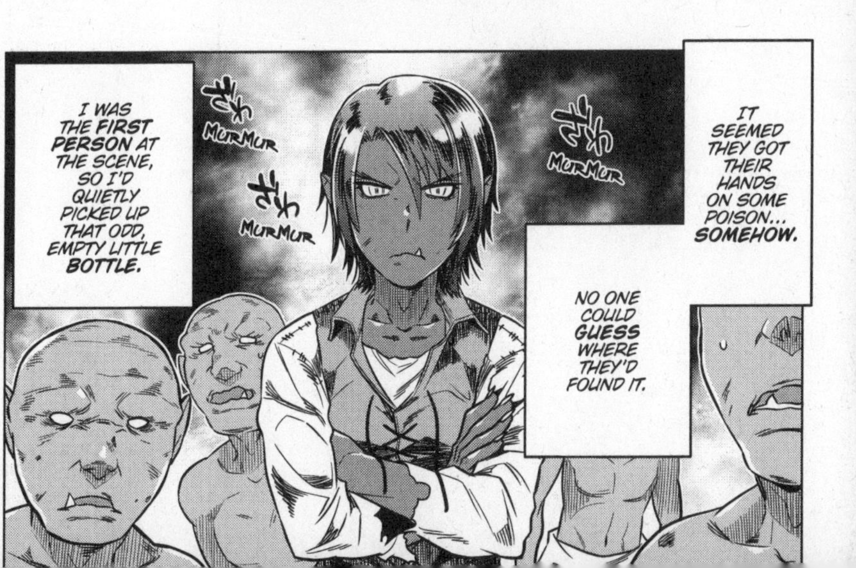
IT SEEMED THEY GOT THEIR HANDS ON SOME POISON... SOMEHOW.
NO ONE COULD GUESS WHERE THEY'D FOUND IT.
ざわ MurMur
ざわ MurMur
ざわ MurMur
I WAS THE FIRST PERSON AT THE SCENE, SO I'D QUIETLY PICKED UP THAT ODD, EMPTY LITTLE BOTTLE.

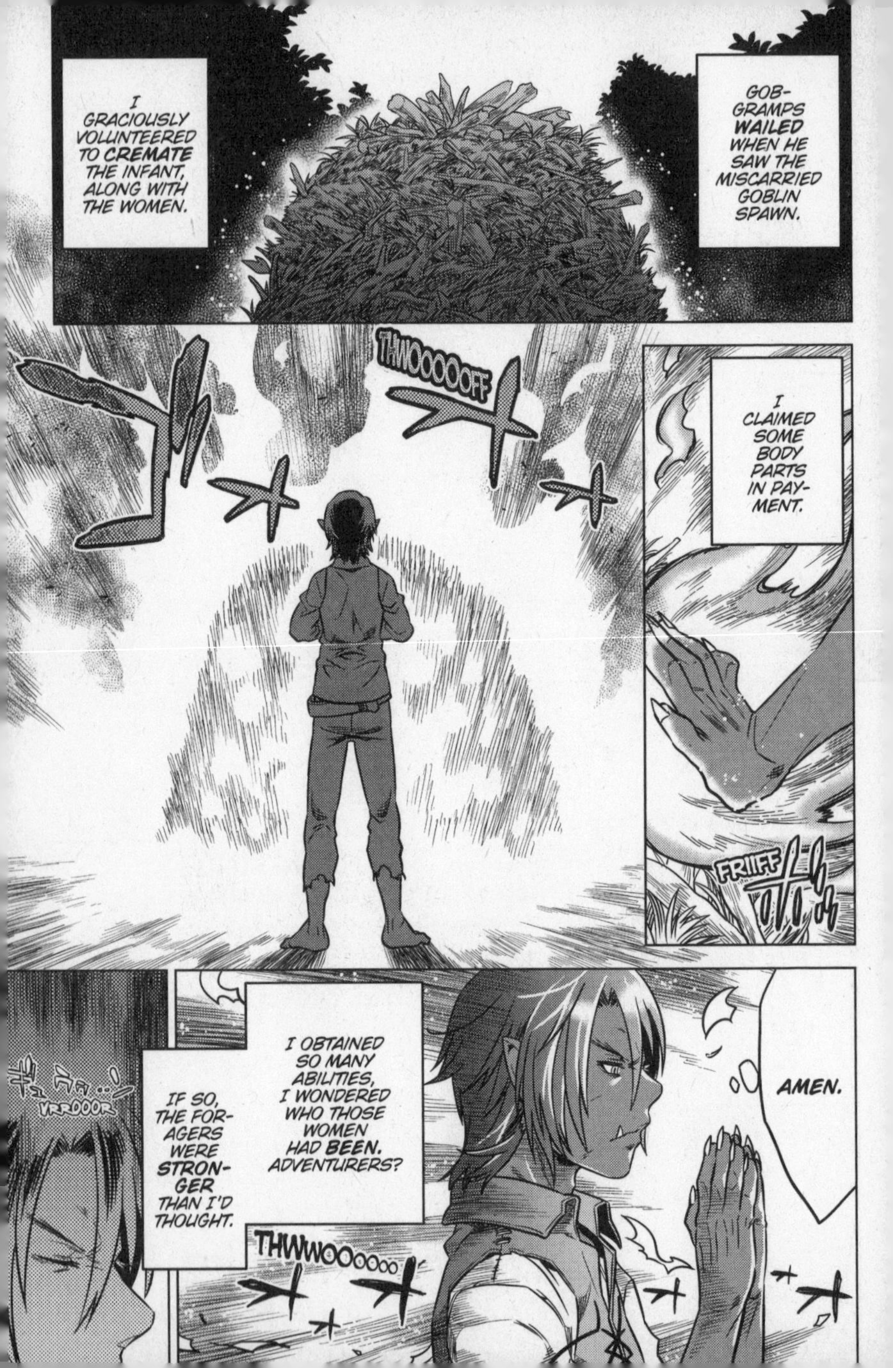
GOB-GRAMPS WAILED WHEN HE SAW THE MISCARRIED GOBLIN SPAWN.
I GRACIOUSLY VOLUNTEERED TO CREMATE THE INFANT, ALONG WITH THE WOMEN.
I CLAIMED SOME BODY PARTS IN PAY-MENT.
FRIIFF
THWOOOOOFF
AMEN.
I OBTAINED SO MANY ABILITIES, I WONDERED WHO THOSE WOMEN HAD BEEN. ADVENTURERS?
IF SO, THE FOR-AGERS WERE STRON-GER THAN I'D THOUGHT.
THWWOOoooo
YRRDOOR

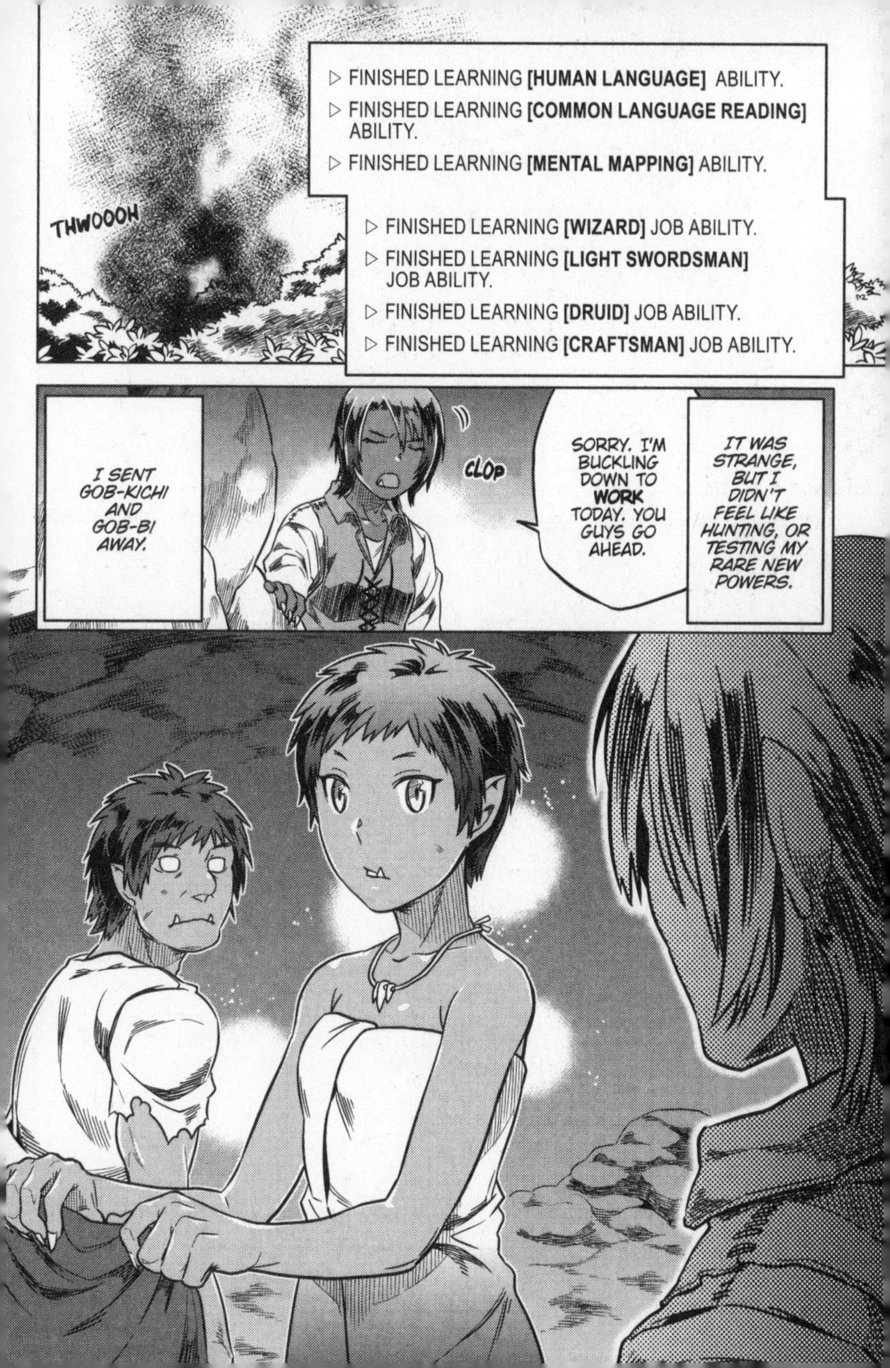
▷ FINISHED LEARNING **[HUMAN LANGUAGE]** ABILITY.
▷ FINISHED LEARNING **[COMMON LANGUAGE READING]** ABILITY.
▷ FINISHED LEARNING **[MENTAL MAPPING]** ABILITY.
▷ FINISHED LEARNING **[WIZARD]** JOB ABILITY.
▷ FINISHED LEARNING **[LIGHT SWORDSMAN]** JOB ABILITY.
▷ FINISHED LEARNING **[DRUID]** JOB ABILITY.
▷ FINISHED LEARNING **[CRAFTSMAN]** JOB ABILITY.
THWOOOH
IT WAS STRANGE, BUT I DIDN'T FEEL LIKE HUNTING, OR TESTING MY RARE NEW POWERS.
SORRY. I'M BUCKLING DOWN TO **WORK** TODAY. YOU GUYS GO AHEAD.
CLOP
I SENT GOB-KICHI AND GOB-BI AWAY.

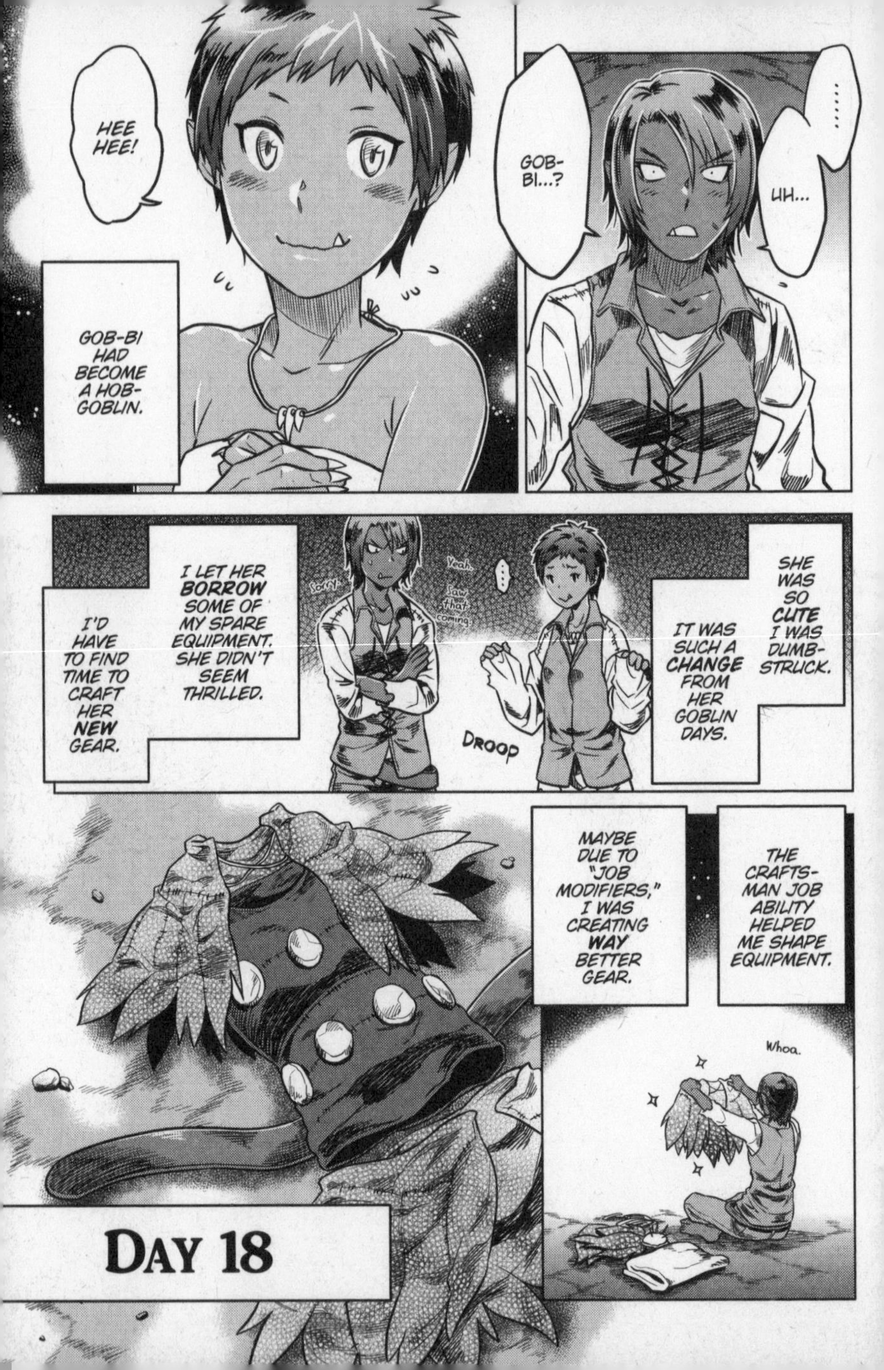
......
UH...
GOB-BI...?
HEE HEE!
GOB-BI HAD BECOME A HOB-GOBLIN.
SHE WAS SO CUTE I WAS DUMB-STRUCK.
IT WAS SUCH A CHANGE FROM HER GOBLIN DAYS.
...
Yeah. Saw that coming.
Sorry.
DROOP
I LET HER BORROW SOME OF MY SPARE EQUIPMENT. SHE DIDN'T SEEM THRILLED.
I'D HAVE TO FIND TIME TO CRAFT HER NEW GEAR.
THE CRAFTS-MAN JOB ABILITY HELPED ME SHAPE EQUIPMENT.
MAYBE DUE TO "JOB MODIFIERS," I WAS CREATING WAY BETTER GEAR.
Whoa.
DAY 18

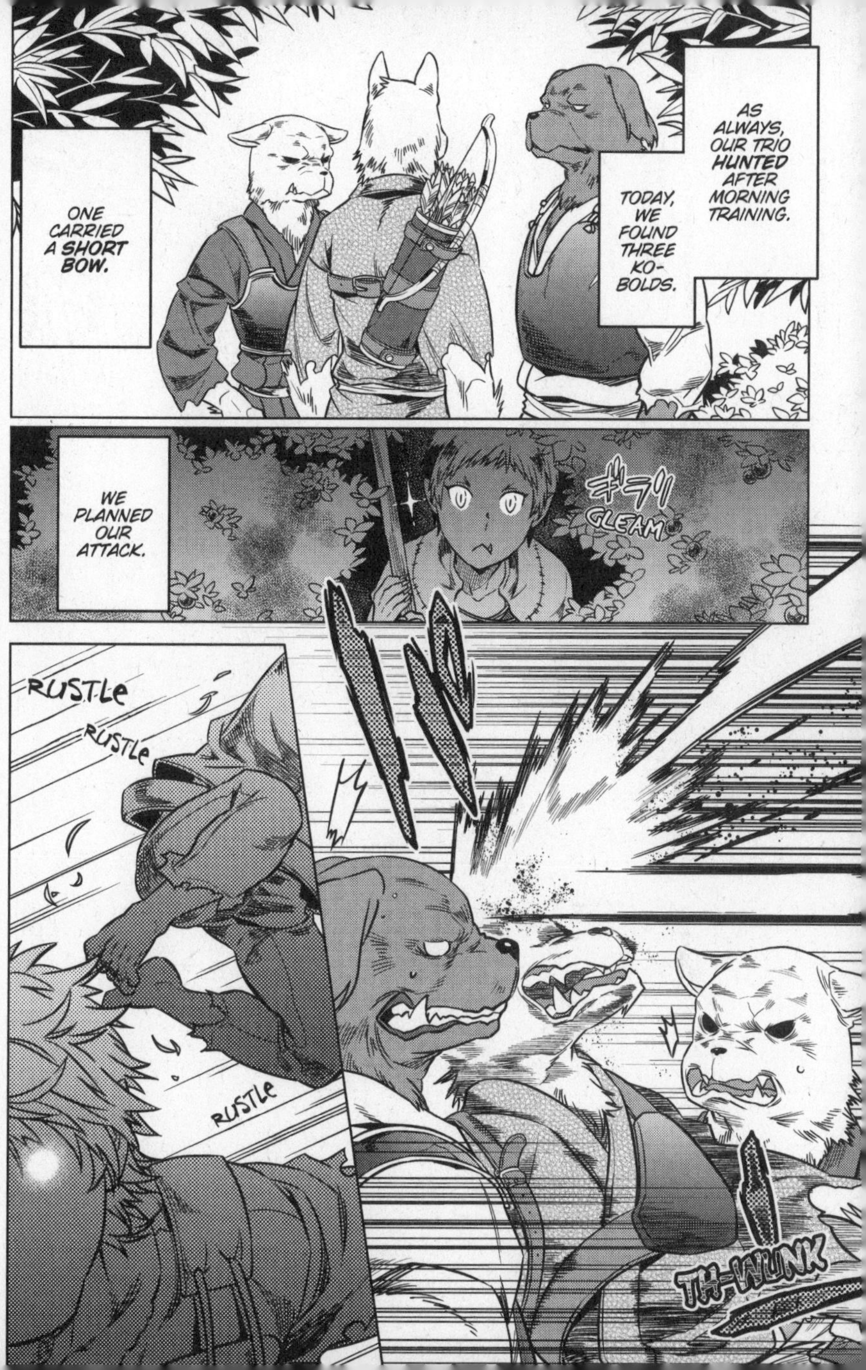
AS ALWAYS, OUR TRIO HUNTED AFTER MORNING TRAINING.
TODAY, WE FOUND THREE KO-BOLDS.
ONE CARRIED A SHORT BOW.
ギラリ
GLEAM
WE PLANNED OUR ATTACK.
RUSTLE
RUSTLE
RUSTLE
TH-WUNK

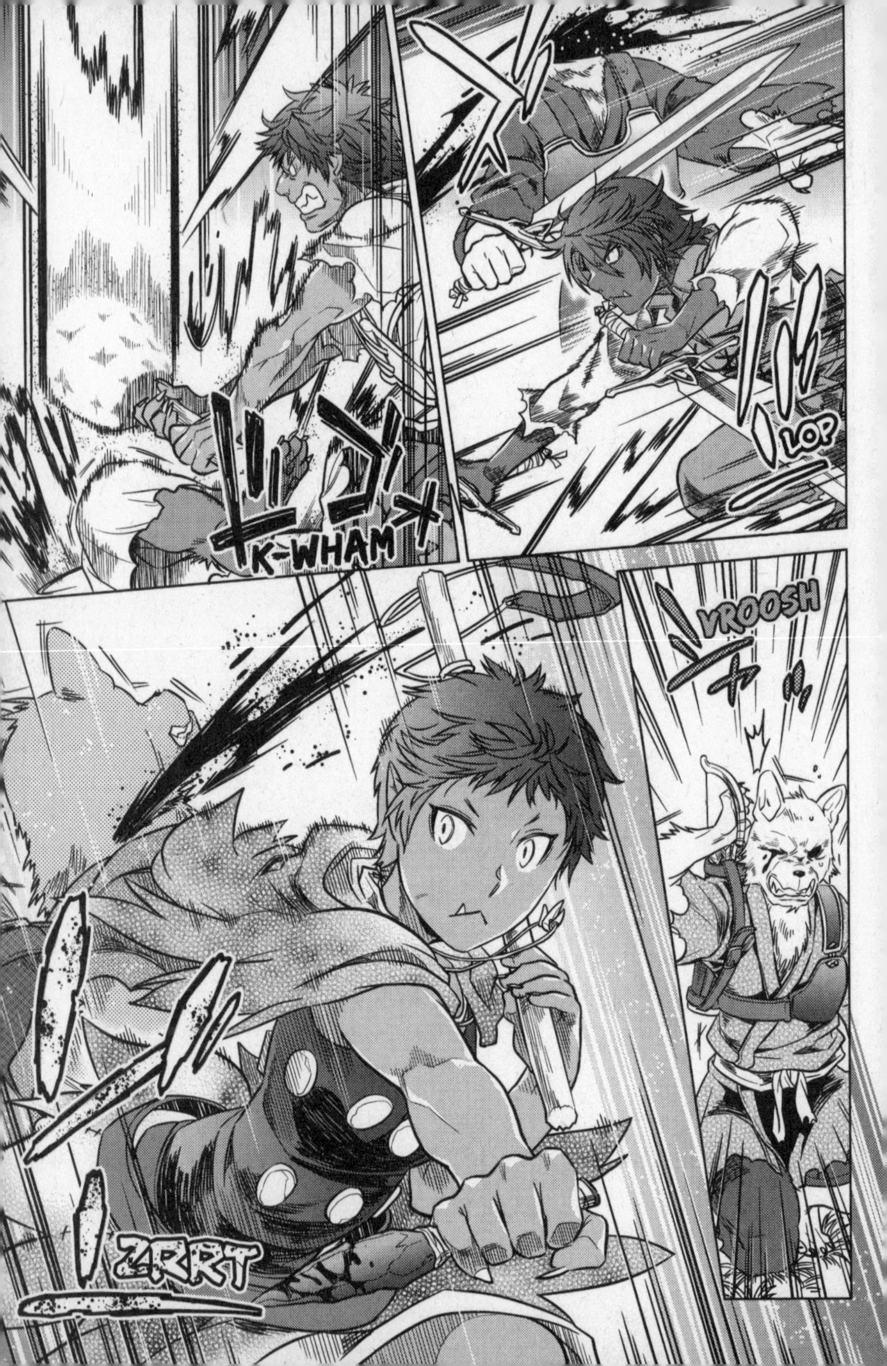
LOP
K-WHAM
VROOSH
ZRRT

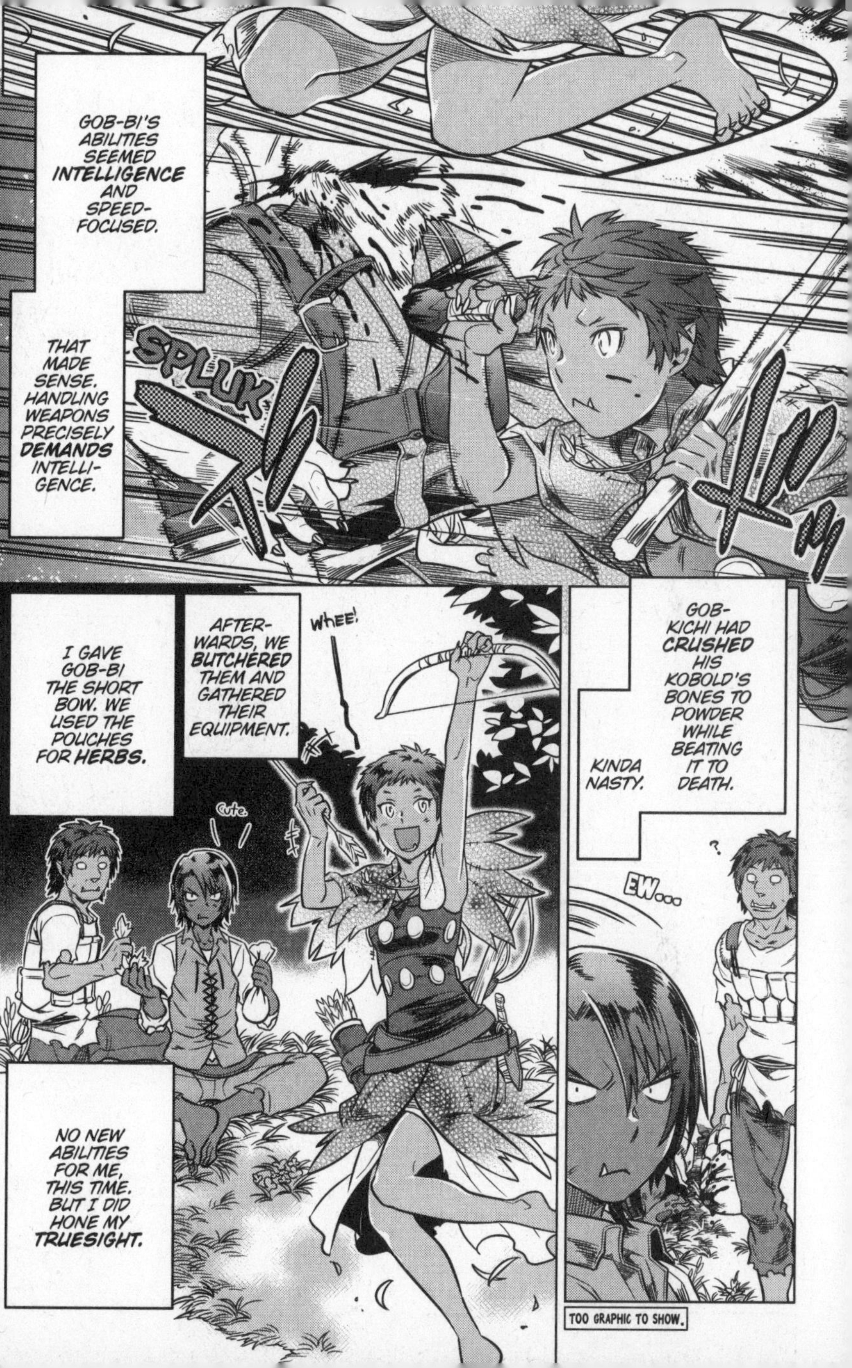
GOB-BI'S ABILITIES SEEMED INTELLIGENCE AND SPEED-FOCUSED.
THAT MADE SENSE. HANDLING WEAPONS PRECISELY DEMANDS INTELLI-GENCE.
SPLUK
GOB-KICHI HAD CRUSHED HIS KOBOLD'S BONES TO POWDER WHILE BEATING IT TO DEATH.
KINDA NASTY.
?
EW...
TOO GRAPHIC TO SHOW.
AFTER-WARDS, WE BUTCHERED THEM AND GATHERED THEIR EQUIPMENT.
Whee!
I GAVE GOB-BI THE SHORT BOW. WE USED THE POUCHES FOR HERBS.
Cute.
NO NEW ABILITIES FOR ME, THIS TIME. BUT I DID HONE MY TRUESIGHT.

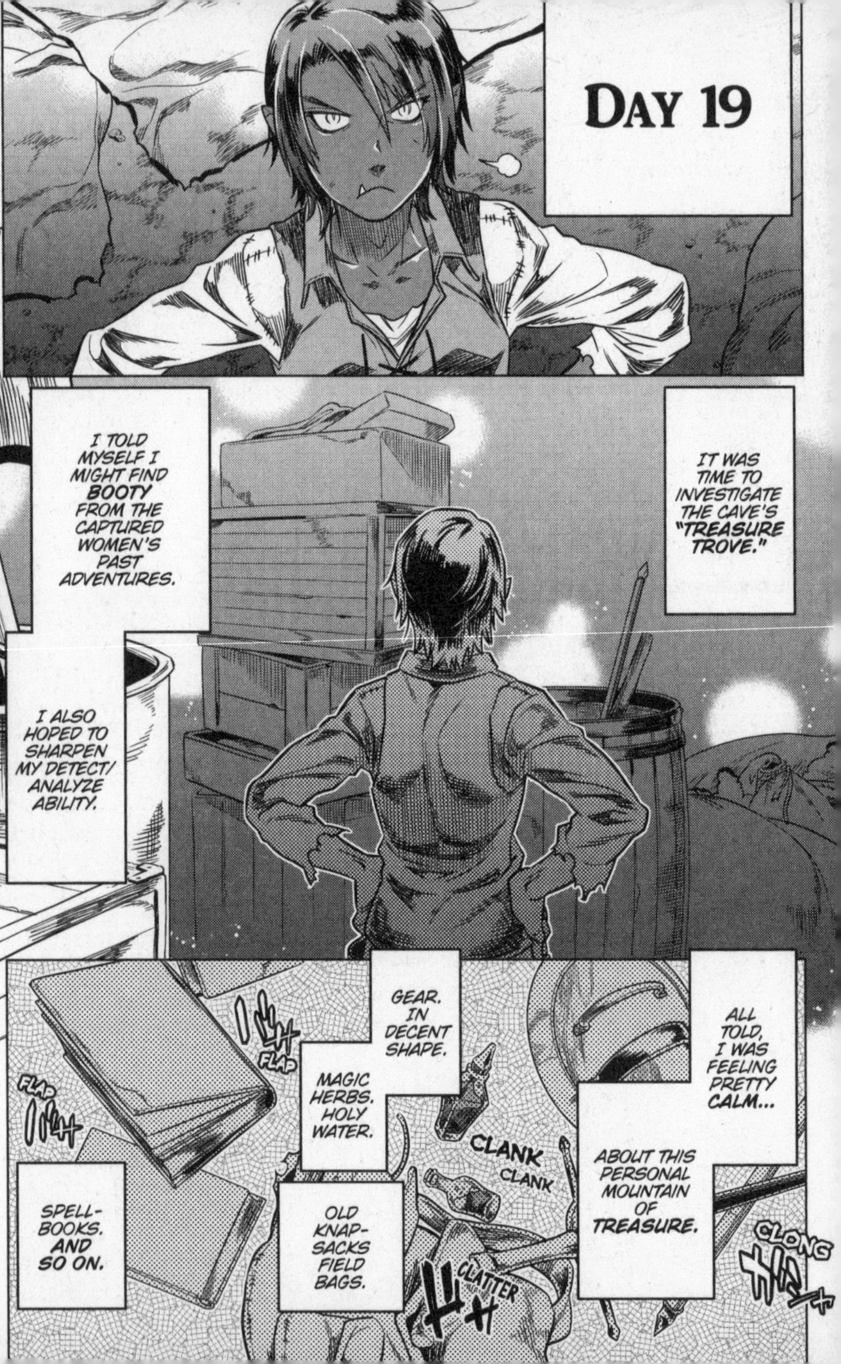
DAY 19
IT WAS TIME TO INVESTIGATE THE CAVE'S "TREASURE TROVE."
I TOLD MYSELF I MIGHT FIND BOOTY FROM THE CAPTURED WOMEN'S PAST ADVENTURES.
I ALSO HOPED TO SHARPEN MY DETECT/ ANALYZE ABILITY.
ALL TOLD, I WAS FEELING PRETTY CALM...
ABOUT THIS PERSONAL MOUNTAIN OF TREASURE.
CLONG
GEAR. IN DECENT SHAPE.
MAGIC HERBS. HOLY WATER.
CLANK
CLANK
OLD KNAP- SACKS FIELD BAGS.
CLATTER
FLAP
FLAP
SPELL- BOOKS. AND SO ON.

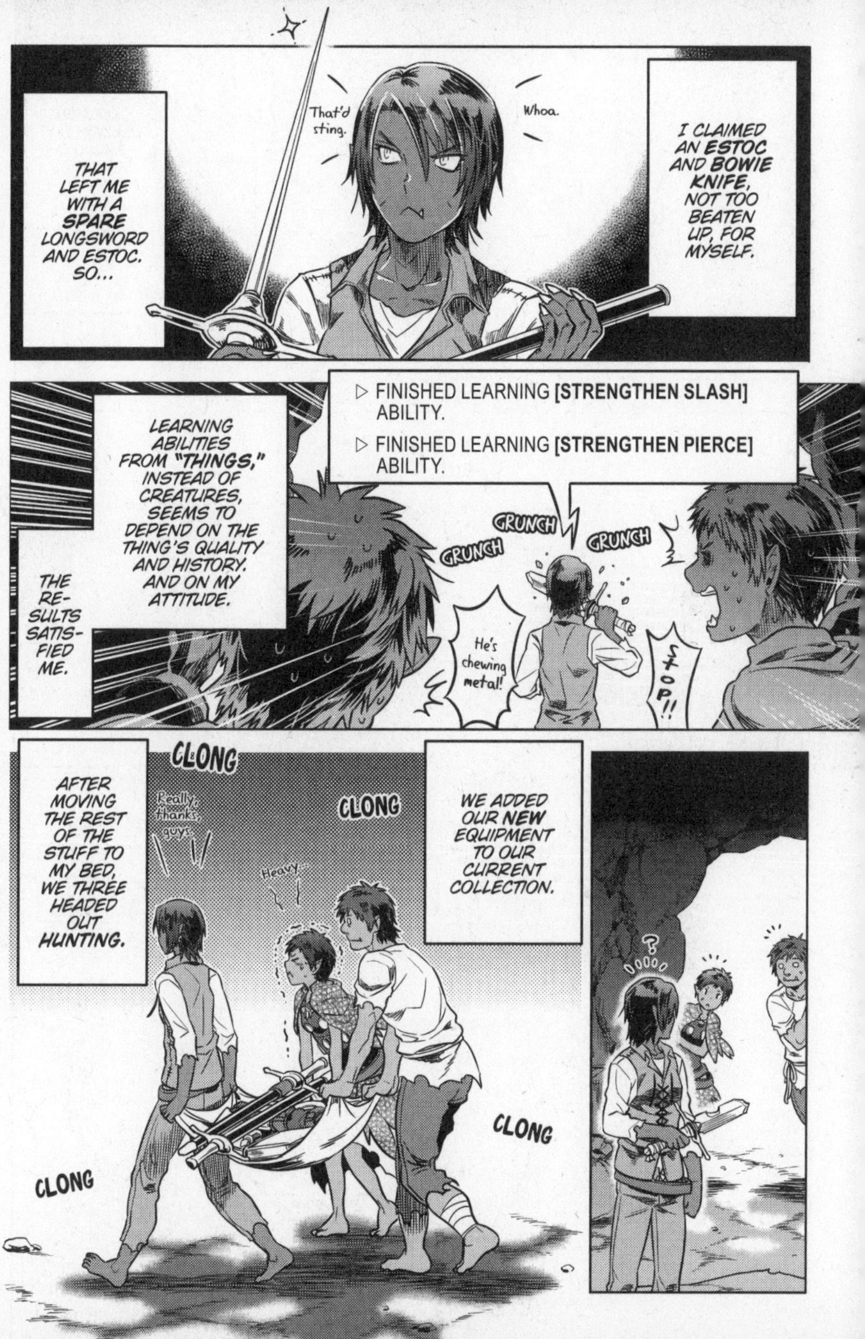

I CLAIMED AN ESTOC AND BOWIE KNIFE, NOT TOO BEATEN UP, FOR MYSELF.
Whoa.
That'd sting.
THAT LEFT ME WITH A SPARE LONGSWORD AND ESTOC. SO...
▷ FINISHED LEARNING [STRENGTHEN SLASH] ABILITY.
▷ FINISHED LEARNING [STRENGTHEN PIERCE] ABILITY.
STOP!!
GRUNCH
GRUNCH
GRUNCH
He's chewing metal!
LEARNING ABILITIES FROM "THINGS," INSTEAD OF CREATURES, SEEMS TO DEPEND ON THE THING'S QUALITY AND HISTORY. AND ON MY ATTITUDE.
THE RE-SULTS SATIS-FIED ME.
?
WE ADDED OUR NEW EQUIPMENT TO OUR CURRENT COLLECTION.
CLONG
CLONG
Really, thanks, guys.
Heavy...
CLONG
AFTER MOVING THE REST OF THE STUFF TO MY BED, WE THREE HEADED OUT HUNTING.
CLONG

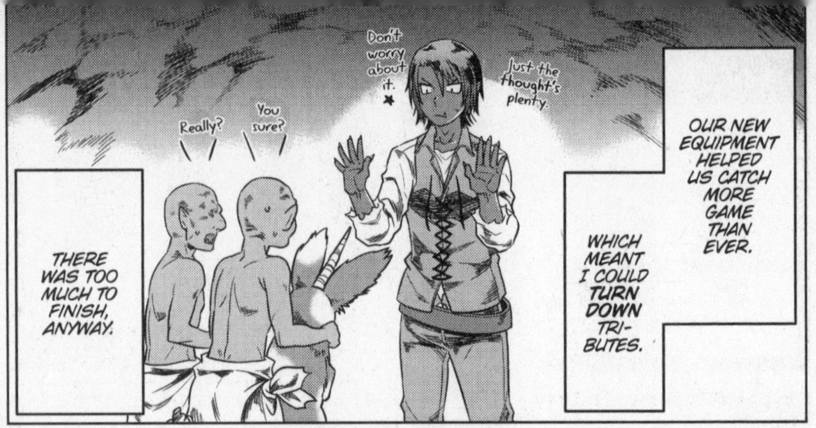
OUR NEW EQUIPMENT HELPED US CATCH MORE GAME THAN EVER.
WHICH MEANT I COULD TURN DOWN TRIBUTES.
Just the thought's plenty.
Don't worry about it.
You sure?
Really?
THERE WAS TOO MUCH TO FINISH, ANYWAY.

DAY 20

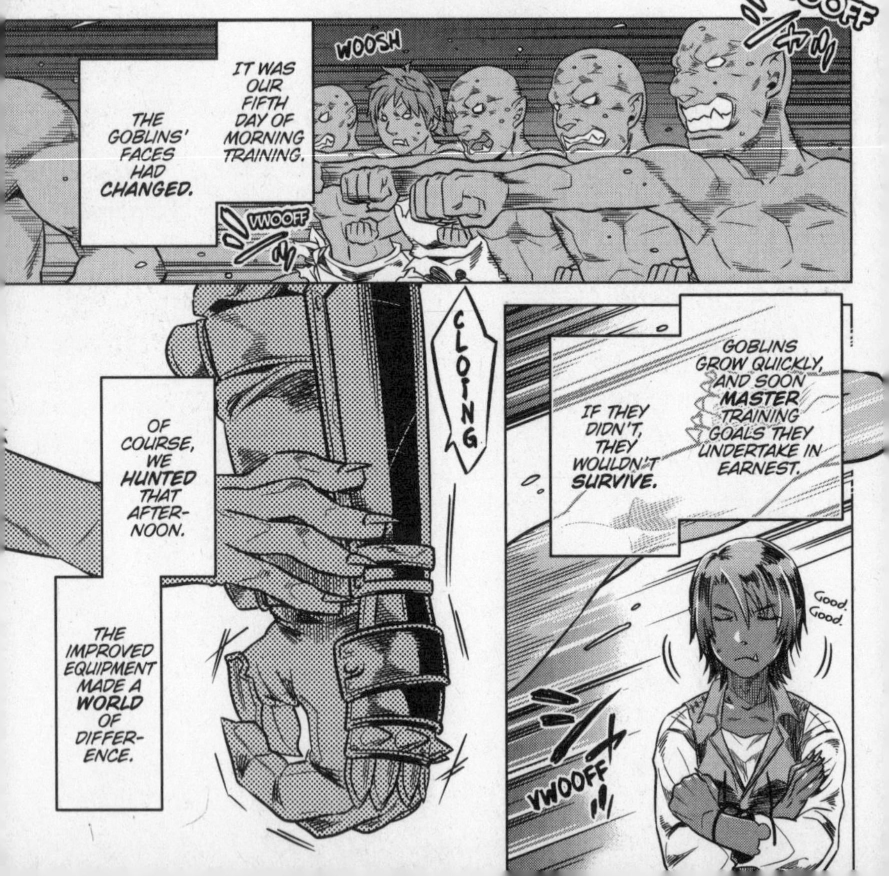
VWOOFF
WOOSH
IT WAS OUR FIFTH DAY OF MORNING TRAINING.
THE GOBLINS' FACES HAD CHANGED.
VWOOFF
GOBLINS GROW QUICKLY, AND SOON MASTER TRAINING GOALS THEY UNDERTAKE IN EARNEST.
IF THEY DIDN'T, THEY WOULDN'T SURVIVE.
Good. Good.
VWOOFF
CLOING
OF COURSE, WE HUNTED THAT AFTERNOON.
THE IMPROVED EQUIPMENT MADE A WORLD OF DIFFERENCE.

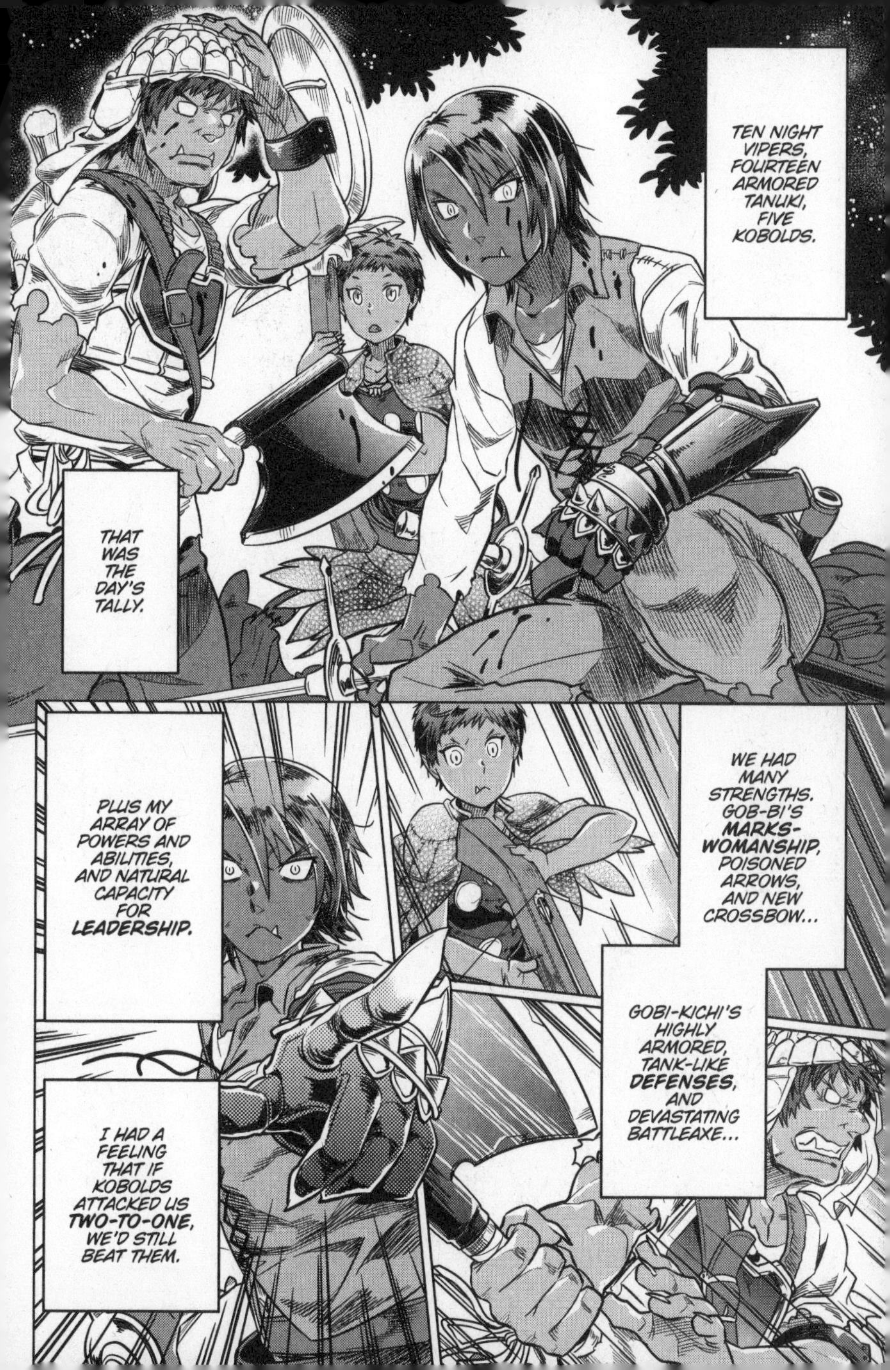
TEN NIGHT VIPERS, FOURTEEN ARMORED TANUKI, FIVE KOBOLDS.
THAT WAS THE DAY'S TALLY.
WE HAD MANY STRENGTHS. GOB-BI'S **MARKS-WOMANSHIP**, POISONED ARROWS, AND NEW CROSSBOW...
GOBI-KICHI'S HIGHLY ARMORED, TANK-LIKE **DEFENSES**, AND DEVASTATING BATTLEAXE...
PLUS MY ARRAY OF POWERS AND ABILITIES, AND NATURAL CAPACITY FOR **LEADERSHIP**.
I HAD A FEELING THAT IF KOBOLDS ATTACKED US **TWO-TO-ONE**, WE'D STILL BEAT THEM.

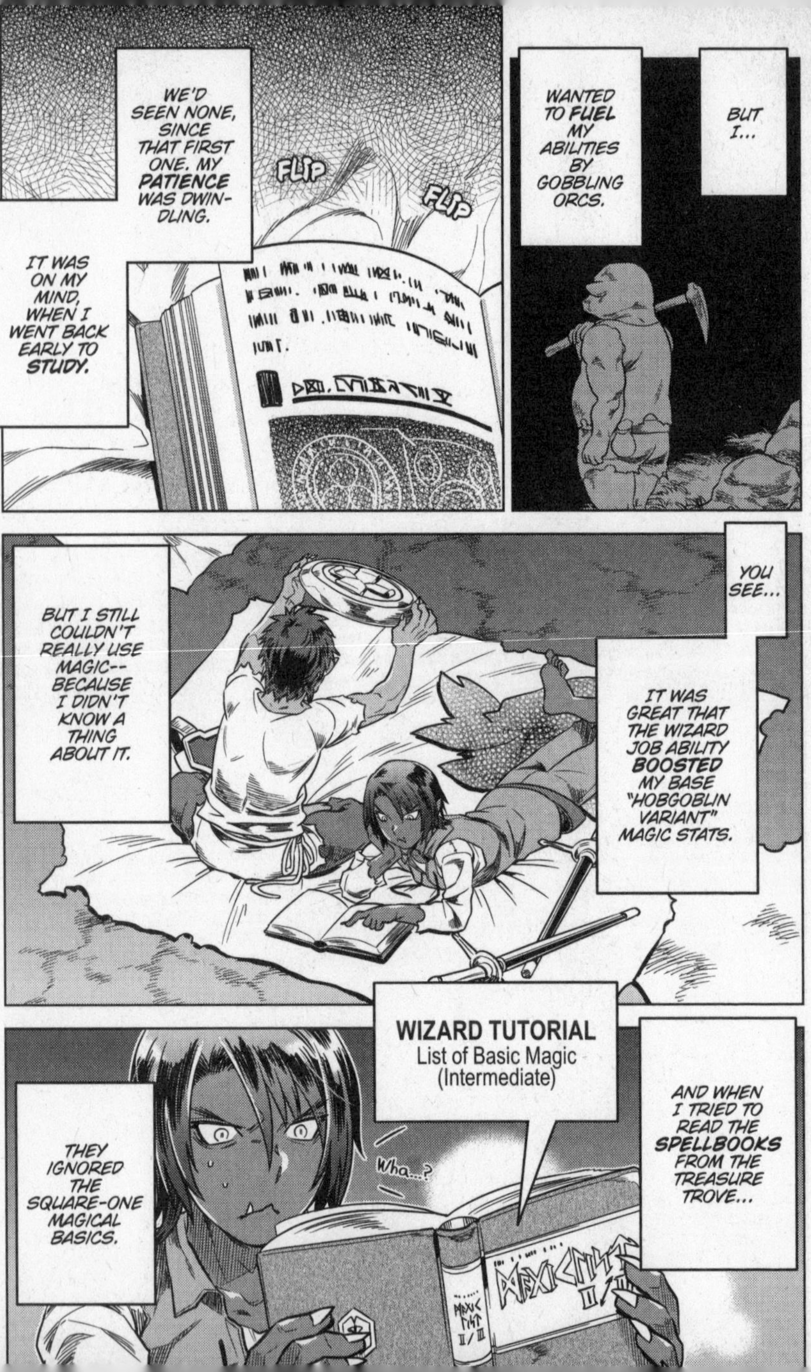

BUT I...
WANTED TO FUEL MY ABILITIES BY GOBBLING ORCS.
WE'D SEEN NONE, SINCE THAT FIRST ONE. MY PATIENCE WAS DWINDLING.
FLIP
FLIP
IT WAS ON MY MIND, WHEN I WENT BACK EARLY TO STUDY.
YOU SEE...
IT WAS GREAT THAT THE WIZARD JOB ABILITY BOOSTED MY BASE "HOBGOBLIN VARIANT" MAGIC STATS.
BUT I STILL COULDN'T REALLY USE MAGIC-- BECAUSE I DIDN'T KNOW A THING ABOUT IT.
AND WHEN I TRIED TO READ THE SPELLBOOKS FROM THE TREASURE TROVE...
WIZARD TUTORIAL
List of Basic Magic
(Intermediate)
Wha...?
THEY IGNORED THE SQUARE-ONE MAGICAL BASICS.

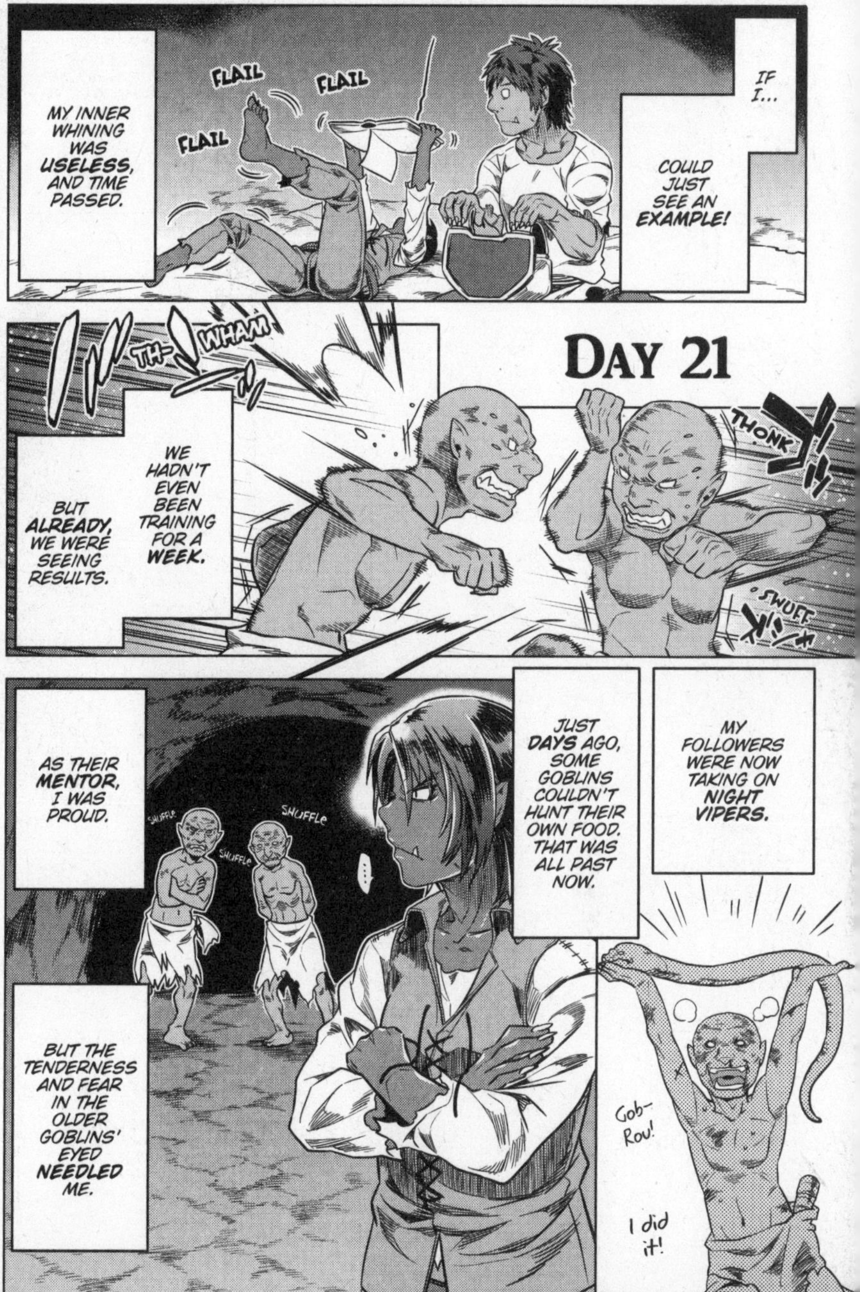
IF I...
COULD JUST SEE AN EXAMPLE!
FLAIL
FLAIL
FLAIL
MY INNER WHINING WAS USELESS, AND TIME PASSED.
DAY 21
THONK
SWUFF
WE HADN'T EVEN BEEN TRAINING FOR A WEEK.
TH- WHAM
BUT ALREADY, WE WERE SEEING RESULTS.
MY FOLLOWERS WERE NOW TAKING ON NIGHT VIPERS.
JUST DAYS AGO, SOME GOBLINS COULDN'T HUNT THEIR OWN FOOD. THAT WAS ALL PAST NOW.
Gob-Rou!
I did it!
AS THEIR MENTOR, I WAS PROUD.
SHUFFLE
SHUFFLE
SHUFFLE
...
BUT THE TENDERNESS AND FEAR IN THE OLDER GOBLINS' EYED NEEDLED ME.

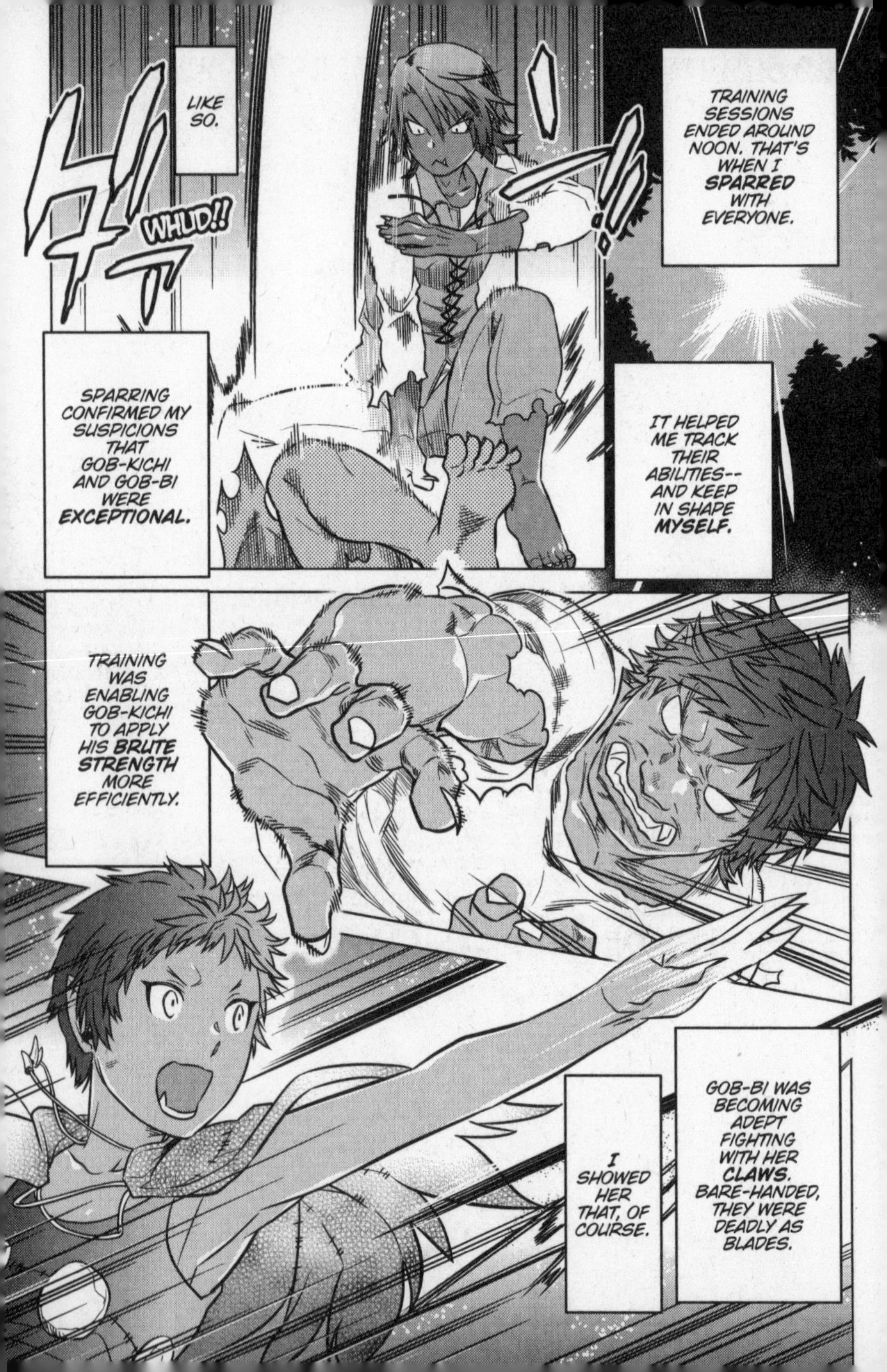
TRAINING SESSIONS ENDED AROUND NOON. THAT'S WHEN I SPARRED WITH EVERYONE.
LIKE SO.
WHUD!!
IT HELPED ME TRACK THEIR ABILITIES-- AND KEEP IN SHAPE MYSELF.
SPARRING CONFIRMED MY SUSPICIONS THAT GOB-KICHI AND GOB-BI WERE EXCEPTIONAL.
TRAINING WAS ENABLING GOB-KICHI TO APPLY HIS BRUTE STRENGTH MORE EFFICIENTLY.
GOB-BI WAS BECOMING ADEPT FIGHTING WITH HER CLAWS. BARE-HANDED, THEY WERE DEADLY AS BLADES.
I SHOWED HER THAT, OF COURSE.

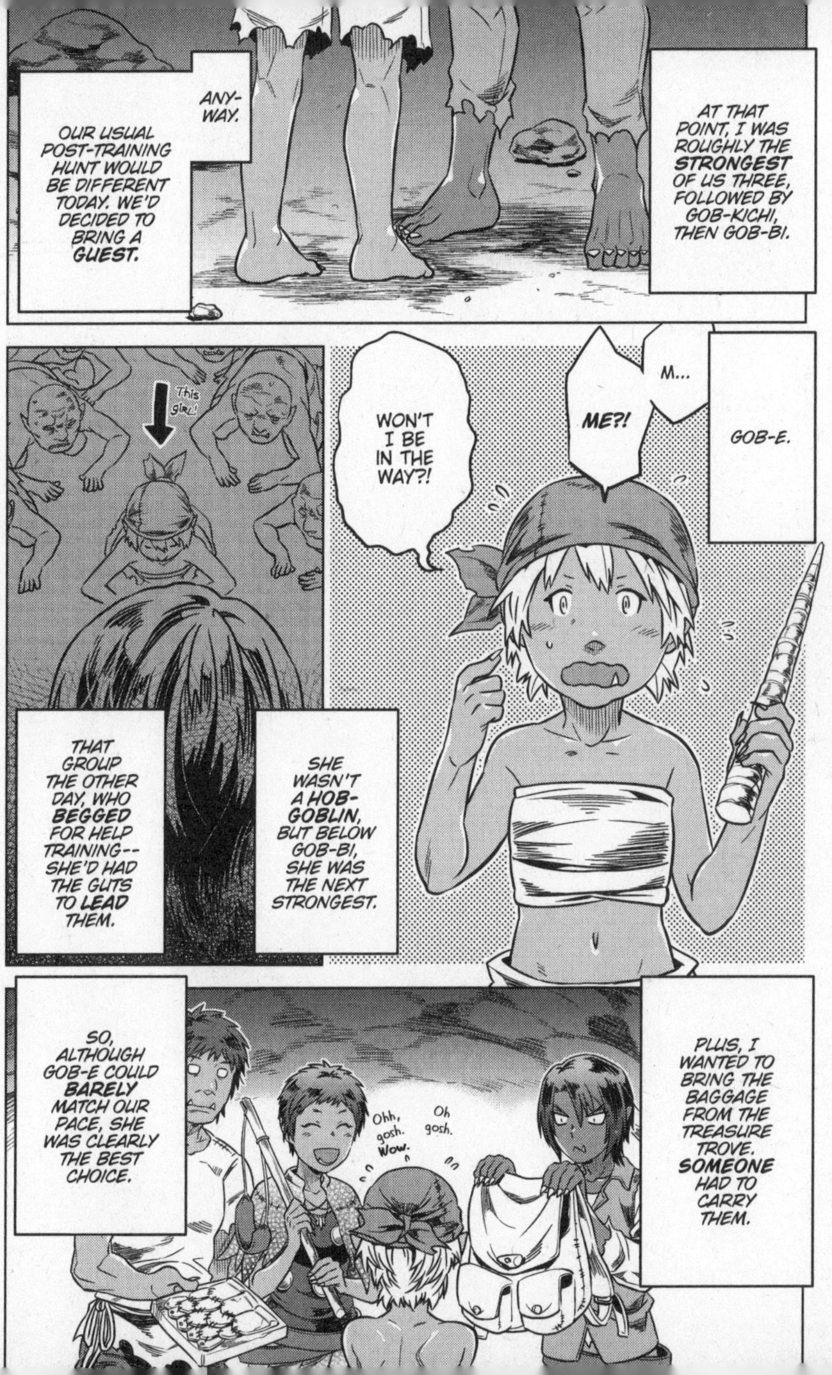
AT THAT POINT, I WAS ROUGHLY THE **STRONGEST** OF US THREE, FOLLOWED BY GOB-KICHI, THEN GOB-BI.
ANY-WAY.
OUR USUAL POST-TRAINING HUNT WOULD BE DIFFERENT TODAY. WE'D DECIDED TO BRING A **GUEST.**
GOB-E.
M...
ME?!
WON'T I BE IN THE WAY?!
This girl!
SHE WASN'T A **HOB-GOBLIN,** BUT BELOW GOB-BI, SHE WAS THE NEXT STRONGEST.
THAT GROUP THE OTHER DAY, WHO **BEGGED** FOR HELP TRAINING-- SHE'D HAD THE GUTS TO **LEAD** THEM.
PLUS, I WANTED TO BRING THE BAGGAGE FROM THE TREASURE TROVE. **SOMEONE** HAD TO CARRY THEM.
Oh gosh.
Ohh, gosh. **Wow.**
SO, ALTHOUGH GOB-E COULD **BARELY** MATCH OUR PACE, SHE WAS CLEARLY THE BEST CHOICE.

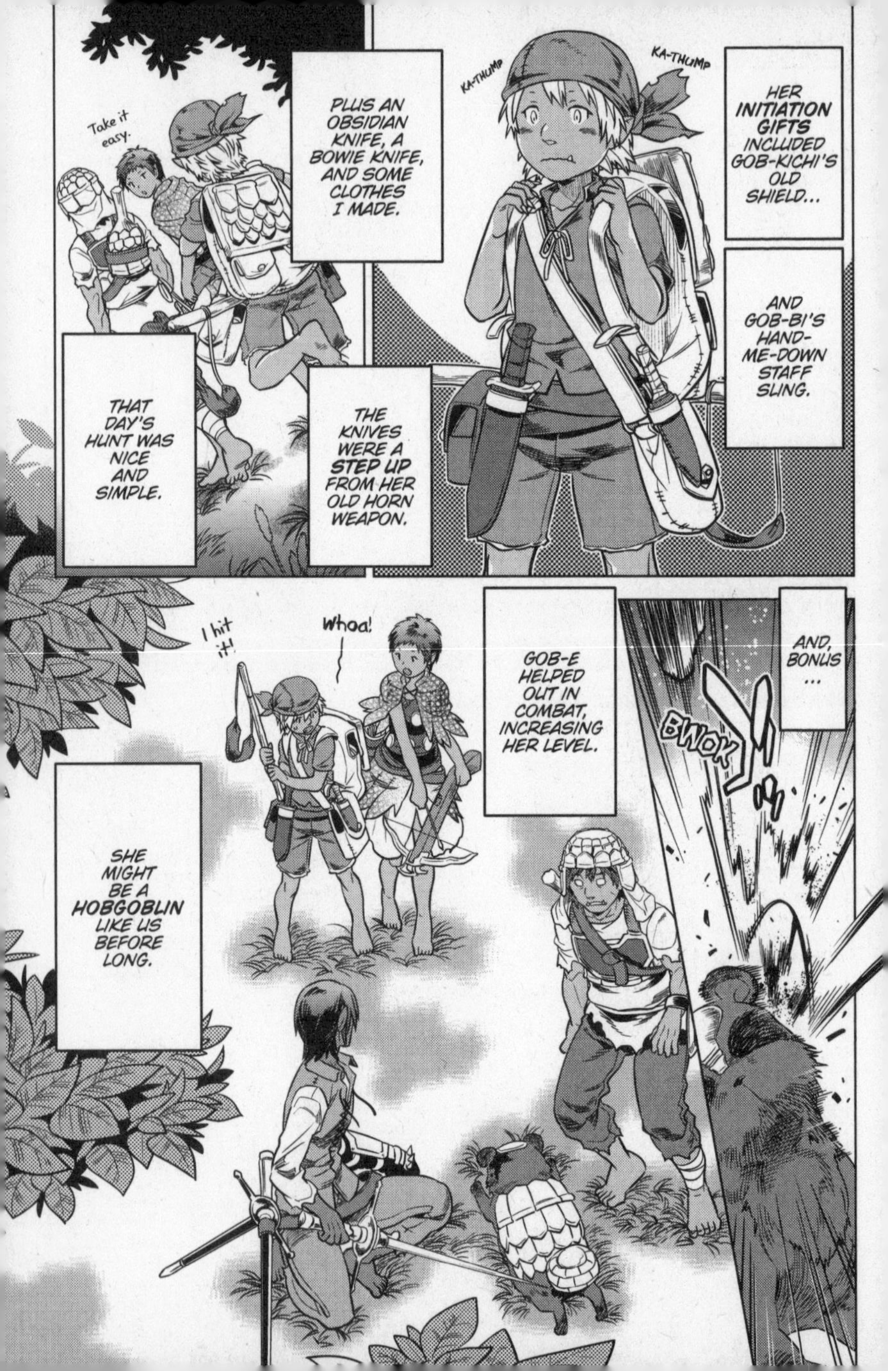
KA-THUMP
KA-THUMP
HER INITIATION GIFTS INCLUDED GOB-KICHI'S OLD SHIELD...
AND GOB-BI'S HAND-ME-DOWN STAFF SLING.
PLUS AN OBSIDIAN KNIFE, A BOWIE KNIFE, AND SOME CLOTHES I MADE.
THE KNIVES WERE A STEP UP FROM HER OLD HORN WEAPON.
Take it easy.
THAT DAY'S HUNT WAS NICE AND SIMPLE.
AND, BONUS...
BWOK
GOB-E HELPED OUT IN COMBAT, INCREASING HER LEVEL.
Whoa!
I hit it!
SHE MIGHT BE A HOBGOBLIN LIKE US BEFORE LONG.

Day 21

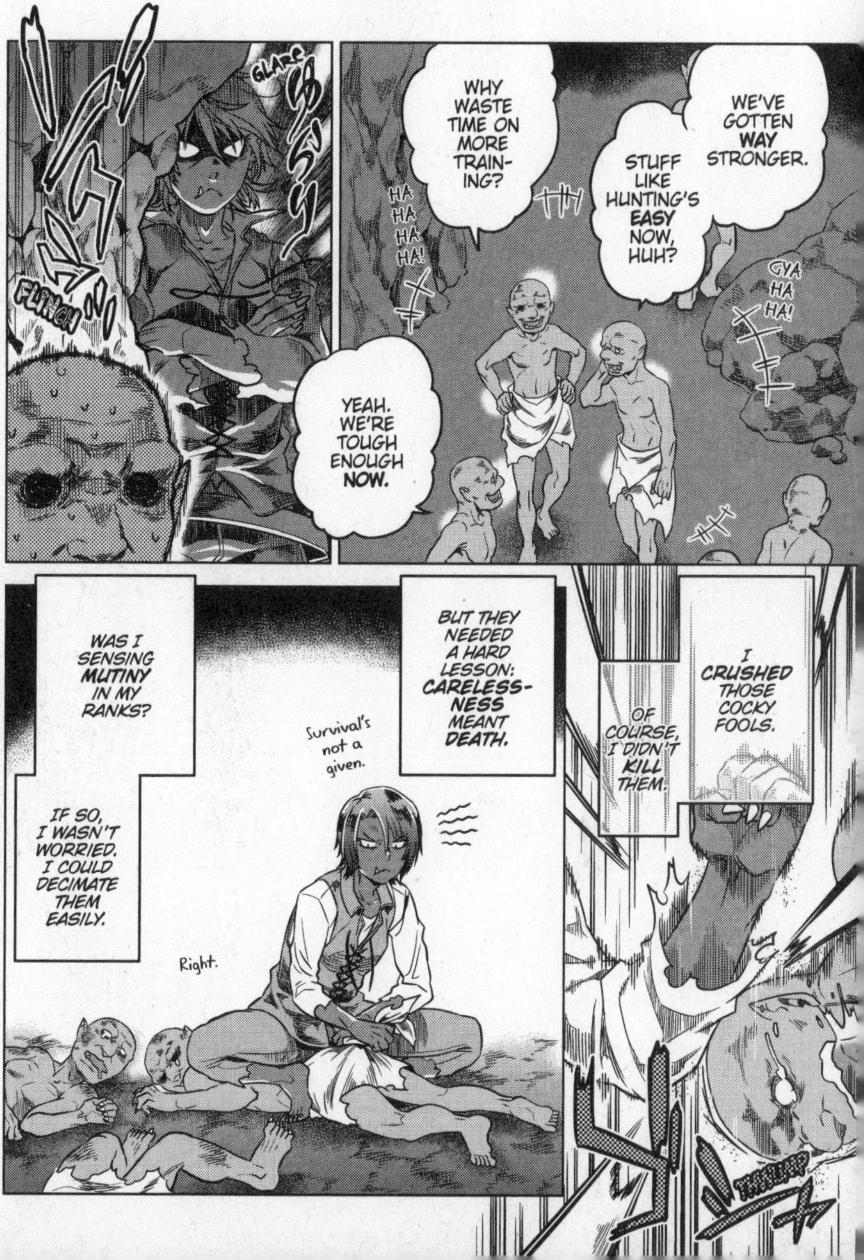
WE'VE GOTTEN WAY STRONGER.
STUFF LIKE HUNTING'S EASY NOW, HUH?
GYA HA HA!
WHY WASTE TIME ON MORE TRAIN-ING?
HA HA HA HA!
YEAH. WE'RE TOUGH ENOUGH NOW.
GLARE
FLINCH
I CRUSHED THOSE COCKY FOOLS.
OF COURSE, I DIDN'T KILL THEM.
THWAP
BUT THEY NEEDED A HARD LESSON: CARELESS-NESS MEANT DEATH.
WAS I SENSING MUTINY IN MY RANKS?
Survival's not a given.
IF SO, I WASN'T WORRIED. I COULD DECIMATE THEM EASILY.
Right.

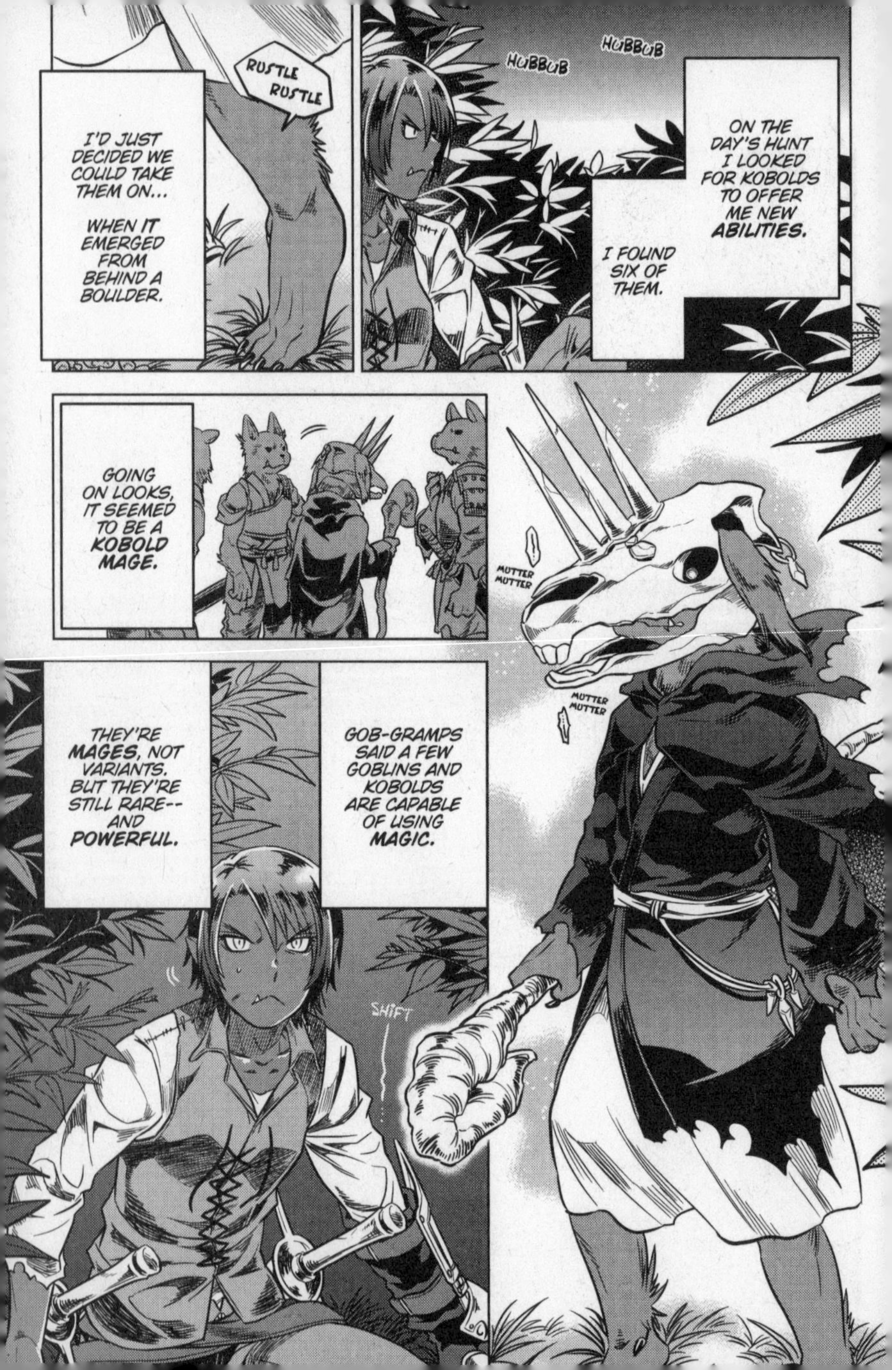
HUBBUB
HUBBUB
ON THE DAY'S HUNT I LOOKED FOR KOBOLDS TO OFFER ME NEW ABILITIES.
I FOUND SIX OF THEM.
RUSTLE RUSTLE
I'D JUST DECIDED WE COULD TAKE THEM ON...
WHEN IT EMERGED FROM BEHIND A BOULDER.
!
MUTTER MUTTER
MUTTER MUTTER
!
GOING ON LOOKS, IT SEEMED TO BE A KOBOLD MAGE.
GOB-GRAMPS SAID A FEW GOBLINS AND KOBOLDS ARE CAPABLE OF USING MAGIC.
THEY'RE MAGES, NOT VARIANTS. BUT THEY'RE STILL RARE--AND POWERFUL.
SHIFT

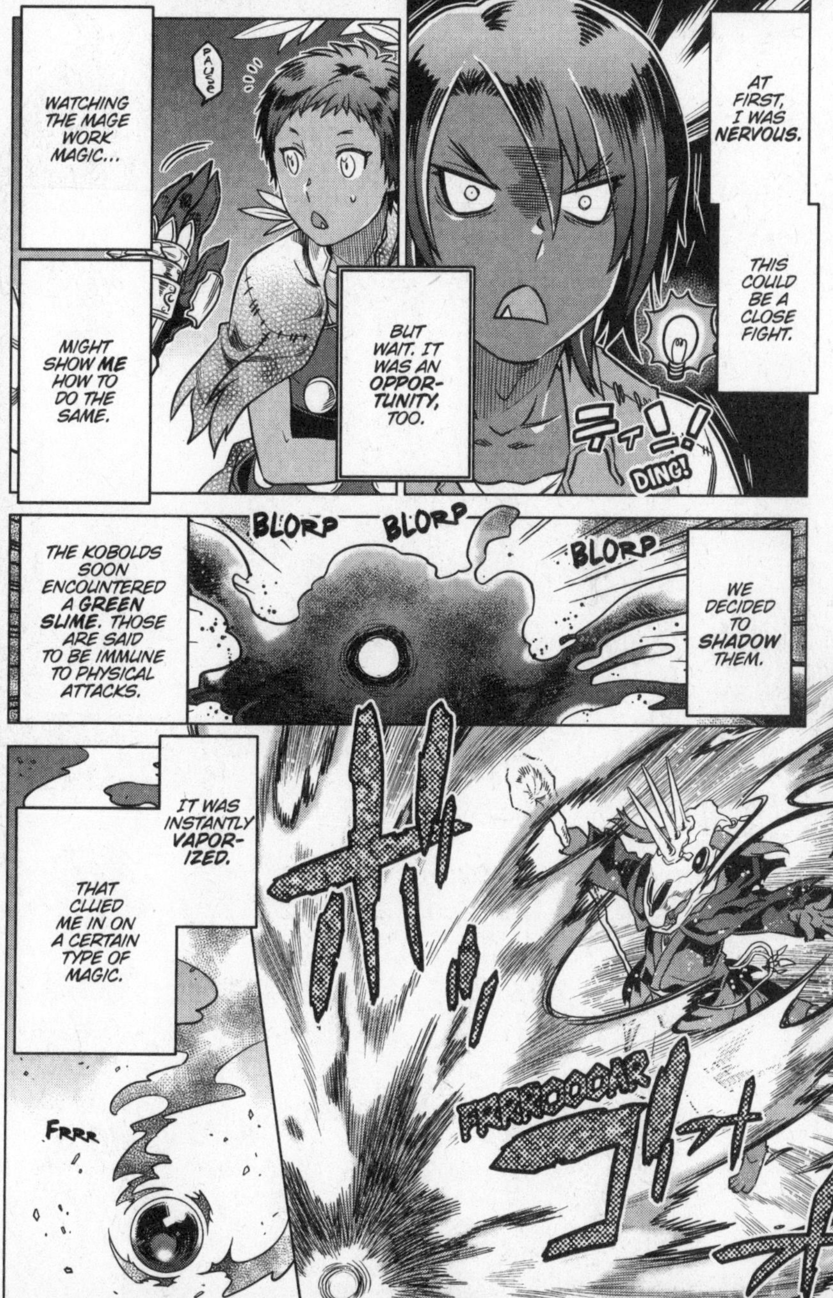
AT FIRST, I WAS NERVOUS.
THIS COULD BE A CLOSE FIGHT.
BUT WAIT. IT WAS AN OPPORTUNITY, TOO.
DING!
PAUSE
WATCHING THE MAGE WORK MAGIC...
MIGHT SHOW ME HOW TO DO THE SAME.
WE DECIDED TO SHADOW THEM.
BLORP
BLORP
BLORP
THE KOBOLDS SOON ENCOUNTERED A GREEN SLIME. THOSE ARE SAID TO BE IMMUNE TO PHYSICAL ATTACKS.
FRRROOOAR
IT WAS INSTANTLY VAPORIZED.
THAT CLUED ME IN ON A CERTAIN TYPE OF MAGIC.
FRRR

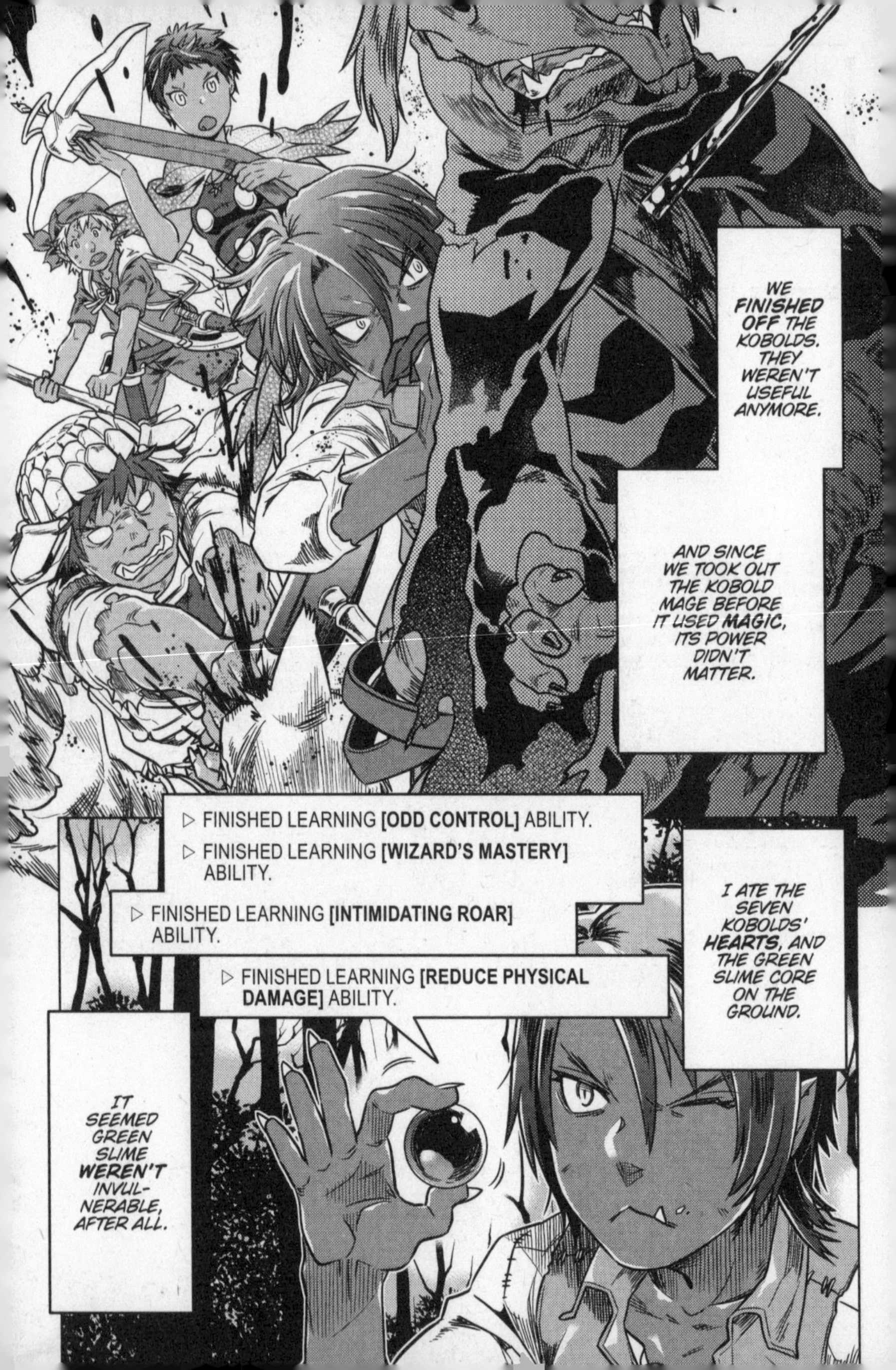
WE FINISHED OFF THE KOBOLDS. THEY WEREN'T USEFUL ANYMORE.
AND SINCE WE TOOK OUT THE KOBOLD MAGE BEFORE IT USED MAGIC, ITS POWER DIDN'T MATTER.
I ATE THE SEVEN KOBOLDS' HEARTS, AND THE GREEN SLIME CORE ON THE GROUND.
▷ FINISHED LEARNING [ODD CONTROL] ABILITY.
▷ FINISHED LEARNING [WIZARD'S MASTERY] ABILITY.
▷ FINISHED LEARNING [INTIMIDATING ROAR] ABILITY.
▷ FINISHED LEARNING [REDUCE PHYSICAL DAMAGE] ABILITY.
IT SEEMED GREEN SLIME WEREN'T INVUL-NERABLE, AFTER ALL.

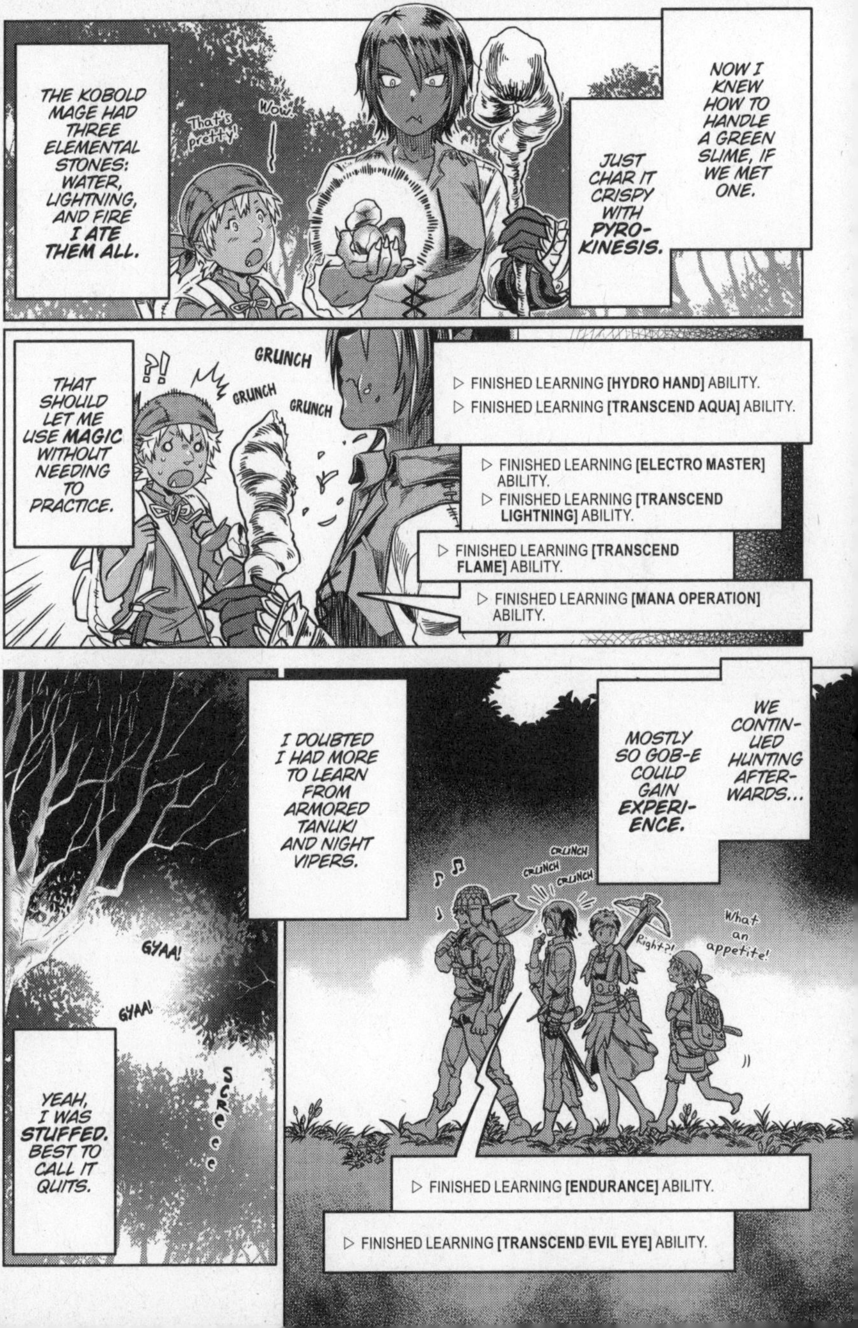
NOW I KNEW HOW TO HANDLE A GREEN SLIME, IF WE MET ONE.
JUST CHAR IT CRISPY WITH PYRO-KINESIS.
Wow.
That's pretty!
THE KOBOLD MAGE HAD THREE ELEMENTAL STONES: WATER, LIGHTNING, AND FIRE I ATE THEM ALL.
▷ FINISHED LEARNING [HYDRO HAND] ABILITY.
▷ FINISHED LEARNING [TRANSCEND AQUA] ABILITY.
▷ FINISHED LEARNING [ELECTRO MASTER] ABILITY.
▷ FINISHED LEARNING [TRANSCEND LIGHTNING] ABILITY.
▷ FINISHED LEARNING [TRANSCEND FLAME] ABILITY.
▷ FINISHED LEARNING [MANA OPERATION] ABILITY.
GRUNCH
GRUNCH
GRUNCH
?!
THAT SHOULD LET ME USE MAGIC WITHOUT NEEDING TO PRACTICE.
WE CONTINUED HUNTING AFTERWARDS...
MOSTLY SO GOB-E COULD GAIN EXPERIENCE.
I DOUBTED I HAD MORE TO LEARN FROM ARMORED TANUKI AND NIGHT VIPERS.
CRUNCH
CRUNCH
CRUNCH
What an appetite!
Right?!
▷ FINISHED LEARNING [ENDURANCE] ABILITY.
▷ FINISHED LEARNING [TRANSCEND EVIL EYE] ABILITY.
GYAA!
GYAA!
SCREeee
YEAH, I WAS STUFFED. BEST TO CALL IT QUITS.

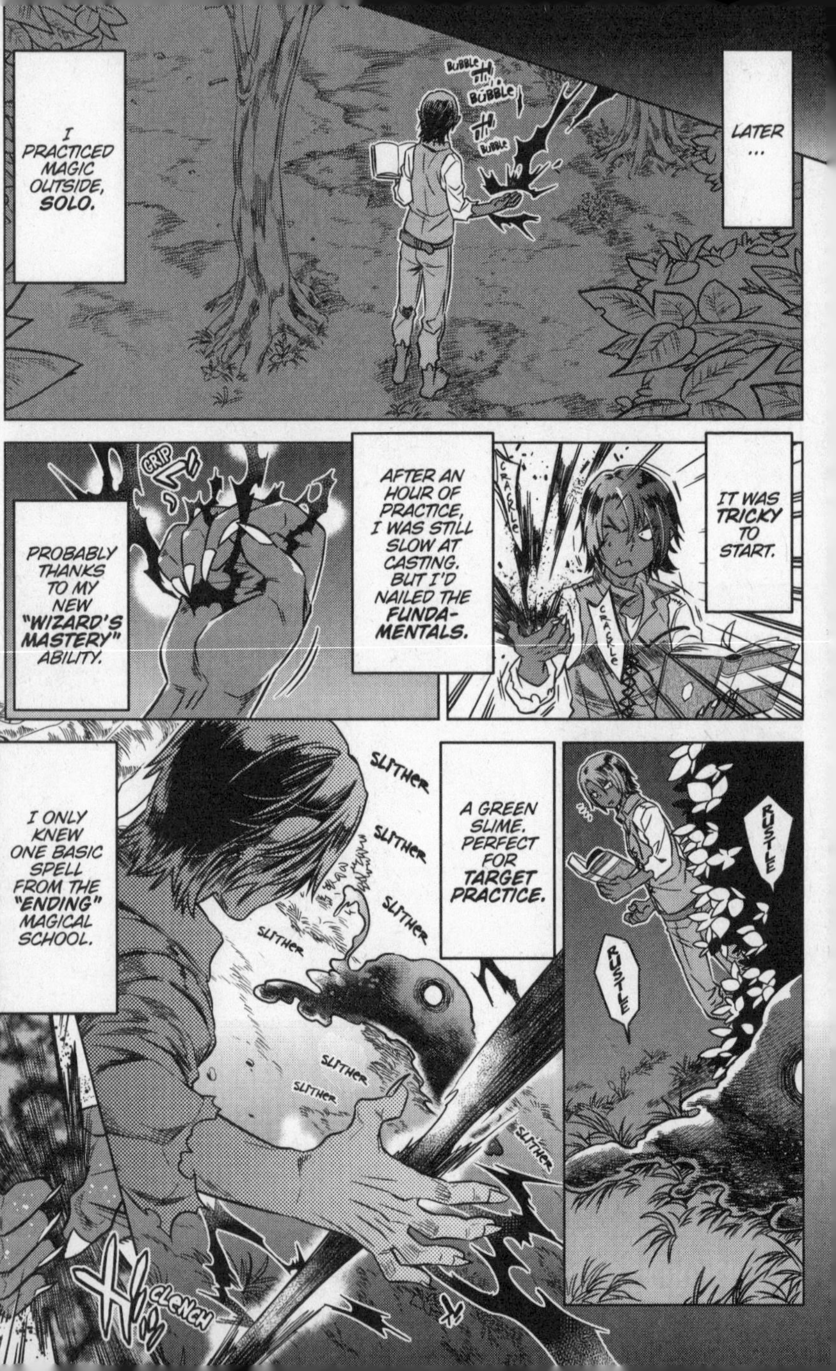
LATER...
BUBBLE
BUBBLE
BUBBLE
I PRACTICED MAGIC OUTSIDE, **SOLO.**
IT WAS **TRICKY** TO START.
CRACKLE
CRACKLE
AFTER AN HOUR OF PRACTICE, I WAS STILL SLOW AT CASTING. BUT I'D NAILED THE **FUNDA-MENTALS.**
GRIP
PROBABLY THANKS TO MY NEW **"WIZARD'S MASTERY"** ABILITY.
RUSTLE
RUSTLE
A GREEN SLIME. PERFECT FOR **TARGET PRACTICE.**
SLITHER
SLITHER
SLITHER
SLITHER
SLITHER
SLITHER
SLITHER
I ONLY KNEW ONE BASIC SPELL FROM THE **"ENDING"** MAGICAL SCHOOL.
CLENCH

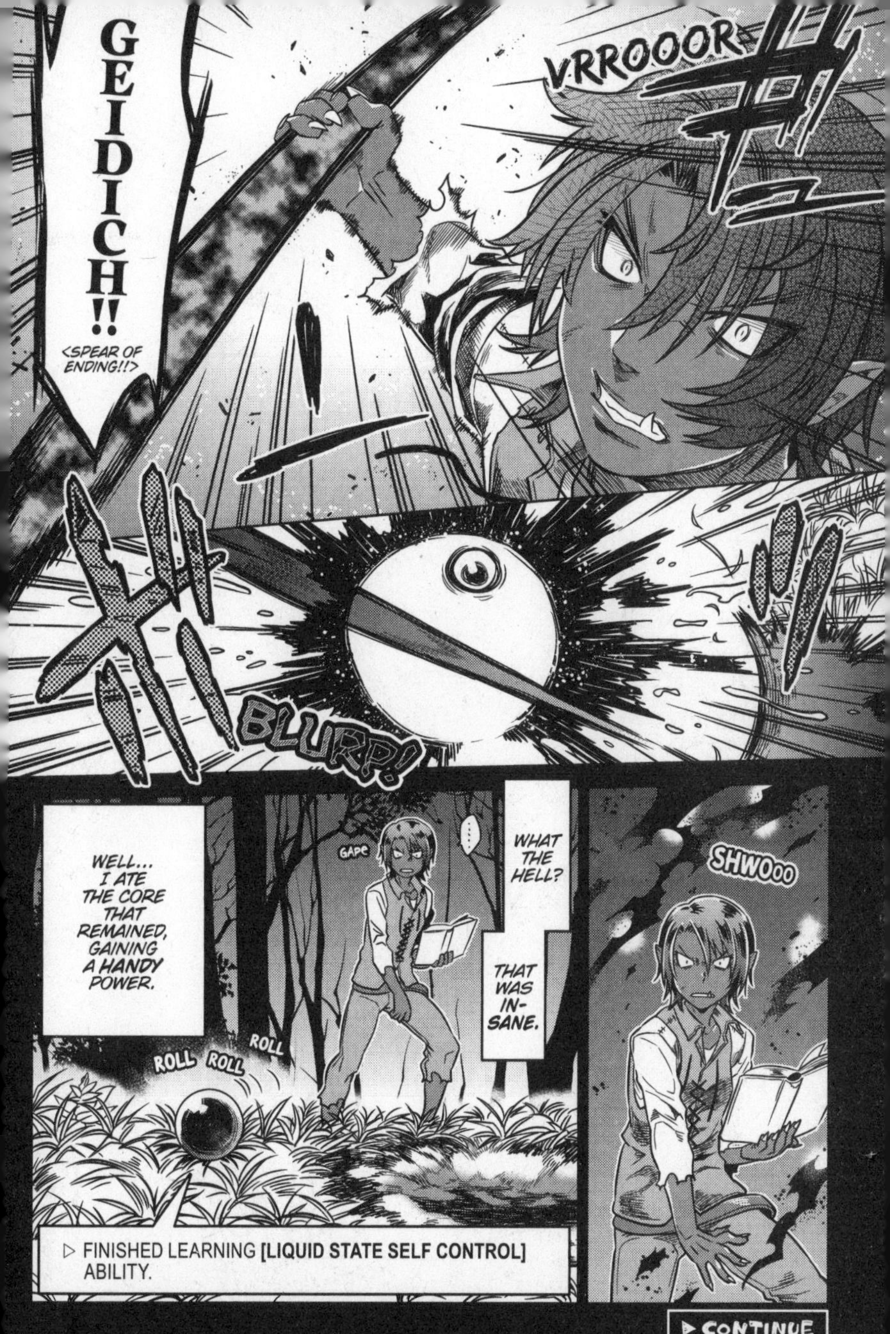
VRROOOR
GEIDICH!!
<SPEAR OF ENDING!!>
BLURP!
SHWOoo
...
GAPE
WHAT THE HELL?
THAT WAS IN-SANE.
WELL... I ATE THE CORE THAT REMAINED, GAINING A HANDY POWER.
ROLL ROLL ROLL
▷ FINISHED LEARNING [LIQUID STATE SELF CONTROL] ABILITY.
▶ CONTINUE

Chapter 6

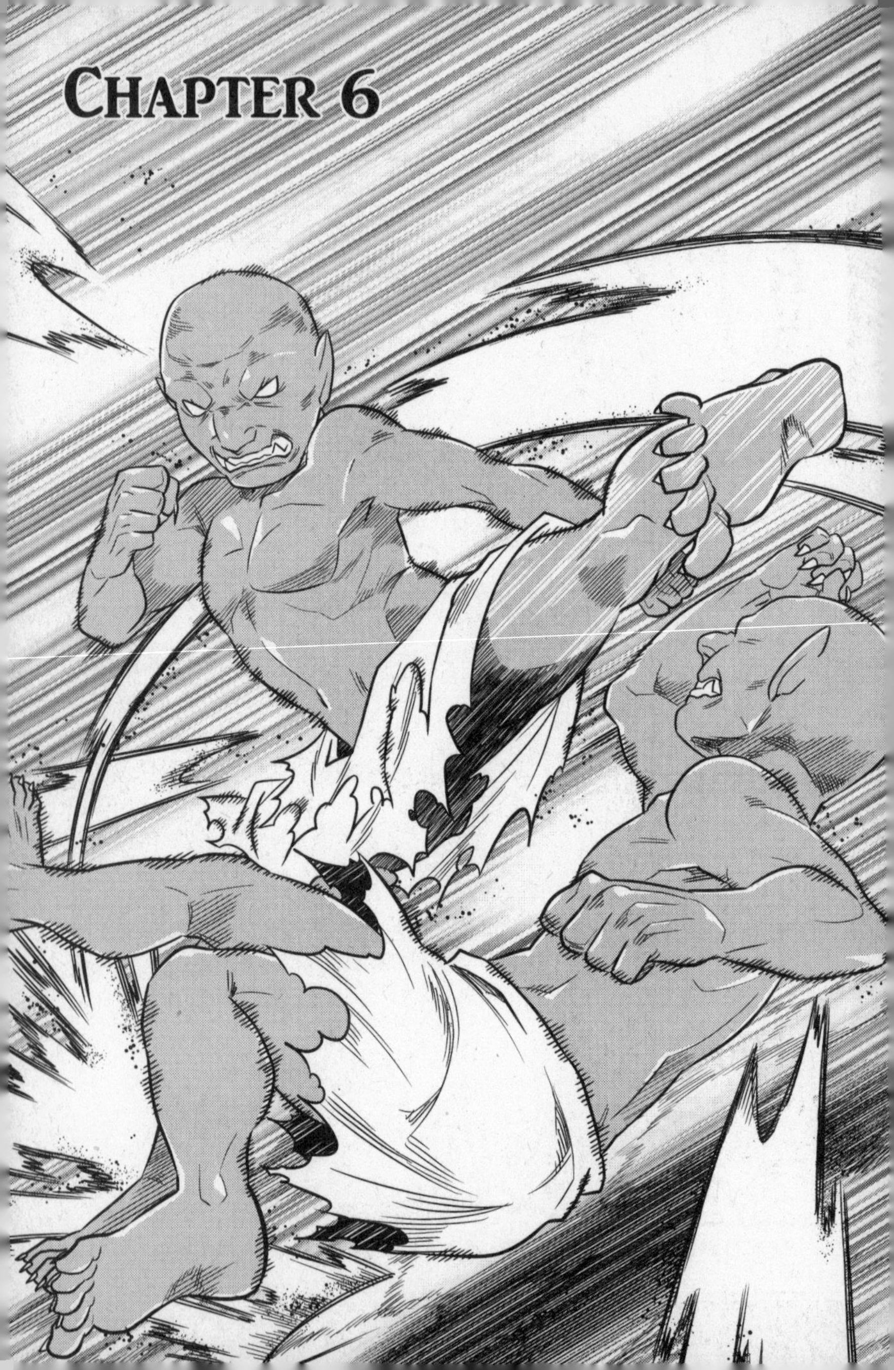

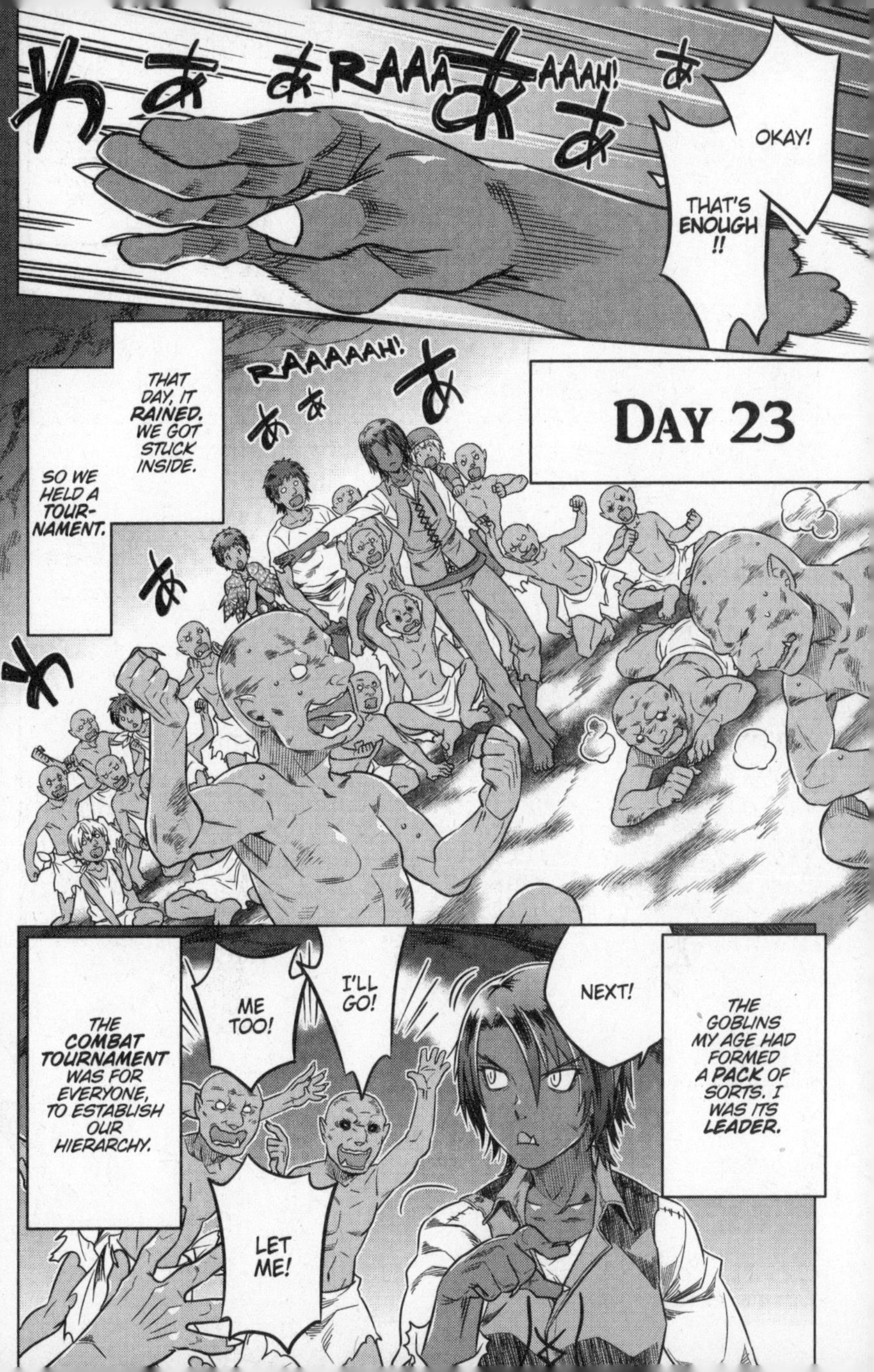
OKAY!
THAT'S ENOUGH!!
RAAAAAAH!
DAY 23
THAT DAY, IT RAINED. WE GOT STUCK INSIDE.
SO WE HELD A TOURNAMENT.
RAAAAAH!
THE GOBLINS MY AGE HAD FORMED A PACK OF SORTS. I WAS ITS LEADER.
NEXT!
I'LL GO!
ME TOO!
THE COMBAT TOURNAMENT WAS FOR EVERYONE, TO ESTABLISH OUR HIERARCHY.
LET ME!

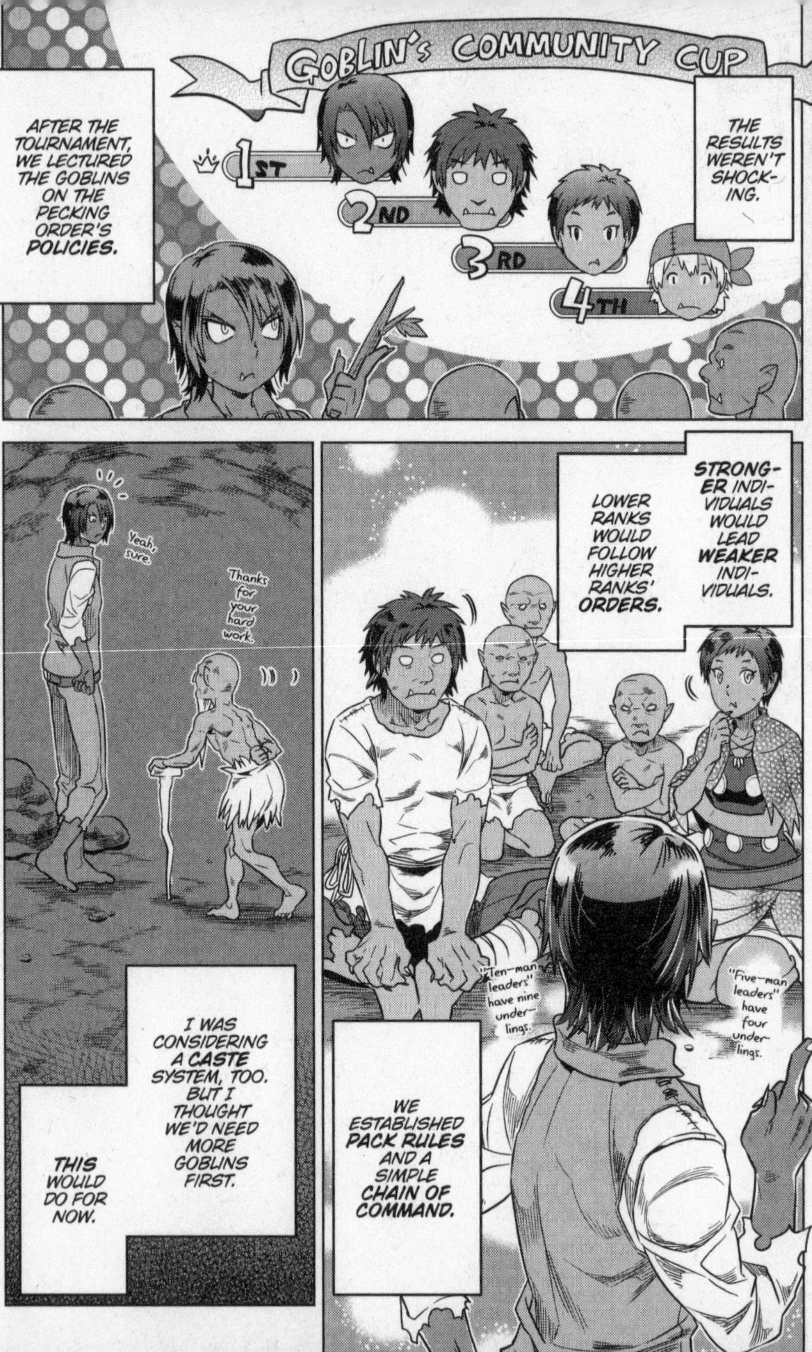
GOBLIN's COMMUNITY CUP
THE RESULTS WEREN'T SHOCKING.
1ST
2ND
3RD
4TH
AFTER THE TOURNAMENT, WE LECTURED THE GOBLINS ON THE PECKING ORDER'S POLICIES.
STRONGER INDIVIDUALS WOULD LEAD WEAKER INDIVIDUALS.
LOWER RANKS WOULD FOLLOW HIGHER RANKS' ORDERS.
"Five-man leaders" have four underlings.
"Ten-man leaders" have nine underlings.
WE ESTABLISHED PACK RULES AND A SIMPLE CHAIN OF COMMAND.
Thanks for your hard work.
Yeah, sure.
I WAS CONSIDERING A CASTE SYSTEM, TOO. BUT I THOUGHT WE'D NEED MORE GOBLINS FIRST.
THIS WOULD DO FOR NOW.

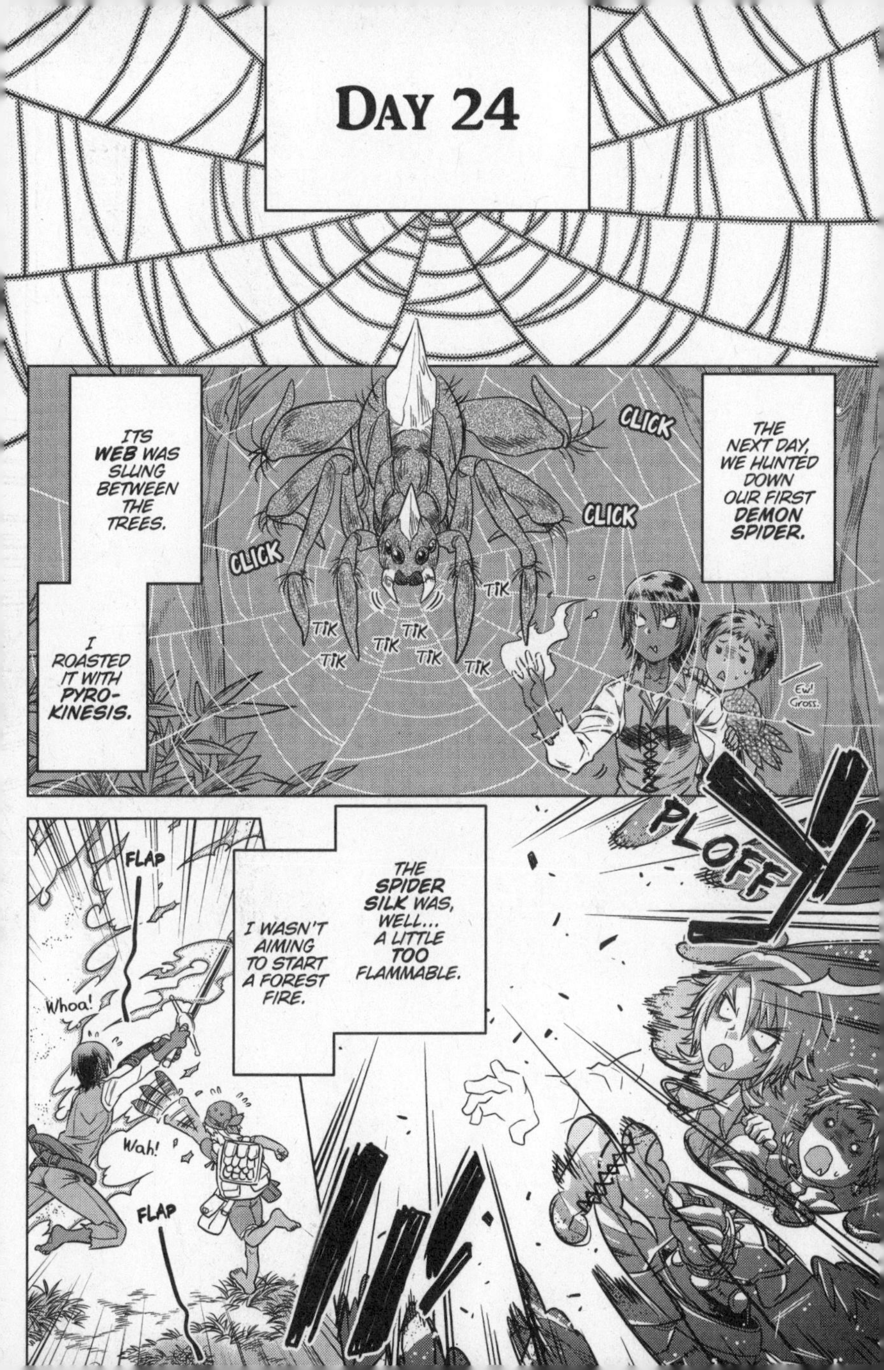
DAY 24
THE NEXT DAY, WE HUNTED DOWN OUR FIRST DEMON SPIDER.
CLICK
CLICK
CLICK
ITS WEB WAS SLUNG BETWEEN THE TREES.
Ew! Gross.
TIK
TIK
TIK
TIK
TIK
TIK
I ROASTED IT WITH PYRO-KINESIS.
PLOFF
THE SPIDER SILK WAS, WELL... A LITTLE TOO FLAMMABLE.
I WASN'T AIMING TO START A FOREST FIRE.
FLAP
Whoa!
Wah!
FLAP

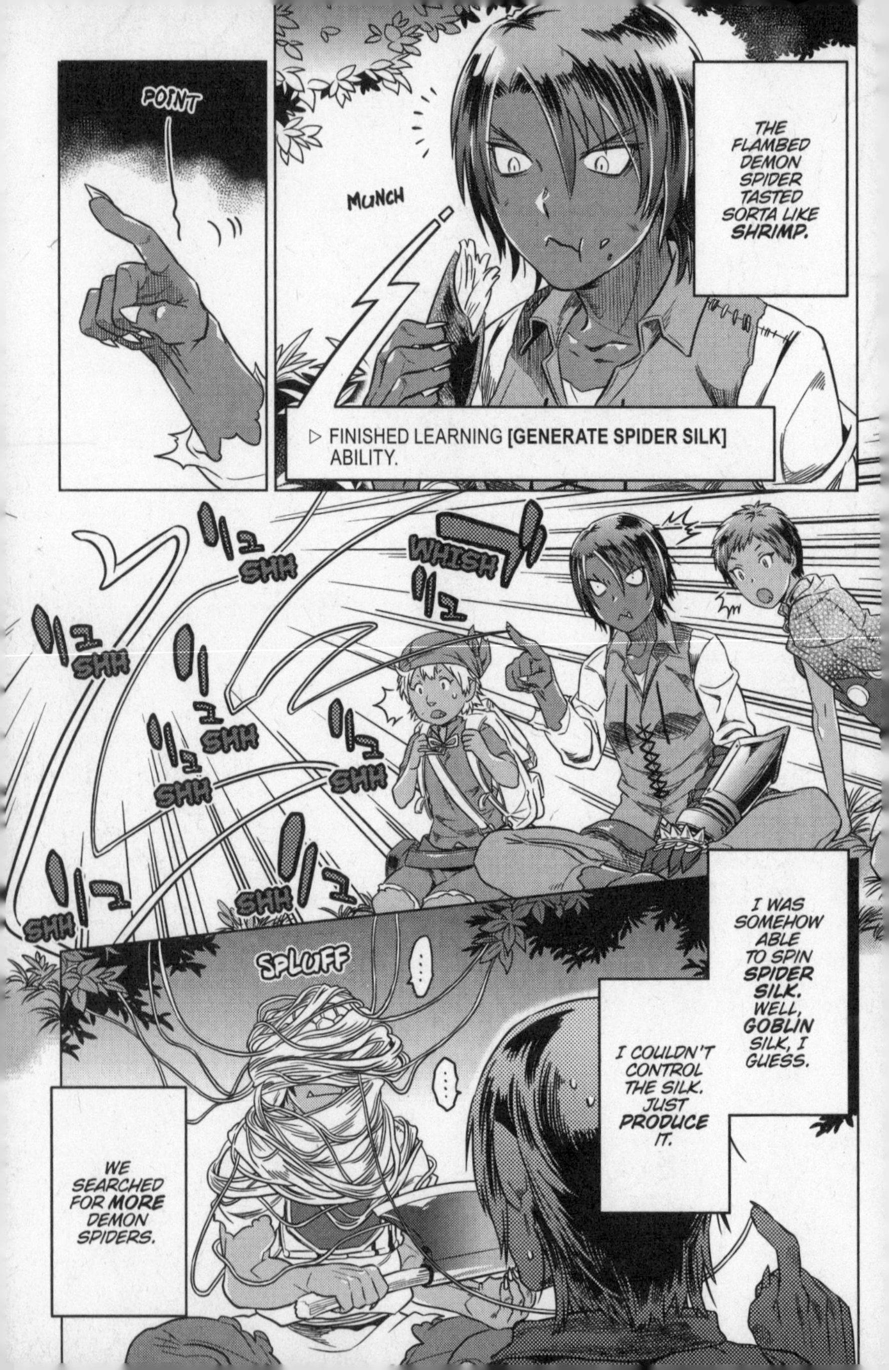
THE FLAMBED DEMON SPIDER TASTED SORTA LIKE SHRIMP.
MUNCH
▷ FINISHED LEARNING [GENERATE SPIDER SILK] ABILITY.
POINT
WHISH
SHH
SHH
SHH
SHH
SHH
SHH
SHH
SHH
I WAS SOMEHOW ABLE TO SPIN SPIDER SILK. WELL, GOBLIN SILK, I GUESS.
I COULDN'T CONTROL THE SILK. JUST PRODUCE IT.
SPLUFF
...
...
WE SEARCHED FOR MORE DEMON SPIDERS.

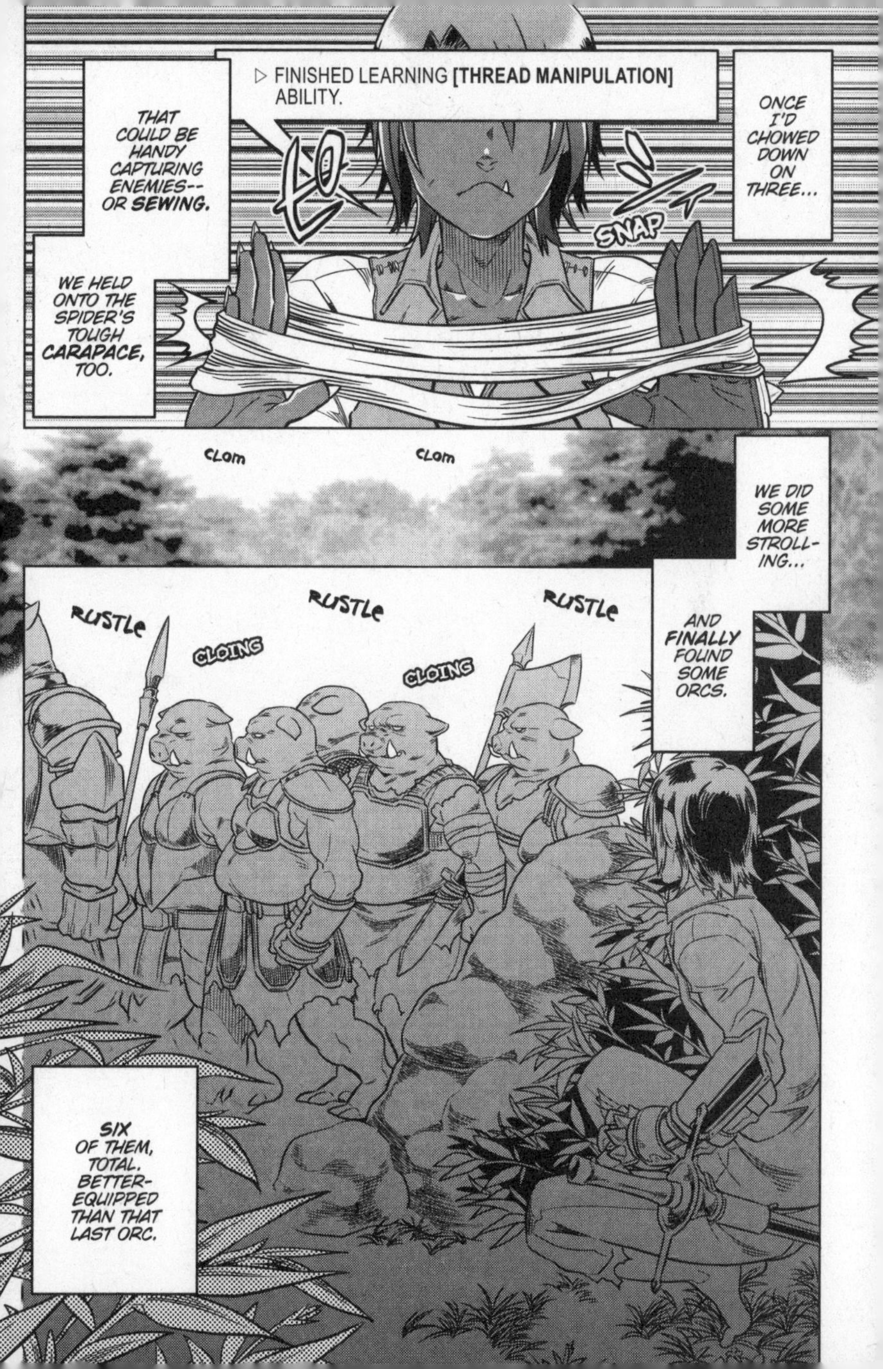

ONCE I'D CHOWED DOWN ON THREE...
▷ FINISHED LEARNING **[THREAD MANIPULATION]** ABILITY.
SNAP
THAT COULD BE HANDY CAPTURING ENEMIES-- OR **SEWING.**
WE HELD ONTO THE SPIDER'S TOUGH **CARAPACE,** TOO.
CLOM
CLOM
WE DID SOME MORE STROLL-ING...
AND **FINALLY** FOUND SOME ORCS.
RUSTLE
RUSTLE
CLOING
RUSTLE
CLOING
SIX OF THEM, TOTAL. BETTER-EQUIPPED THAN THAT LAST ORC.

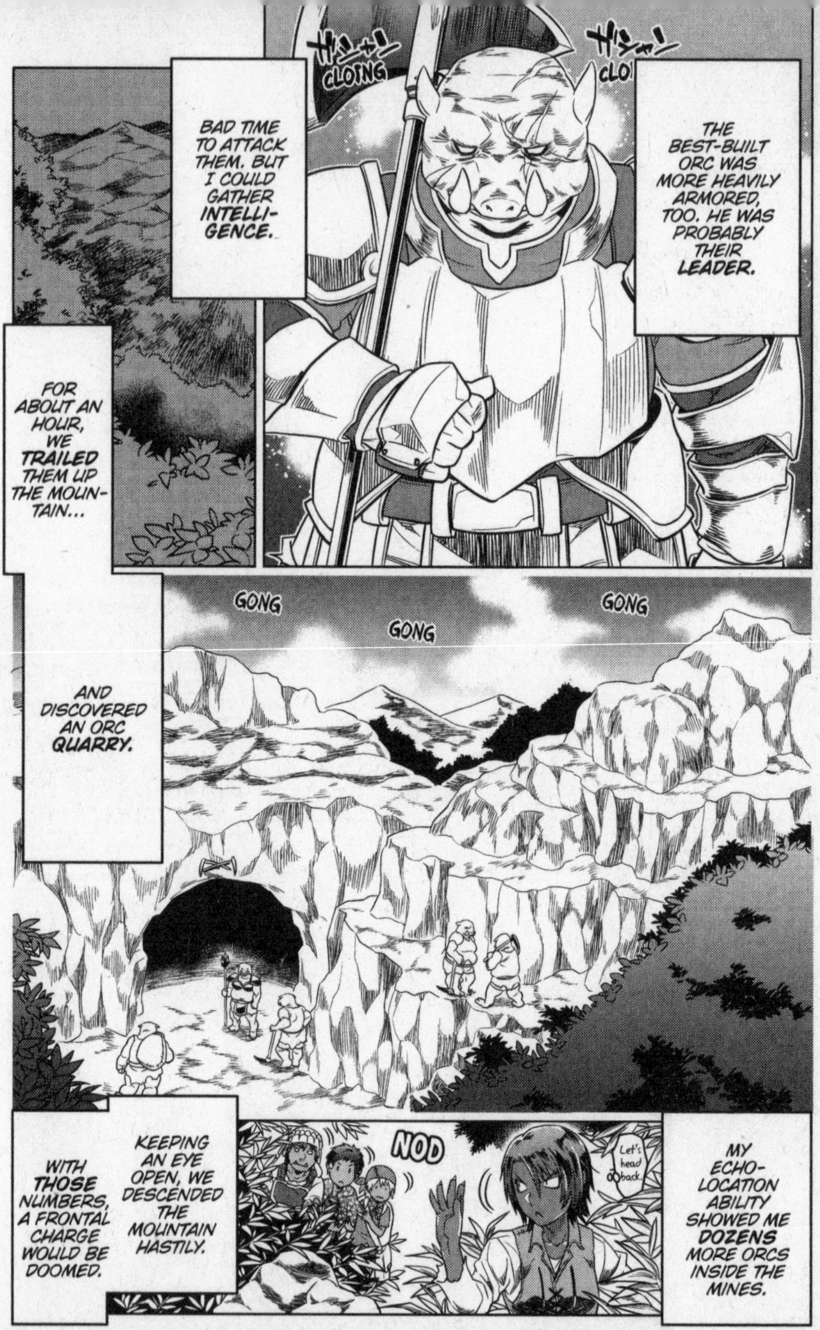

ガシャン
CLO!
THE BEST-BUILT ORC WAS MORE HEAVILY ARMORED, TOO. HE WAS PROBABLY THEIR **LEADER.**
ガシャン
CLOING
BAD TIME TO ATTACK THEM. BUT I COULD GATHER **INTELLIGENCE.**
FOR ABOUT AN HOUR, WE **TRAILED** THEM UP THE MOUNTAIN...
GONG
GONG
GONG
AND DISCOVERED AN ORC **QUARRY.**
MY ECHOLOCATION ABILITY SHOWED ME **DOZENS** MORE ORCS INSIDE THE MINES.
Let's head back.
NOD
KEEPING AN EYE OPEN, WE DESCENDED THE MOUNTAIN HASTILY.
WITH **THOSE** NUMBERS, A FRONTAL CHARGE WOULD BE DOOMED.

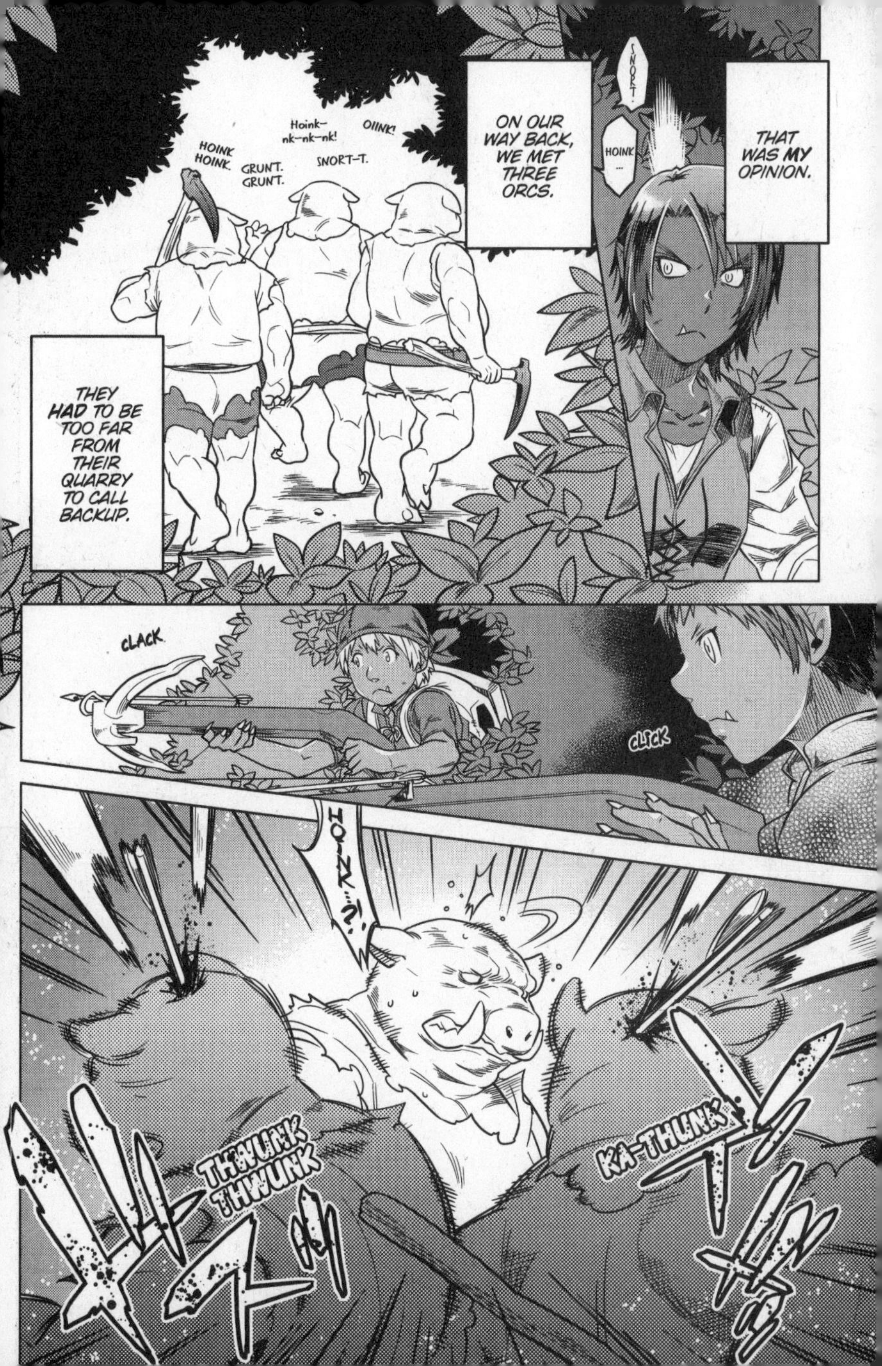
THAT WAS MY OPINION.
SNORT.
HOINK...
ON OUR WAY BACK, WE MET THREE ORCS.
OIINK!
Hoink-nk-nk-nk!
SNORT-T.
HOINK HOINK.
GRUNT. GRUNT.
THEY HAD TO BE TOO FAR FROM THEIR QUARRY TO CALL BACKUP.
CLICK
CLACK
HOINK...?!
KA-THUNK
THWUNK THWUNK

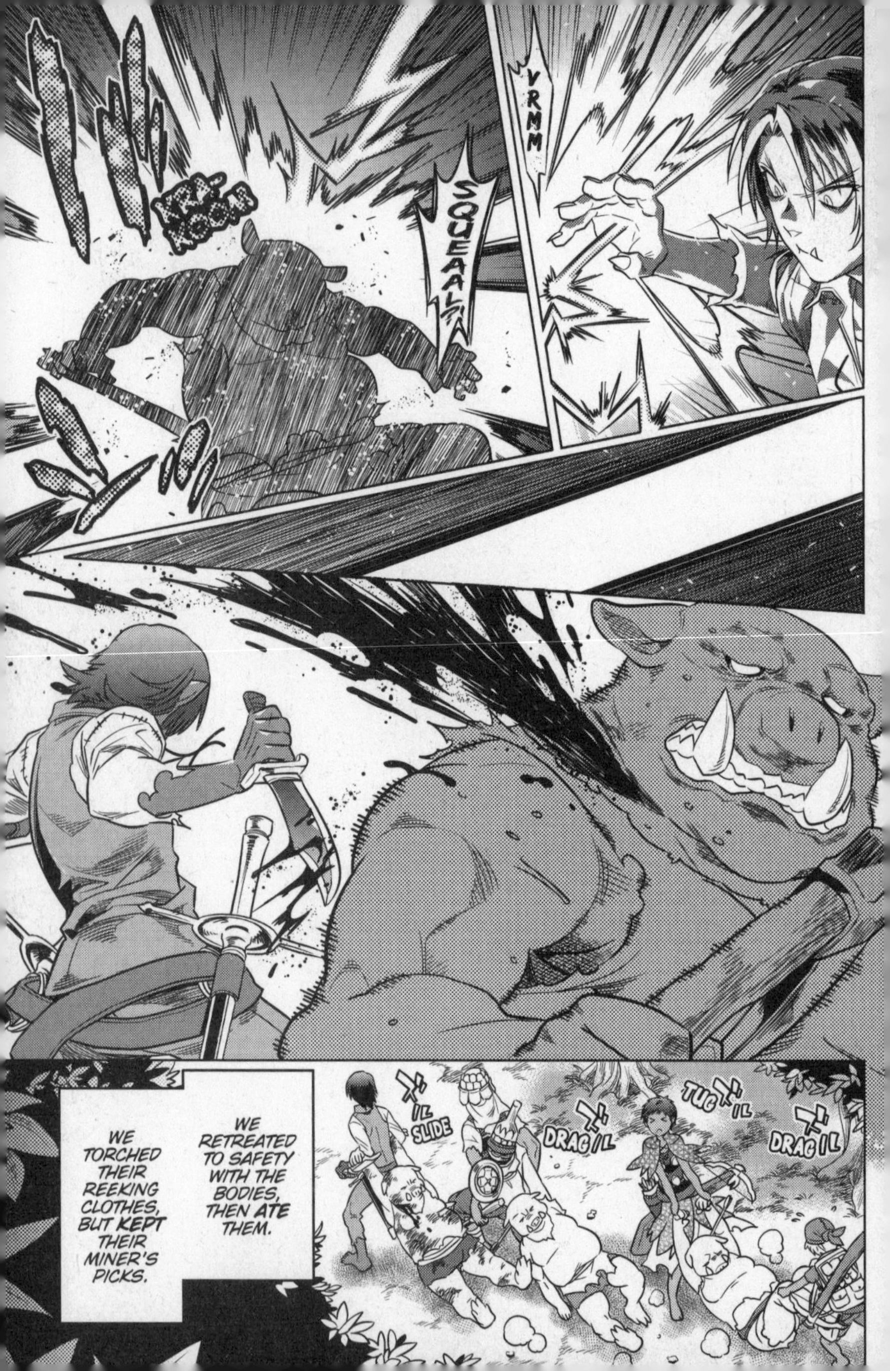
VRMM
SQUEAAAL!?
TUG
DRAG
DRAG
SLIDE
WE RETREATED TO SAFETY WITH THE BODIES, THEN ATE THEM.
WE TORCHED THEIR REEKING CLOTHES, BUT KEPT THEIR MINER'S PICKS.

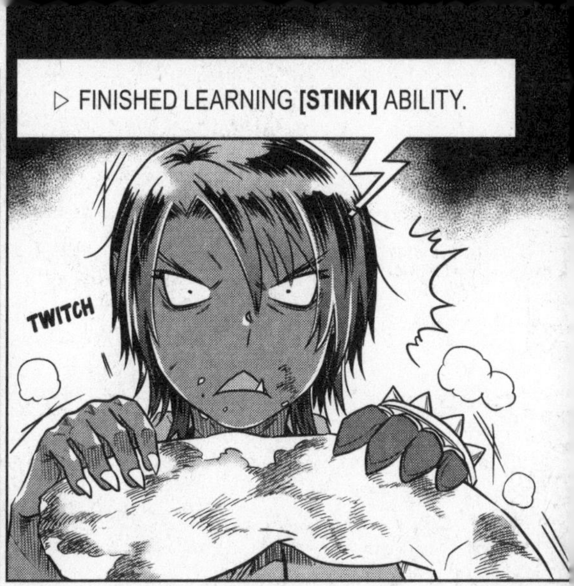
▷ FINISHED LEARNING [STINK] ABILITY.
TWITCH
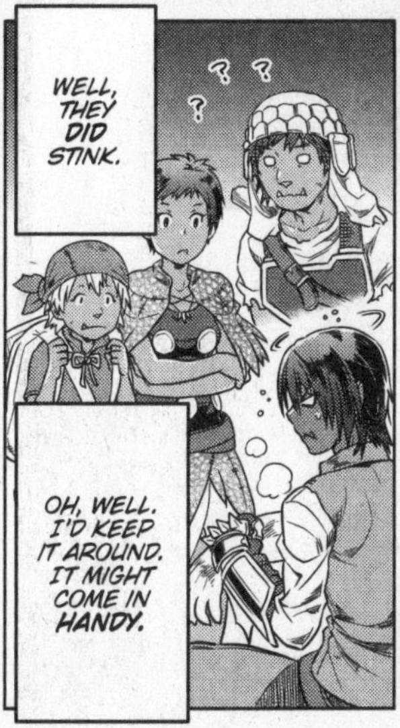
WELL, THEY DID STINK.
OH, WELL. I'D KEEP IT AROUND. IT MIGHT COME IN HANDY.

DAY 25

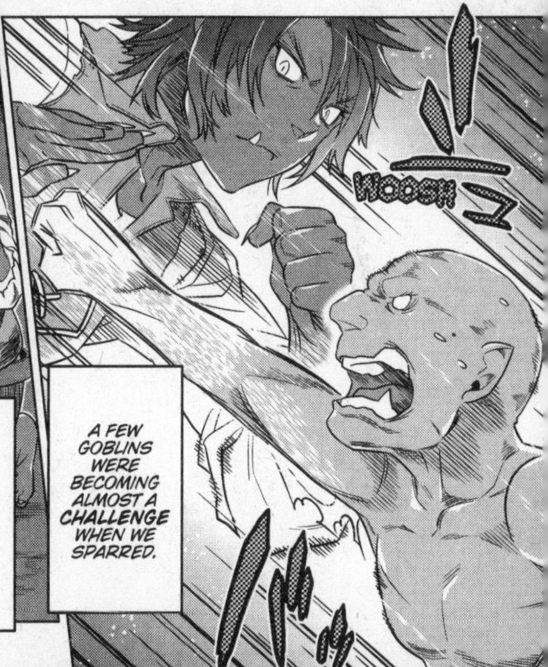
WOOSH
A FEW GOBLINS WERE BECOMING ALMOST A CHALLENGE WHEN WE SPARRED.
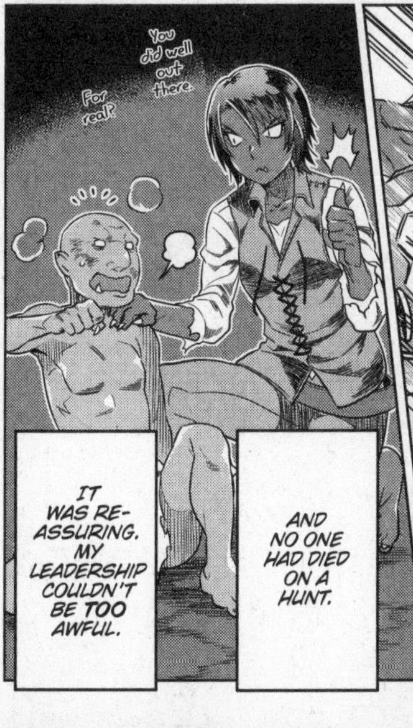
You did well out there.
For real?
AND NO ONE HAD DIED ON A HUNT.
IT WAS RE-ASSURING. MY LEADERSHIP COULDN'T BE TOO AWFUL.

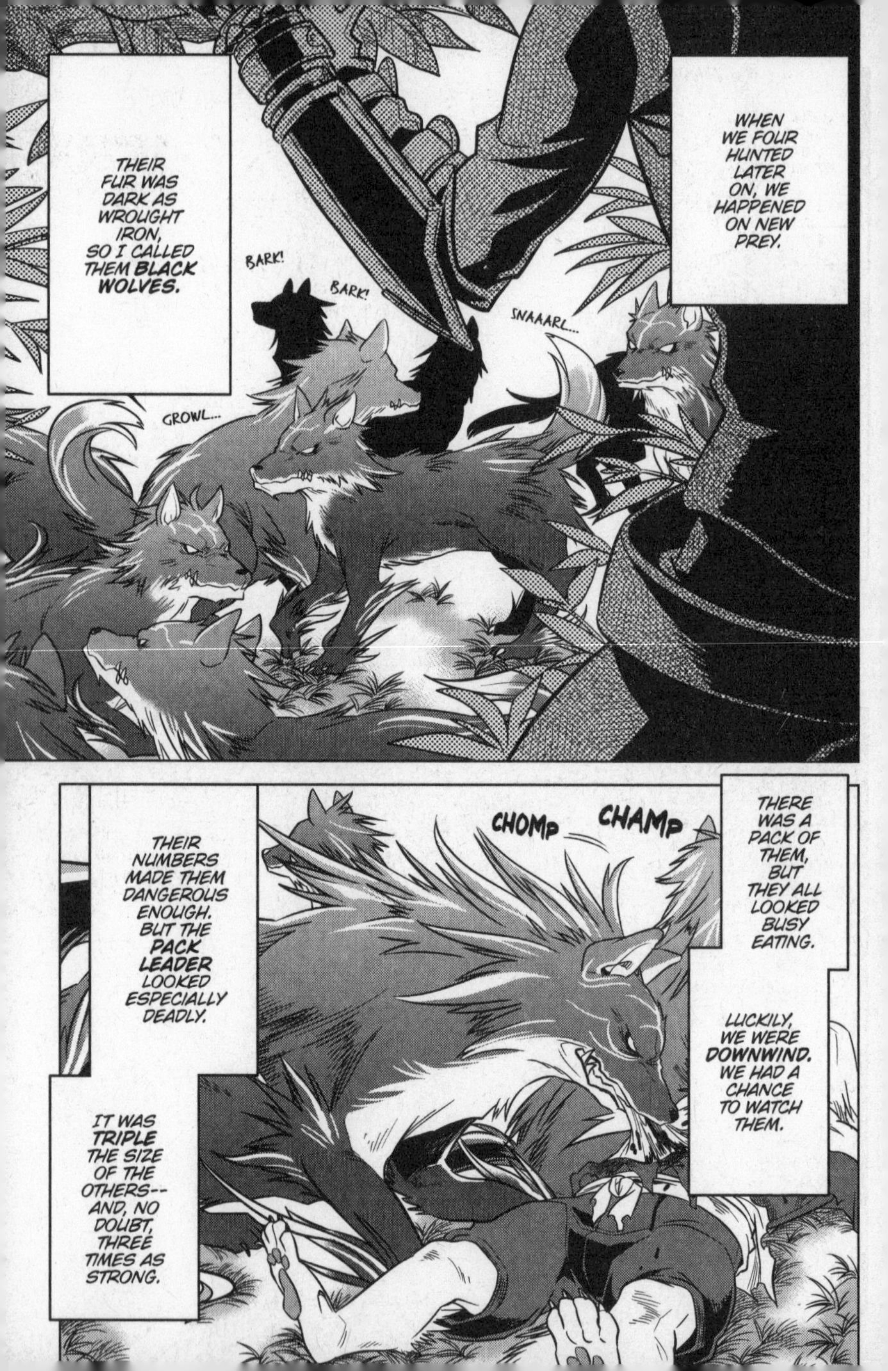
WHEN WE FOUR HUNTED LATER ON, WE HAPPENED ON NEW PREY.
SNAAARL...
BARK!
BARK!
THEIR FUR WAS DARK AS WROUGHT IRON, SO I CALLED THEM **BLACK WOLVES.**
GROWL...
THERE WAS A PACK OF THEM, BUT THEY ALL LOOKED BUSY EATING.
CHAMP
CHOMP
LUCKILY, WE WERE **DOWNWIND.** WE HAD A CHANCE TO WATCH THEM.
THEIR NUMBERS MADE THEM DANGEROUS ENOUGH. BUT THE **PACK LEADER** LOOKED ESPECIALLY DEADLY.
IT WAS **TRIPLE** THE SIZE OF THE OTHERS-- AND, NO DOUBT, THREE TIMES AS STRONG.

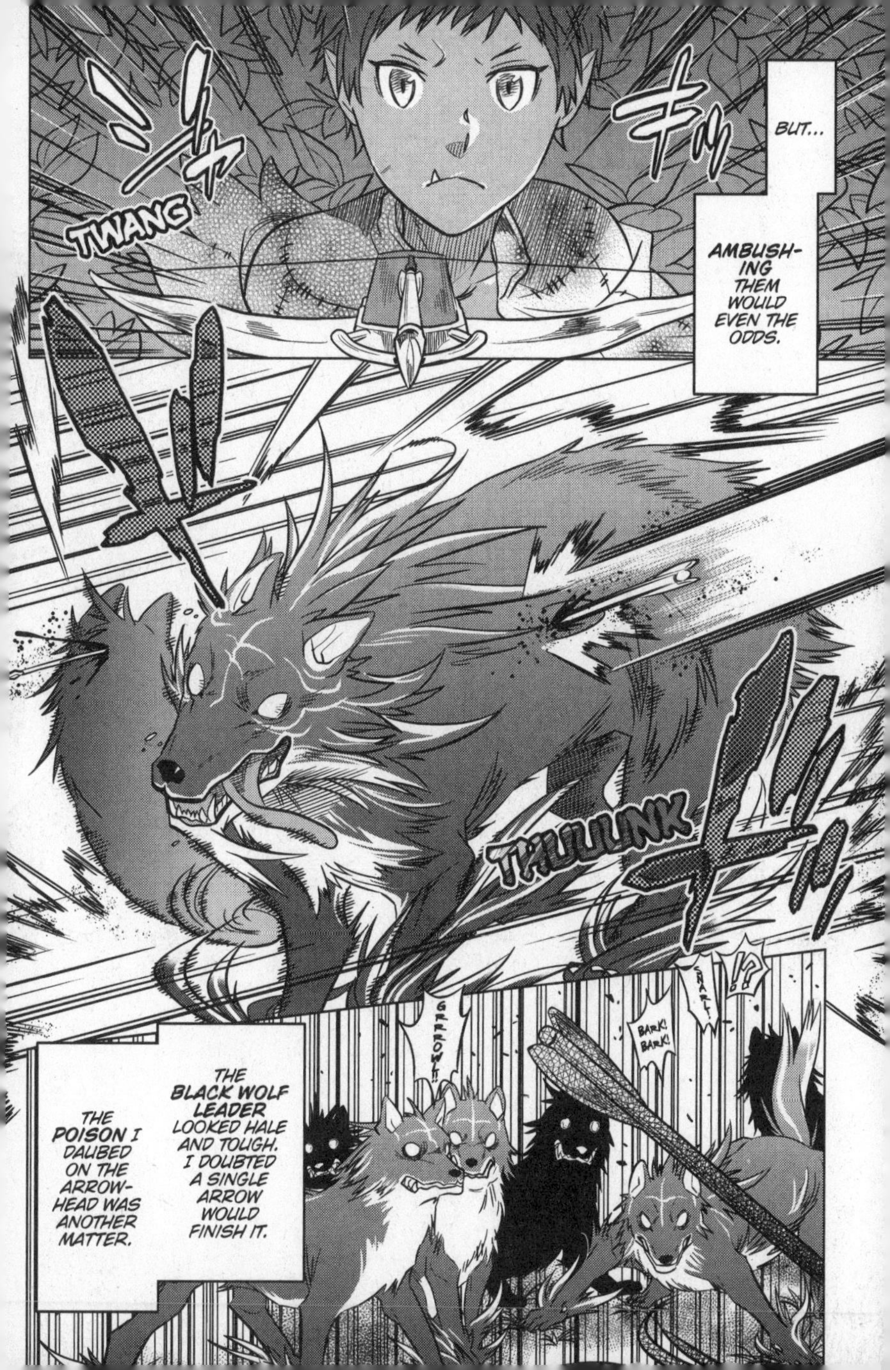
BUT...
AMBUSHING THEM WOULD EVEN THE ODDS.
TWANG
THUUUNK
!!?
SNARL!
BARK! BARK!
GRRROWL!!
THE BLACK WOLF LEADER LOOKED HALE AND TOUGH. I DOUBTED A SINGLE ARROW WOULD FINISH IT.
THE POISON I DAUBED ON THE ARROWHEAD WAS ANOTHER MATTER.

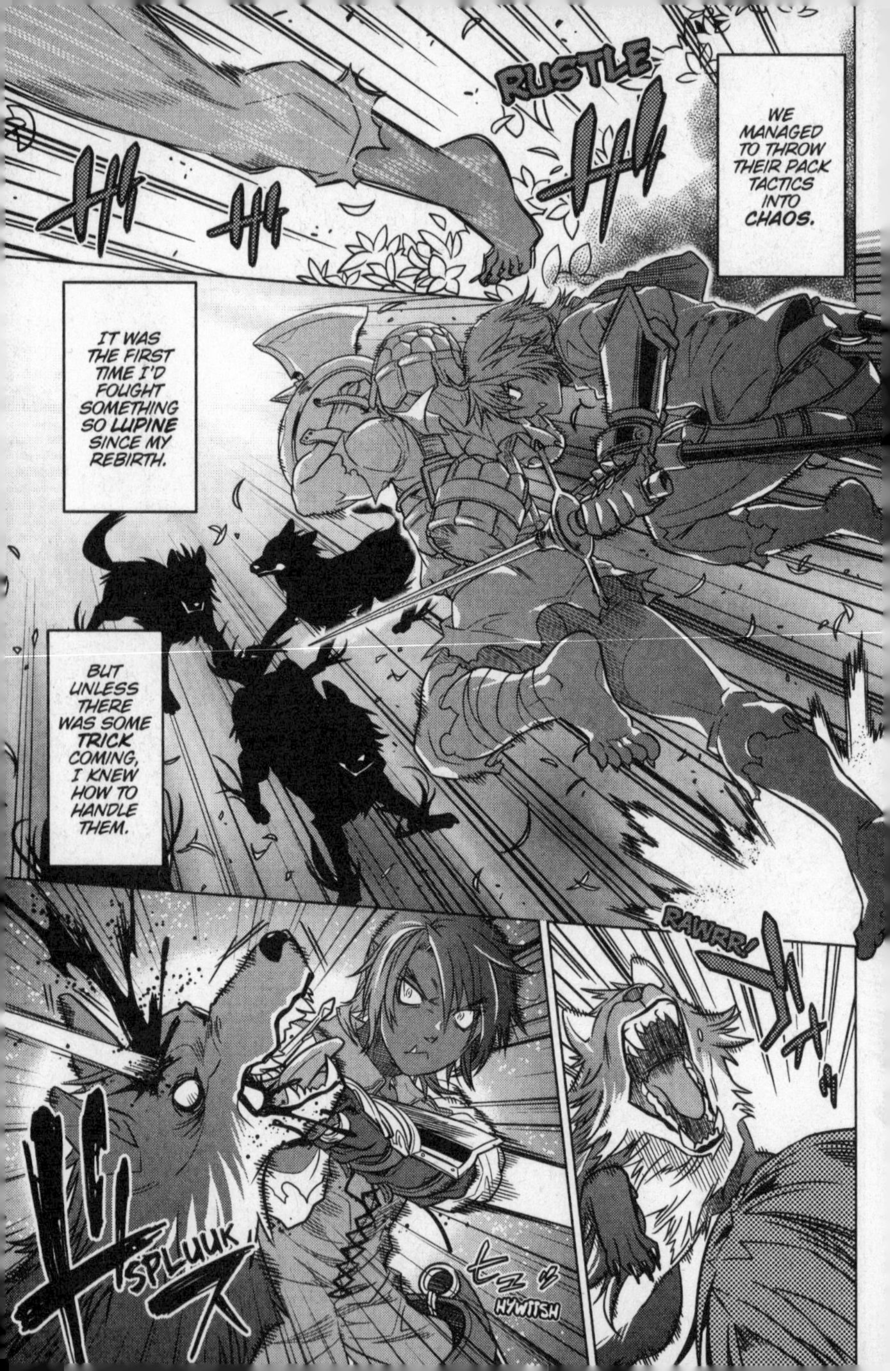

RUSTLE
WE MANAGED TO THROW THEIR PACK TACTICS INTO CHAOS.
IT WAS THE FIRST TIME I'D FOUGHT SOMETHING SO LUPINE SINCE MY REBIRTH.
BUT UNLESS THERE WAS SOME TRICK COMING, I KNEW HOW TO HANDLE THEM.
RAWRR!
SPLUUK
HYWITSH

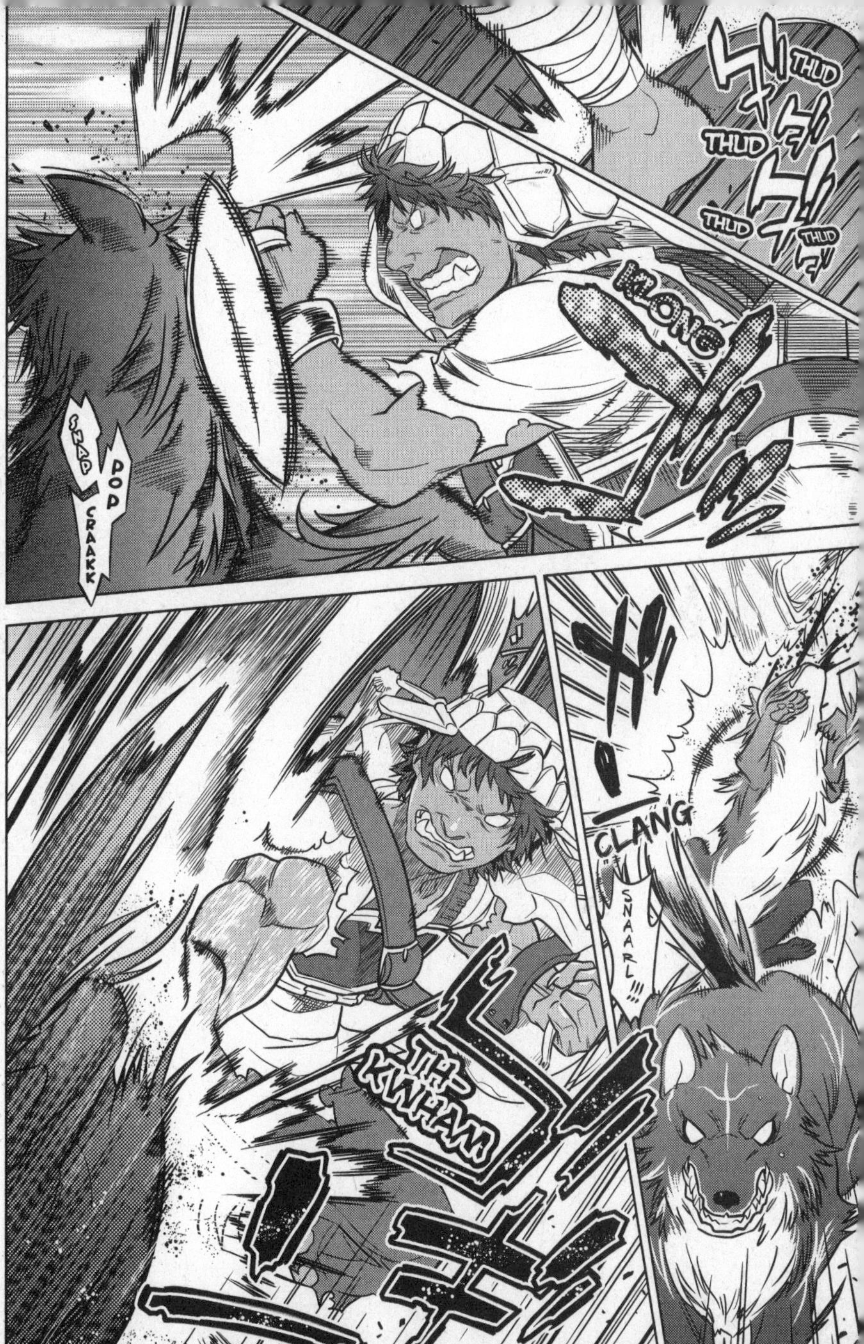
THUD
THUD
THUD
THUD
KLONG
SNAP
POP
CRAAKK
CLANG
SNAAARL!!!
THI-KWHAM

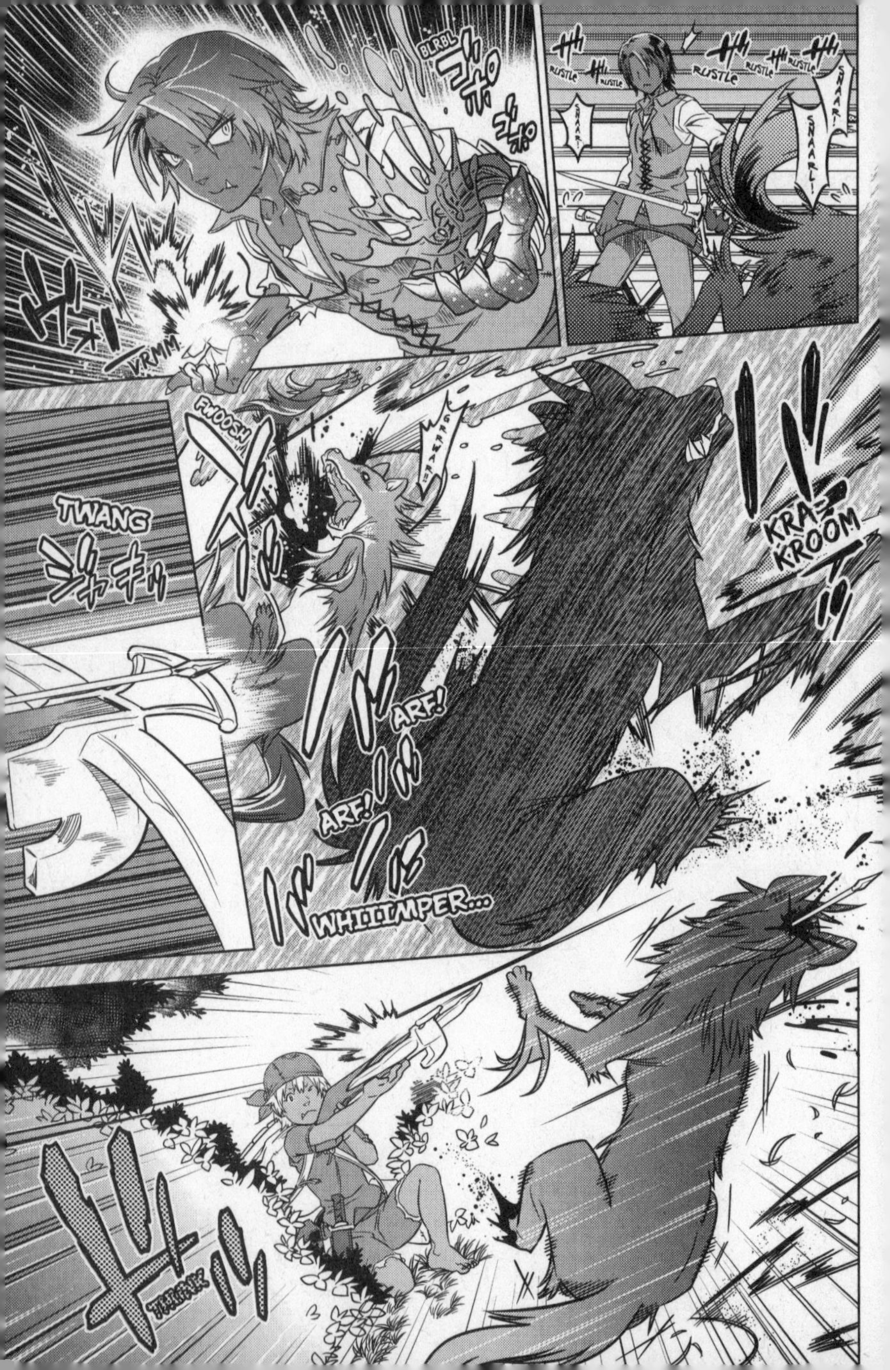
RUSTLE
RUSTLE
RUSTLE
RUSTLE
RUSTLE
SNAAR!
SNAARL!
SNAAR!
BLRBL
ゴポ
ゴポ
VRMM
KRA-KROOM
GRRWAR!!
FWOOSH
TWANG
シャキッ
ARF!
ARF!
WHIIIMPER...

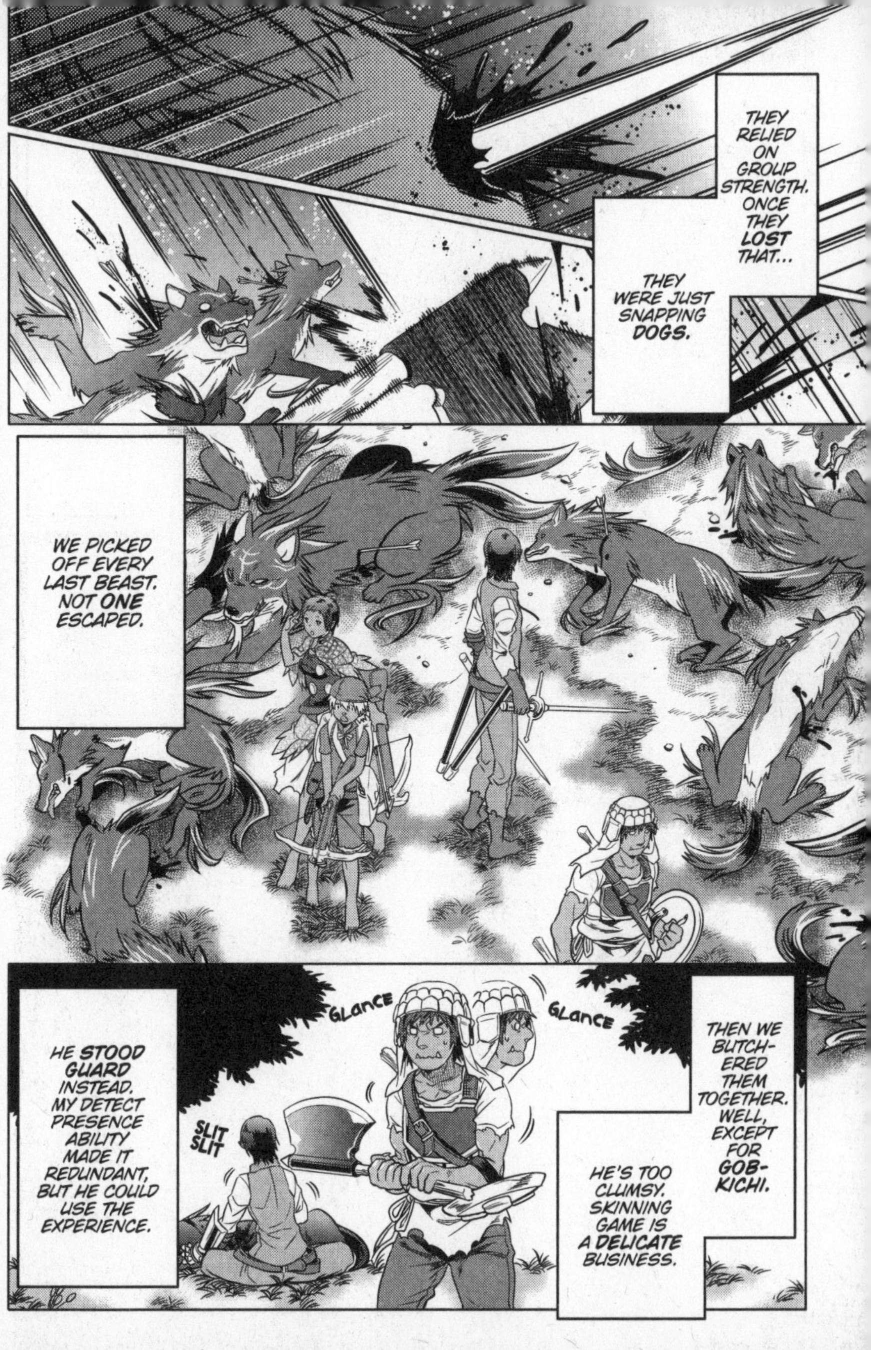
THEY RELIED ON GROUP STRENGTH. ONCE THEY LOST THAT...
THEY WERE JUST SNAPPING DOGS.
WE PICKED OFF EVERY LAST BEAST. NOT ONE ESCAPED.
THEN WE BUTCHERED THEM TOGETHER. WELL, EXCEPT FOR GOBKICHI.
HE'S TOO CLUMSY. SKINNING GAME IS A DELICATE BUSINESS.
GLANCE
GLANCE
SLIT SLIT
HE STOOD GUARD INSTEAD. MY DETECT PRESENCE ABILITY MADE IT REDUNDANT, BUT HE COULD USE THE EXPERIENCE.

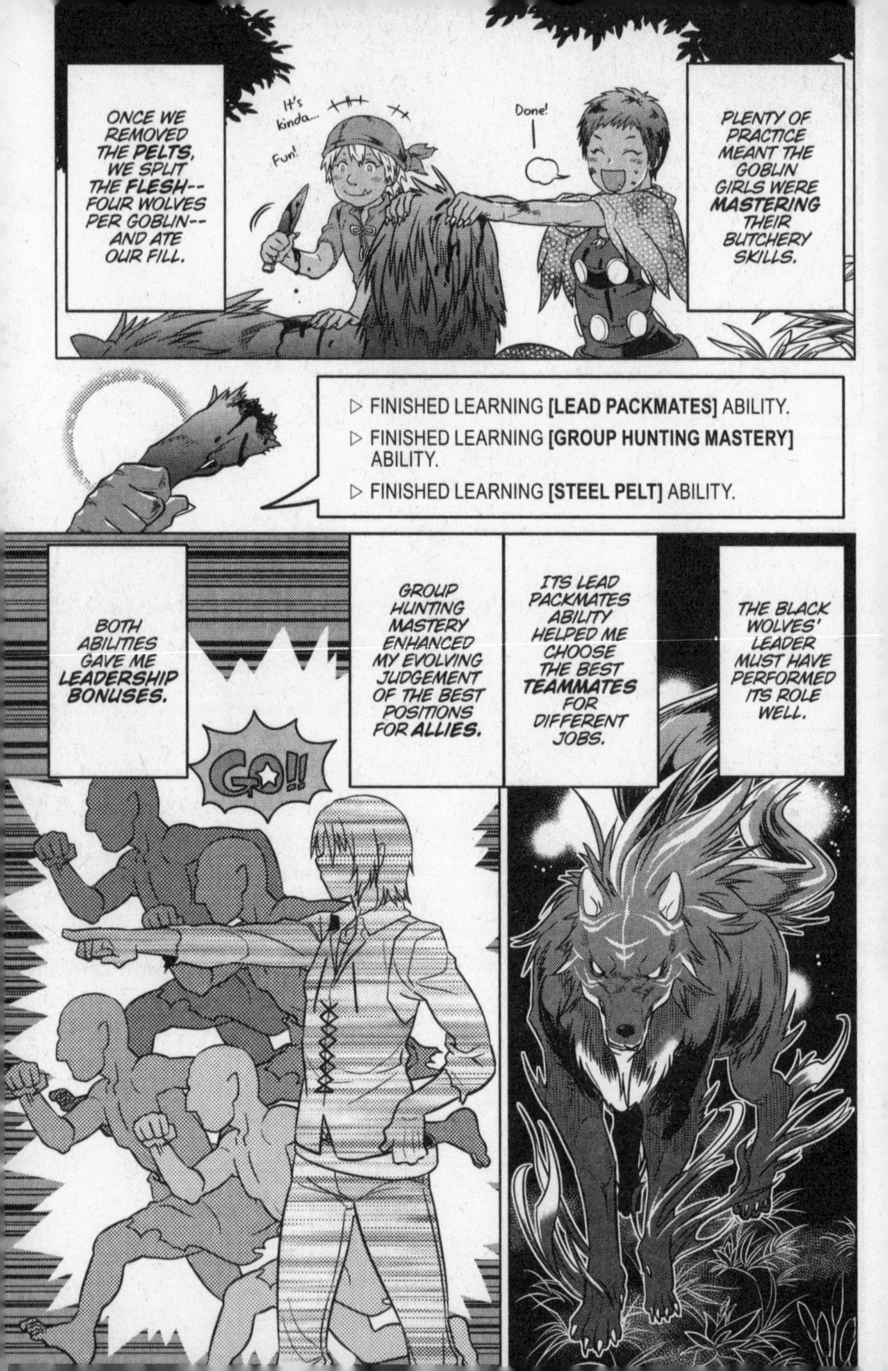
PLENTY OF PRACTICE MEANT THE GOBLIN GIRLS WERE MASTERING THEIR BUTCHERY SKILLS.
Done!
It's kinda... Fun!
ONCE WE REMOVED THE PELTS, WE SPLIT THE FLESH--FOUR WOLVES PER GOBLIN--AND ATE OUR FILL.
▷ FINISHED LEARNING [LEAD PACKMATES] ABILITY.
▷ FINISHED LEARNING [GROUP HUNTING MASTERY] ABILITY.
▷ FINISHED LEARNING [STEEL PELT] ABILITY.
THE BLACK WOLVES' LEADER MUST HAVE PERFORMED ITS ROLE WELL.
ITS LEAD PACKMATES ABILITY HELPED ME CHOOSE THE BEST TEAMMATES FOR DIFFERENT JOBS.
GROUP HUNTING MASTERY ENHANCED MY EVOLVING JUDGEMENT OF THE BEST POSITIONS FOR ALLIES.
BOTH ABILITIES GAVE ME LEADERSHIP BONUSES.
GO!!

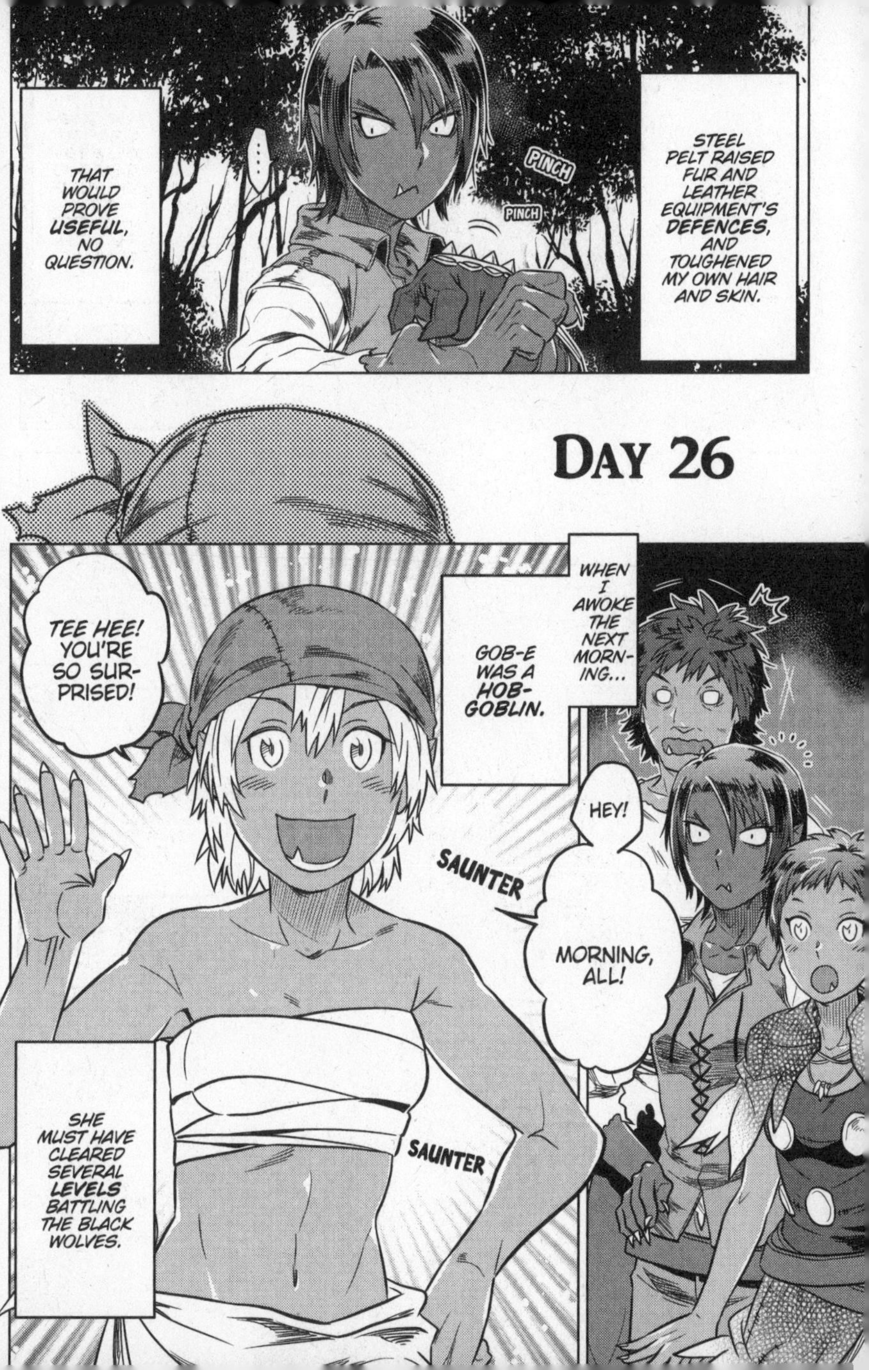
STEEL PELT RAISED FUR AND LEATHER EQUIPMENT'S DEFENCES, AND TOUGHENED MY OWN HAIR AND SKIN.
PINCH
PINCH
...
THAT WOULD PROVE USEFUL, NO QUESTION.
DAY 26
WHEN I AWOKE THE NEXT MORNING...
GOB-E WAS A HOBGOBLIN.
HEY!
MORNING, ALL!
SAUNTER
TEE HEE! YOU'RE SO SURPRISED!
SAUNTER
SHE MUST HAVE CLEARED SEVERAL LEVELS BATTLING THE BLACK WOLVES.

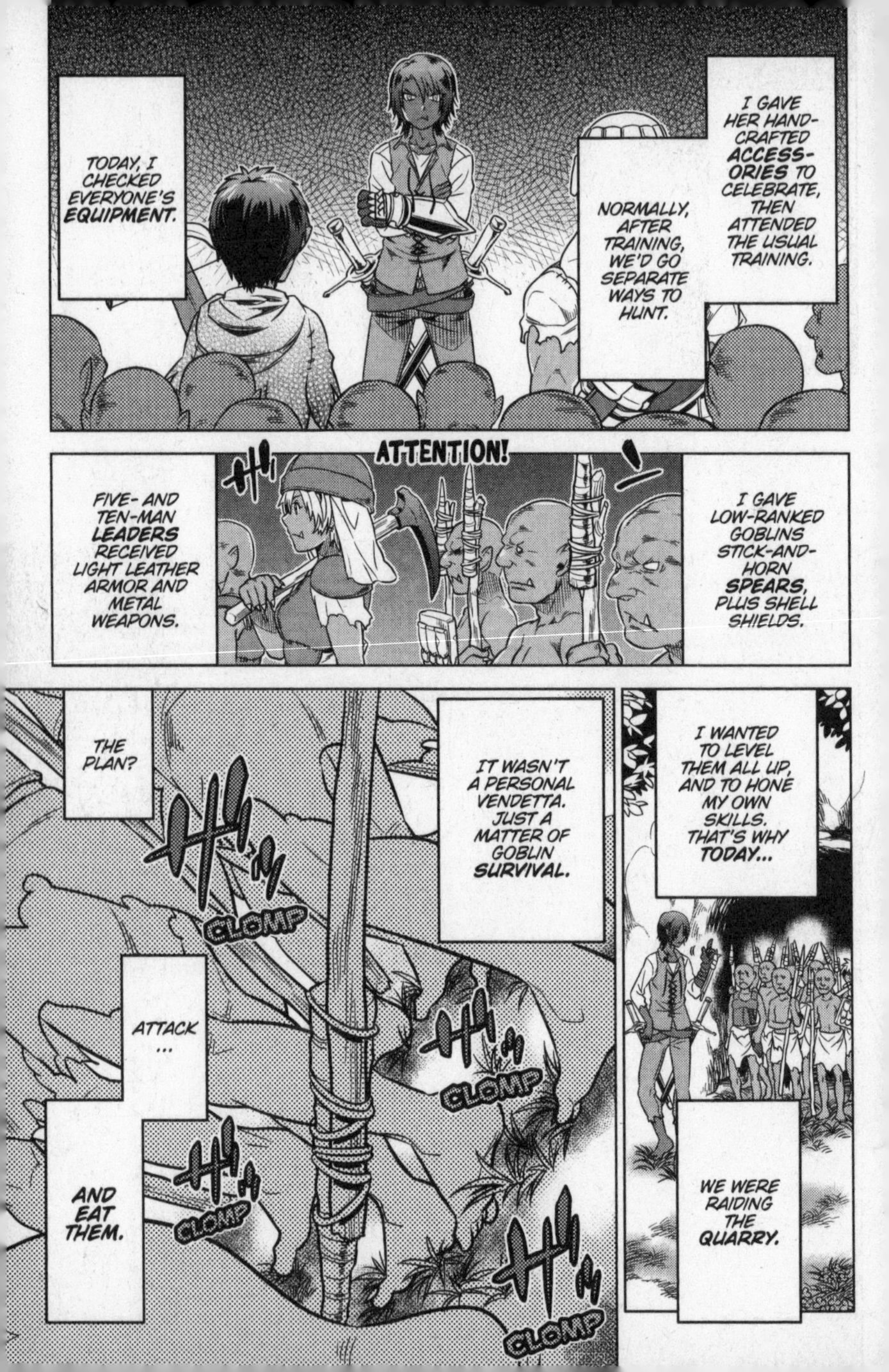
I GAVE HER HAND-CRAFTED ACCESSORIES TO CELEBRATE, THEN ATTENDED THE USUAL TRAINING.
NORMALLY, AFTER TRAINING, WE'D GO SEPARATE WAYS TO HUNT.
TODAY, I CHECKED EVERYONE'S EQUIPMENT.
I GAVE LOW-RANKED GOBLINS STICK-AND-HORN SPEARS, PLUS SHELL SHIELDS.
ATTENTION!
FIVE- AND TEN-MAN LEADERS RECEIVED LIGHT LEATHER ARMOR AND METAL WEAPONS.
I WANTED TO LEVEL THEM ALL UP, AND TO HONE MY OWN SKILLS. THAT'S WHY TODAY...
WE WERE RAIDING THE QUARRY.
IT WASN'T A PERSONAL VENDETTA. JUST A MATTER OF GOBLIN SURVIVAL.
THE PLAN?
CLOMP
ATTACK ...
CLOMP
AND EAT THEM.
CLOMP
CLOMP

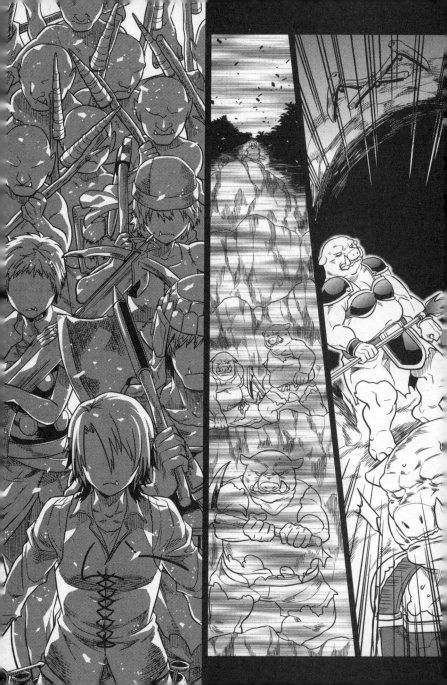

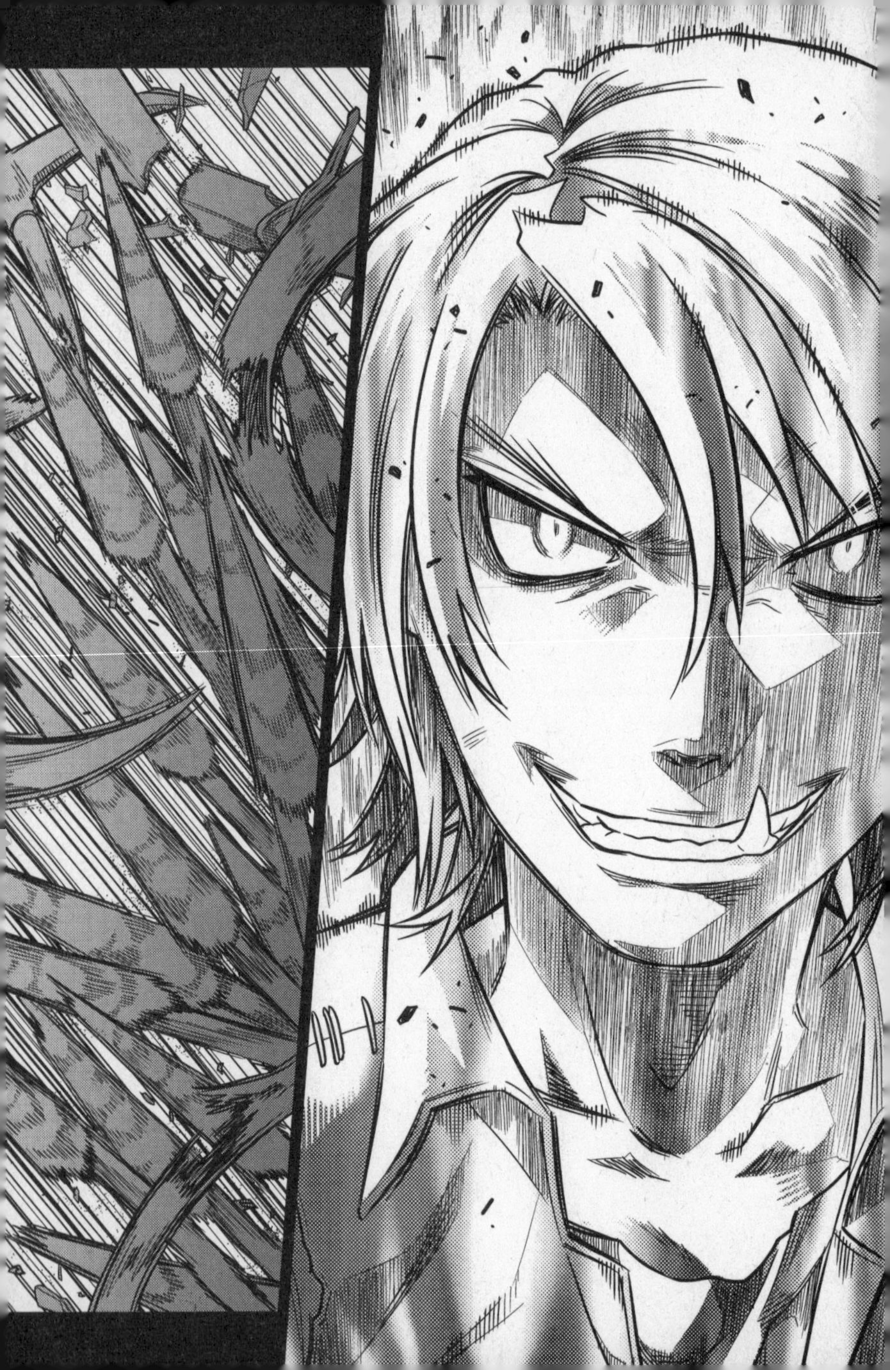

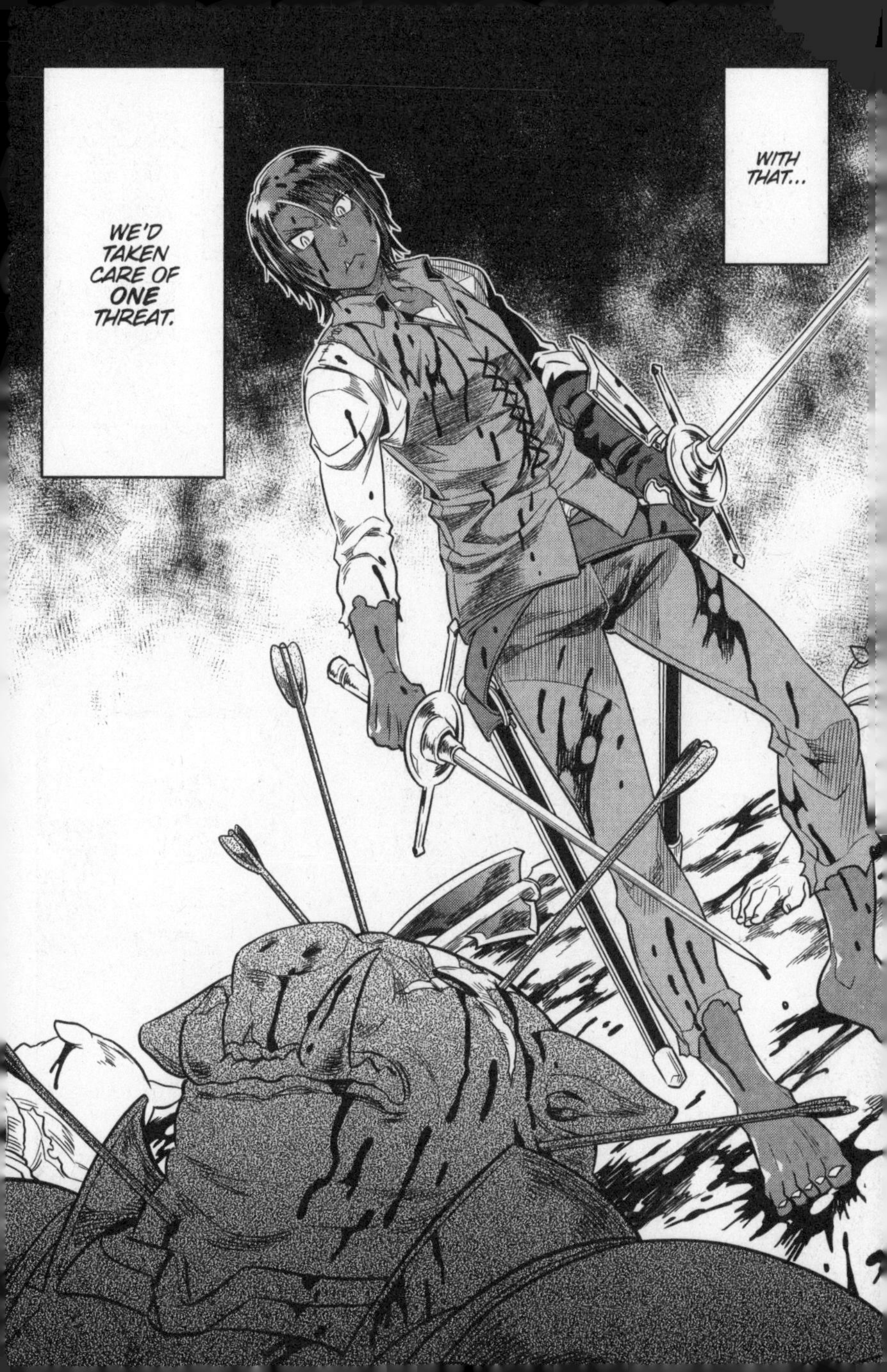
WITH THAT...
WE'D TAKEN CARE OF ONE THREAT.

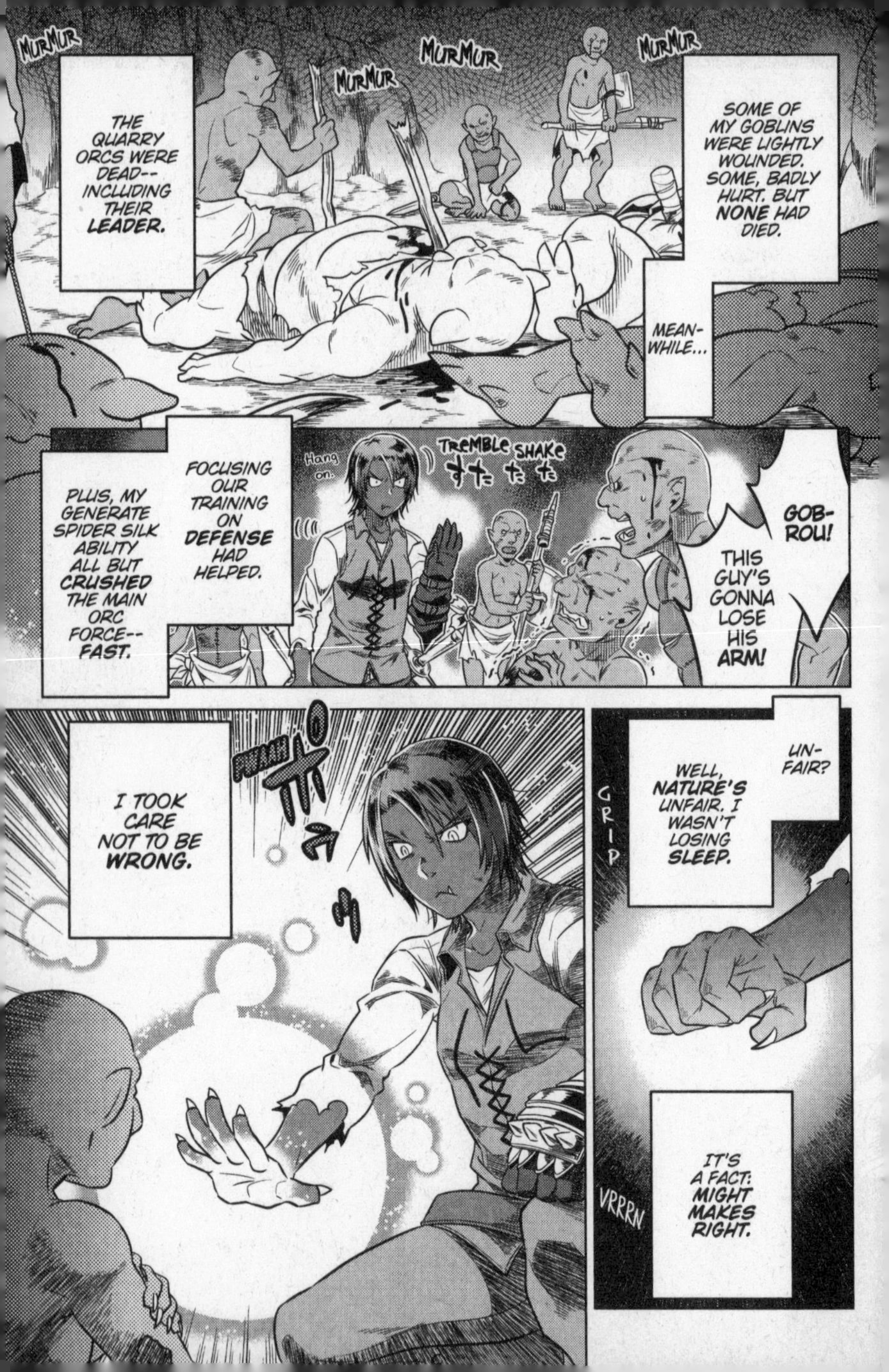
MURMUR
SOME OF MY GOBLINS WERE LIGHTLY WOUNDED. SOME, BADLY HURT. BUT NONE HAD DIED.
MURMUR
MURMUR
THE QUARRY ORCS WERE DEAD-- INCLUDING THEIR LEADER.
MURMUR
MEAN-WHILE...
GOB-ROU!
THIS GUY'S GONNA LOSE HIS ARM!
TREMBLE SHAKE
Hang on.
FOCUSING OUR TRAINING ON DEFENSE HAD HELPED.
PLUS, MY GENERATE SPIDER SILK ABILITY ALL BUT CRUSHED THE MAIN ORC FORCE-- FAST.
UN-FAIR?
WELL, NATURE'S UNFAIR. I WASN'T LOSING SLEEP.
GRIP
IT'S A FACT: MIGHT MAKES RIGHT.
VRRRN
PWAAH
I TOOK CARE NOT TO BE WRONG.

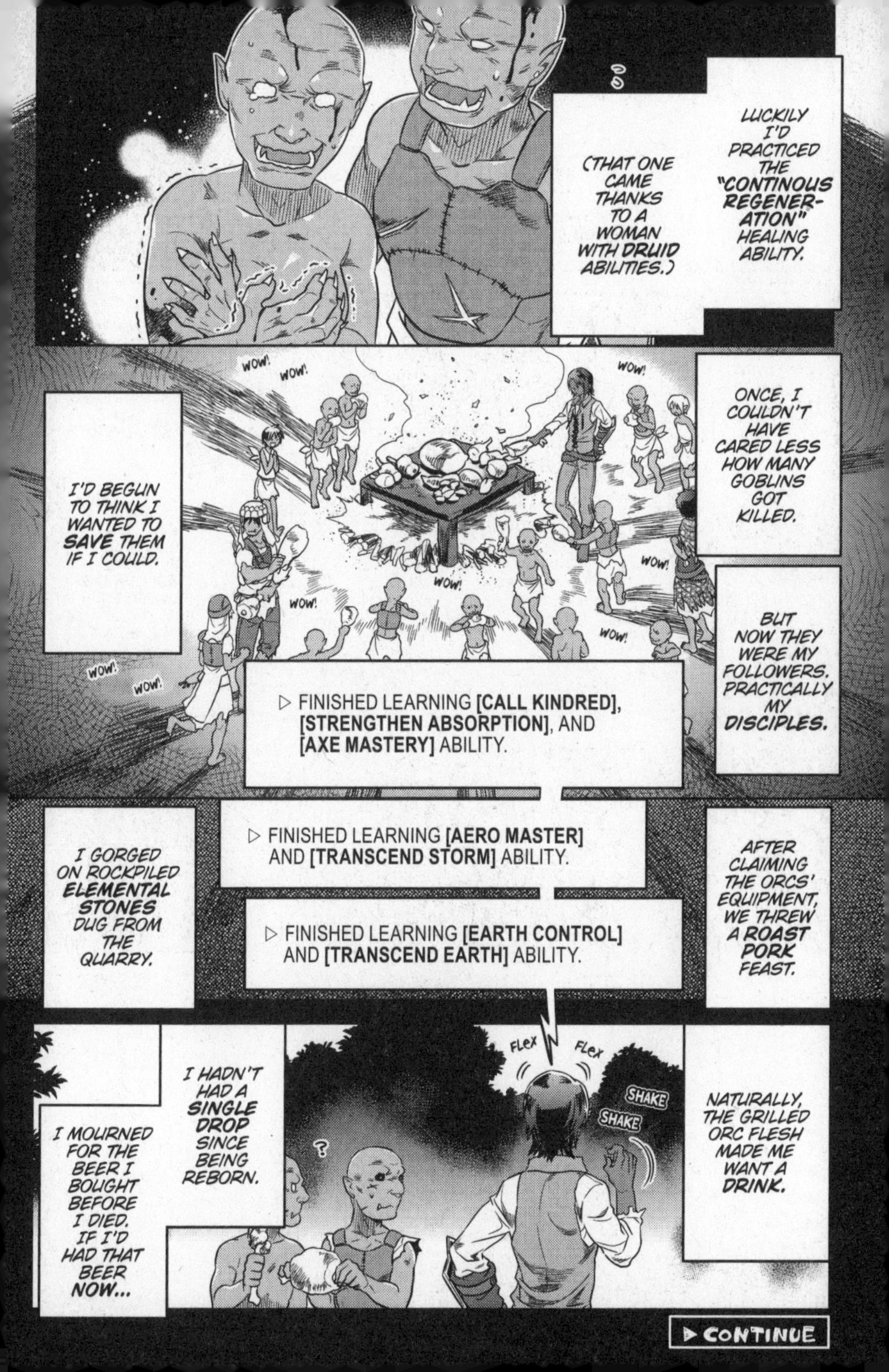
LUCKILY I'D PRACTICED THE "CONTINOUS REGENERATION" HEALING ABILITY.
(THAT ONE CAME THANKS TO A WOMAN WITH DRUID ABILITIES.)
ONCE, I COULDN'T HAVE CARED LESS HOW MANY GOBLINS GOT KILLED.
BUT NOW THEY WERE MY FOLLOWERS. PRACTICALLY MY DISCIPLES.
WOW!
WOW!
WOW!
WOW!
WOW!
WOW!
WOW!
WOW!
WOW!
I'D BEGUN TO THINK I WANTED TO SAVE THEM IF I COULD.
▷ FINISHED LEARNING [CALL KINDRED], [STRENGTHEN ABSORPTION], AND [AXE MASTERY] ABILITY.
AFTER CLAIMING THE ORCS' EQUIPMENT, WE THREW A ROAST PORK FEAST.
▷ FINISHED LEARNING [AERO MASTER] AND [TRANSCEND STORM] ABILITY.
▷ FINISHED LEARNING [EARTH CONTROL] AND [TRANSCEND EARTH] ABILITY.
I GORGED ON ROCKPILED ELEMENTAL STONES DUG FROM THE QUARRY.
NATURALLY, THE GRILLED ORC FLESH MADE ME WANT A DRINK.
FLEX
FLEX
SHAKE
SHAKE
?
I HADN'T HAD A SINGLE DROP SINCE BEING REBORN.
I MOURNED FOR THE BEER I BOUGHT BEFORE I DIED. IF I'D HAD THAT BEER NOW...
▷ CONTINUE

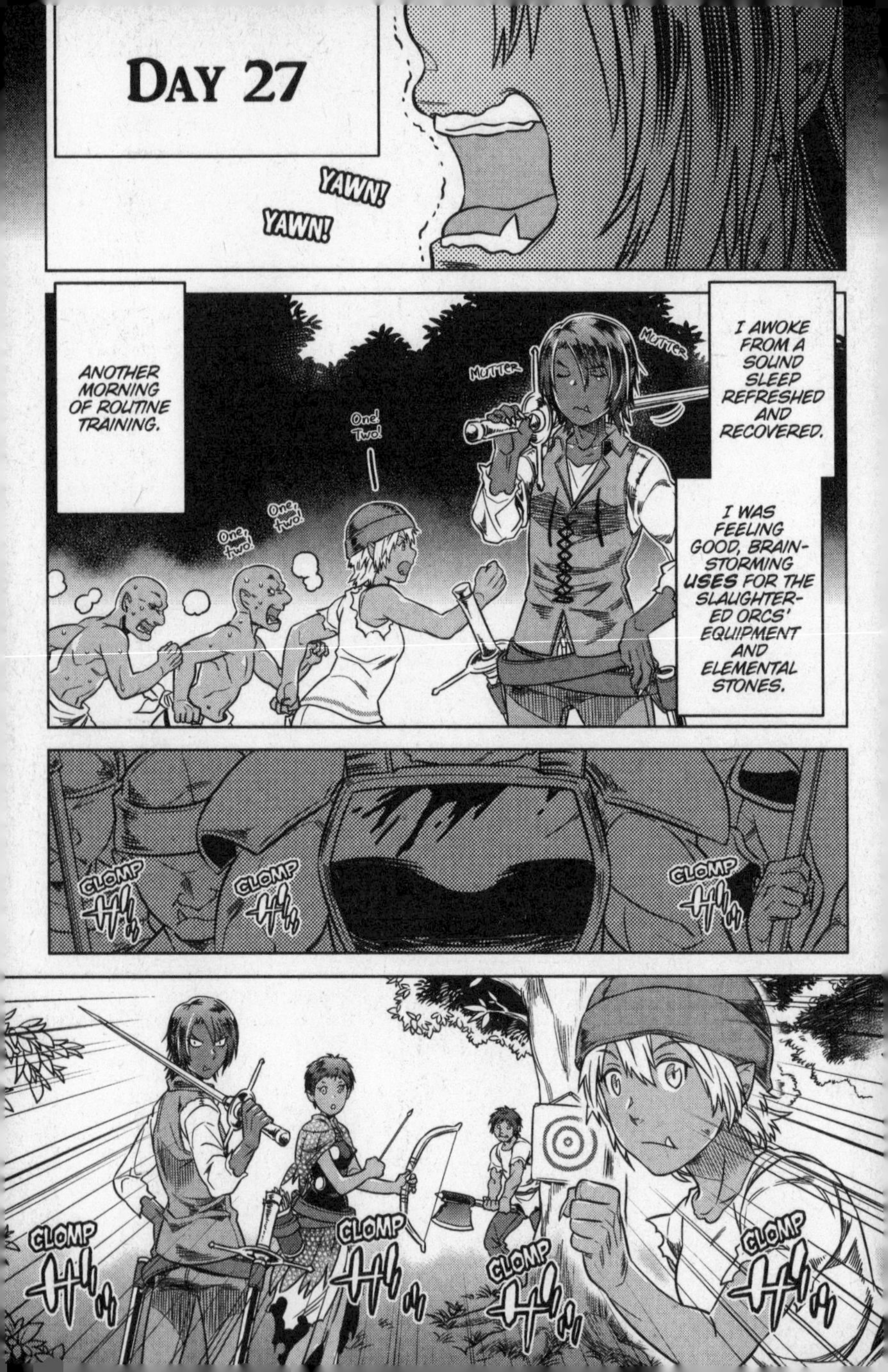
DAY 27
YAWN!
YAWN!
I AWOKE FROM A SOUND SLEEP REFRESHED AND RECOVERED.
MUTTER
MUTTER
I WAS FEELING GOOD, BRAIN-STORMING USES FOR THE SLAUGHTER-ED ORCS' EQUIPMENT AND ELEMENTAL STONES.
One! Two!
ANOTHER MORNING OF ROUTINE TRAINING.
One, two!
One, two!
CLOMP
CLOMP
CLOMP
CLOMP
CLOMP
CLOMP
CLOMP

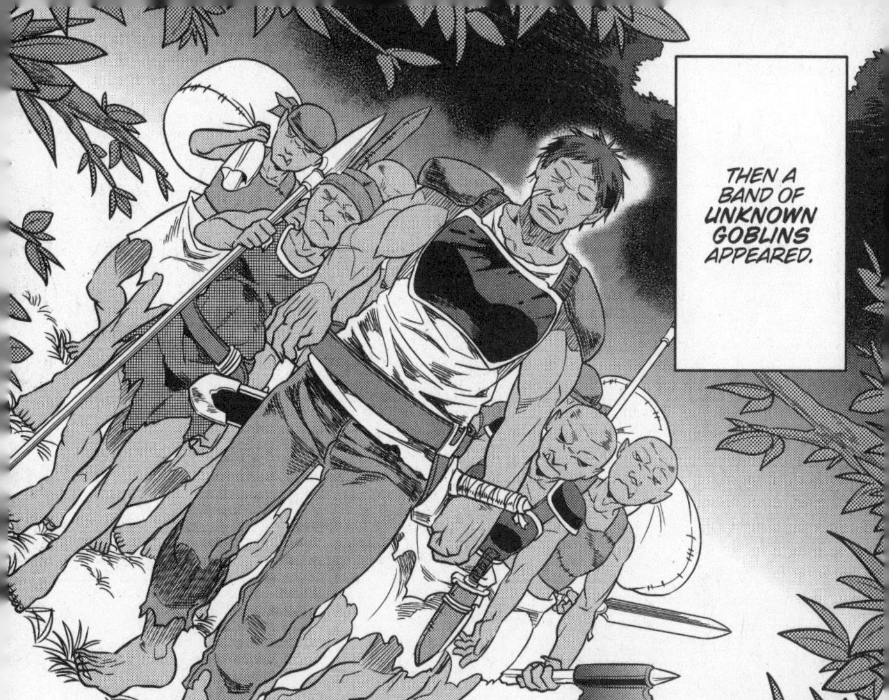
THEN A BAND OF UNKNOWN GOBLINS APPEARED.
CHAPTER 7

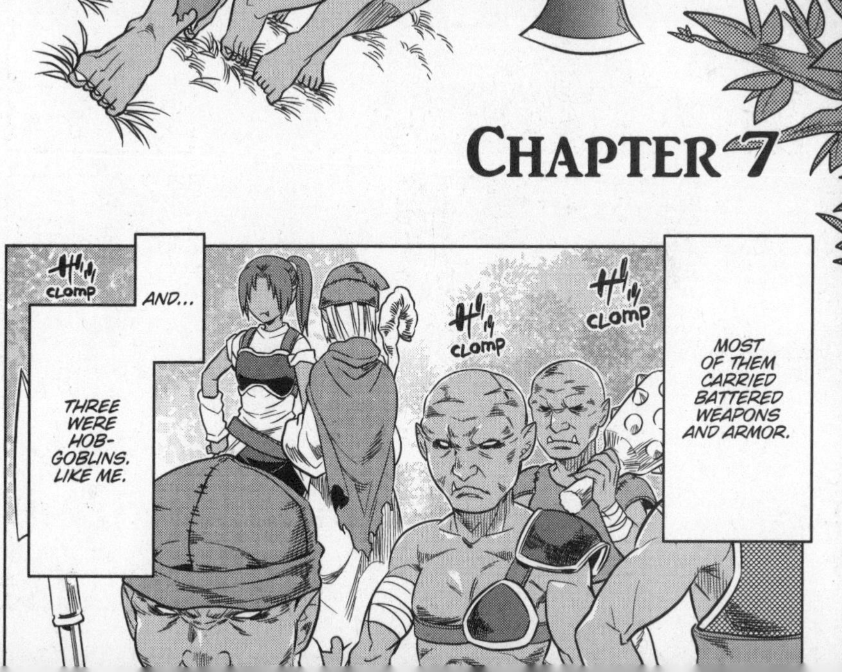
MOST OF THEM CARRIED BATTERED WEAPONS AND ARMOR.
CLOMP
CLOMP
CLOMP
AND...
THREE WERE HOB-GOBLINS. LIKE ME.

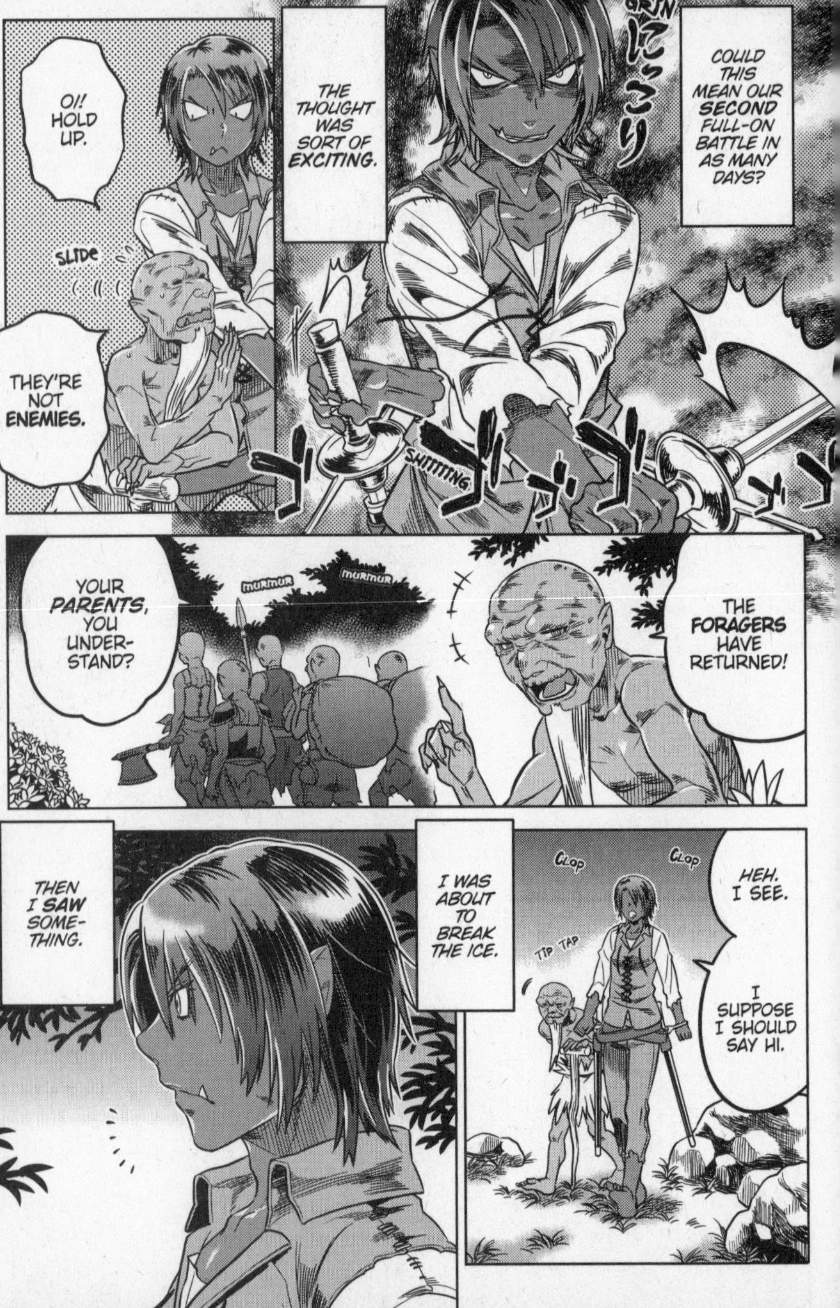
COULD THIS MEAN OUR SECOND FULL-ON BATTLE IN AS MANY DAYS?
GRIN
にっこり
THE THOUGHT WAS SORT OF EXCITING.
SHIIIIING
OI! HOLD UP.
SLIDE
THEY'RE NOT ENEMIES.
THE FORAGERS HAVE RETURNED!
murmur
murmur
YOUR PARENTS, YOU UNDER-STAND?
HEH. I SEE.
I SUPPOSE I SHOULD SAY HI.
CLOP
CLOP
I WAS ABOUT TO BREAK THE ICE.
TIP TAP
THEN I SAW SOME-THING.

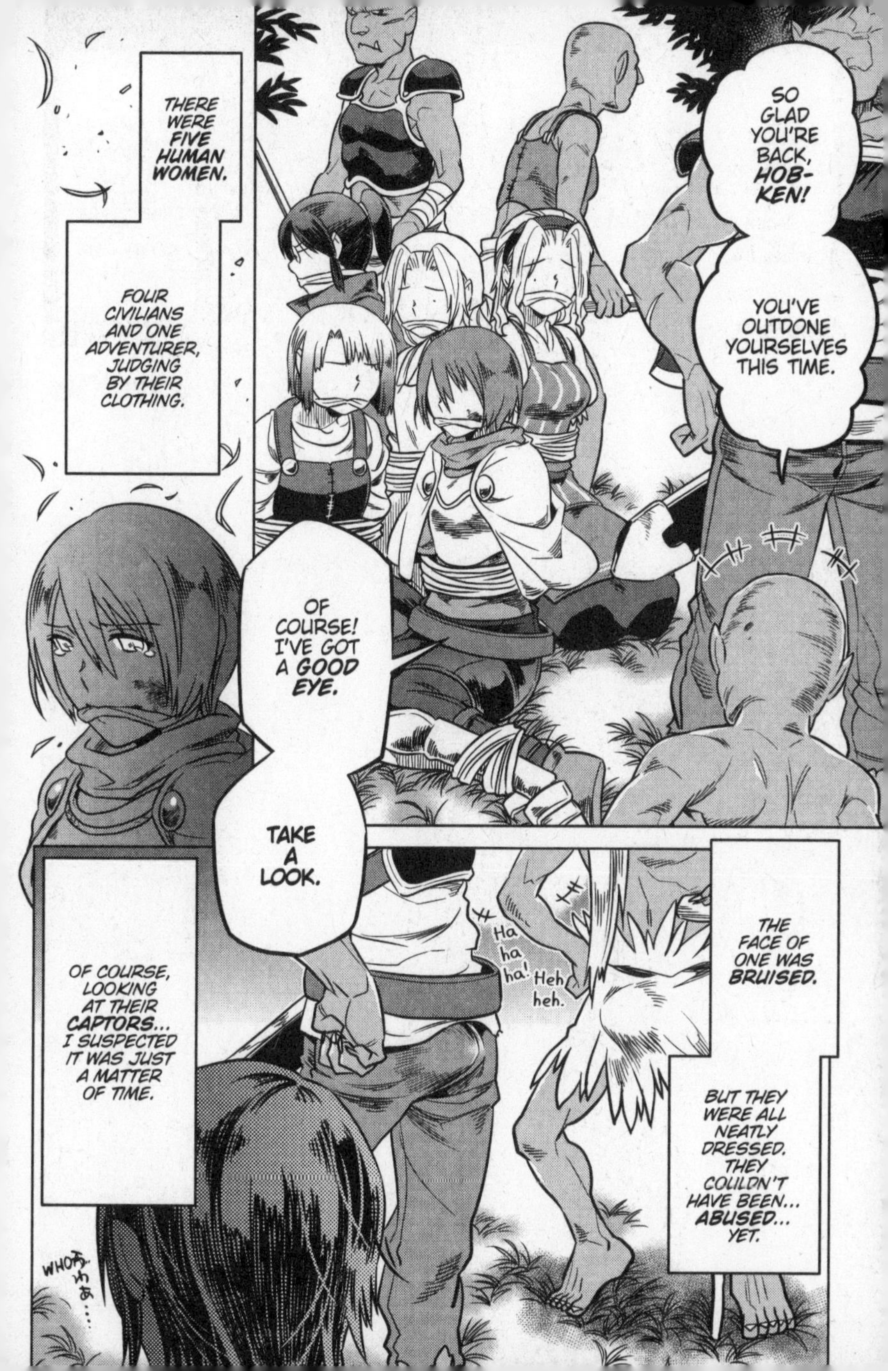
SO GLAD YOU'RE BACK, HOB-KEN!
YOU'VE OUTDONE YOURSELVES THIS TIME.
OF COURSE! I'VE GOT A GOOD EYE.
TAKE A LOOK.
THERE WERE FIVE HUMAN WOMEN.
FOUR CIVILIANS AND ONE ADVENTURER, JUDGING BY THEIR CLOTHING.
THE FACE OF ONE WAS BRUISED.
BUT THEY WERE ALL NEATLY DRESSED. THEY COULDN'T HAVE BEEN... ABUSED... YET.
Ha ha ha!
Heh heh.
OF COURSE, LOOKING AT THEIR CAPTORS... I SUSPECTED IT WAS JUST A MATTER OF TIME.
WHOA....

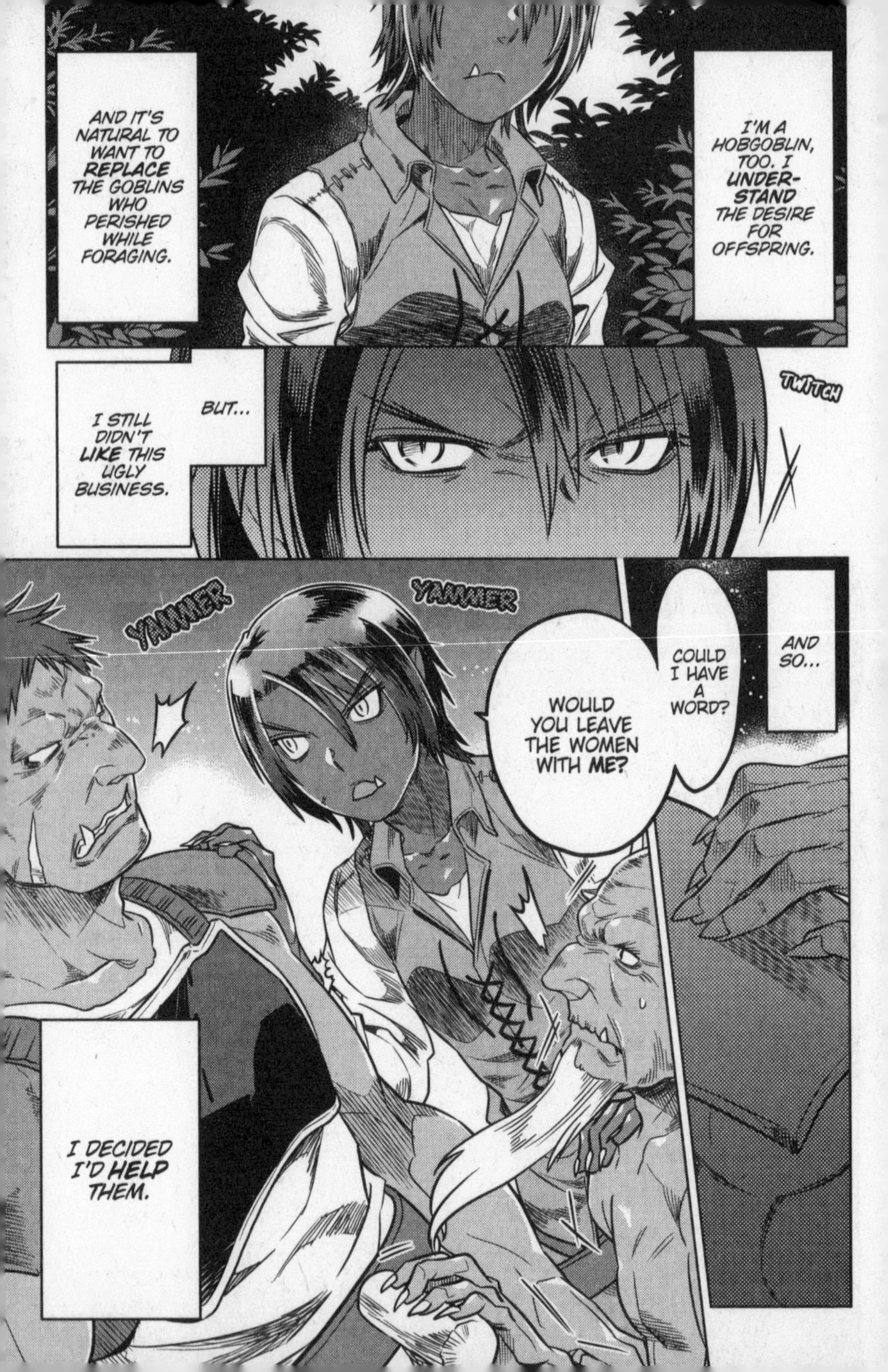
I'M A HOBGOBLIN, TOO. I UNDERSTAND THE DESIRE FOR OFFSPRING.
AND IT'S NATURAL TO WANT TO REPLACE THE GOBLINS WHO PERISHED WHILE FORAGING.
TWITCH
BUT...
I STILL DIDN'T LIKE THIS UGLY BUSINESS.
AND SO...
COULD I HAVE A WORD?
WOULD YOU LEAVE THE WOMEN WITH ME?
YAMMER
YAMMER
I DECIDED I'D HELP THEM.

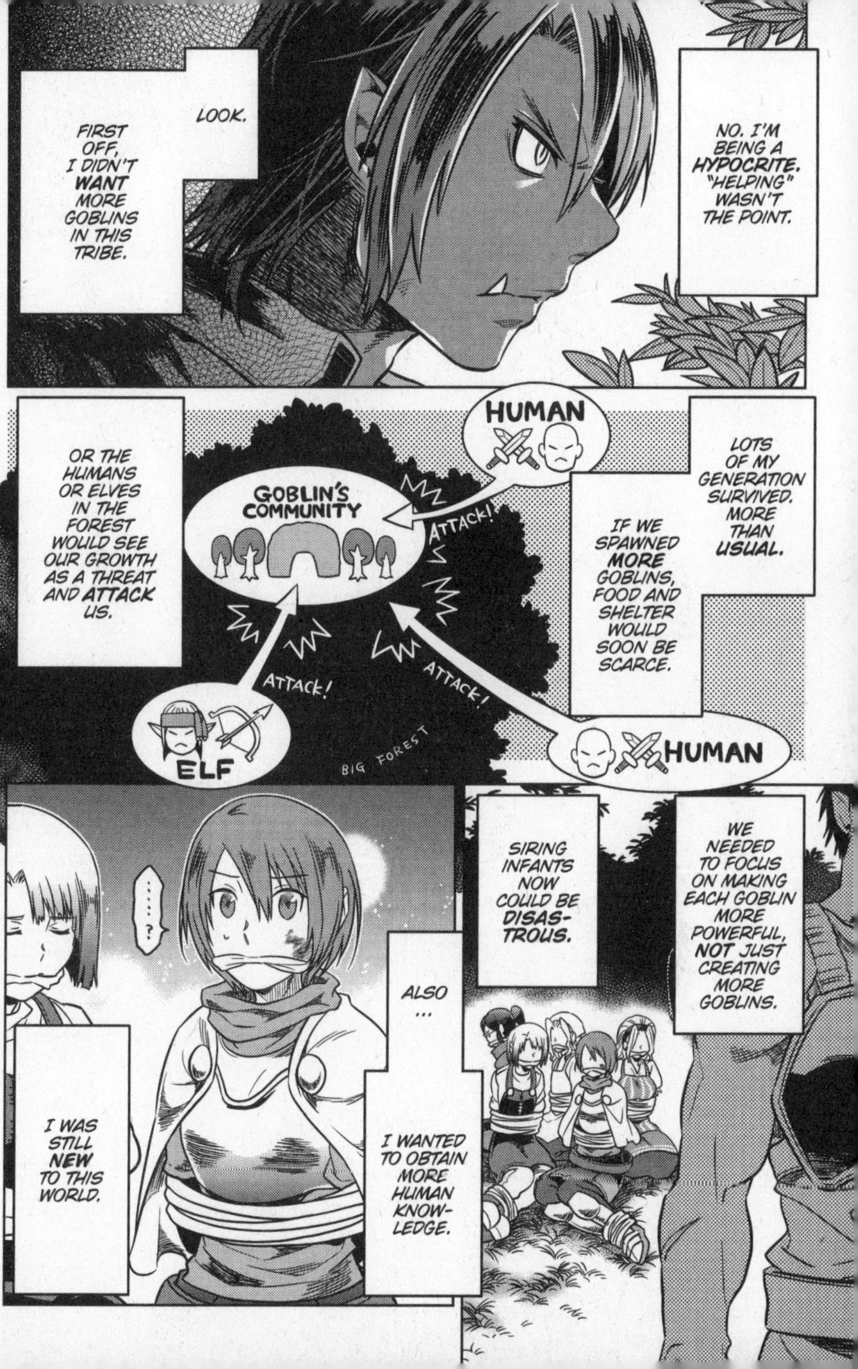

NO. I'M BEING A HYPOCRITE. "HELPING" WASN'T THE POINT.
LOOK.
FIRST OFF, I DIDN'T WANT MORE GOBLINS IN THIS TRIBE.
LOTS OF MY GENERATION SURVIVED. MORE THAN USUAL.
IF WE SPAWNED MORE GOBLINS, FOOD AND SHELTER WOULD SOON BE SCARCE.
HUMAN
ATTACK!
GOBLIN'S COMMUNITY
ATTACK!
HUMAN
ATTACK!
ELF
BIG FOREST
OR THE HUMANS OR ELVES IN THE FOREST WOULD SEE OUR GROWTH AS A THREAT AND ATTACK US.
WE NEEDED TO FOCUS ON MAKING EACH GOBLIN MORE POWERFUL, NOT JUST CREATING MORE GOBLINS.
SIRING INFANTS NOW COULD BE DISASTROUS.
.....?
ALSO ...
I WANTED TO OBTAIN MORE HUMAN KNOWLEDGE.
I WAS STILL NEW TO THIS WORLD.

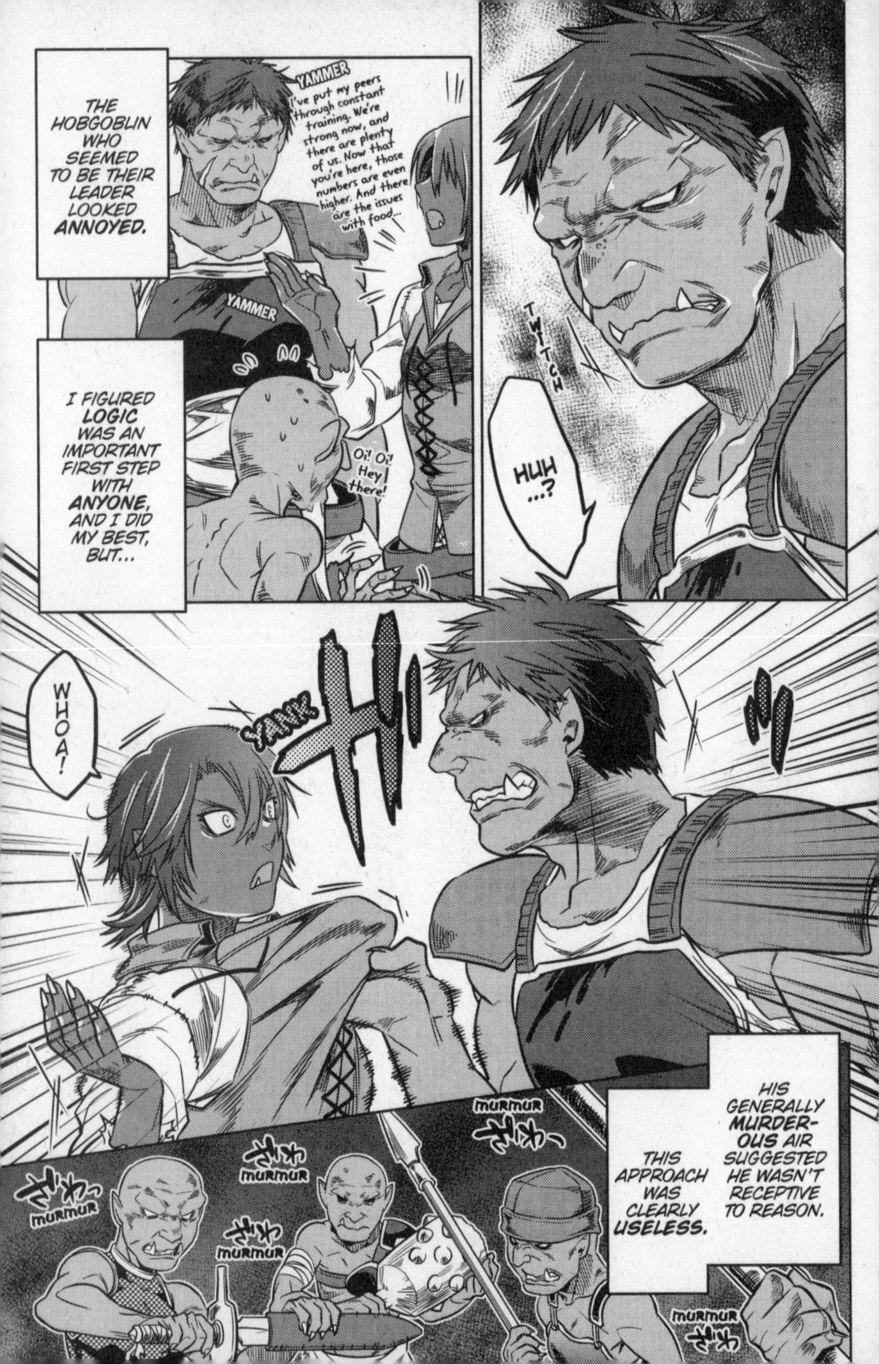
TWITCH
HUH ...?
YAMMER
I've put my peers through constant training. We're strong now, and there are plenty of us. Now that you're here, those numbers are even higher. And there are the issues with food...
THE HOBGOBLIN WHO SEEMED TO BE THEIR LEADER LOOKED ANNOYED.
YAMMER
Oi! Oi! Hey there!
I FIGURED LOGIC WAS AN IMPORTANT FIRST STEP WITH ANYONE, AND I DID MY BEST, BUT...
YANK
WHOA!
HIS GENERALLY MURDEROUS AIR SUGGESTED HE WASN'T RECEPTIVE TO REASON.
THIS APPROACH WAS CLEARLY USELESS.
murmur
murmur
murmur
murmur
murmur

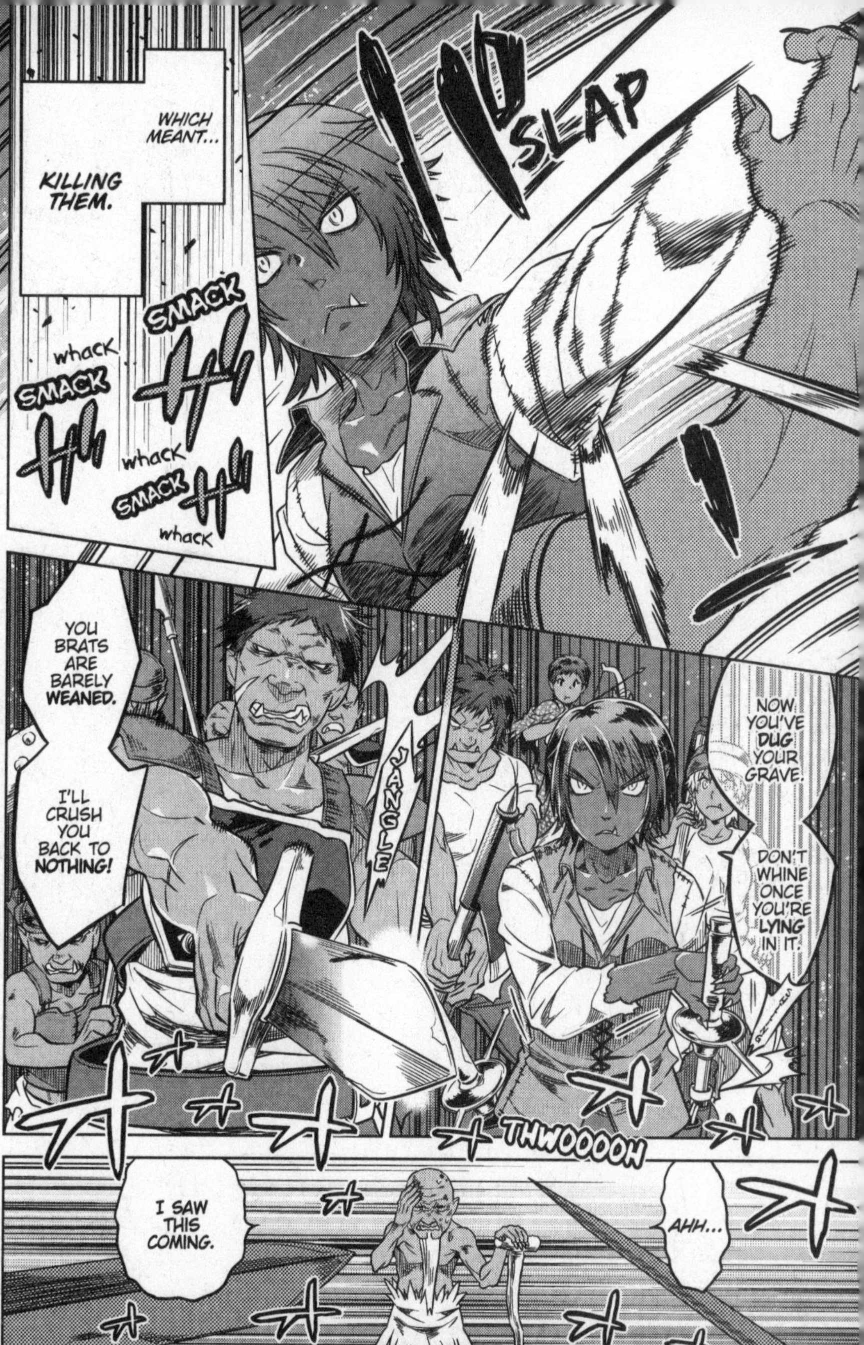
SLAP
WHICH MEANT...
KILLING THEM.
SMACK
whack
SMACK
whack
SMACK
whack
NOW YOU'VE DUG YOUR GRAVE.
DON'T WHINE ONCE YOU'RE LYING IN IT.
JANGLE
YOU BRATS ARE BARELY WEANED.
I'LL CRUSH YOU BACK TO NOTHING!
THWOOOOOH
AHH...
I SAW THIS COMING.

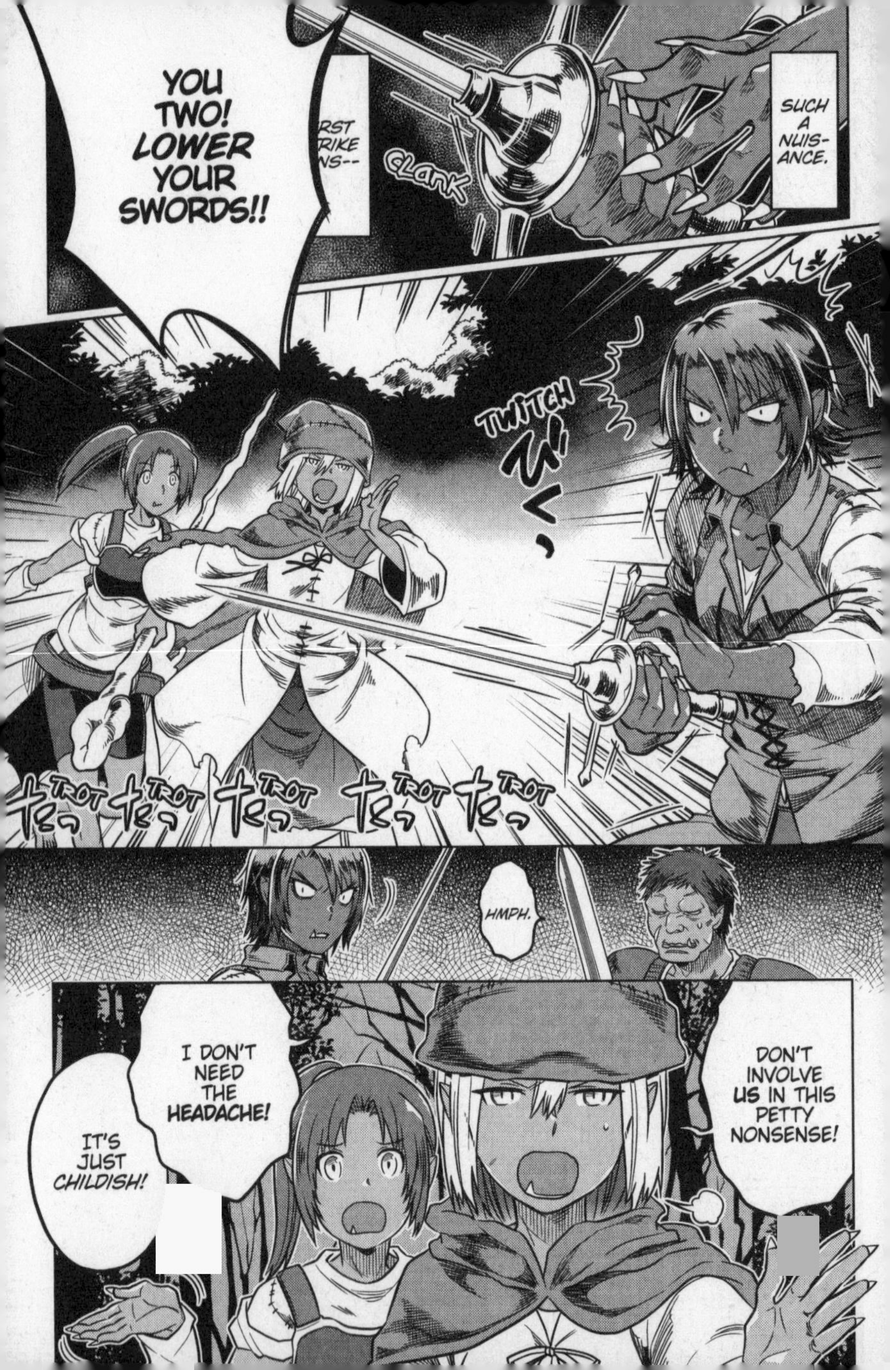
SUCH A NUISANCE.
CLANK
YOU TWO! LOWER YOUR SWORDS!!
TWITCH
ぴくっ
TROT
たっ
TROT
たっ
TROT
たっ
TROT
たっ
TROT
たっ
HMPH.
DON'T INVOLVE US IN THIS PETTY NONSENSE!
I DON'T NEED THE HEADACHE!
IT'S JUST CHILDISH!

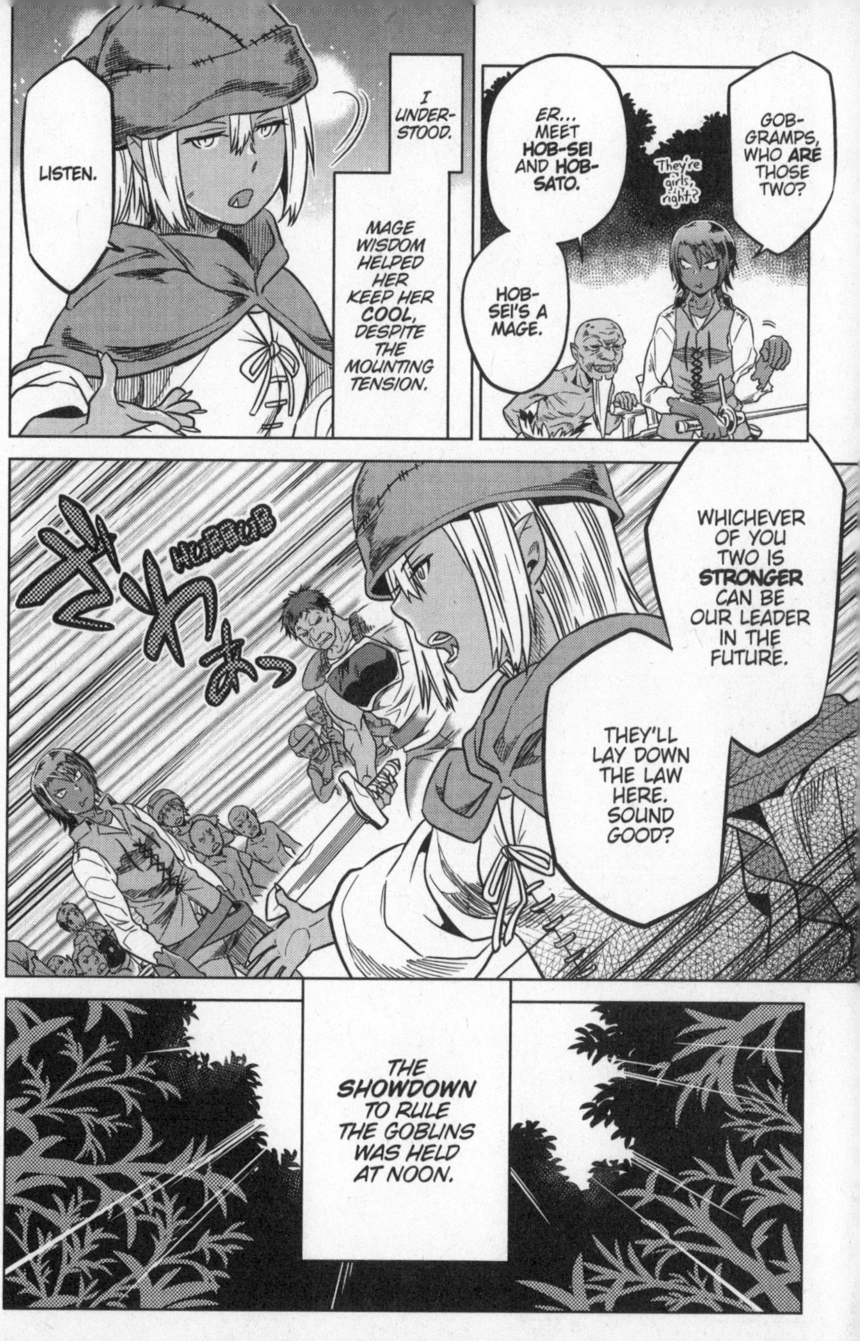
GOB-GRAMPS, WHO ARE THOSE TWO?
They're girls, right?
ER... MEET HOB-SEI AND HOB-SATO.
HOB-SEI'S A MAGE.
I UNDERSTOOD.
MAGE WISDOM HELPED HER KEEP HER COOL, DESPITE THE MOUNTING TENSION.
LISTEN.
WHICHEVER OF YOU TWO IS STRONGER CAN BE OUR LEADER IN THE FUTURE.
THEY'LL LAY DOWN THE LAW HERE. SOUND GOOD?
ざわあっ
THE SHOWDOWN TO RULE THE GOBLINS WAS HELD AT NOON.

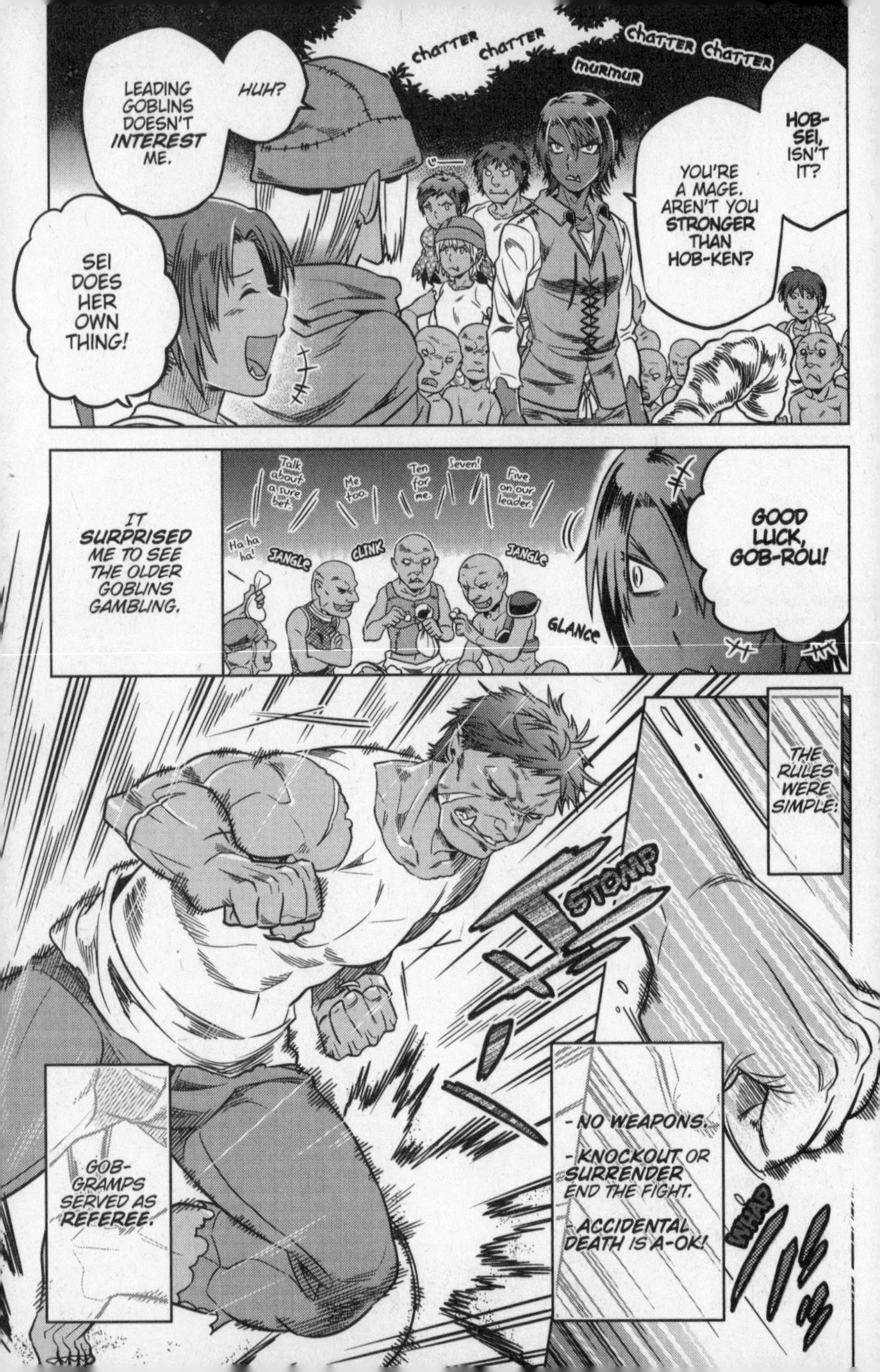
CHATTER CHATTER
CHATTER CHATTER
MURMUR
HOB-SEI, ISN'T IT?
YOU'RE A MAGE. AREN'T YOU STRONGER THAN HOB-KEN?
HUH?
LEADING GOBLINS DOESN'T INTEREST ME.
SEI DOES HER OWN THING!
GOOD LUCK, GOB-ROU!
GLANCE
Five on our leader.
Seven!
Ten for me.
Me too.
Talk about a sure bet.
JANGLE
CLINK
JANGLE
Ha ha ha!
IT SURPRISED ME TO SEE THE OLDER GOBLINS GAMBLING.
THE RULES WERE SIMPLE:
STOMP
- NO WEAPONS.
- KNOCKOUT OR SURRENDER END THE FIGHT.
- ACCIDENTAL DEATH IS A-OK!
WHAP
GOB-GRAMPS SERVED AS REFEREE.

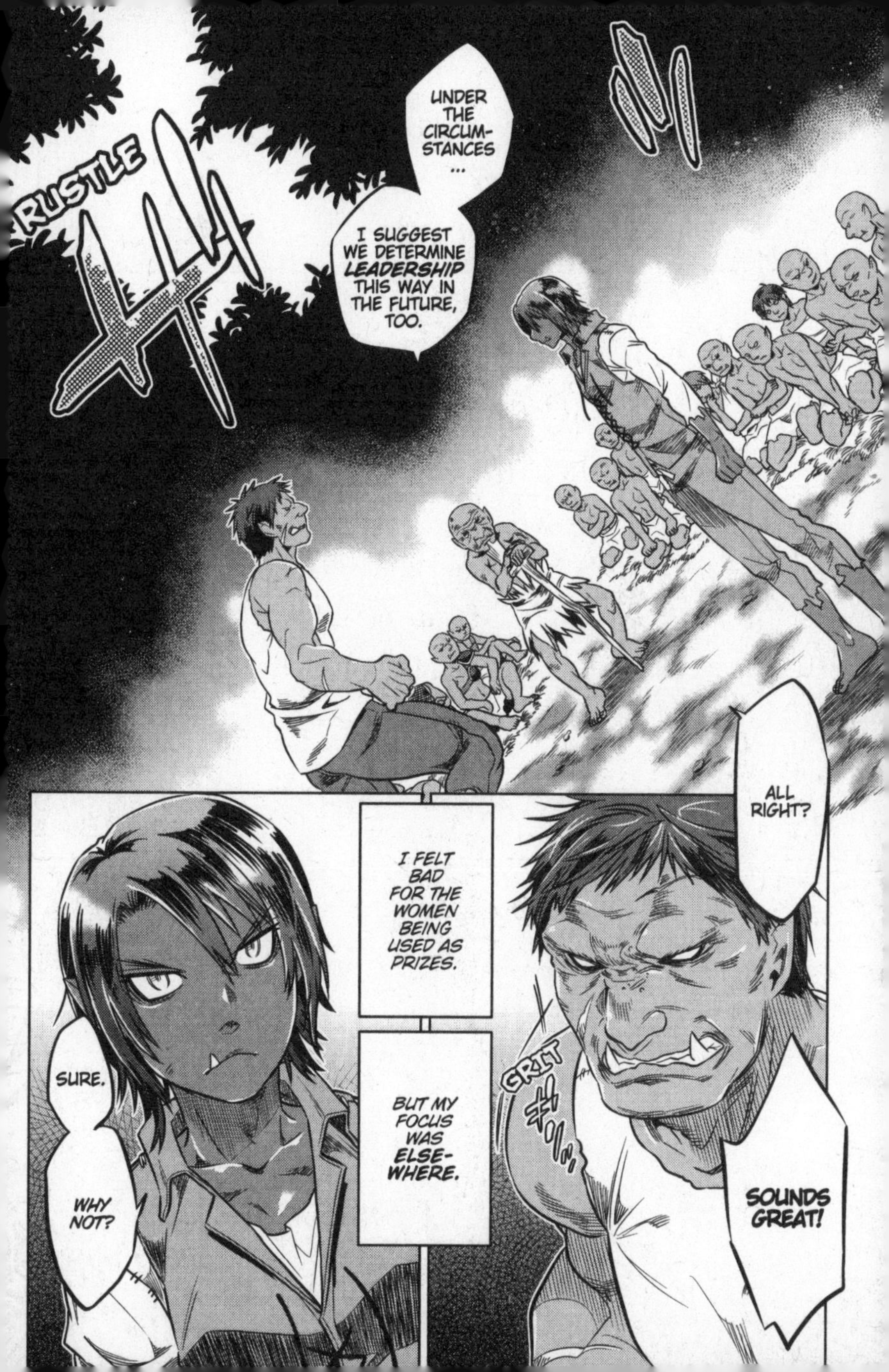
UNDER THE CIRCUM-STANCES...
I SUGGEST WE DETERMINE LEADERSHIP THIS WAY IN THE FUTURE, TOO.
RUSTLE
ALL RIGHT?
GRIT
SOUNDS GREAT!
I FELT BAD FOR THE WOMEN BEING USED AS PRIZES.
BUT MY FOCUS WAS ELSE-WHERE.
SURE.
WHY NOT?

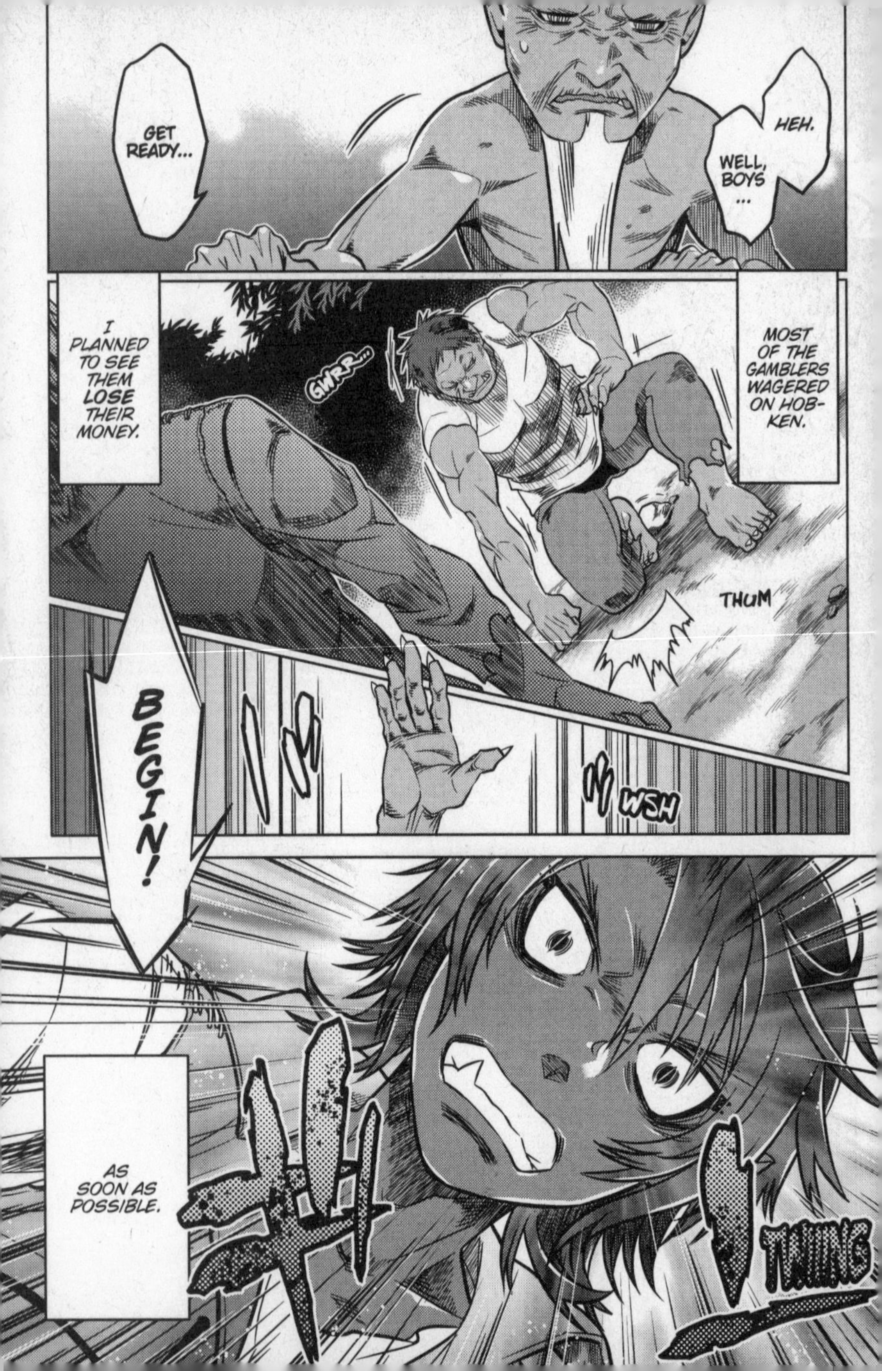
HEH.
WELL, BOYS ...
GET READY...
MOST OF THE GAMBLERS WAGERED ON HOB-KEN.
GWRR...
THUM
I PLANNED TO SEE THEM LOSE THEIR MONEY.
WSH
BEGIN!
TWING
AS SOON AS POSSIBLE.

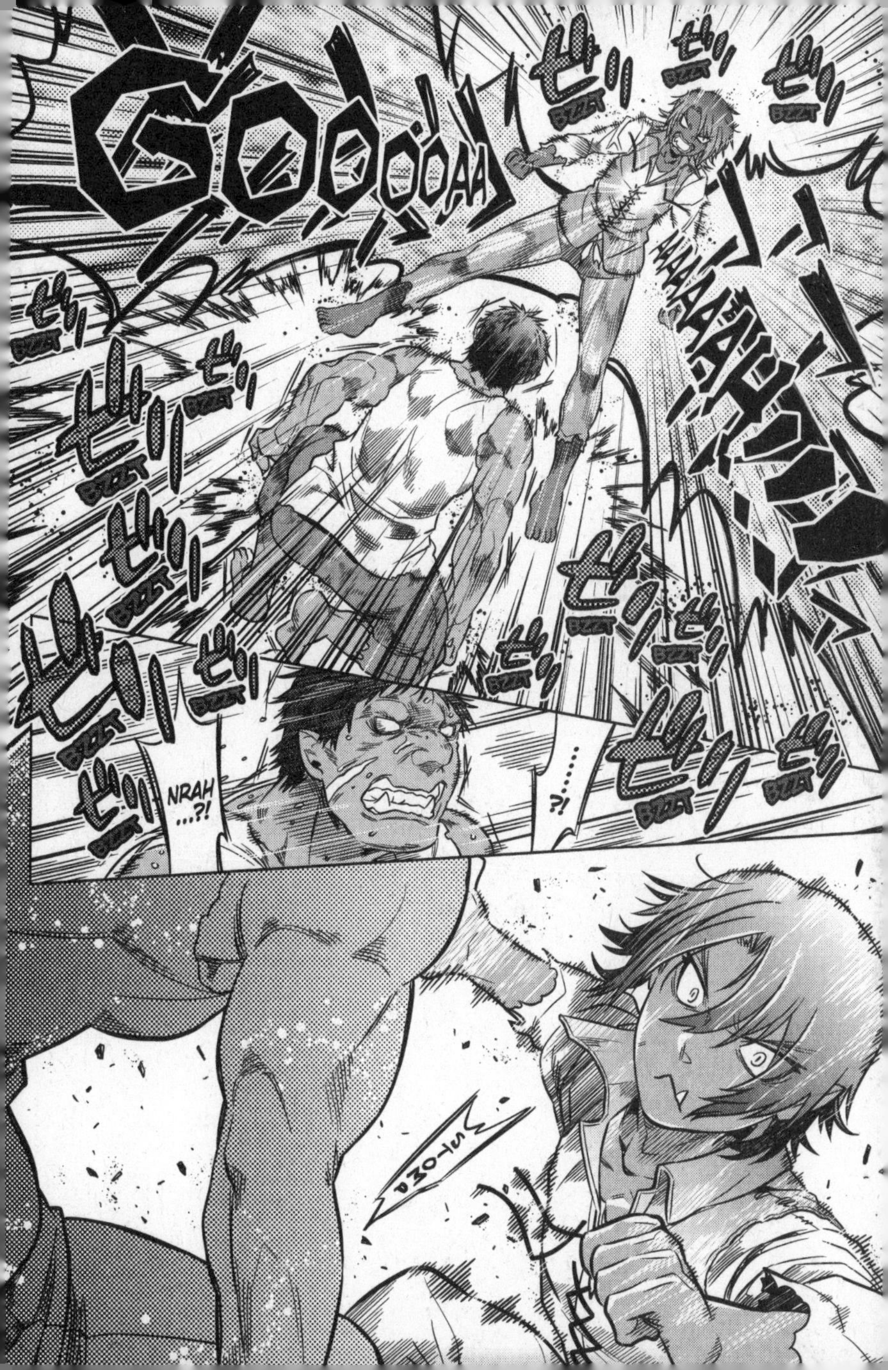

ぜ BZZT
ぜ BZZT
ぜ BZZT
GOOOOAA
AAAAAAAAH
ぜ BZZT
ぜ BZZT
ぜ BZZT
ぜ BZZT
ぜ BZZT
ぜ BZZT
ぜ BZZT
ぜ BZZT
ぜ BZZT
ぜ BZZT
......?!
NRAH ...?!
ぜ BZZT

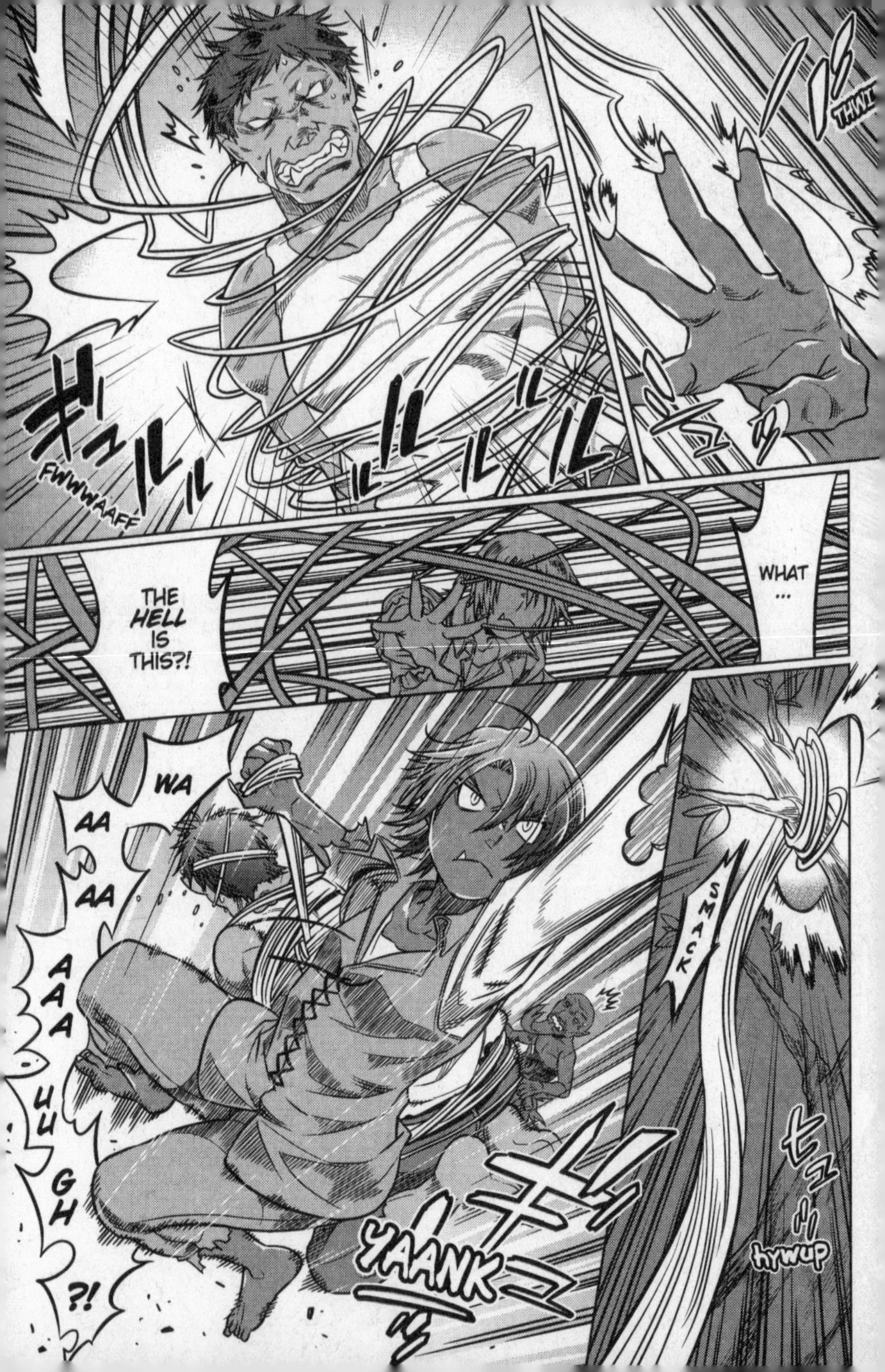

THWI
ギュルルルルルル
FWWWAAFF
WHAT...
THE HELL IS THIS?!
SMACK
ヒュッ
hywup
ギュ
YAANK
WA AA AA AAAA UUGH GH?!

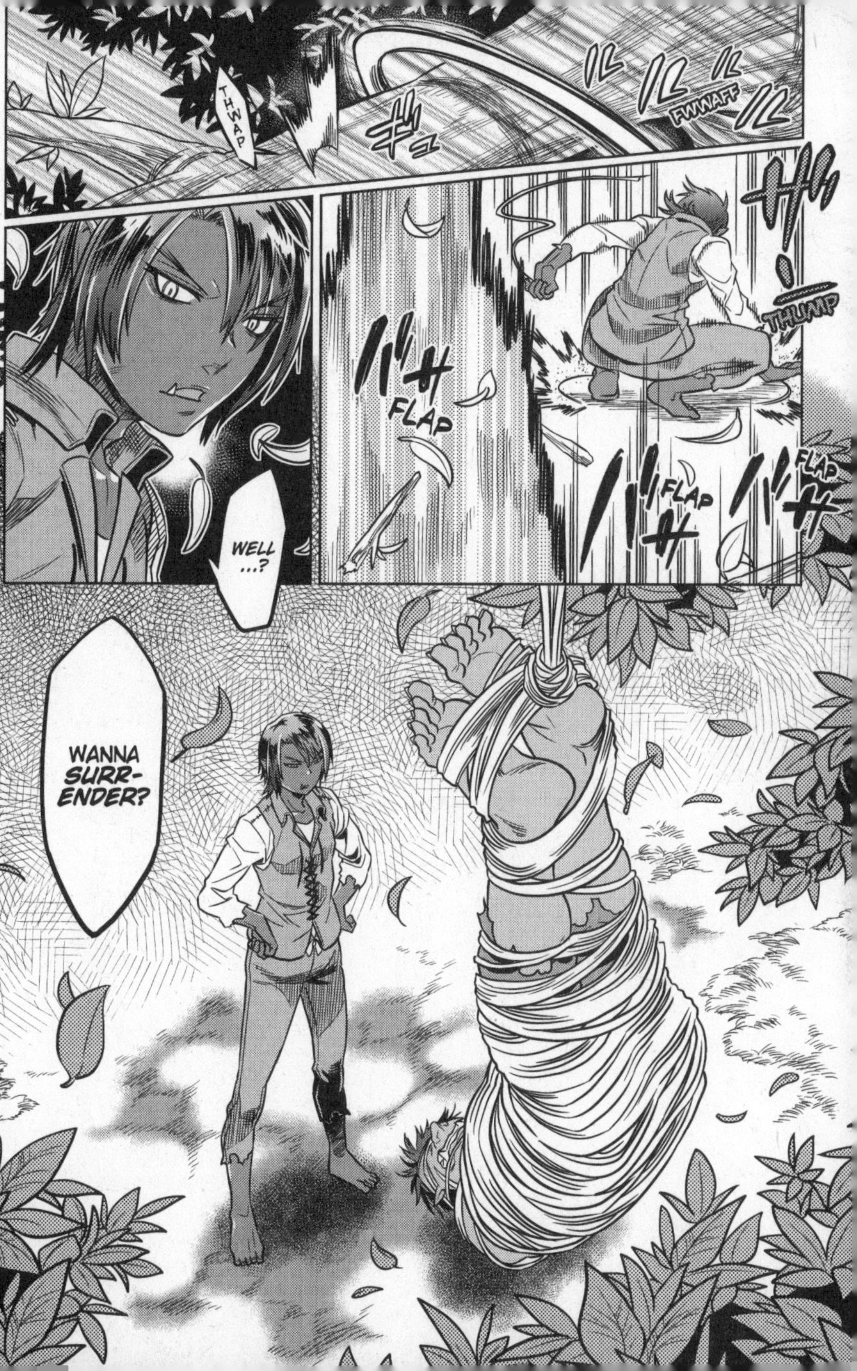

FWWAFF
THWAP
THUMP
FLAP
FLAP
FLAP
WELL ...?
WANNA SURR-ENDER?

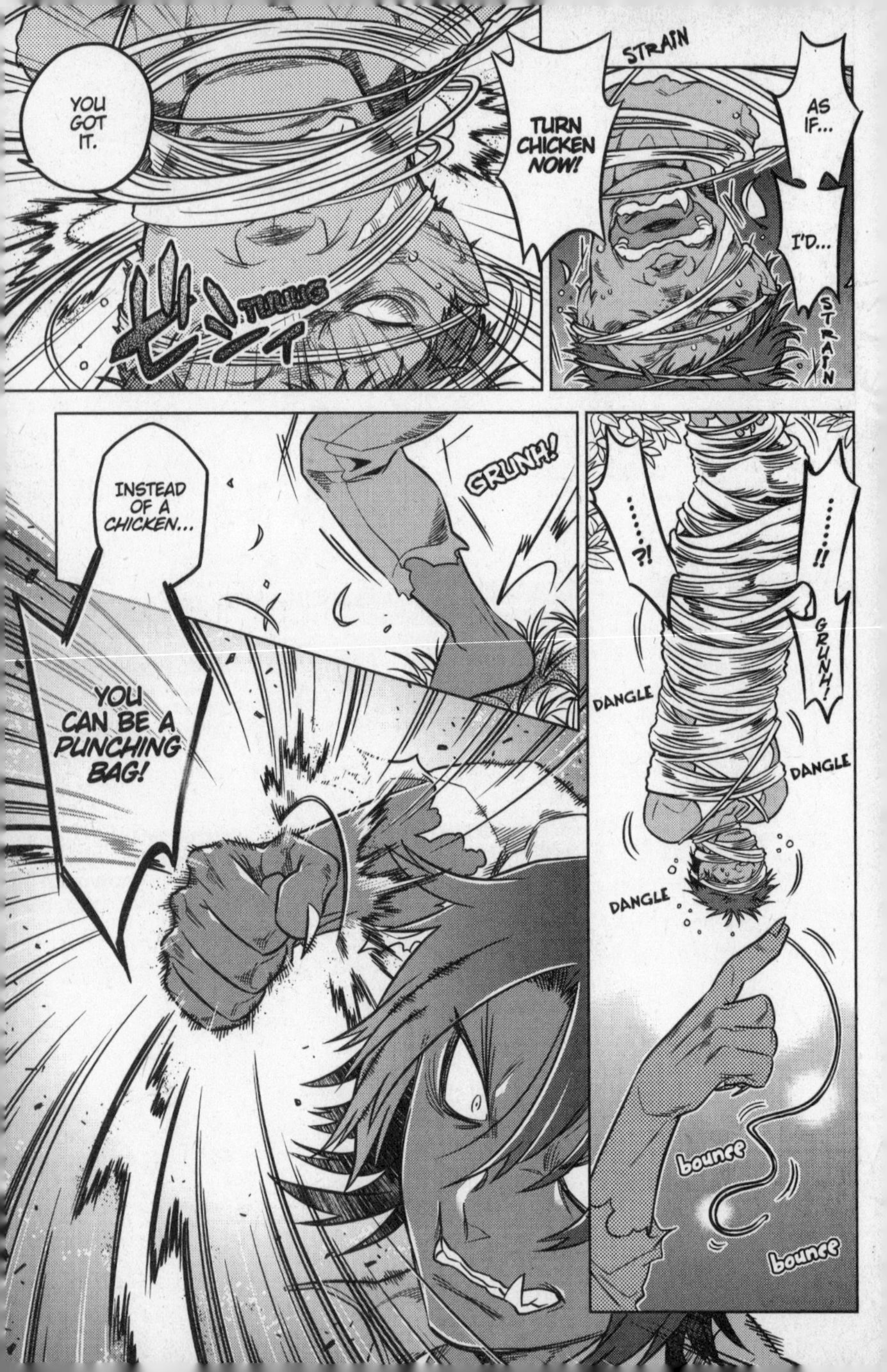
STRAIN
TURN CHICKEN NOW!
AS IF...
I'D...
STRAIN
YOU GOT IT.
......!!
......?!
GRUNH!
DANGLE
DANGLE
DANGLE
bounce
bounce
GRUNH!
INSTEAD OF A CHICKEN...
YOU CAN BE A PUNCHING BAG!

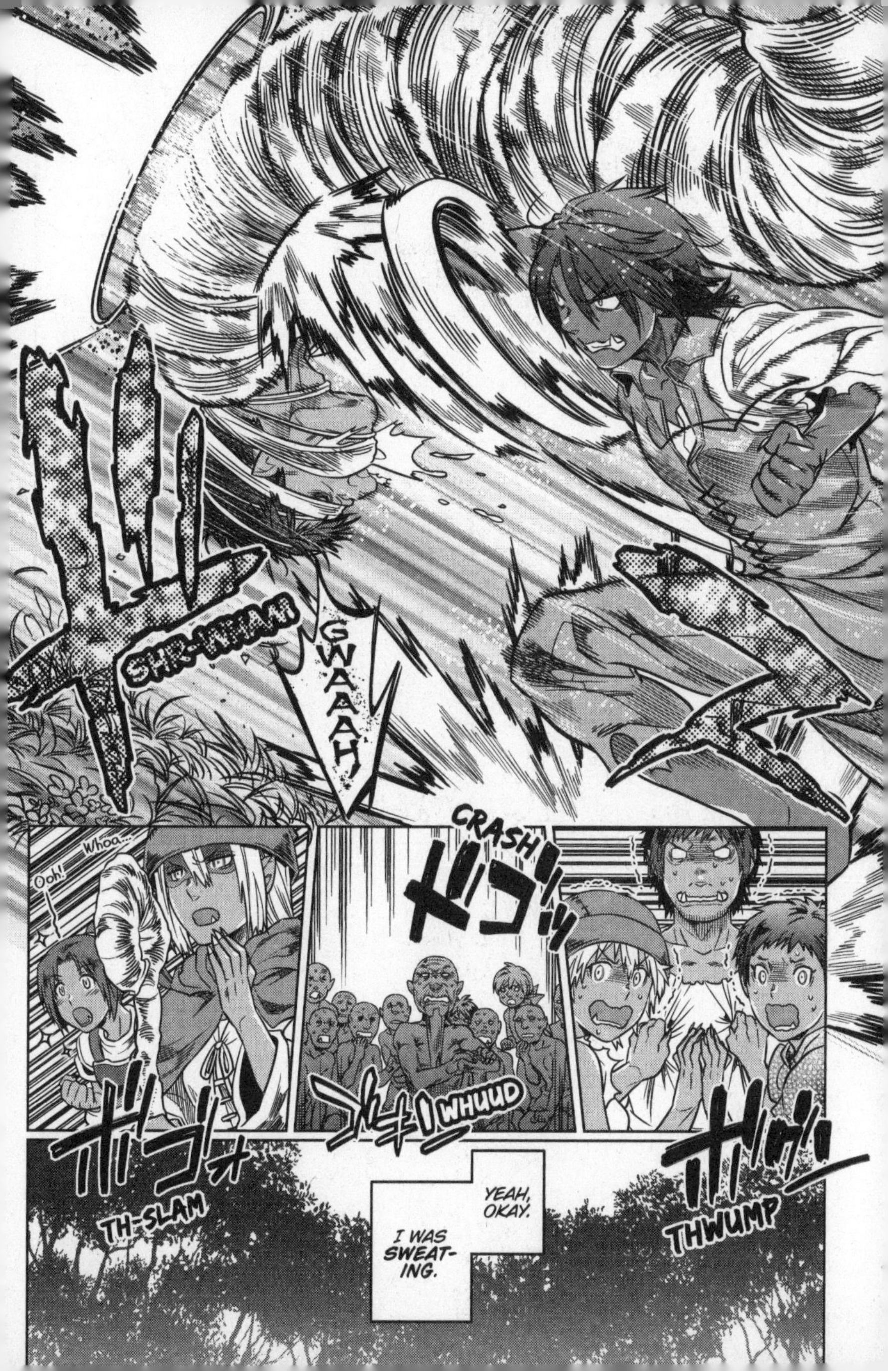
GWAAAH
SHR-WHAM!
CRASH
WHUUD
Whoa...
Ooh!
THWUMP
YEAH, OKAY.
I WAS SWEAT-ING.
TH-SLAM

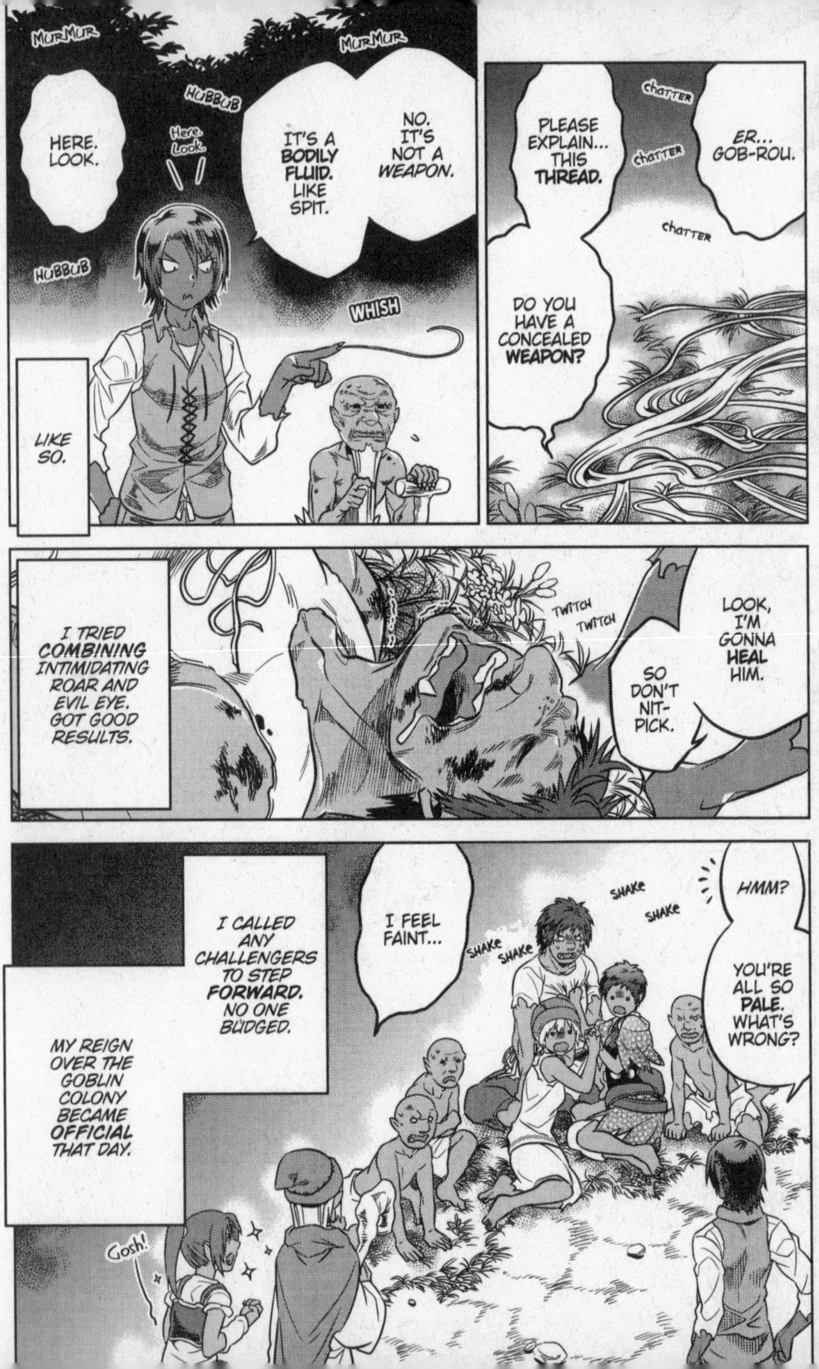

ER... GOB-ROU.
chatter
PLEASE EXPLAIN... THIS THREAD.
chatter
chatter
DO YOU HAVE A CONCEALED WEAPON?
MURMUR
MURMUR
NO. IT'S NOT A WEAPON.
IT'S A BODILY FLUID. LIKE SPIT.
HUBBUB
HERE. LOOK.
Here. Look.
HUBBUB
WHISH
LIKE SO.
LOOK, I'M GONNA HEAL HIM.
SO DON'T NIT-PICK.
TWITCH
TWITCH
I TRIED COMBINING INTIMIDATING ROAR AND EVIL EYE. GOT GOOD RESULTS.
HMM?
YOU'RE ALL SO PALE. WHAT'S WRONG?
SHAKE
SHAKE
SHAKE
SHAKE
I FEEL FAINT...
I CALLED ANY CHALLENGERS TO STEP FORWARD. NO ONE BUDGED.
MY REIGN OVER THE GOBLIN COLONY BECAME OFFICIAL THAT DAY.
Gosh!

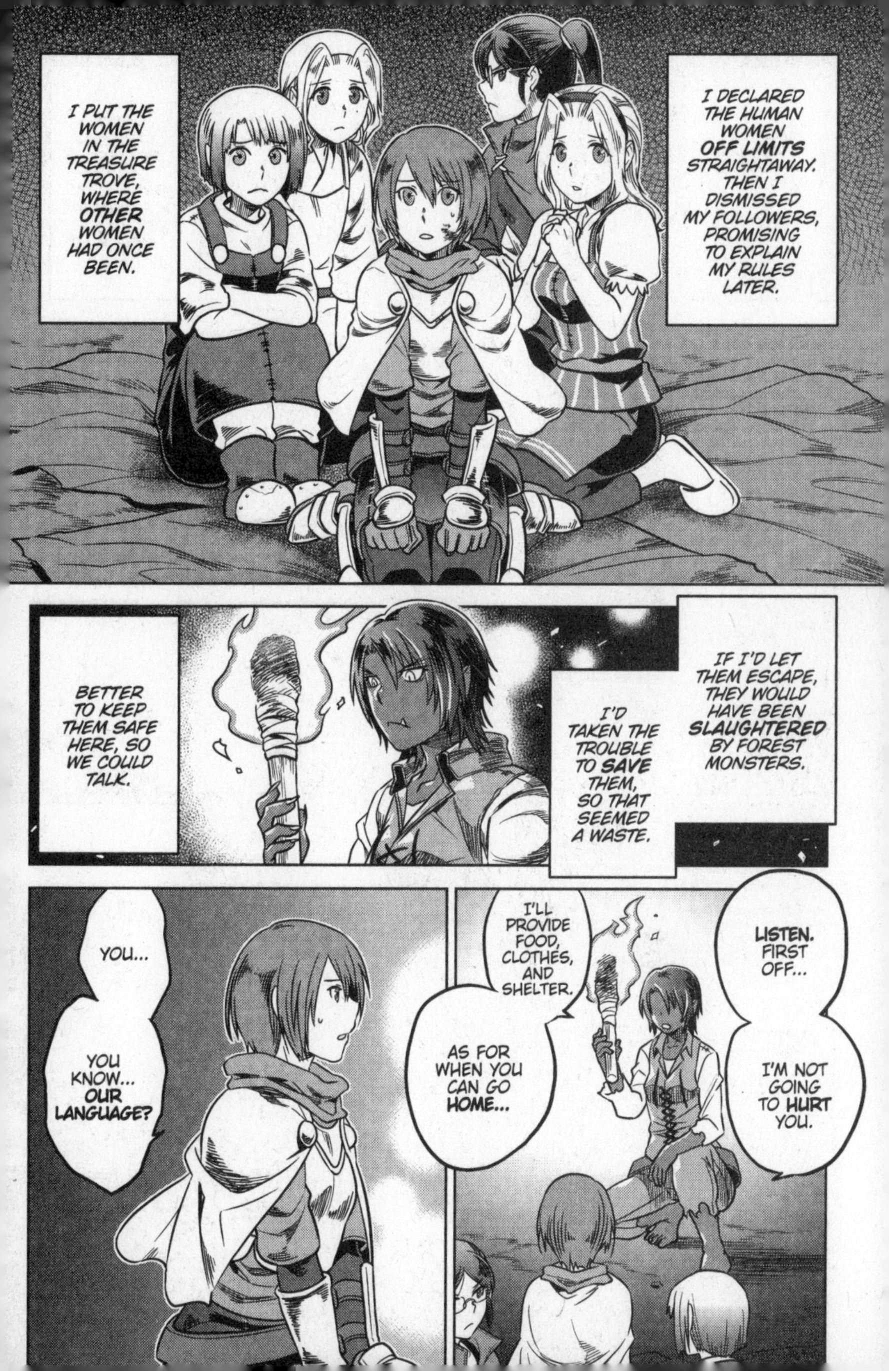
I DECLARED THE HUMAN WOMEN **OFF LIMITS** STRAIGHTAWAY. THEN I DISMISSED MY FOLLOWERS, PROMISING TO EXPLAIN MY RULES LATER.
I PUT THE WOMEN IN THE TREASURE TROVE, WHERE **OTHER** WOMEN HAD ONCE BEEN.
IF I'D LET THEM ESCAPE, THEY WOULD HAVE BEEN **SLAUGHTERED** BY FOREST MONSTERS.
I'D TAKEN THE TROUBLE TO **SAVE** THEM, SO THAT SEEMED A WASTE.
BETTER TO KEEP THEM SAFE HERE, SO WE COULD TALK.
LISTEN. FIRST OFF...
I'M NOT GOING TO **HURT** YOU.
I'LL PROVIDE FOOD, CLOTHES, AND SHELTER.
AS FOR WHEN YOU CAN GO **HOME**...
YOU...
YOU KNOW... **OUR LANGUAGE?**

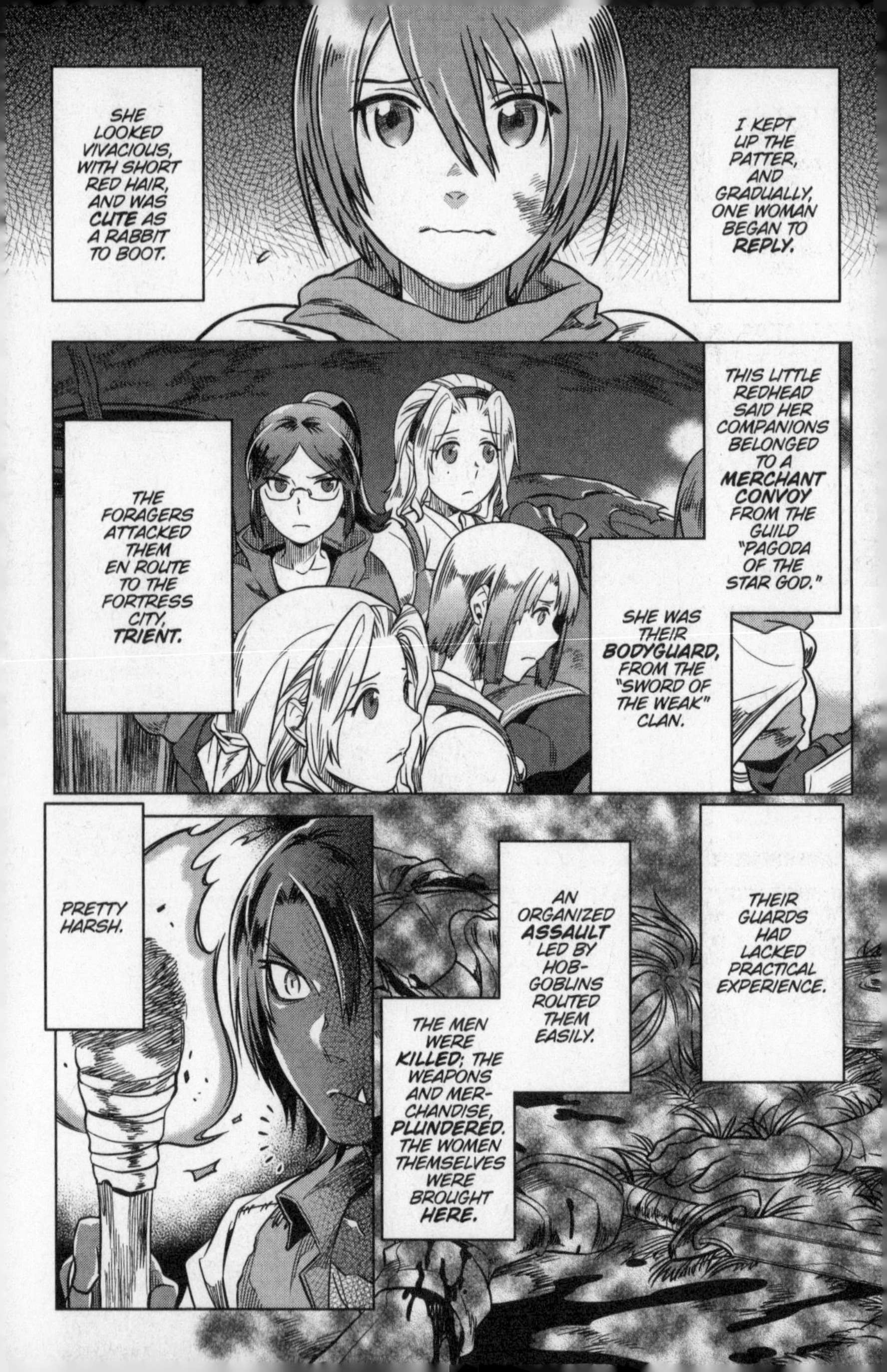
I KEPT UP THE PATTER, AND GRADUALLY, ONE WOMAN BEGAN TO REPLY.
SHE LOOKED VIVACIOUS, WITH SHORT RED HAIR, AND WAS CUTE AS A RABBIT TO BOOT.
THIS LITTLE REDHEAD SAID HER COMPANIONS BELONGED TO A MERCHANT CONVOY FROM THE GUILD "PAGODA OF THE STAR GOD."
SHE WAS THEIR BODYGUARD, FROM THE "SWORD OF THE WEAK" CLAN.
THE FORAGERS ATTACKED THEM EN ROUTE TO THE FORTRESS CITY, TRIENT.
THEIR GUARDS HAD LACKED PRACTICAL EXPERIENCE.
AN ORGANIZED ASSAULT LED BY HOB-GOBLINS ROUTED THEM EASILY.
THE MEN WERE KILLED; THE WEAPONS AND MER-CHANDISE, PLUNDERED. THE WOMEN THEMSELVES WERE BROUGHT HERE.
PRETTY HARSH.

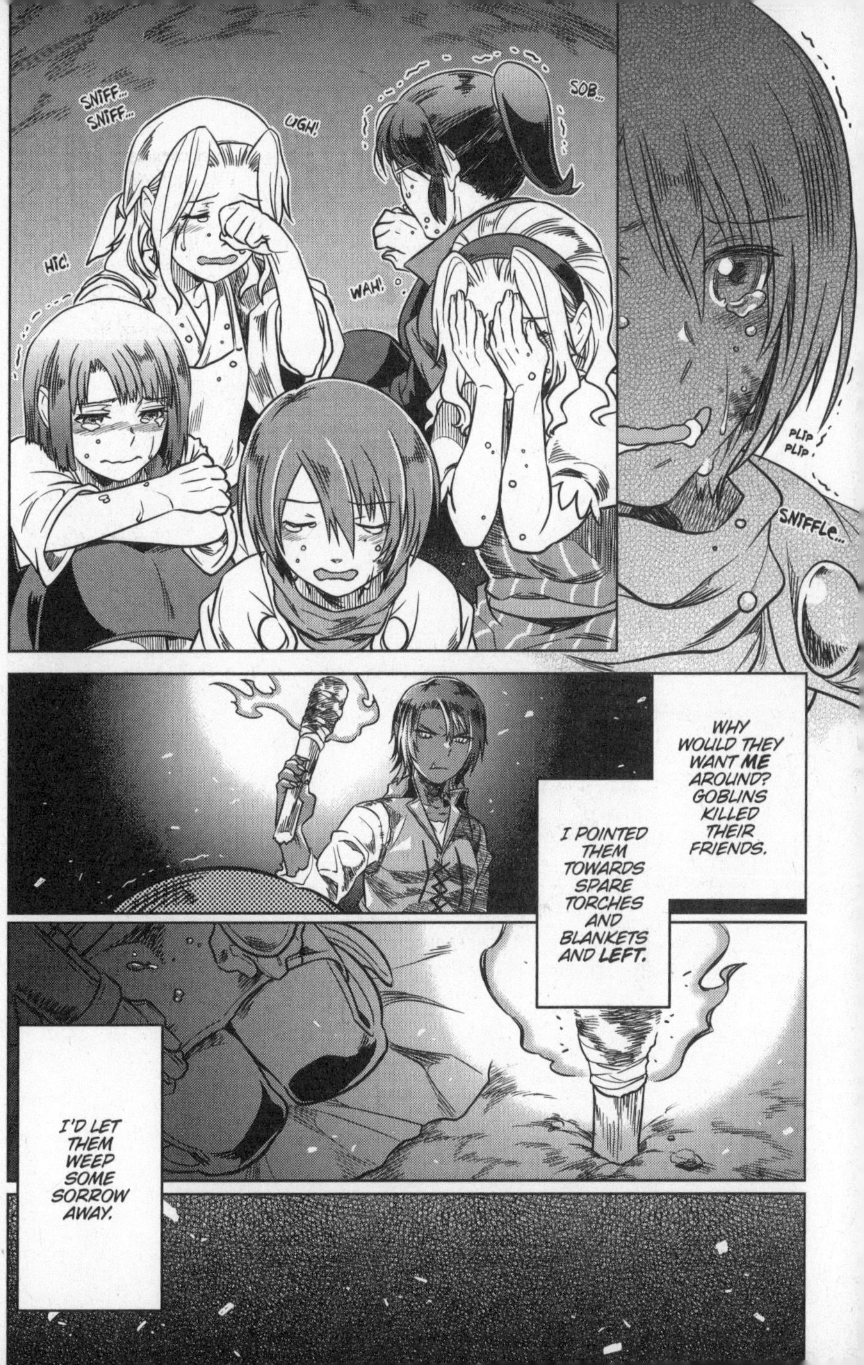
PLIP PLIP
SNIFFLE...
SOB...
UGH!
SNIFF... SNIFF...
WAH!
HIC!
WHY WOULD THEY WANT **ME** AROUND? GOBLINS KILLED THEIR FRIENDS.
I POINTED THEM TOWARDS SPARE TORCHES AND BLANKETS AND **LEFT.**
I'D LET THEM WEEP SOME SORROW AWAY.

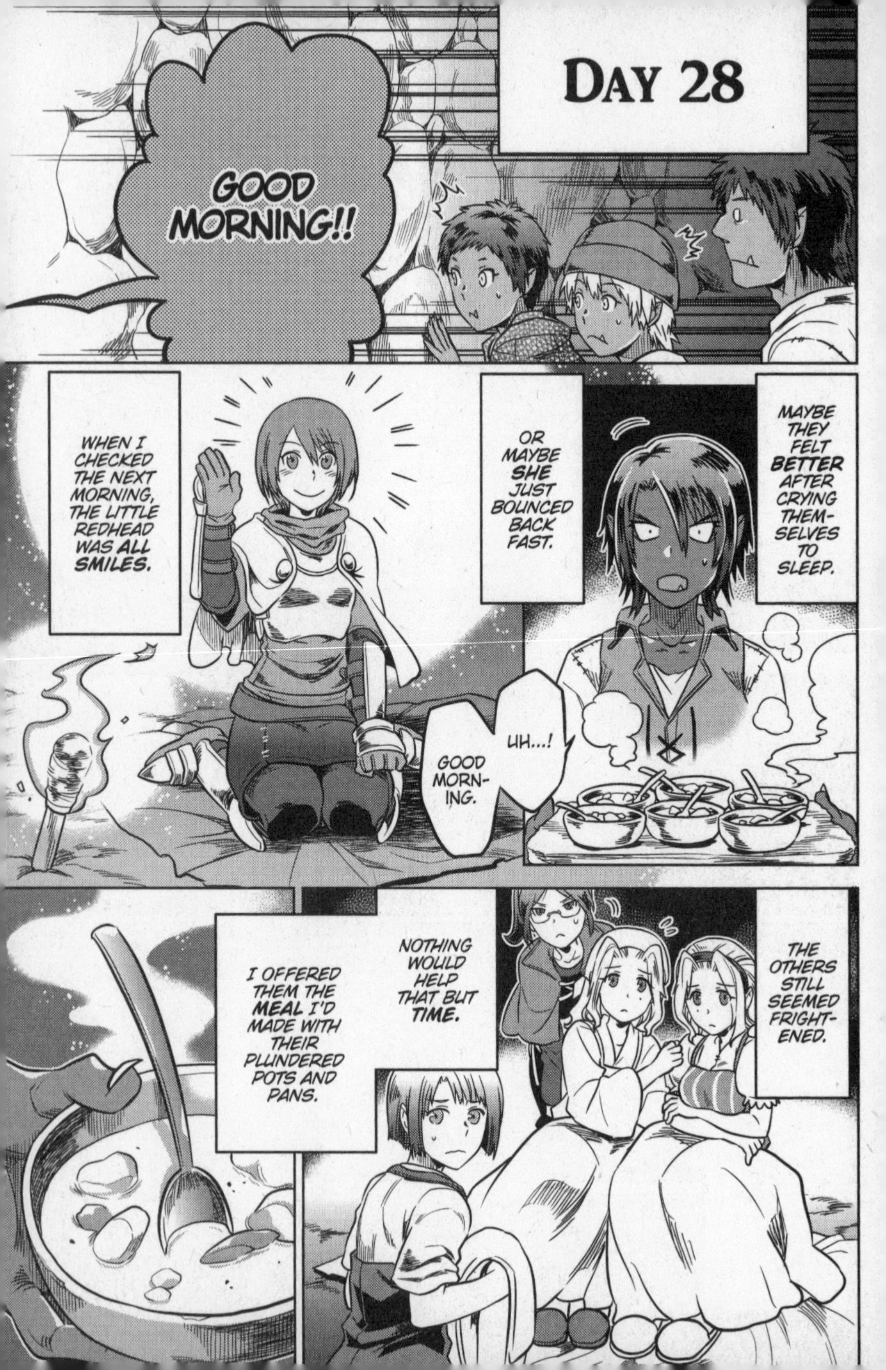
DAY 28
GOOD MORNING!!
MAYBE THEY FELT BETTER AFTER CRYING THEMSELVES TO SLEEP.
OR MAYBE SHE JUST BOUNCED BACK FAST.
UH...!
WHEN I CHECKED THE NEXT MORNING, THE LITTLE REDHEAD WAS ALL SMILES.
GOOD MORNING.
THE OTHERS STILL SEEMED FRIGHTENED.
NOTHING WOULD HELP THAT BUT TIME.
I OFFERED THEM THE MEAL I'D MADE WITH THEIR PLUNDERED POTS AND PANS.

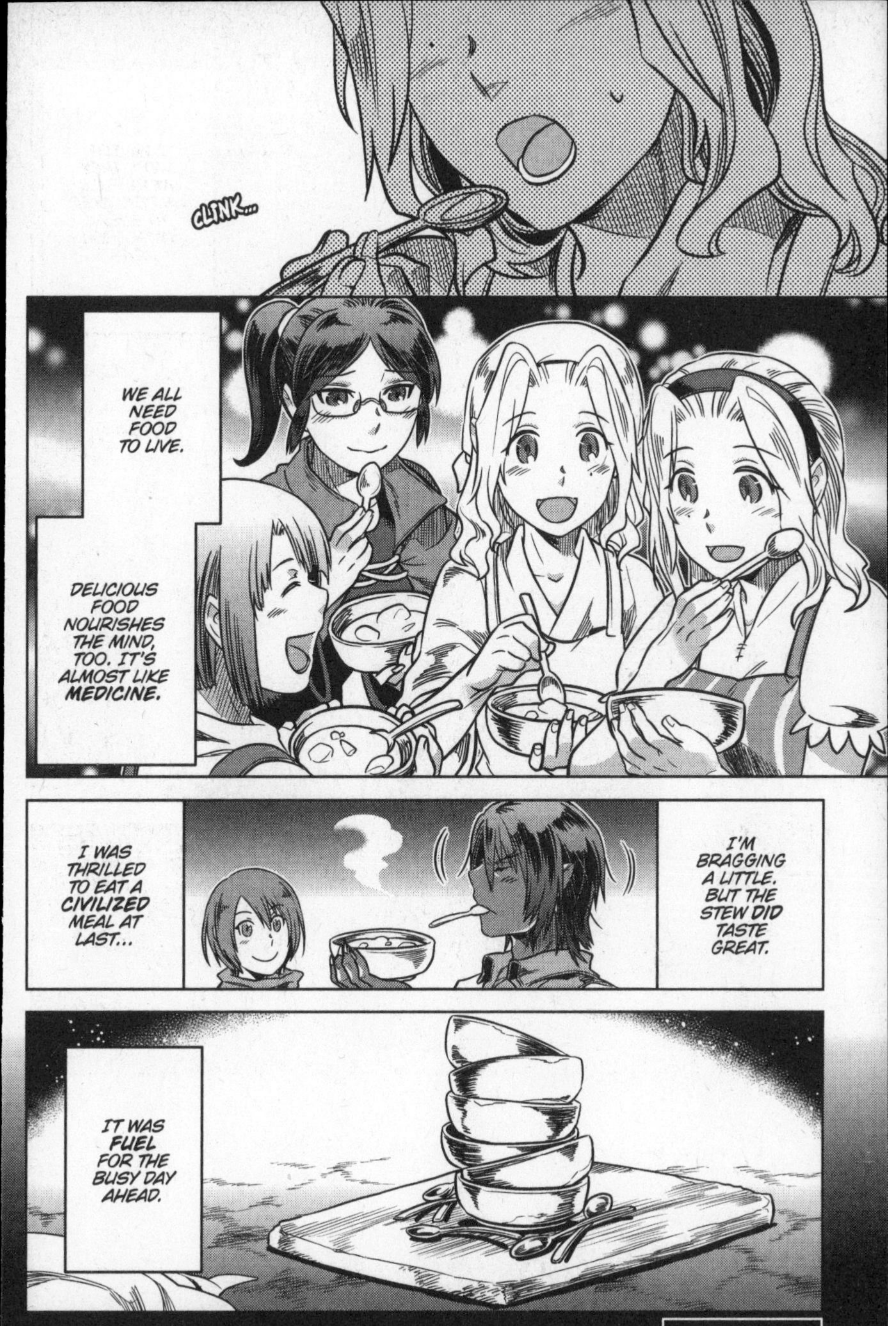
CLINK...
WE ALL NEED FOOD TO LIVE.
DELICIOUS FOOD NOURISHES THE MIND, TOO. IT'S ALMOST LIKE MEDICINE.
I'M BRAGGING A LITTLE. BUT THE STEW DID TASTE GREAT.
I WAS THRILLED TO EAT A CIVILIZED MEAL AT LAST...
IT WAS FUEL FOR THE BUSY DAY AHEAD.

▶ CONTINUE

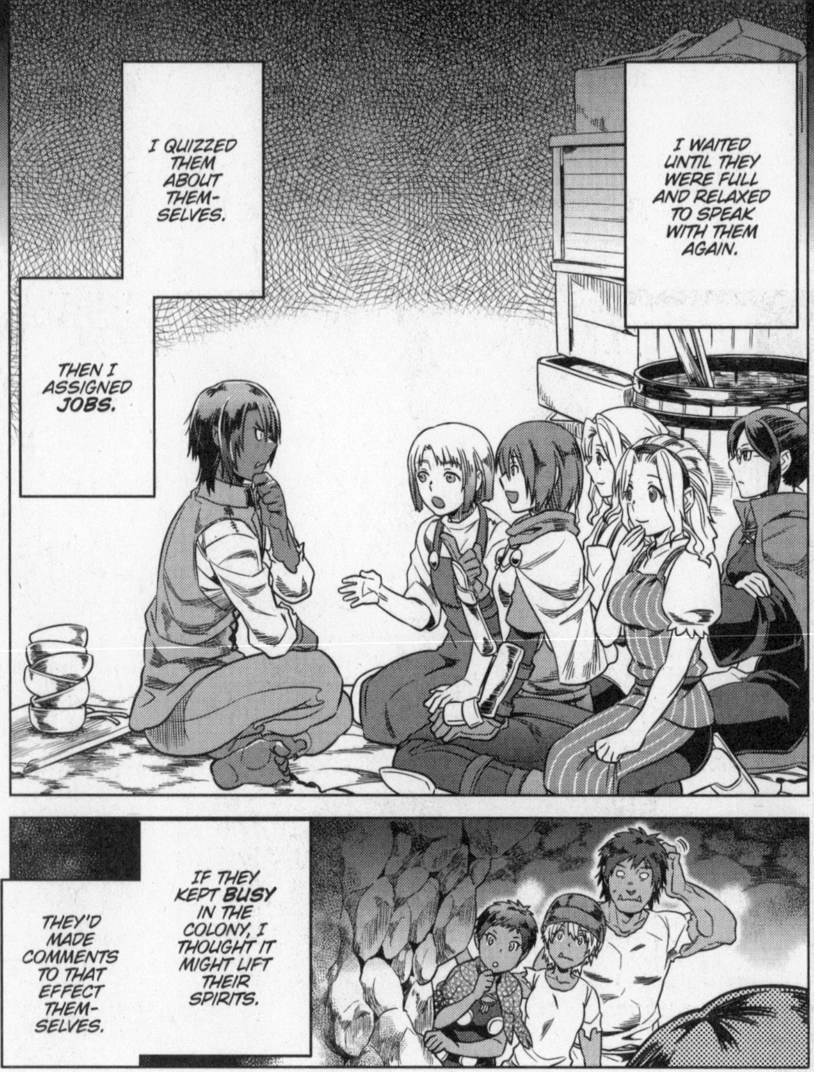
I WAITED UNTIL THEY WERE FULL AND RELAXED TO SPEAK WITH THEM AGAIN.
I QUIZZED THEM ABOUT THEM-SELVES.
THEN I ASSIGNED JOBS.
IF THEY KEPT BUSY IN THE COLONY, I THOUGHT IT MIGHT LIFT THEIR SPIRITS.
THEY'D MADE COMMENTS TO THAT EFFECT THEM-SELVES.

CHAPTER 8

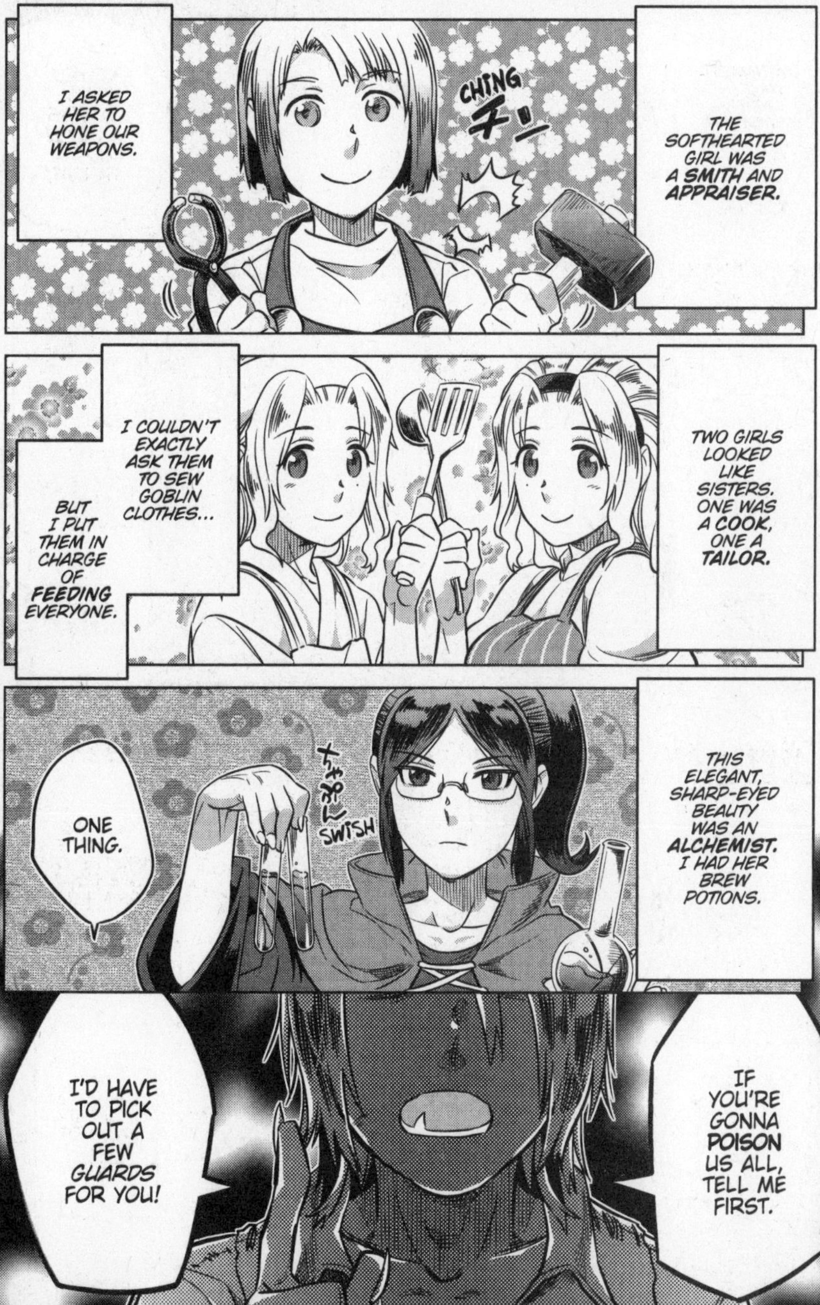
THE SOFTHEARTED GIRL WAS A **SMITH** AND **APPRAISER.**
CHING
チン
I ASKED HER TO HONE OUR WEAPONS.
TWO GIRLS LOOKED LIKE SISTERS. ONE WAS A **COOK**, ONE A **TAILOR.**
I COULDN'T EXACTLY ASK THEM TO SEW GOBLIN CLOTHES...
BUT I PUT THEM IN CHARGE OF **FEEDING** EVERYONE.
THIS ELEGANT, SHARP-EYED BEAUTY WAS AN **ALCHEMIST.** I HAD HER BREW POTIONS.
ちゃぷん
SWISH
ONE THING.
IF YOU'RE GONNA **POISON** US ALL, TELL ME FIRST.
I'D HAVE TO PICK OUT A FEW GUARDS FOR YOU!

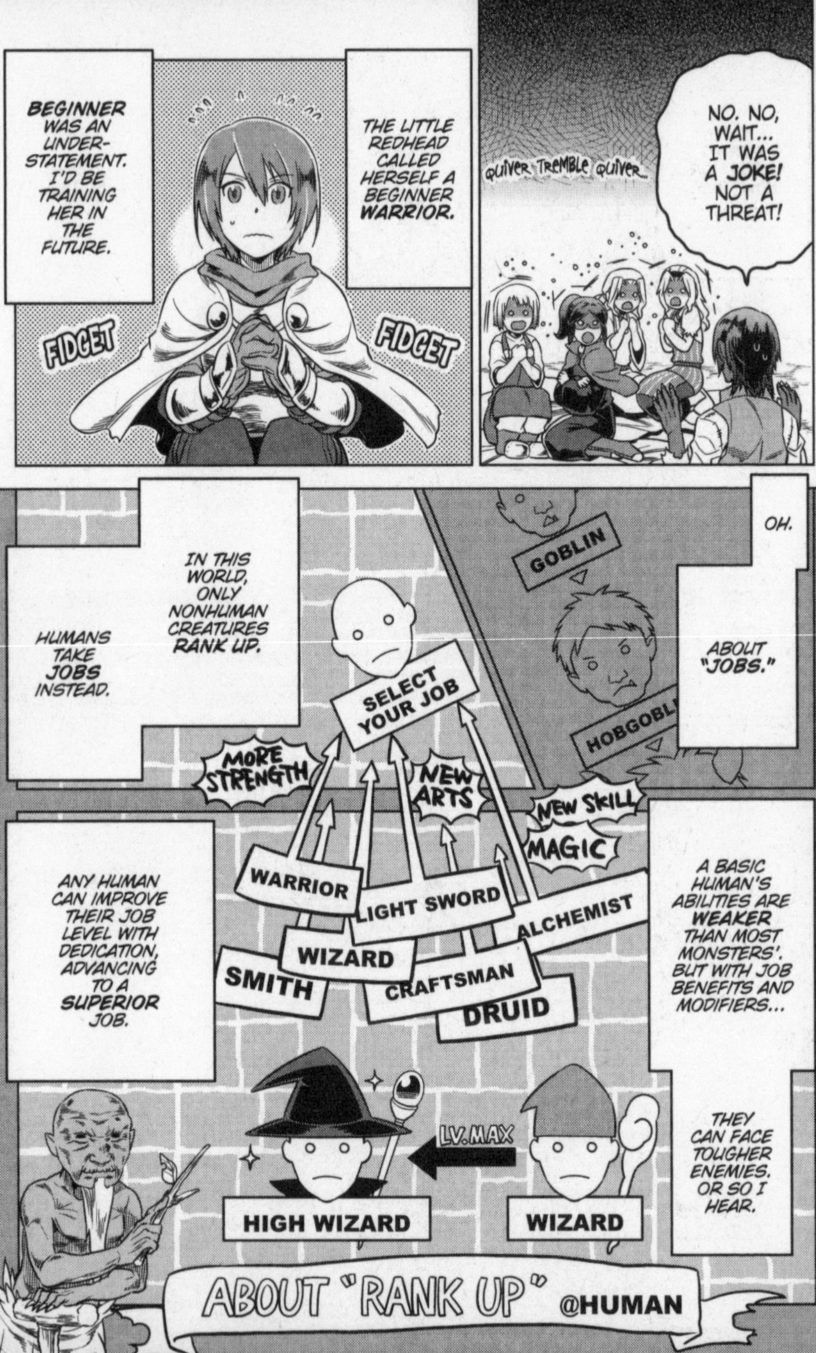
NO. NO, WAIT... IT WAS A JOKE! NOT A THREAT!
QUIVER TREMBLE QUIVER...
THE LITTLE REDHEAD CALLED HERSELF A BEGINNER WARRIOR.
BEGINNER WAS AN UNDER-STATEMENT. I'D BE TRAINING HER IN THE FUTURE.
FIDGET
FIDGET
OH.
ABOUT "JOBS."
GOBLIN
HOBGOBL
IN THIS WORLD, ONLY NONHUMAN CREATURES RANK UP.
HUMANS TAKE JOBS INSTEAD.
SELECT YOUR JOB
MORE STRENGTH
NEW ARTS
NEW SKILL
MAGIC
WARRIOR
LIGHT SWORD
ALCHEMIST
WIZARD
SMITH
CRAFTSMAN
DRUID
A BASIC HUMAN'S ABILITIES ARE WEAKER THAN MOST MONSTERS'. BUT WITH JOB BENEFITS AND MODIFIERS...
ANY HUMAN CAN IMPROVE THEIR JOB LEVEL WITH DEDICATION, ADVANCING TO A SUPERIOR JOB.
THEY CAN FACE TOUGHER ENEMIES. OR SO I HEAR.
LV.MAX
WIZARD
HIGH WIZARD
ABOUT "RANK UP" @HUMAN

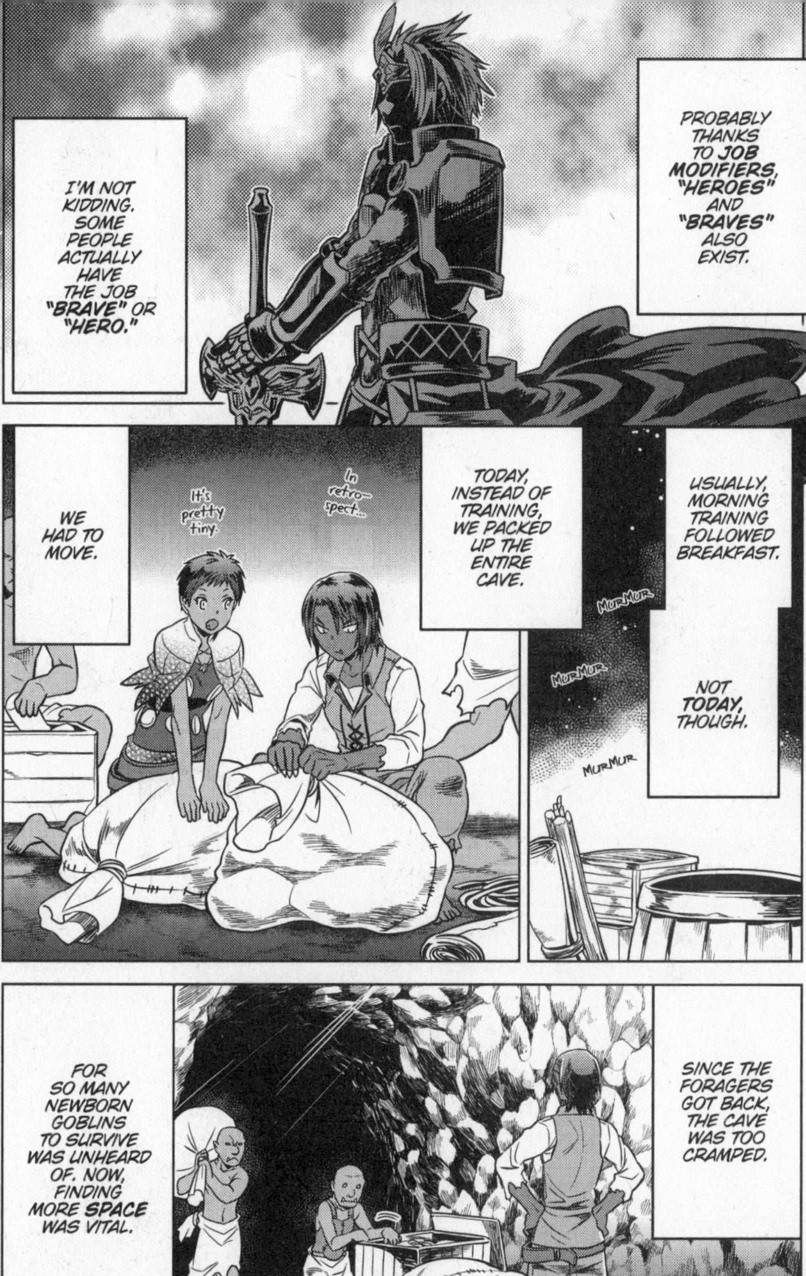
PROBABLY THANKS TO JOB MODIFIERS, "HEROES" AND "BRAVES" ALSO EXIST.
I'M NOT KIDDING. SOME PEOPLE ACTUALLY HAVE THE JOB "BRAVE" OR "HERO."
USUALLY, MORNING TRAINING FOLLOWED BREAKFAST.
MURMUR
MURMUR
MURMUR
NOT TODAY, THOUGH.
TODAY, INSTEAD OF TRAINING, WE PACKED UP THE ENTIRE CAVE.
In retro-spect...
It's pretty tiny.
WE HAD TO MOVE.
SINCE THE FORAGERS GOT BACK, THE CAVE WAS TOO CRAMPED.
FOR SO MANY NEWBORN GOBLINS TO SURVIVE WAS UNHEARD OF. NOW, FINDING MORE SPACE WAS VITAL.

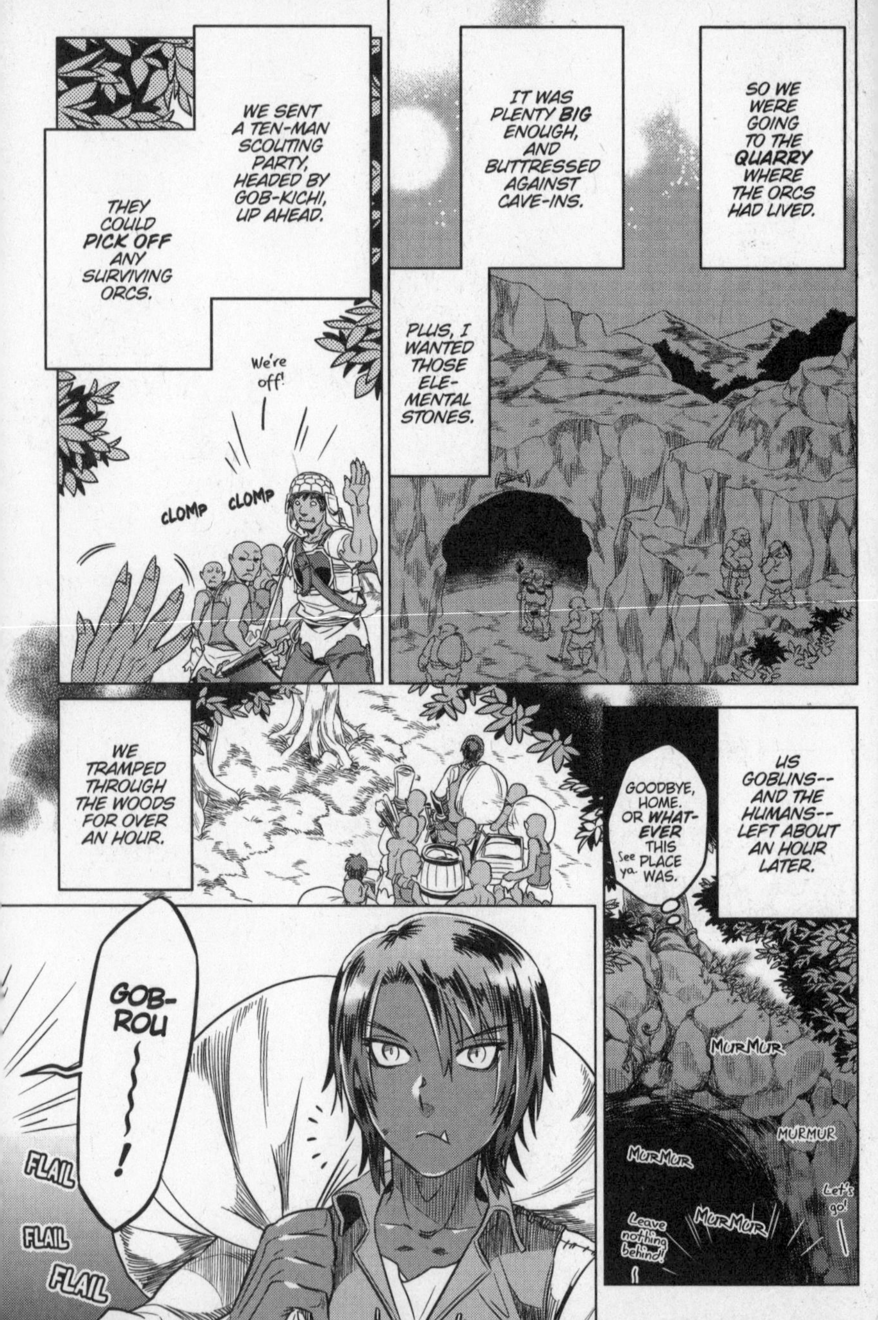
SO WE WERE GOING TO THE QUARRY WHERE THE ORCS HAD LIVED.
IT WAS PLENTY BIG ENOUGH, AND BUTTRESSED AGAINST CAVE-INS.
PLUS, I WANTED THOSE ELE-MENTAL STONES.
WE SENT A TEN-MAN SCOUTING PARTY, HEADED BY GOB-KICHI, UP AHEAD.
THEY COULD PICK OFF ANY SURVIVING ORCS.
We're off!
CLOMP CLOMP
US GOBLINS--AND THE HUMANS--LEFT ABOUT AN HOUR LATER.
GOODBYE, HOME. OR WHATEVER THIS PLACE WAS.
See ya.
MURMUR
MURMUR
MURMUR
Let's go!
MURMUR
Leave nothing behind!
WE TRAMPED THROUGH THE WOODS FOR OVER AN HOUR.
GOB-ROU~~!
FLAIL
FLAIL
FLAIL

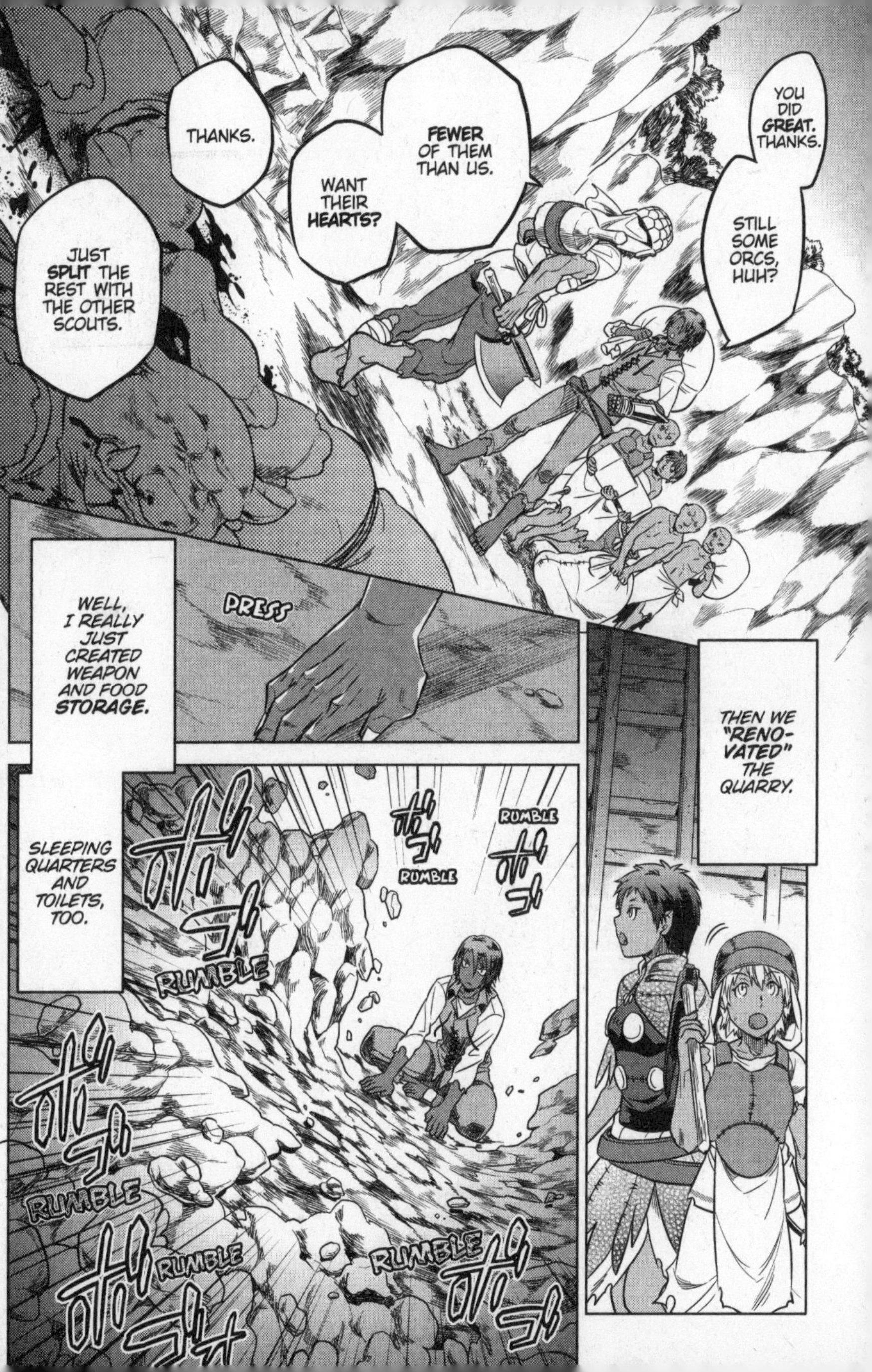
YOU DID GREAT. THANKS.
STILL SOME ORCS, HUH?
FEWER OF THEM THAN US.
WANT THEIR HEARTS?
THANKS.
JUST SPLIT THE REST WITH THE OTHER SCOUTS.
THEN WE "RENOVATED" THE QUARRY.
WELL, I REALLY JUST CREATED WEAPON AND FOOD STORAGE.
PRESS
SLEEPING QUARTERS AND TOILETS, TOO.
RUMBLE
RUMBLE
RUMBLE
RUMBLE
RUMBLE
RUMBLE

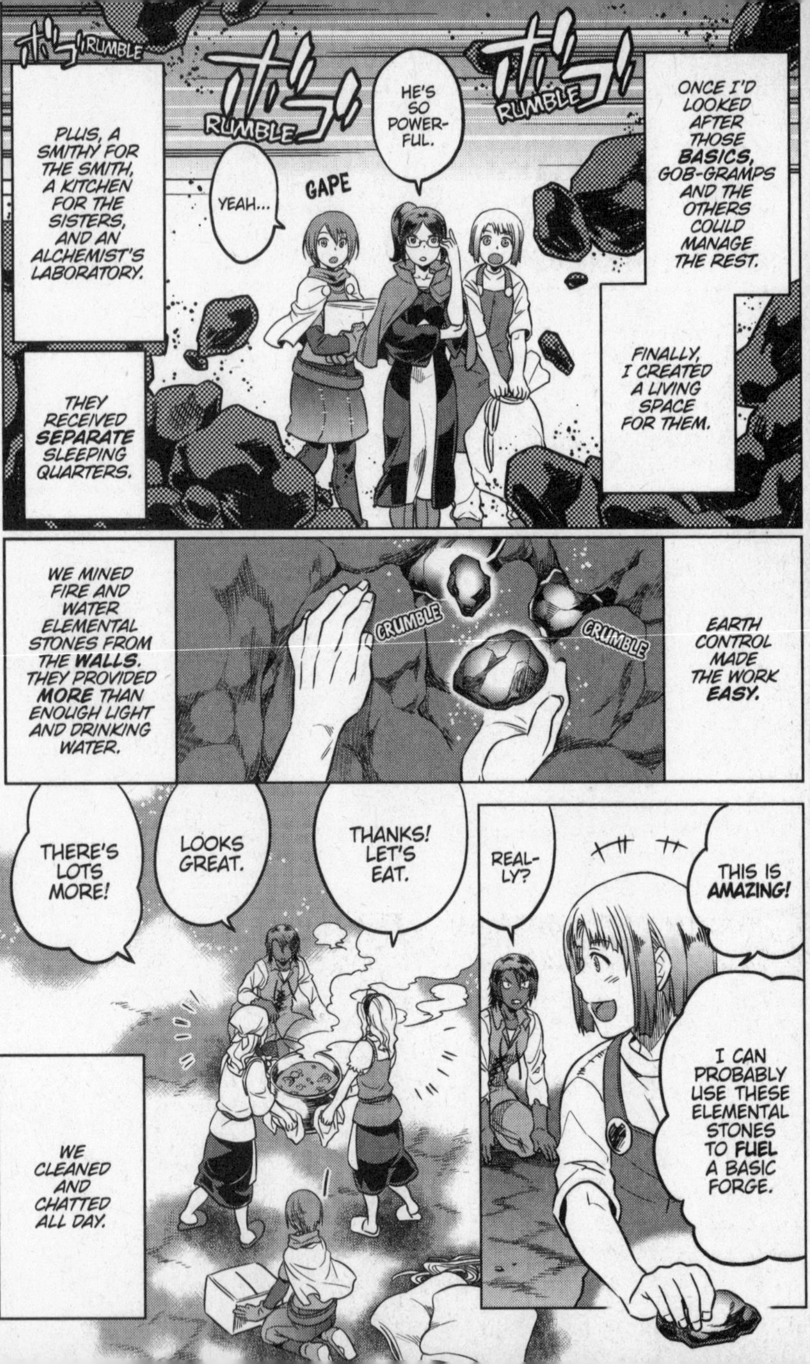
ONCE I'D LOOKED AFTER THOSE BASICS, GOB-GRAMPS AND THE OTHERS COULD MANAGE THE REST.
FINALLY, I CREATED A LIVING SPACE FOR THEM.
RUMBLE
HE'S SO POWERFUL.
RUMBLE
YEAH...
GAPE
RUMBLE
PLUS, A SMITHY FOR THE SMITH, A KITCHEN FOR THE SISTERS, AND AN ALCHEMIST'S LABORATORY.
THEY RECEIVED SEPARATE SLEEPING QUARTERS.
EARTH CONTROL MADE THE WORK EASY.
CRUMBLE
CRUMBLE
WE MINED FIRE AND WATER ELEMENTAL STONES FROM THE WALLS. THEY PROVIDED MORE THAN ENOUGH LIGHT AND DRINKING WATER.
THIS IS AMAZING!
REALLY?
I CAN PROBABLY USE THESE ELEMENTAL STONES TO FUEL A BASIC FORGE.
THANKS! LET'S EAT.
LOOKS GREAT.
THERE'S LOTS MORE!
WE CLEANED AND CHATTED ALL DAY.

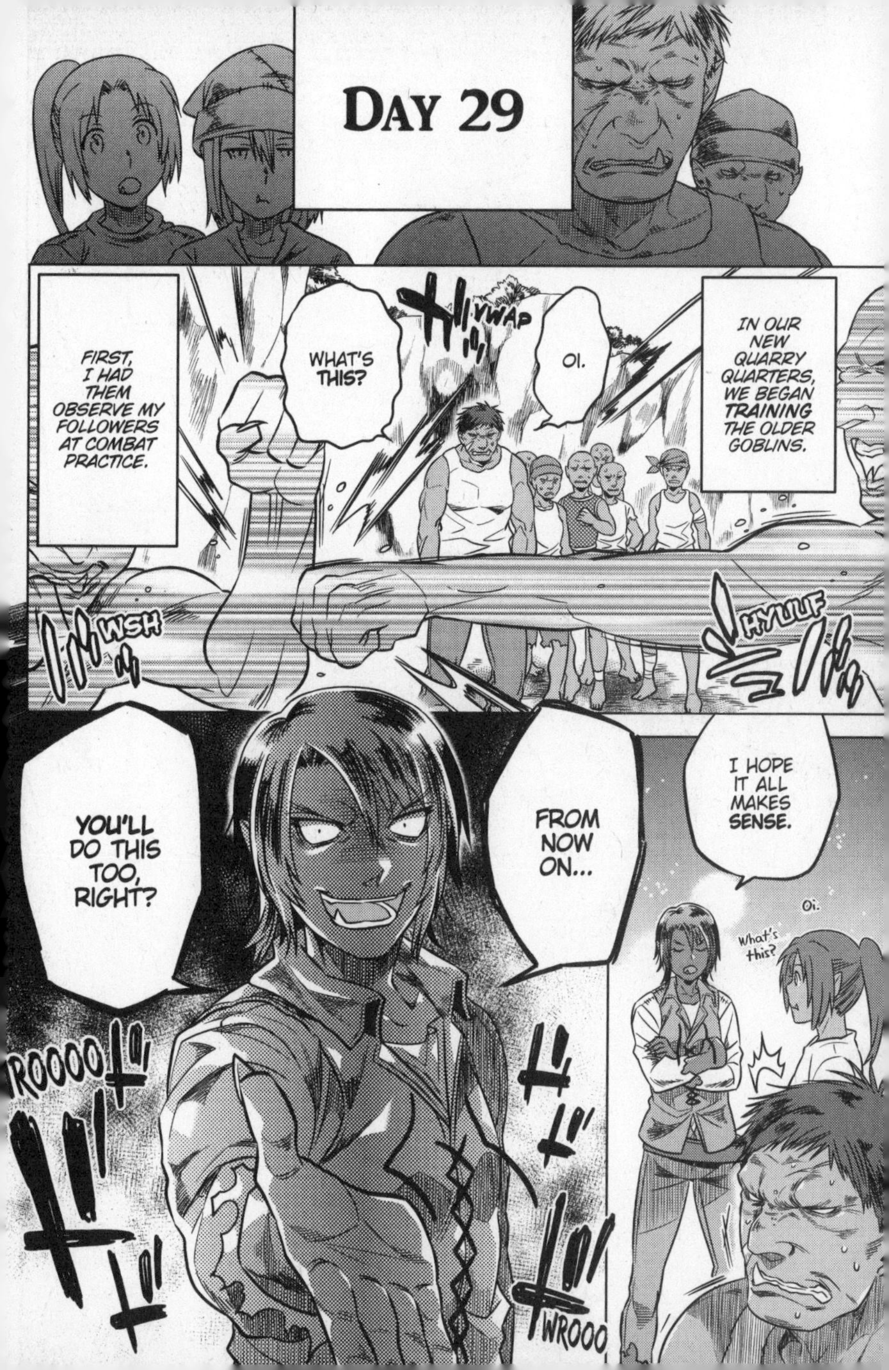
DAY 29
IN OUR NEW QUARRY QUARTERS, WE BEGAN TRAINING THE OLDER GOBLINS.
VWAP
OI.
WHAT'S THIS?
FIRST, I HAD THEM OBSERVE MY FOLLOWERS AT COMBAT PRACTICE.
HYUUF
WSH
I HOPE IT ALL MAKES SENSE.
Oi.
What's this?
FROM NOW ON...
YOU'LL DO THIS TOO, RIGHT?
WROOO
ROOOO

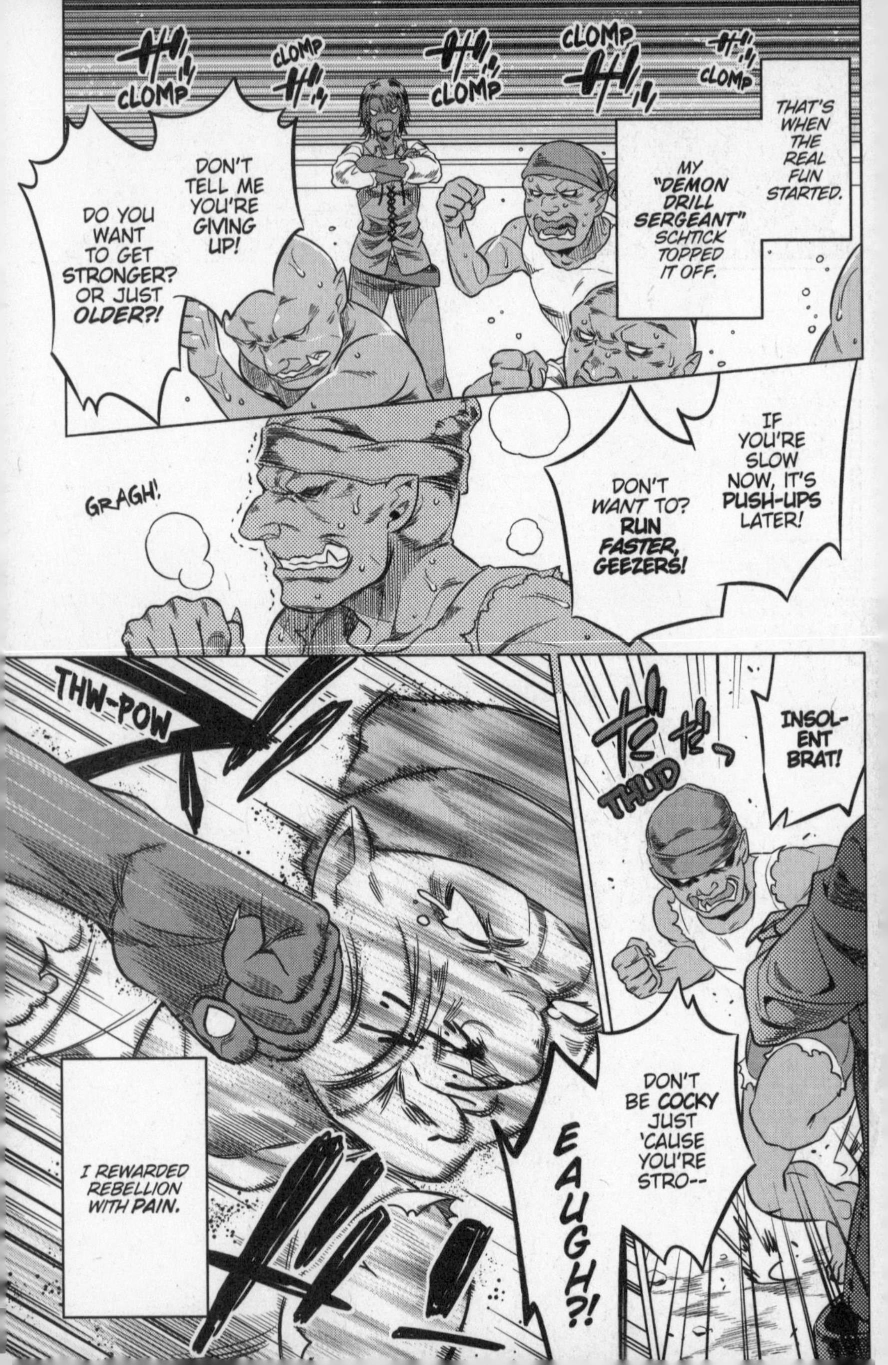
CLOMP
CLOMP
CLOMP
CLOMP
CLOMP
THAT'S WHEN THE REAL FUN STARTED.
MY "DEMON DRILL SERGEANT" SCHTICK TOPPED IT OFF.
DON'T TELL ME YOU'RE GIVING UP!
DO YOU WANT TO GET STRONGER? OR JUST OLDER?!
IF YOU'RE SLOW NOW, IT'S PUSH-UPS LATER!
DON'T WANT TO? RUN FASTER, GEEZERS!
GRAGH!
INSOL-ENT BRAT!
THUD
DON'T BE COCKY JUST 'CAUSE YOU'RE STRO--
THW-POW
EAUGH?!
I REWARDED REBELLION WITH PAIN.

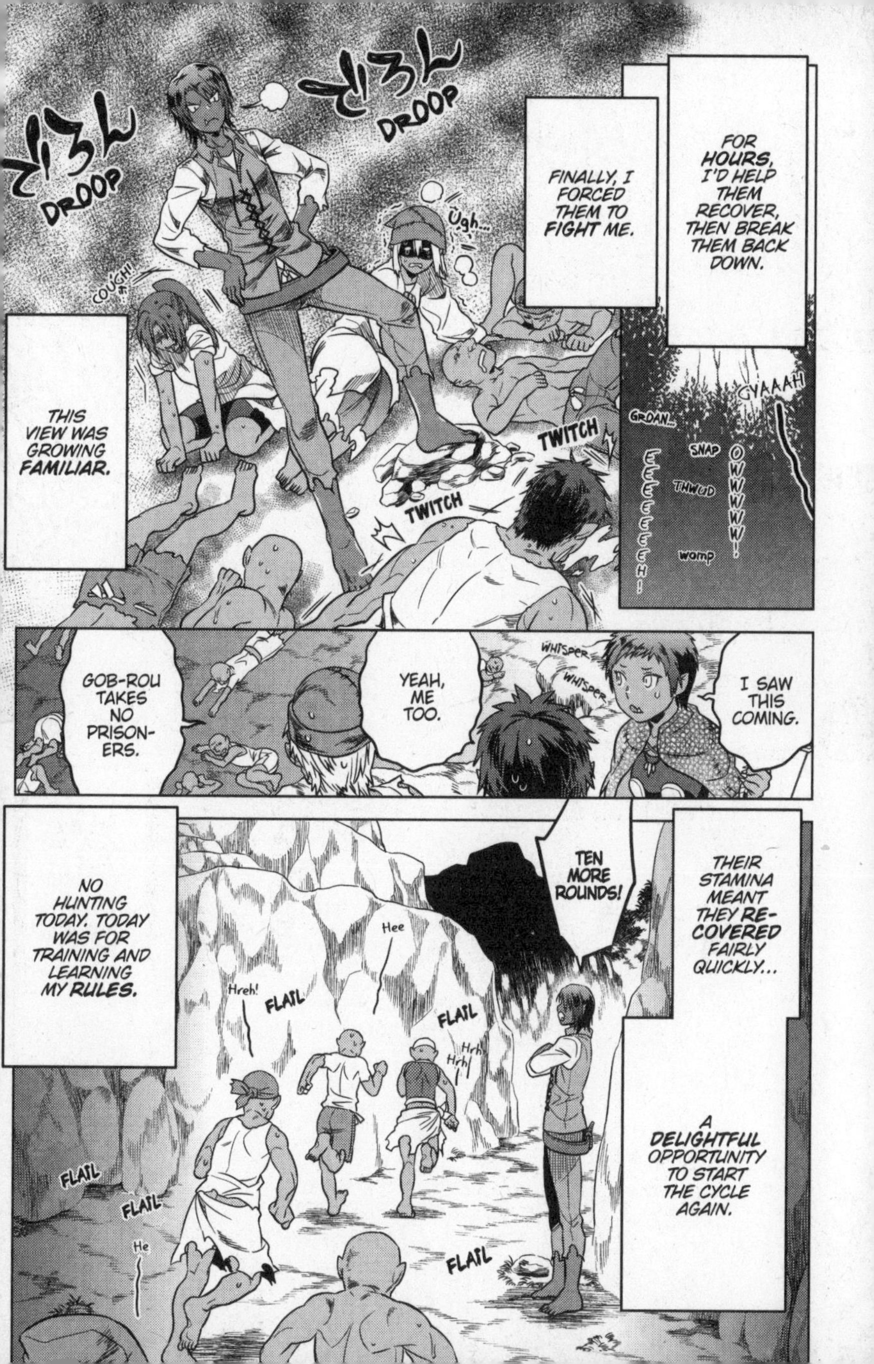

FOR HOURS, I'D HELP THEM RECOVER, THEN BREAK THEM BACK DOWN.
FINALLY, I FORCED THEM TO FIGHT ME.
GYAAAH
OWWWWWW!
EEEEEEEEH!
GROAN...
SNAP
THWUD
womp
DROOP
DROOP
Ugh...
COUGH!
THIS VIEW WAS GROWING FAMILIAR.
TWITCH
TWITCH
I SAW THIS COMING.
whisper
whisper
YEAH, ME TOO.
GOB-ROU TAKES NO PRISONERS.
THEIR STAMINA MEANT THEY RECOVERED FAIRLY QUICKLY...
A DELIGHTFUL OPPORTUNITY TO START THE CYCLE AGAIN.
TEN MORE ROUNDS!
NO HUNTING TODAY. TODAY WAS FOR TRAINING AND LEARNING MY RULES.
Hee
FLAIL
FLAIL
Hreh!
Hrh
Hrh
FLAIL
FLAIL
He
FLAIL

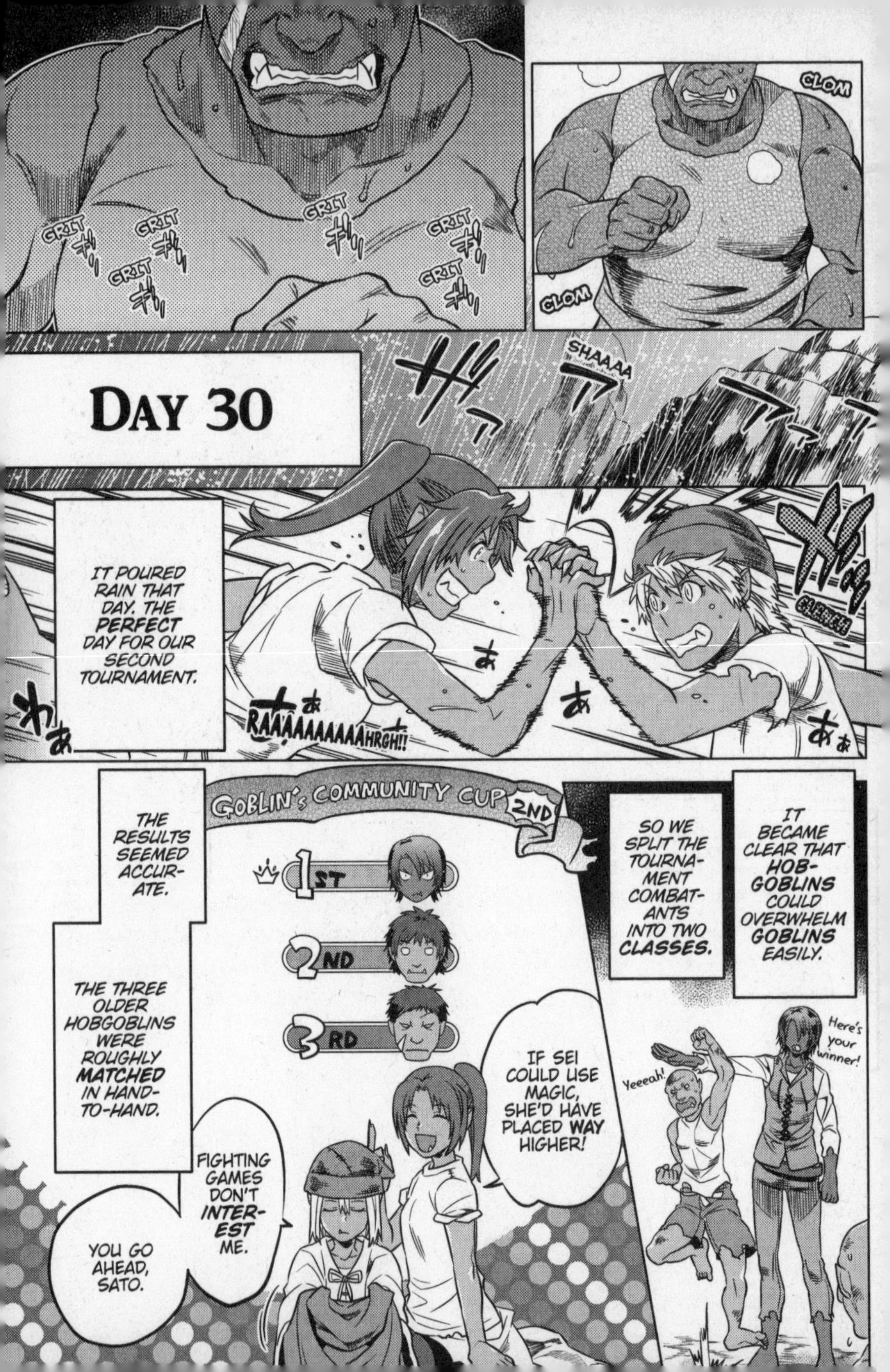

CLOM
CLOM
GRIT
GRIT
GRIT
GRIT
GRIT
DAY 30
SHAAAA
IT POURED RAIN THAT DAY. THE PERFECT DAY FOR OUR SECOND TOURNAMENT.
CLENCH
RAAAAAAAAAAHRGH!!
IT BECAME CLEAR THAT HOBGOBLINS COULD OVERWHELM GOBLINS EASILY.
SO WE SPLIT THE TOURNAMENT COMBATANTS INTO TWO CLASSES.
Here's your winner!
Yeeeah!
GOBLIN's COMMUNITY CUP 2ND
THE RESULTS SEEMED ACCURATE.
1ST
2ND
3RD
IF SEI COULD USE MAGIC, SHE'D HAVE PLACED WAY HIGHER!
THE THREE OLDER HOBGOBLINS WERE ROUGHLY MATCHED IN HAND-TO-HAND.
FIGHTING GAMES DON'T INTEREST ME.
YOU GO AHEAD, SATO.

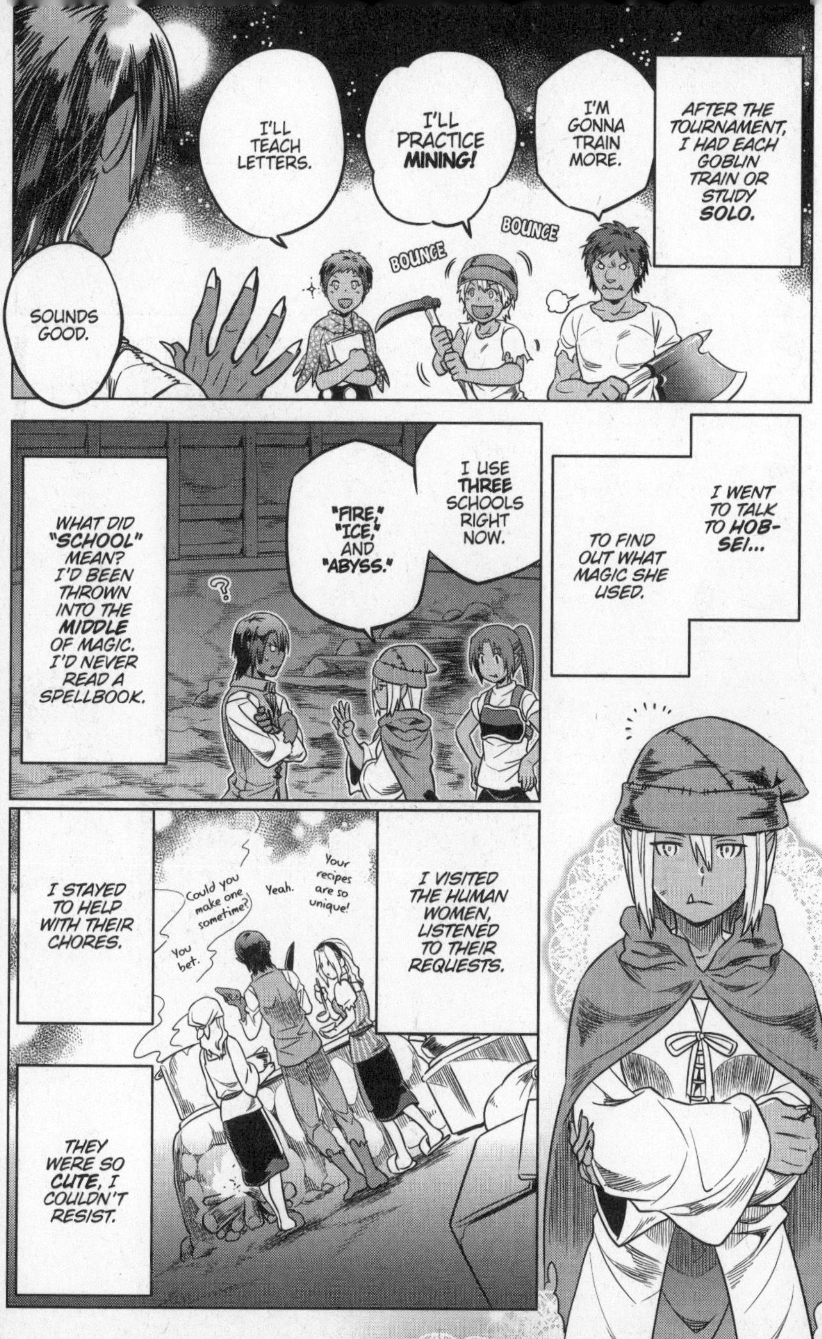
AFTER THE TOURNAMENT, I HAD EACH GOBLIN TRAIN OR STUDY SOLO.
I'M GONNA TRAIN MORE.
BOUNCE
I'LL PRACTICE MINING!
BOUNCE
I'LL TEACH LETTERS.
SOUNDS GOOD.
I WENT TO TALK TO HOB-SEI...
TO FIND OUT WHAT MAGIC SHE USED.
I USE THREE SCHOOLS RIGHT NOW.
"FIRE," "ICE," AND "ABYSS."
?
WHAT DID "SCHOOL" MEAN? I'D BEEN THROWN INTO THE MIDDLE OF MAGIC. I'D NEVER READ A SPELLBOOK.
I VISITED THE HUMAN WOMEN, LISTENED TO THEIR REQUESTS.
Your recipes are so unique!
Yeah.
Could you make one sometime?
You bet.
I STAYED TO HELP WITH THEIR CHORES.
THEY WERE SO CUTE, I COULDN'T RESIST.

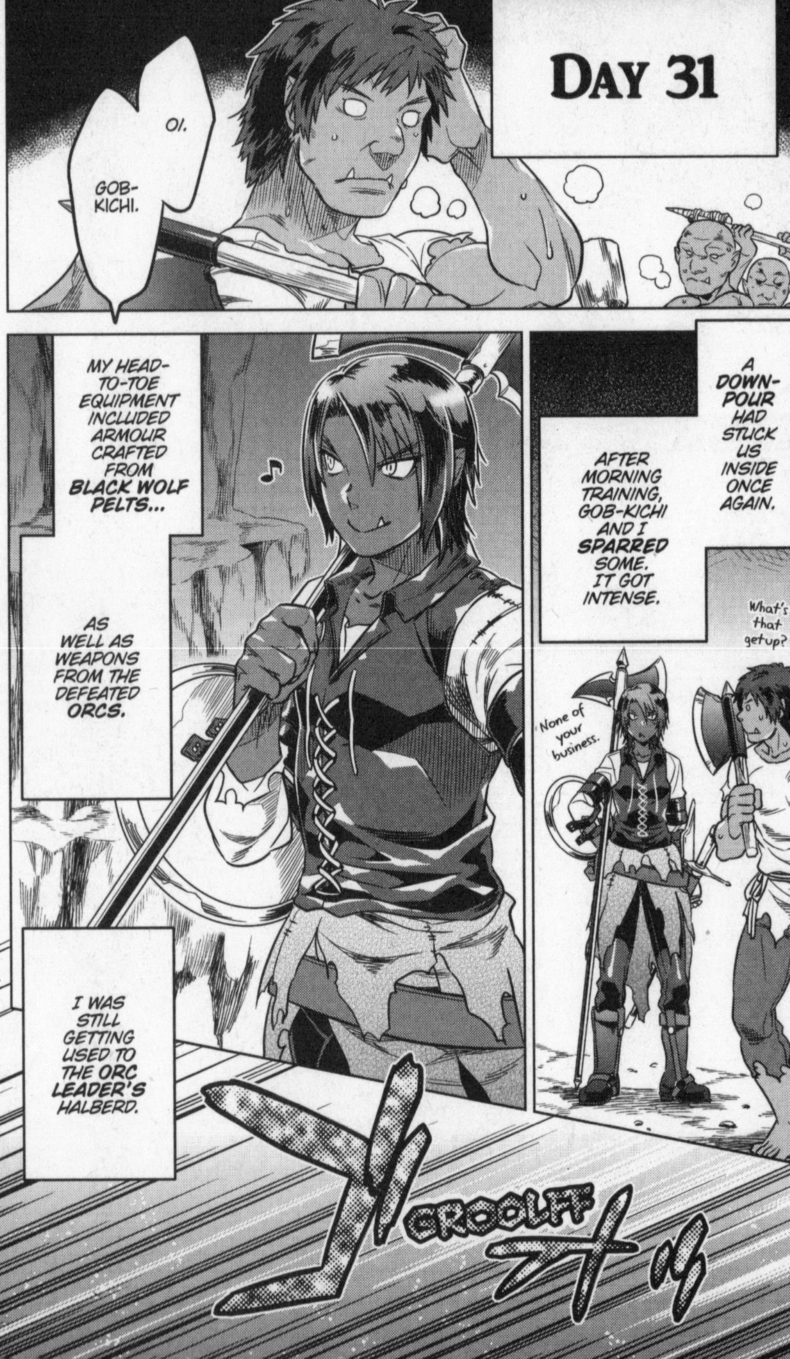
DAY 31
OI.
GOB-KICHI.
A DOWNPOUR HAD STUCK US INSIDE ONCE AGAIN.
AFTER MORNING TRAINING, GOB-KICHI AND I SPARRED SOME. IT GOT INTENSE.
What's that getup?
None of your business.
MY HEAD-TO-TOE EQUIPMENT INCLUDED ARMOUR CRAFTED FROM BLACK WOLF PELTS...
AS WELL AS WEAPONS FROM THE DEFEATED ORCS.
I WAS STILL GETTING USED TO THE ORC LEADER'S HALBERD.
GROOLFF

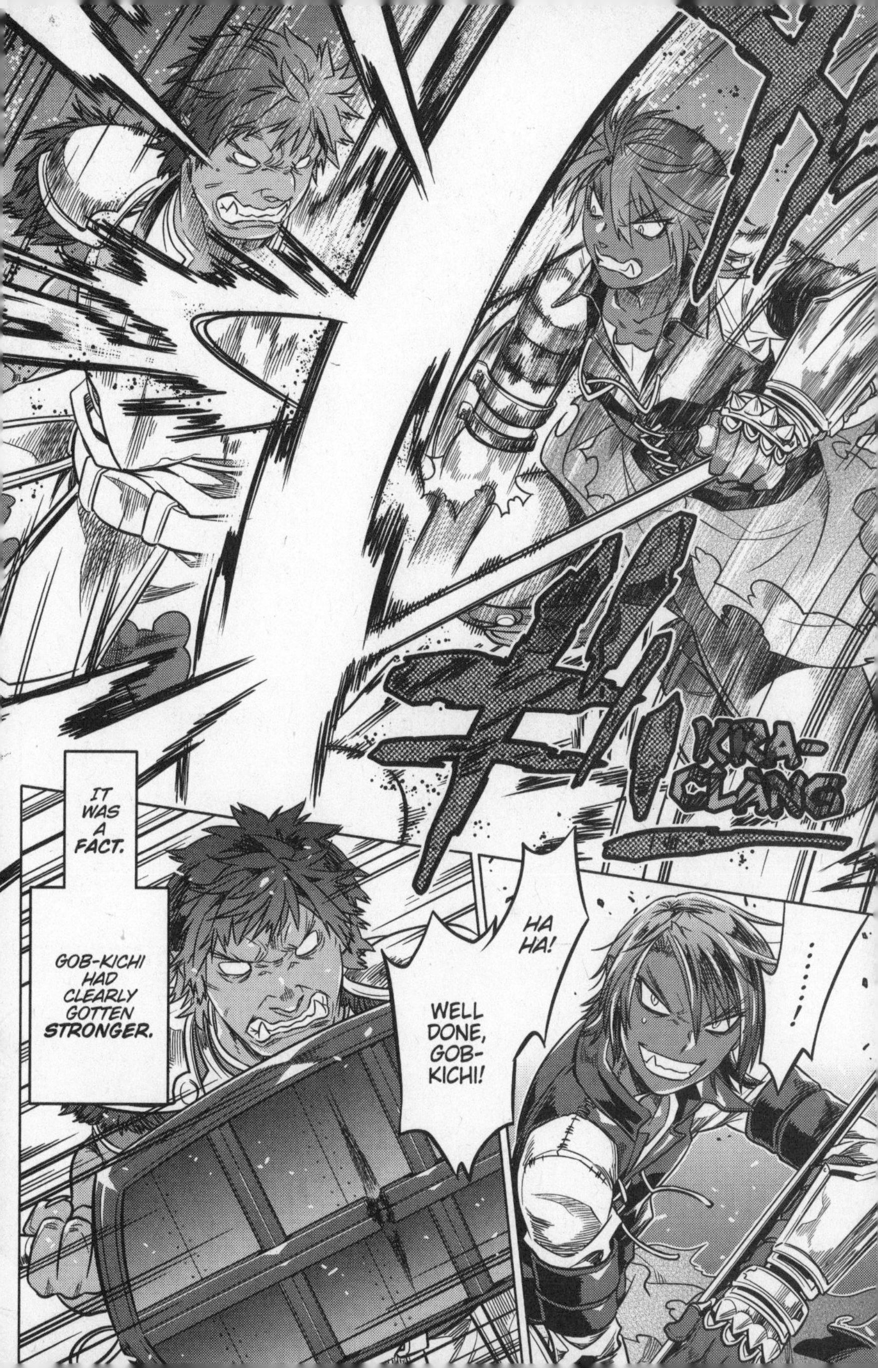
KIRA-CLANG
......!
HA HA!
WELL DONE, GOB-KICHI!
IT WAS A FACT.
GOB-KICHI HAD CLEARLY GOTTEN STRONGER.

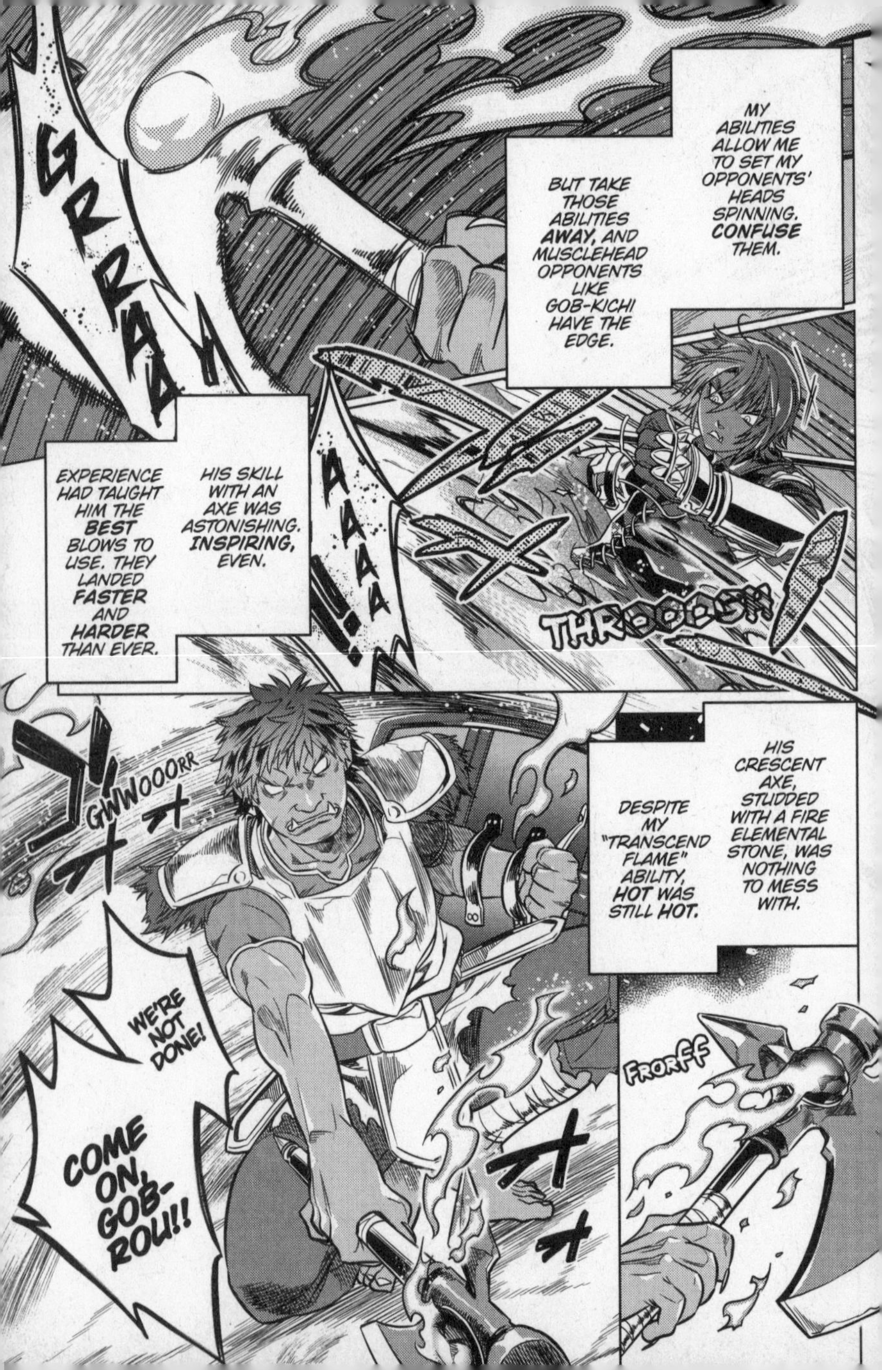

MY ABILITIES ALLOW ME TO SET MY OPPONENTS' HEADS SPINNING. **CONFUSE** THEM.
BUT TAKE THOSE ABILITIES **AWAY**, AND MUSCLEHEAD OPPONENTS LIKE GOB-KICHI HAVE THE EDGE.
GRRAAA
AAAA!!
THROOOOSH!!
HIS SKILL WITH AN AXE WAS ASTONISHING. **INSPIRING**, EVEN.
EXPERIENCE HAD TAUGHT HIM THE **BEST** BLOWS TO USE. THEY LANDED **FASTER** AND **HARDER** THAN EVER.
HIS CRESCENT AXE, STUDDED WITH A FIRE ELEMENTAL STONE, WAS NOTHING TO MESS WITH.
DESPITE MY "TRANSCEND FLAME" ABILITY, **HOT** WAS STILL **HOT**.
FRORFF
GWWOOORR
WE'RE NOT DONE!
COME ON, GOB-ROU!!

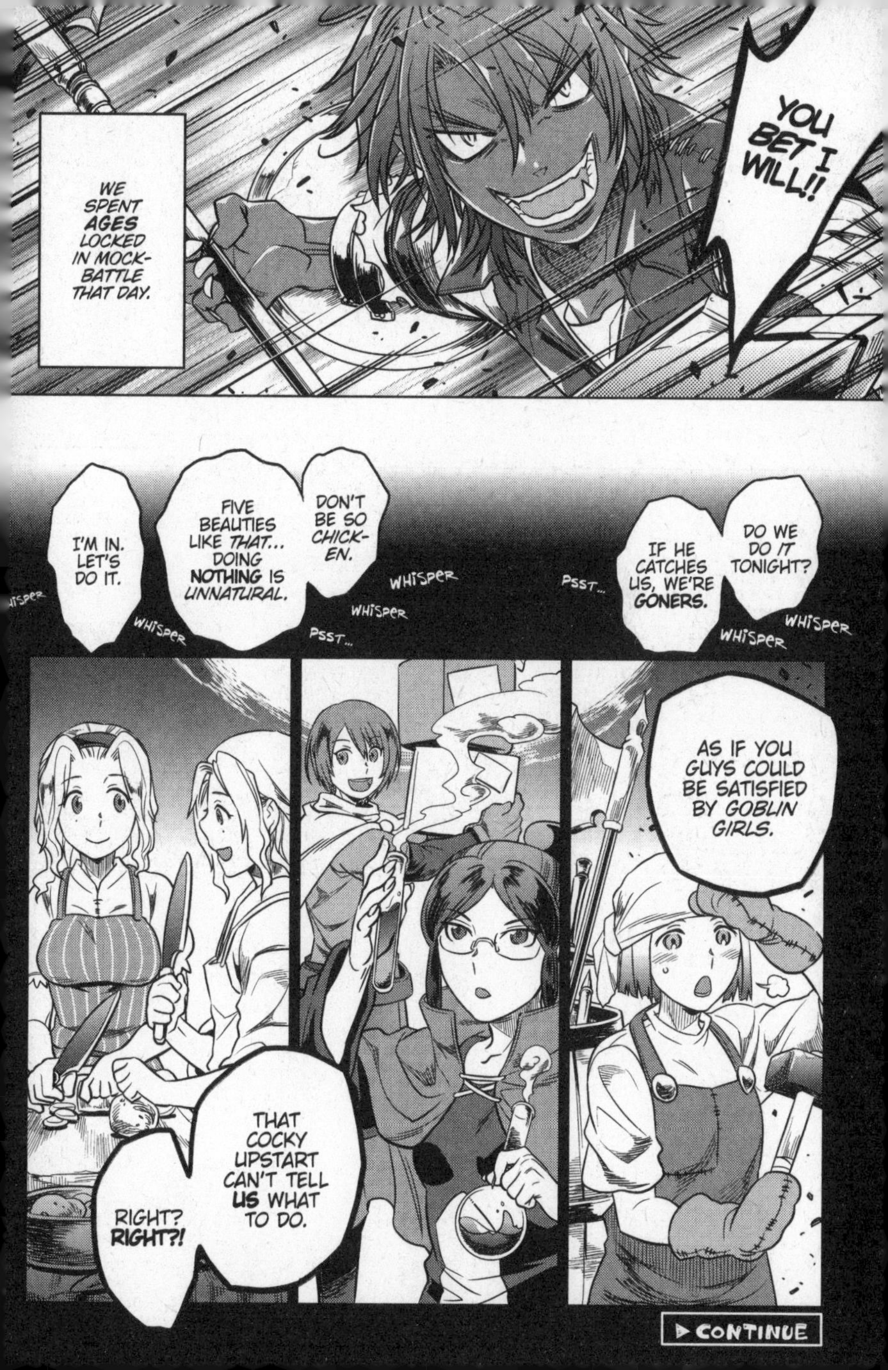

YOU BET I WILL!!
WE SPENT AGES LOCKED IN MOCK-BATTLE THAT DAY.
DO WE DO IT TONIGHT?
WHISPER
WHISPER
IF HE CATCHES US, WE'RE GONERS.
PSST...
WHISPER
DON'T BE SO CHICKEN.
WHISPER
PSST...
FIVE BEAUTIES LIKE THAT... DOING NOTHING IS UNNATURAL.
WHISPER
I'M IN. LET'S DO IT.
WHISPER
AS IF YOU GUYS COULD BE SATISFIED BY GOBLIN GIRLS.
THAT COCKY UPSTART CAN'T TELL US WHAT TO DO.
RIGHT? RIGHT?!
CONTINUE

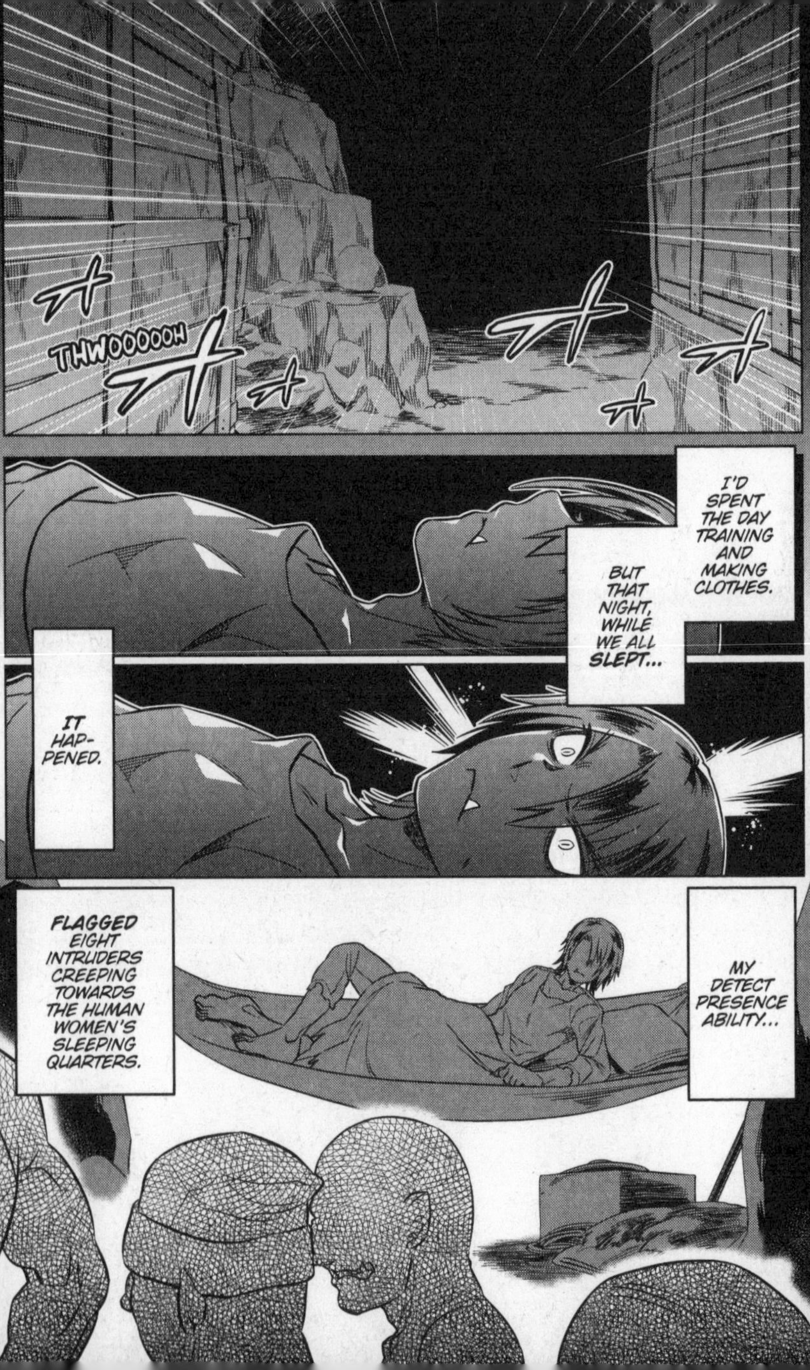
THWOOOOOH
I'D SPENT THE DAY TRAINING AND MAKING CLOTHES.
BUT THAT NIGHT, WHILE WE ALL SLEPT...
IT HAP-PENED.
MY DETECT PRESENCE ABILITY...
FLAGGED EIGHT INTRUDERS CREEPING TOWARDS THE HUMAN WOMEN'S SLEEPING QUARTERS.

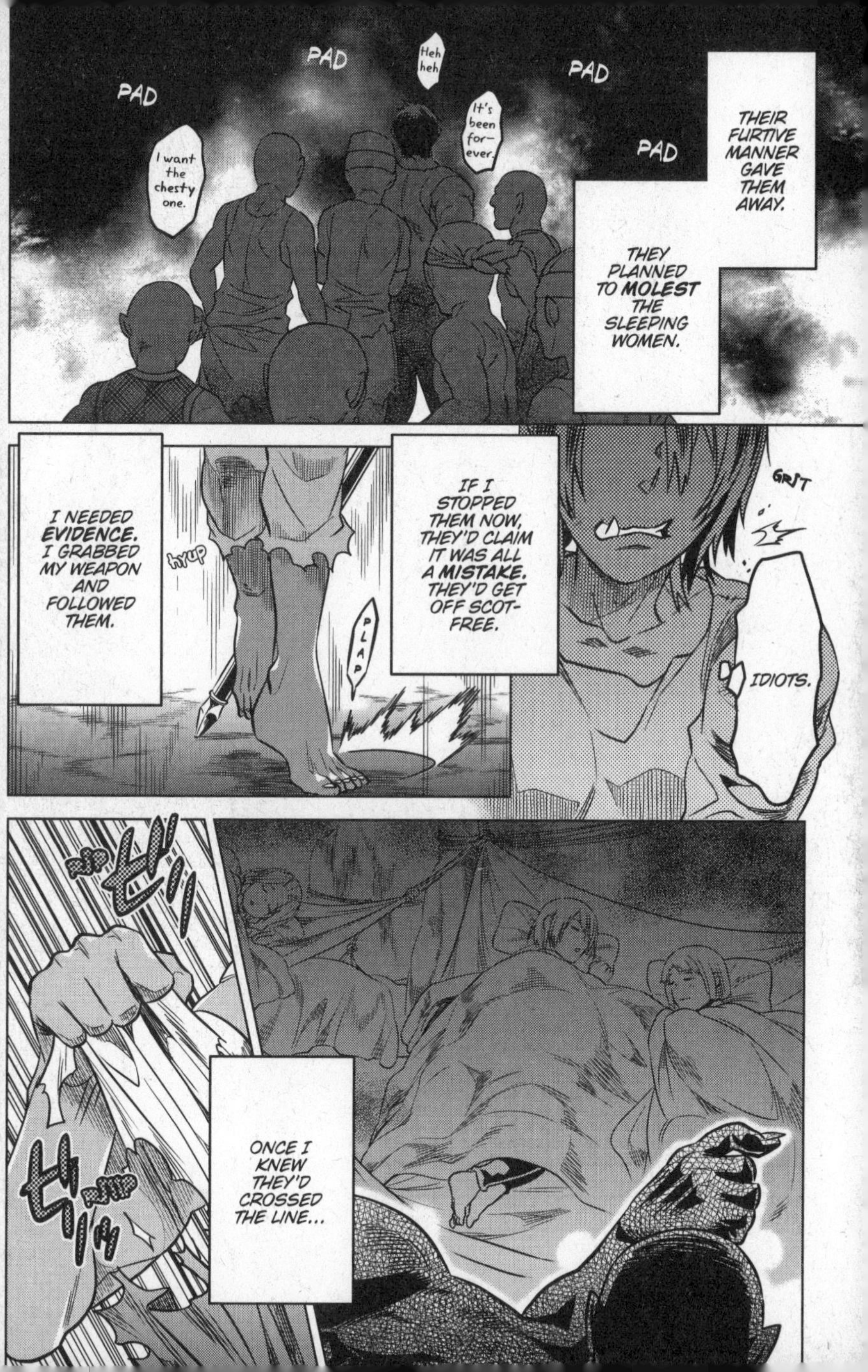
THEIR FURTIVE MANNER GAVE THEM AWAY.
THEY PLANNED TO **MOLEST** THE SLEEPING WOMEN.
PAD
PAD
Heh heh
It's been for-ever.
PAD
PAD
I want the chesty one.
GRIT
IDIOTS.
IF I STOPPED THEM NOW, THEY'D CLAIM IT WAS ALL A **MISTAKE.** THEY'D GET OFF SCOT-FREE.
I NEEDED **EVIDENCE.** I GRABBED MY WEAPON AND FOLLOWED THEM.
hyup
PLAP
ONCE I KNEW THEY'D CROSSED THE LINE...
RIP
RRIP

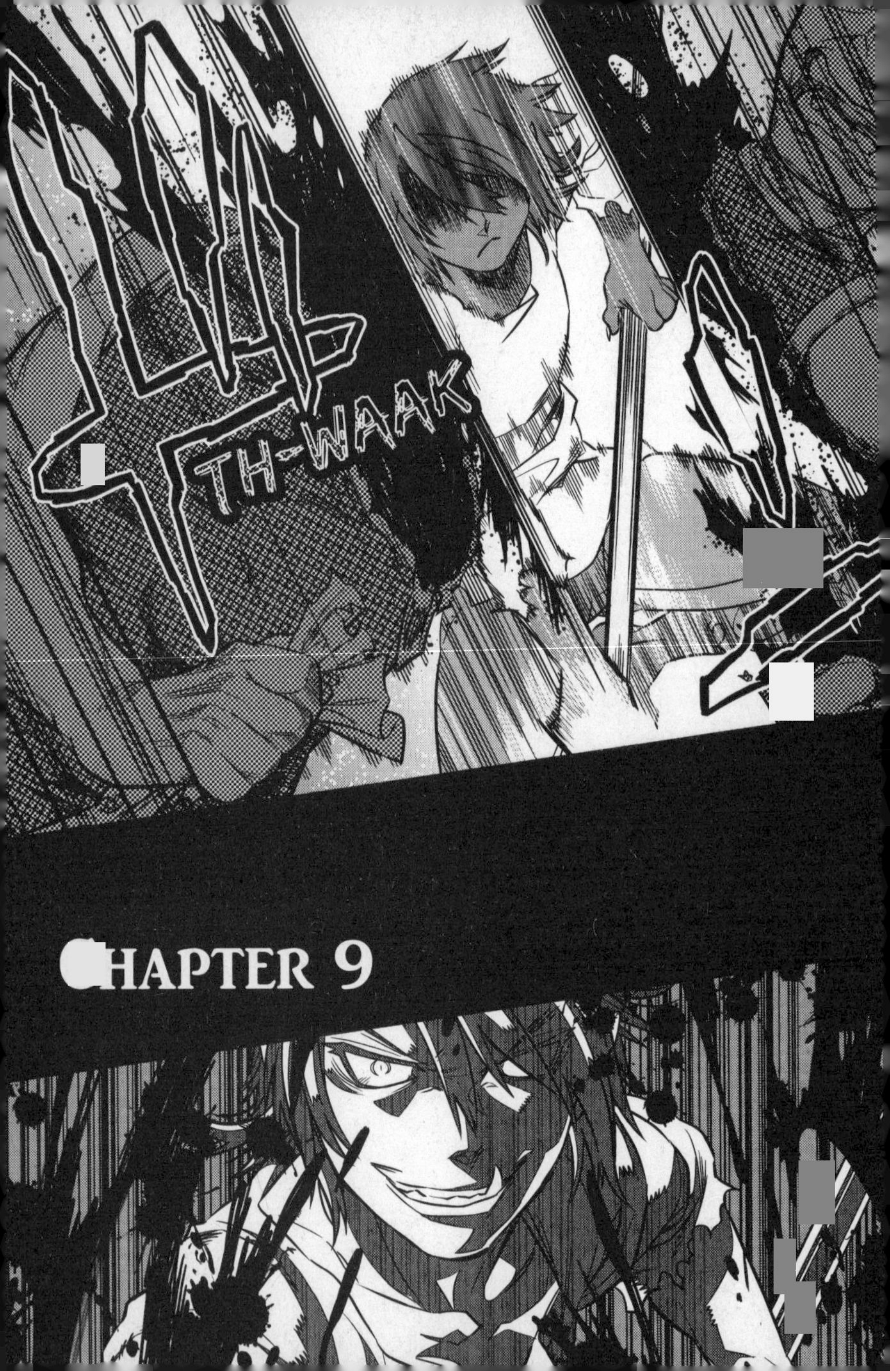
TH-WAAK
CHAPTER 9

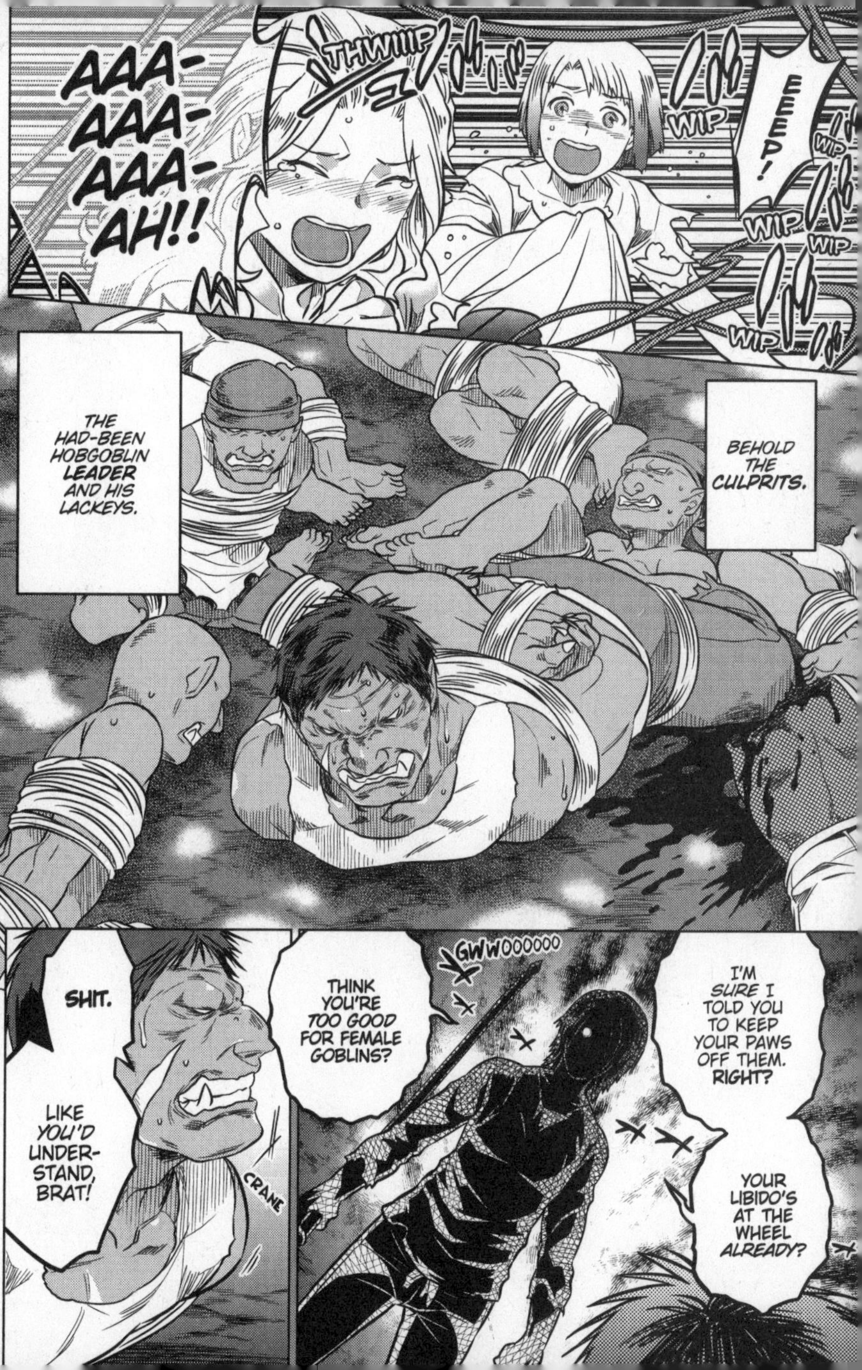
EEEEP!
WIP
WIP
WIP
WIP
WIP
THWIIIP
AAAAAAAAAAAH!!
BEHOLD THE CULPRITS.
THE HAD-BEEN HOBGOBLIN LEADER AND HIS LACKEYS.
I'M SURE I TOLD YOU TO KEEP YOUR PAWS OFF THEM. RIGHT?
GWWOOOOOO
YOUR LIBIDO'S AT THE WHEEL ALREADY?
THINK YOU'RE TOO GOOD FOR FEMALE GOBLINS?
SHIT.
CRANE
LIKE YOU'D UNDER-STAND, BRAT!

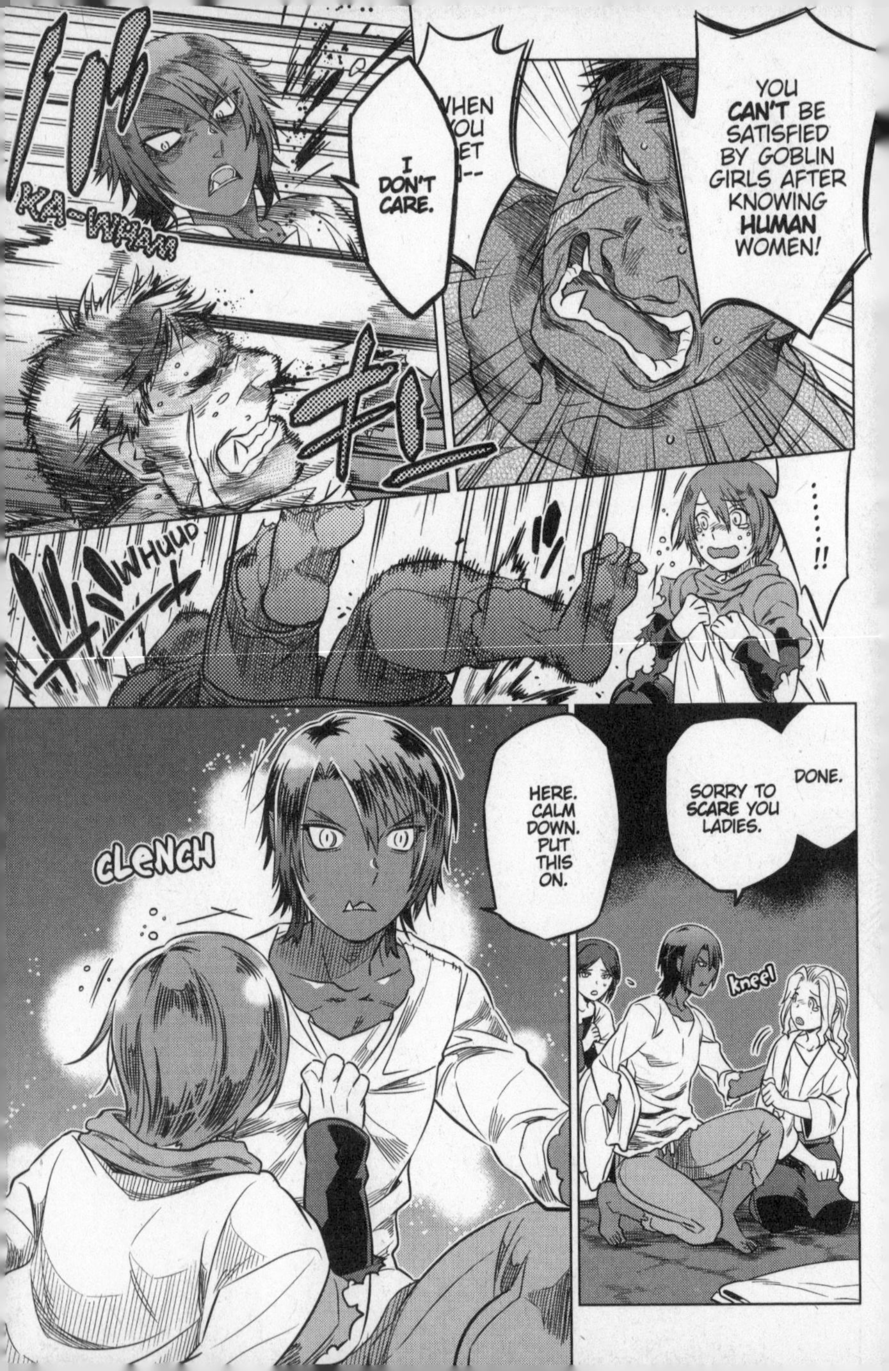
YOU CAN'T BE SATISFIED BY GOBLIN GIRLS AFTER KNOWING HUMAN WOMEN!
I DON'T CARE.
KA-WHAM
......!!
WHUUD
DONE.
SORRY TO SCARE YOU LADIES.
kneel
HERE. CALM DOWN. PUT THIS ON.
CLENCH

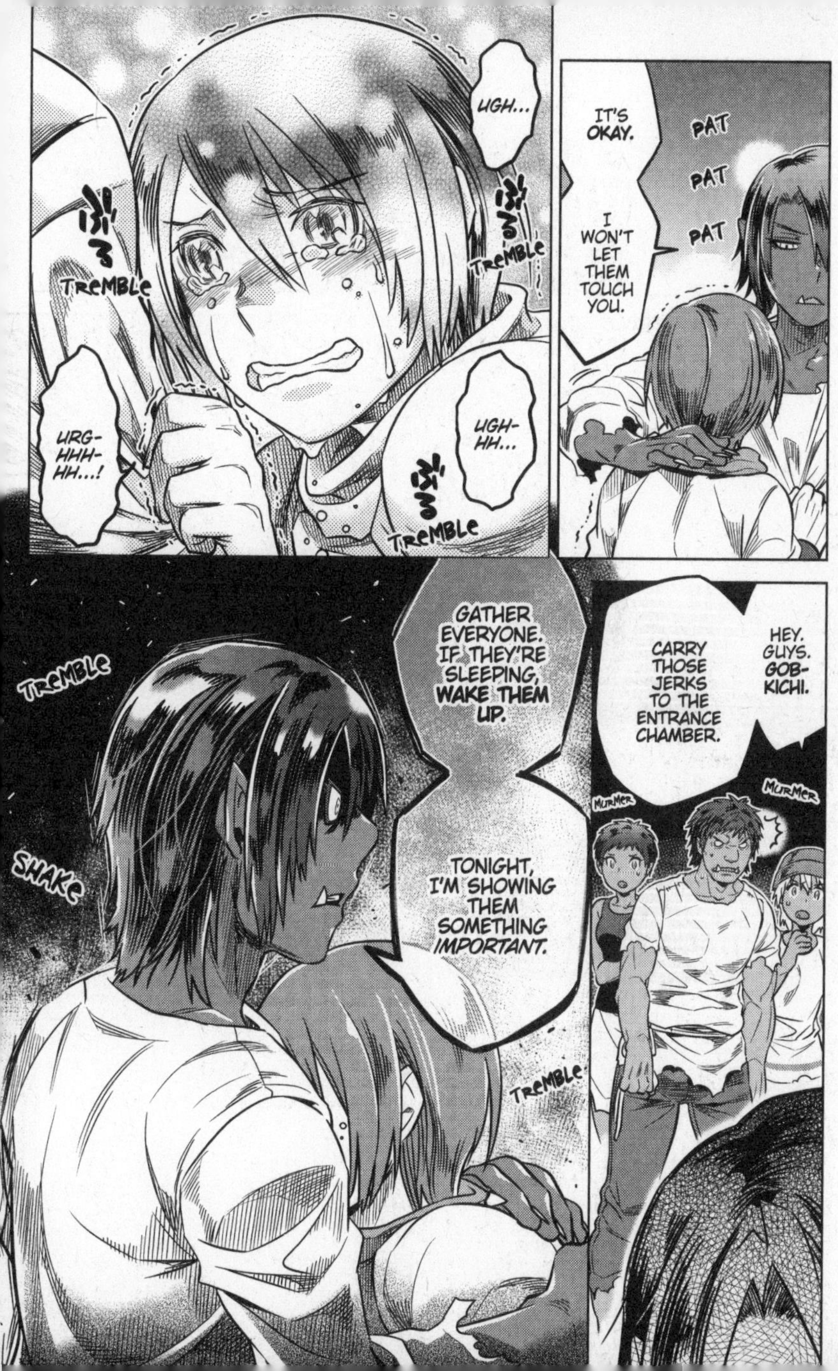
IT'S OKAY.
I WON'T LET THEM TOUCH YOU.
PAT
PAT
PAT
UGH...
TREMBLE
TREMBLE
URG-HHH-HH...!
UGH-HH...
TREMBLE
HEY. GUYS. GOB-KICHI.
CARRY THOSE JERKS TO THE ENTRANCE CHAMBER.
MURMER
MURMER
GATHER EVERYONE. IF THEY'RE SLEEPING, WAKE THEM UP.
TONIGHT, I'M SHOWING THEM SOMETHING IMPORTANT.
TREMBLE
SHAKE
TREMBLE

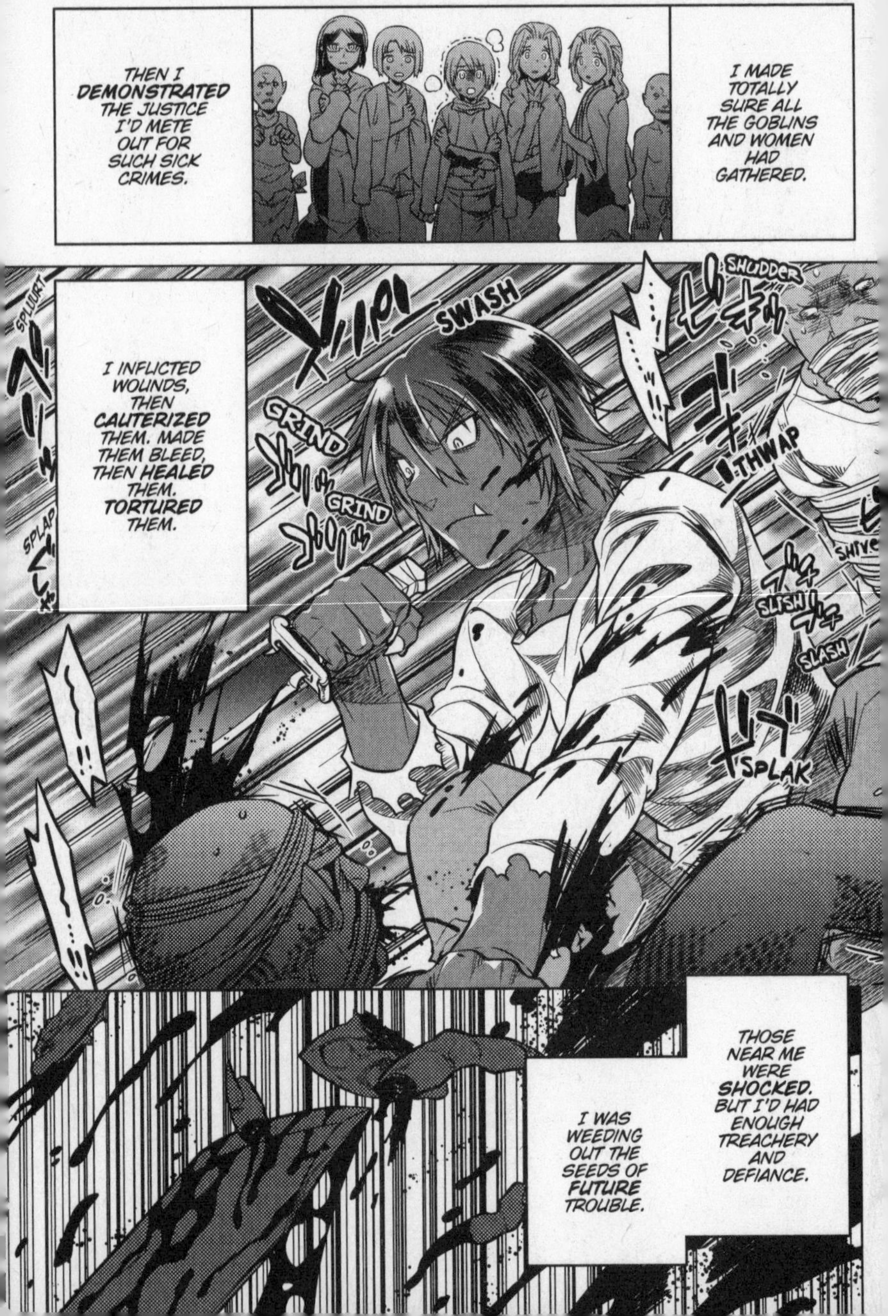

I MADE TOTALLY SURE ALL THE GOBLINS AND WOMEN HAD GATHERED.
THEN I DEMONSTRATED THE JUSTICE I'D METE OUT FOR SUCH SICK CRIMES.
SHUDDER
SWASH
THWAP
SLISH
SLASH
SPLAK
I INFLICTED WOUNDS, THEN CAUTERIZED THEM. MADE THEM BLEED, THEN HEALED THEM. TORTURED THEM.
GRIND
GRIND
SPLUURT
SPLAP
THOSE NEAR ME WERE SHOCKED. BUT I'D HAD ENOUGH TREACHERY AND DEFIANCE.
I WAS WEEDING OUT THE SEEDS OF FUTURE TROUBLE.

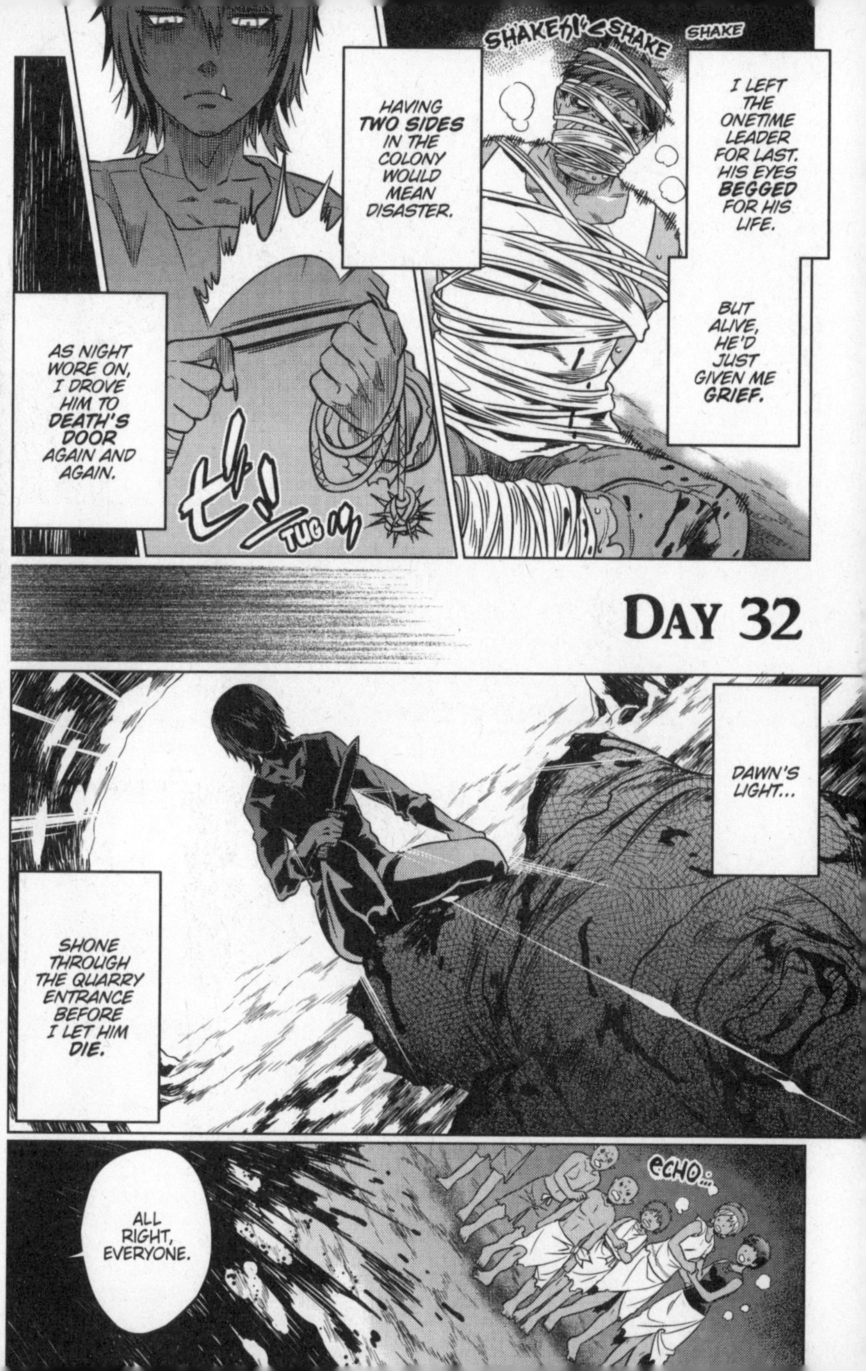

SHAKE SHAKE
SHAKE
I LEFT THE ONETIME LEADER FOR LAST. HIS EYES BEGGED FOR HIS LIFE.
BUT ALIVE, HE'D JUST GIVEN ME GRIEF.
HAVING TWO SIDES IN THE COLONY WOULD MEAN DISASTER.
AS NIGHT WORE ON, I DROVE HIM TO DEATH'S DOOR AGAIN AND AGAIN.
TUG
DAY 32
DAWN'S LIGHT...
SHONE THROUGH THE QUARRY ENTRANCE BEFORE I LET HIM DIE.
ECHO...
ALL RIGHT, EVERYONE.

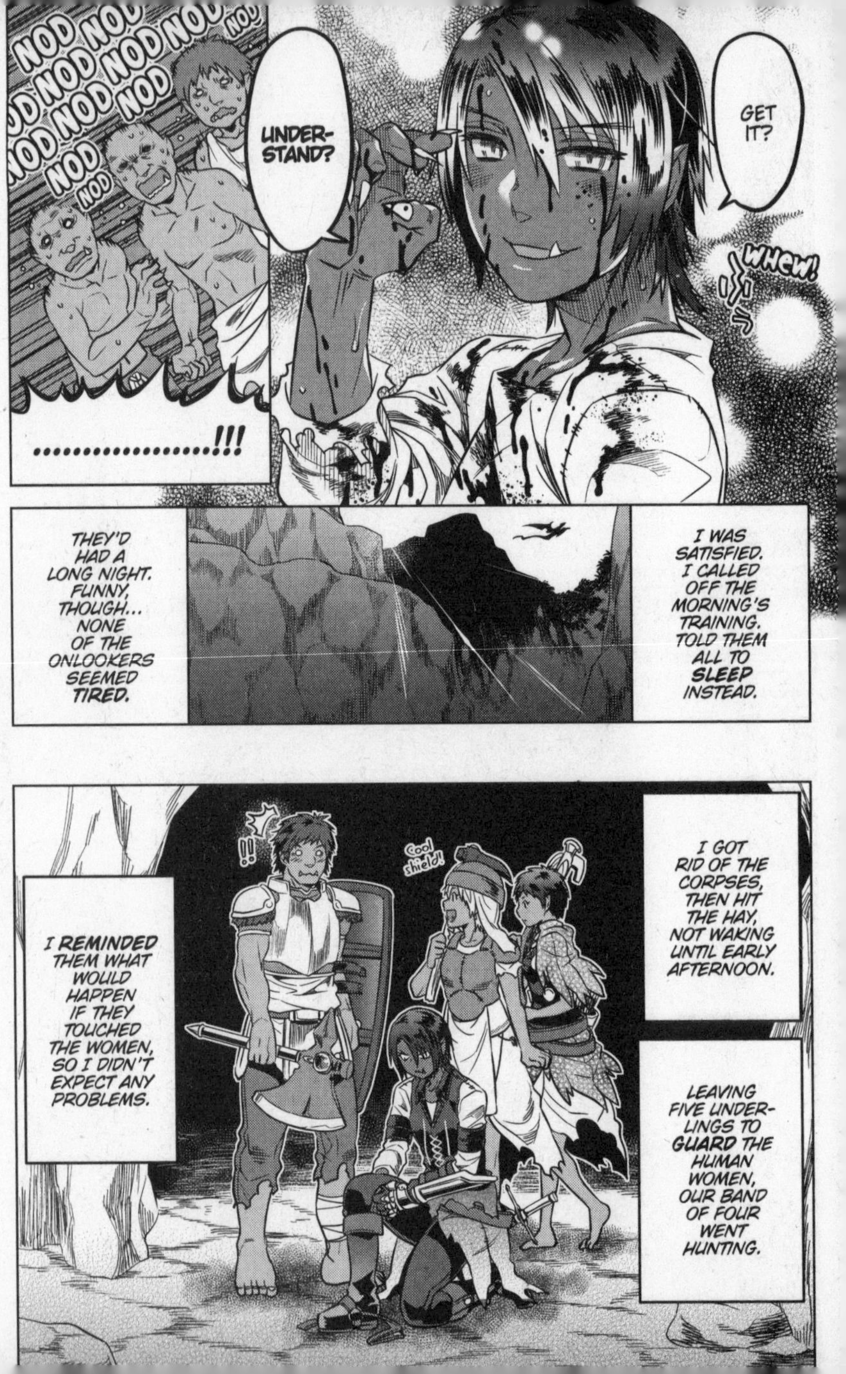
GET IT?
WHEW!
UNDER-STAND?
NOD NOD NOD NOD NOD NOD NOD NOD NOD NOD NOD
..................!!!
I WAS SATISFIED. I CALLED OFF THE MORNING'S TRAINING. TOLD THEM ALL TO SLEEP INSTEAD.
THEY'D HAD A LONG NIGHT. FUNNY, THOUGH... NONE OF THE ONLOOKERS SEEMED TIRED.
I GOT RID OF THE CORPSES, THEN HIT THE HAY, NOT WAKING UNTIL EARLY AFTERNOON.
LEAVING FIVE UNDER-LINGS TO GUARD THE HUMAN WOMEN, OUR BAND OF FOUR WENT HUNTING.
Cool shield!
!!
I REMINDED THEM WHAT WOULD HAPPEN IF THEY TOUCHED THE WOMEN, SO I DIDN'T EXPECT ANY PROBLEMS.

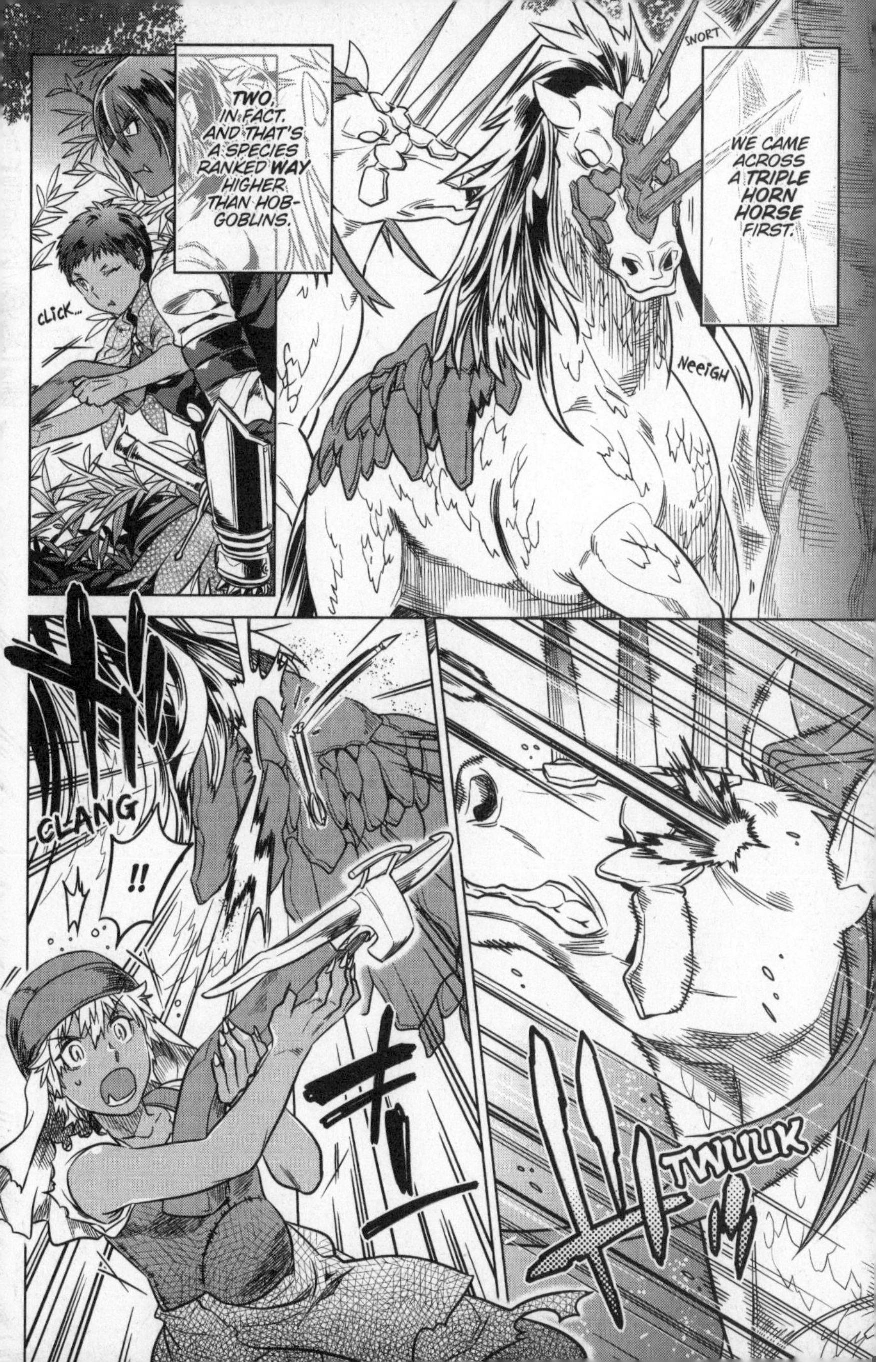
SNORT
WE CAME ACROSS A TRIPLE HORN HORSE FIRST.
NEEIGH
TWO, IN FACT. AND THAT'S A SPECIES RANKED WAY HIGHER THAN HOB-GOBLINS.
CLICK...
TWUUK
CLANG
!!

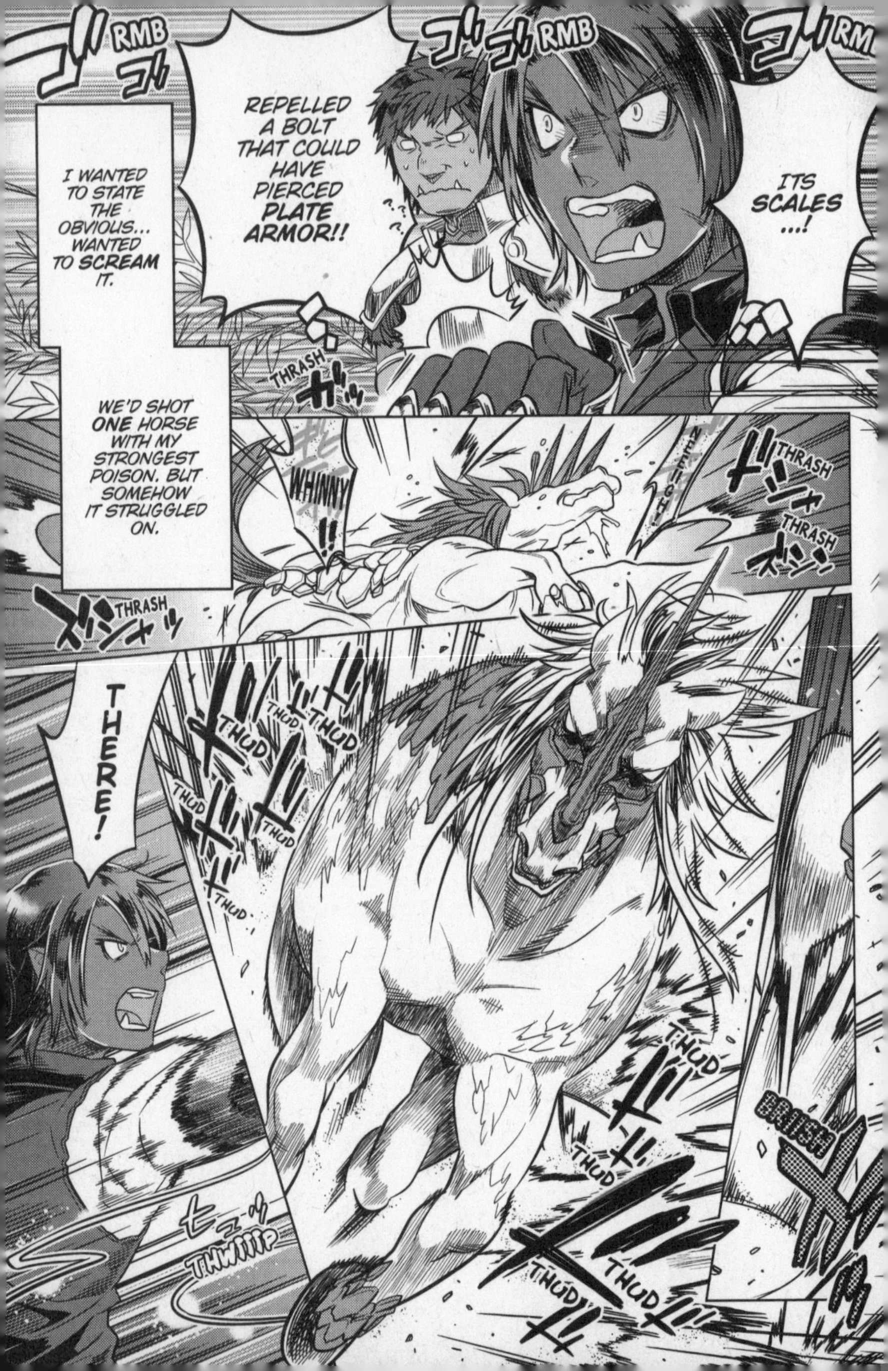
RM
ITS SCALES ...!
RMB
REPELLED A BOLT THAT COULD HAVE PIERCED PLATE ARMOR!!
RMB
I WANTED TO STATE THE OBVIOUS... WANTED TO SCREAM IT.
THRASH
THRASH
THRASH
NEEIGH!
WHINNY!!
WE'D SHOT ONE HORSE WITH MY STRONGEST POISON. BUT SOMEHOW IT STRUGGLED ON.
THRASH
THUD
THUD
THUD
THUD
THUD
THUD
THERE!
THUD
THUD
THUD
THUD
THWIIIP

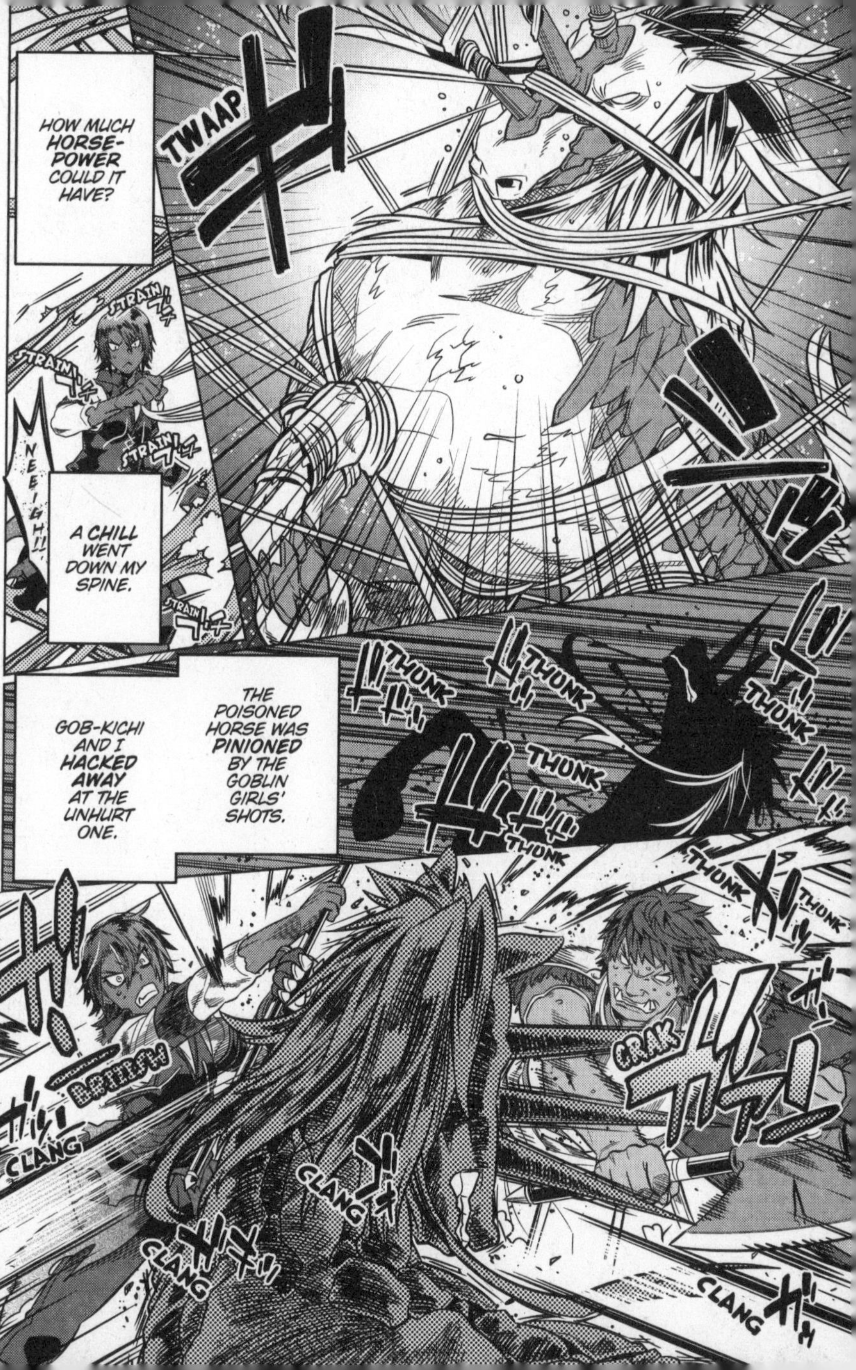
TWAAP
HOW MUCH HORSE-POWER COULD IT HAVE?
STRAIN
STRAIN
STRAIN
NEEEIGH!!
A CHILL WENT DOWN MY SPINE.
STRAIN
THUNK
THUNK
THUNK
THUNK
THUNK
THE POISONED HORSE WAS **PINIONED** BY THE GOBLIN GIRLS' SHOTS.
GOB-KICHI AND I **HACKED AWAY** AT THE UNHURT ONE.
THUNK
THUNK
CRAK
CLANG
CLANG
CLANG
CLANG

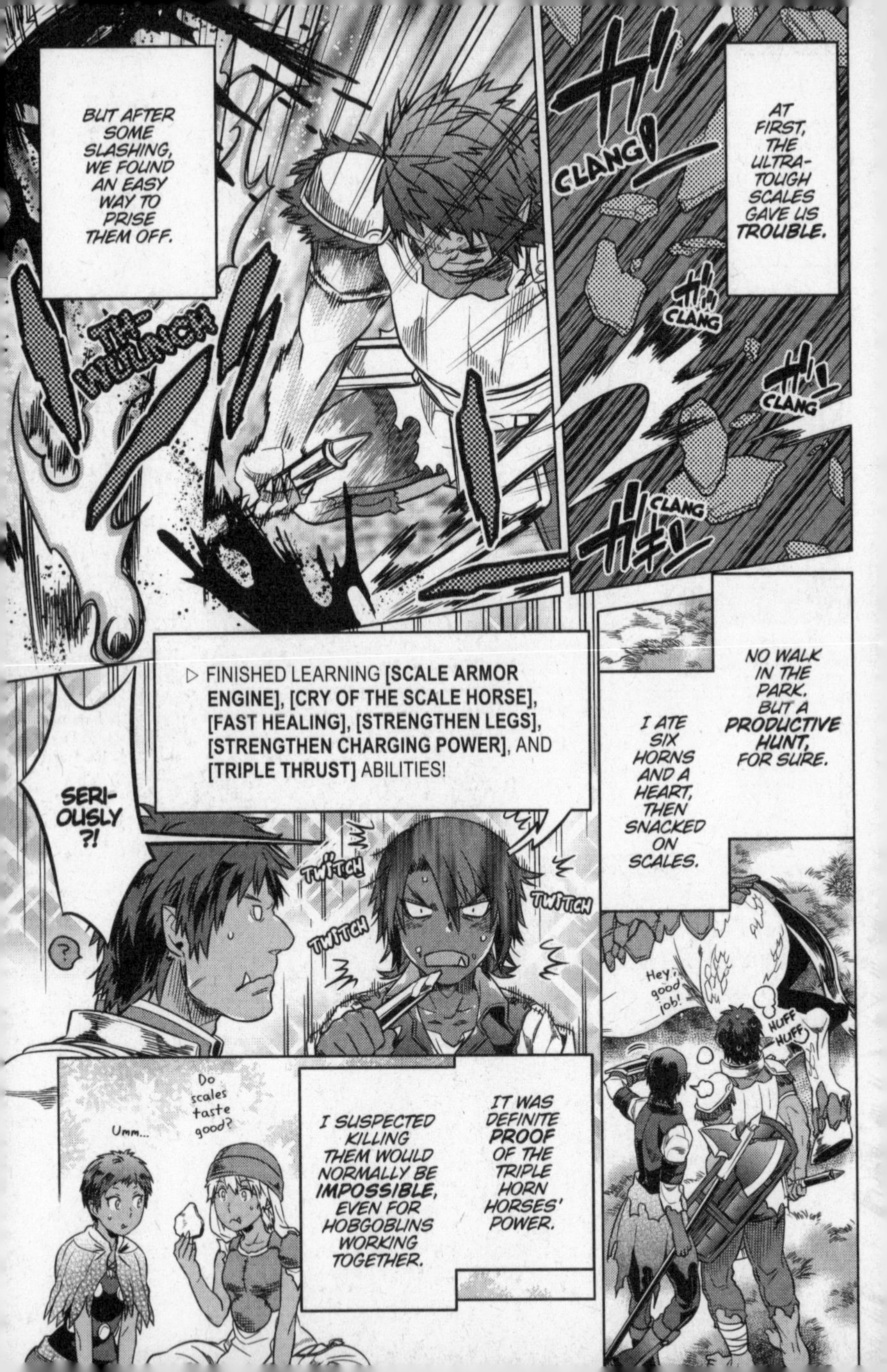
AT FIRST, THE ULTRA-TOUGH SCALES GAVE US TROUBLE.
CLANG!
CLANG
CLANG
CLANG
BUT AFTER SOME SLASHING, WE FOUND AN EASY WAY TO PRISE THEM OFF.
THWUNCH
NO WALK IN THE PARK. BUT A PRODUCTIVE HUNT, FOR SURE.
I ATE SIX HORNS AND A HEART, THEN SNACKED ON SCALES.
Hey, good job!
HUFF HUFF
▷ FINISHED LEARNING [SCALE ARMOR ENGINE], [CRY OF THE SCALE HORSE], [FAST HEALING], [STRENGTHEN LEGS], [STRENGTHEN CHARGING POWER], AND [TRIPLE THRUST] ABILITIES!
SERI-OUSLY ?!
TWITCH
TWITCH
TWITCH
?
IT WAS DEFINITE PROOF OF THE TRIPLE HORN HORSES' POWER.
I SUSPECTED KILLING THEM WOULD NORMALLY BE IMPOSSIBLE, EVEN FOR HOBGOBLINS WORKING TOGETHER.
Do scales taste good?
Umm...

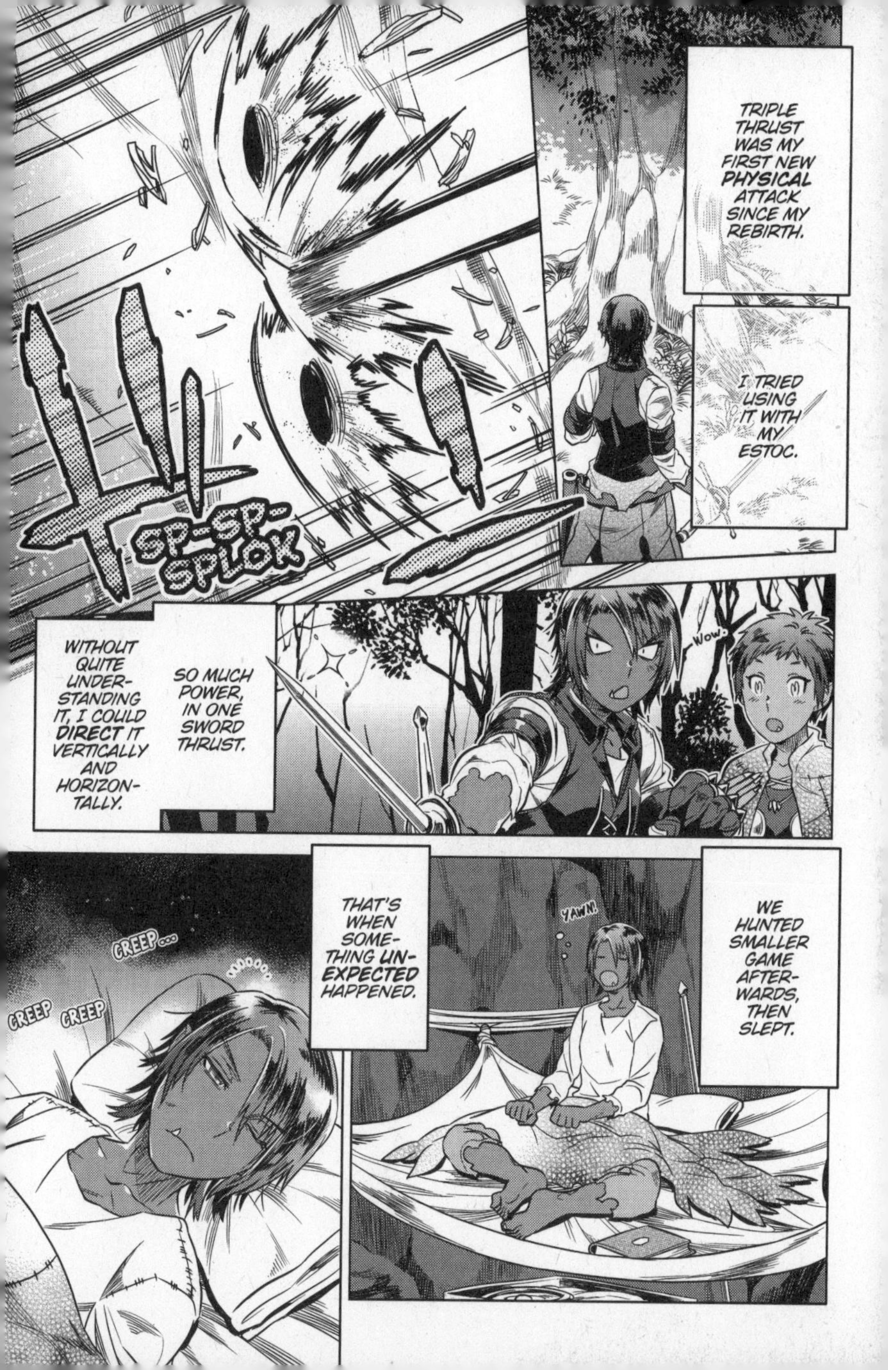
TRIPLE THRUST WAS MY FIRST NEW PHYSICAL ATTACK SINCE MY REBIRTH.
I TRIED USING IT WITH MY ESTOC.
SP-SP-SPLOK
WOW.
SO MUCH POWER, IN ONE SWORD THRUST.
WITHOUT QUITE UNDERSTANDING IT, I COULD DIRECT IT VERTICALLY AND HORIZONTALLY.
WE HUNTED SMALLER GAME AFTERWARDS, THEN SLEPT.
YAWN.
THAT'S WHEN SOMETHING UNEXPECTED HAPPENED.
CREEP...
CREEP
CREEP

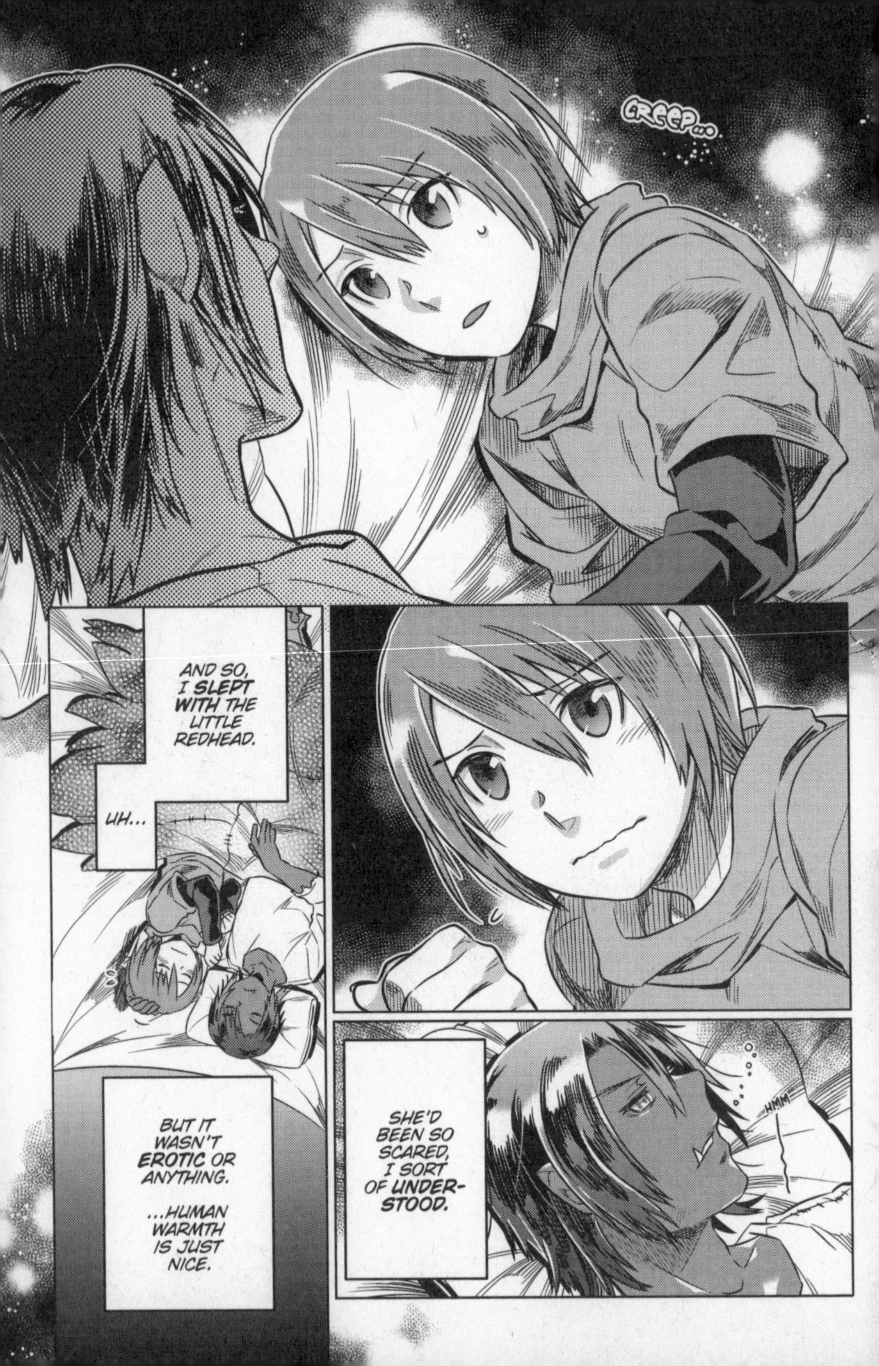
CREEP...
SHE'D BEEN SO SCARED, I SORT OF UNDERSTOOD.
HMM
AND SO, I SLEPT WITH THE LITTLE REDHEAD.
UH...
BUT IT WASN'T EROTIC OR ANYTHING.
...HUMAN WARMTH IS JUST NICE.

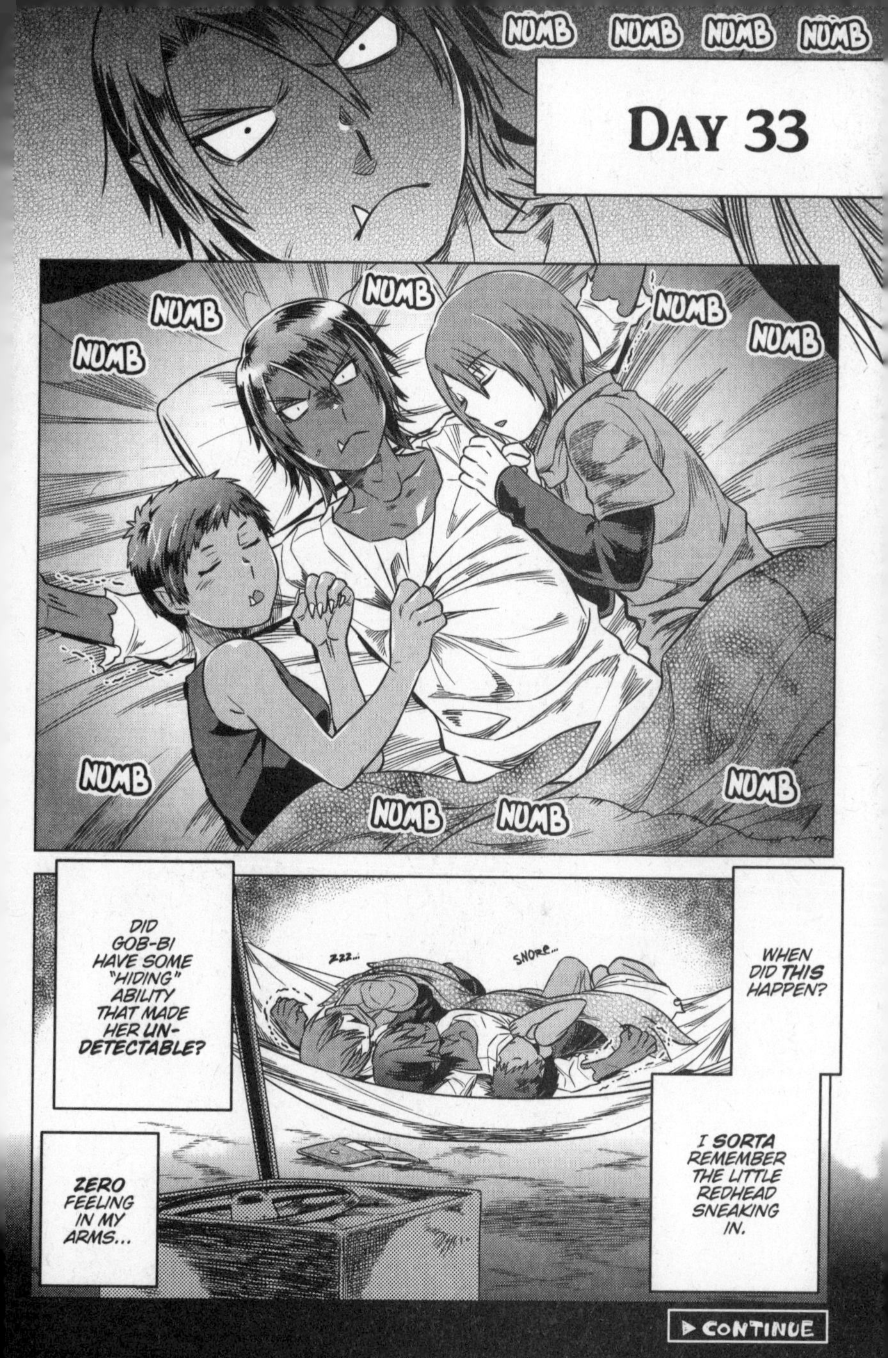
NUMB NUMB NUMB NUMB
DAY 33
NUMB
NUMB
NUMB
NUMB
NUMB
NUMB
NUMB
NUMB
NUMB
WHEN DID THIS HAPPEN?
I SORTA REMEMBER THE LITTLE REDHEAD SNEAKING IN.
SNORE...
ZZZ...
DID GOB-BI HAVE SOME "HIDING" ABILITY THAT MADE HER UN-DETECTABLE?
ZERO FEELING IN MY ARMS...
▶ CONTINUE

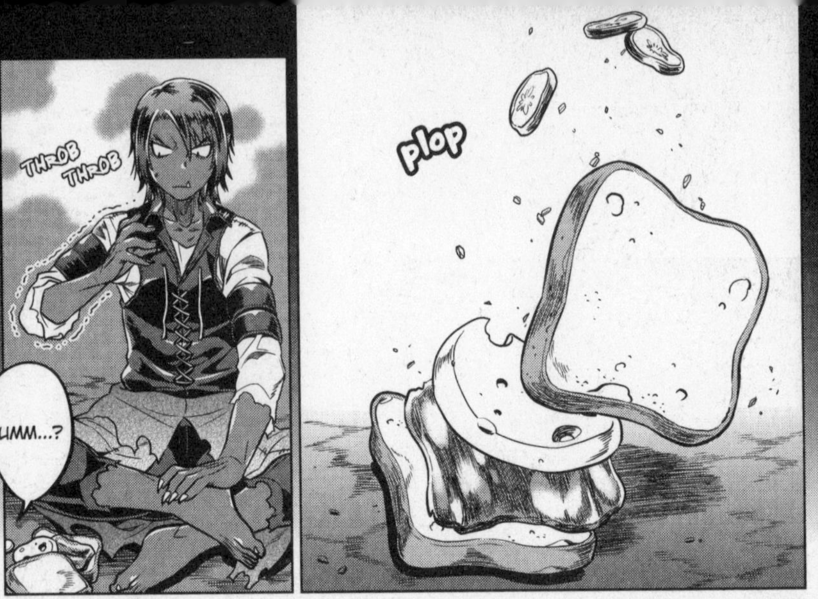
plop
THROB THROB
UMM...?

CHAPTER 10

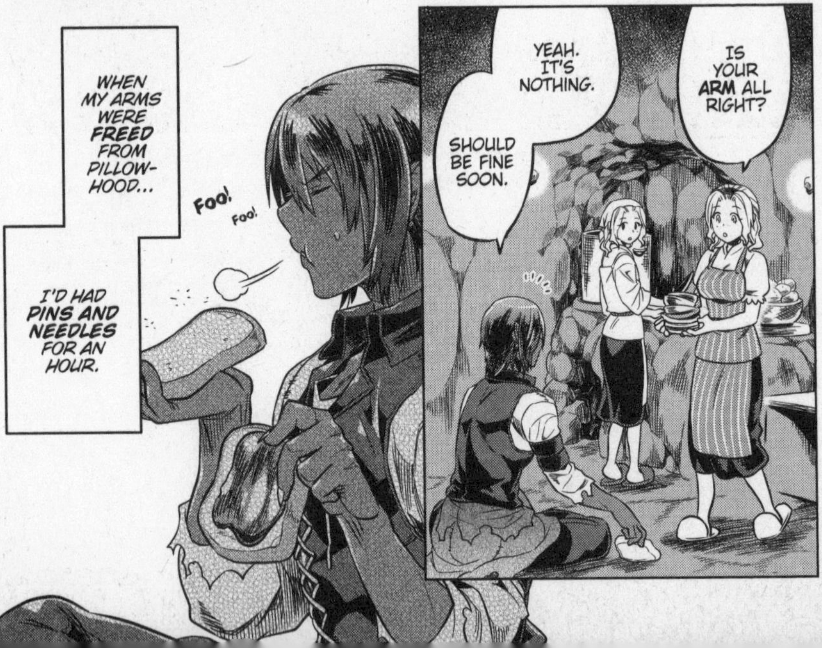
IS YOUR ARM ALL RIGHT?
YEAH. IT'S NOTHING.
SHOULD BE FINE SOON.
WHEN MY ARMS WERE FREED FROM PILLOW-HOOD...
I'D HAD PINS AND NEEDLES FOR AN HOUR.
FOO! FOO!

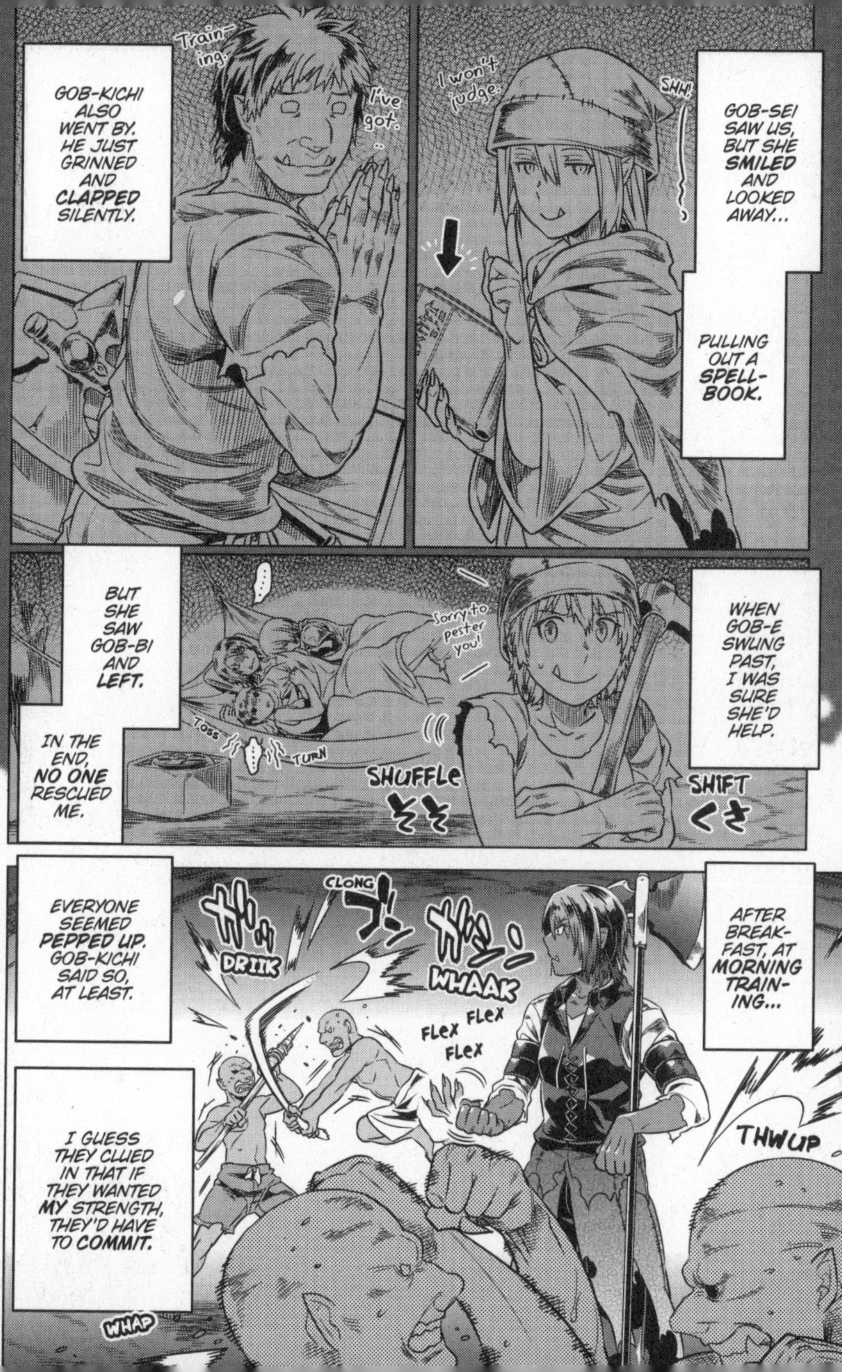

GOB-SEI SAW US, BUT SHE SMILED AND LOOKED AWAY...
SHH!
I won't judge.
PULLING OUT A SPELL-BOOK.
GOB-KICHI ALSO WENT BY. HE JUST GRINNED AND CLAPPED SILENTLY.
Train-ing.
I've got.
WHEN GOB-E SWUNG PAST, I WAS SURE SHE'D HELP.
SHIFT
くき
Sorry to pester you!
SHUFFLE
そそ
BUT SHE SAW GOB-BI AND LEFT.
TOSS
TURN
IN THE END, NO ONE RESCUED ME.
AFTER BREAK-FAST, AT MORNING TRAIN-ING...
CLONG
WHAAK
DRIIK
FLEX
FLEX
FLEX
THWUP
EVERYONE SEEMED PEPPED UP. GOB-KICHI SAID SO, AT LEAST.
I GUESS THEY CLUED IN THAT IF THEY WANTED MY STRENGTH, THEY'D HAVE TO COMMIT.
WHAP

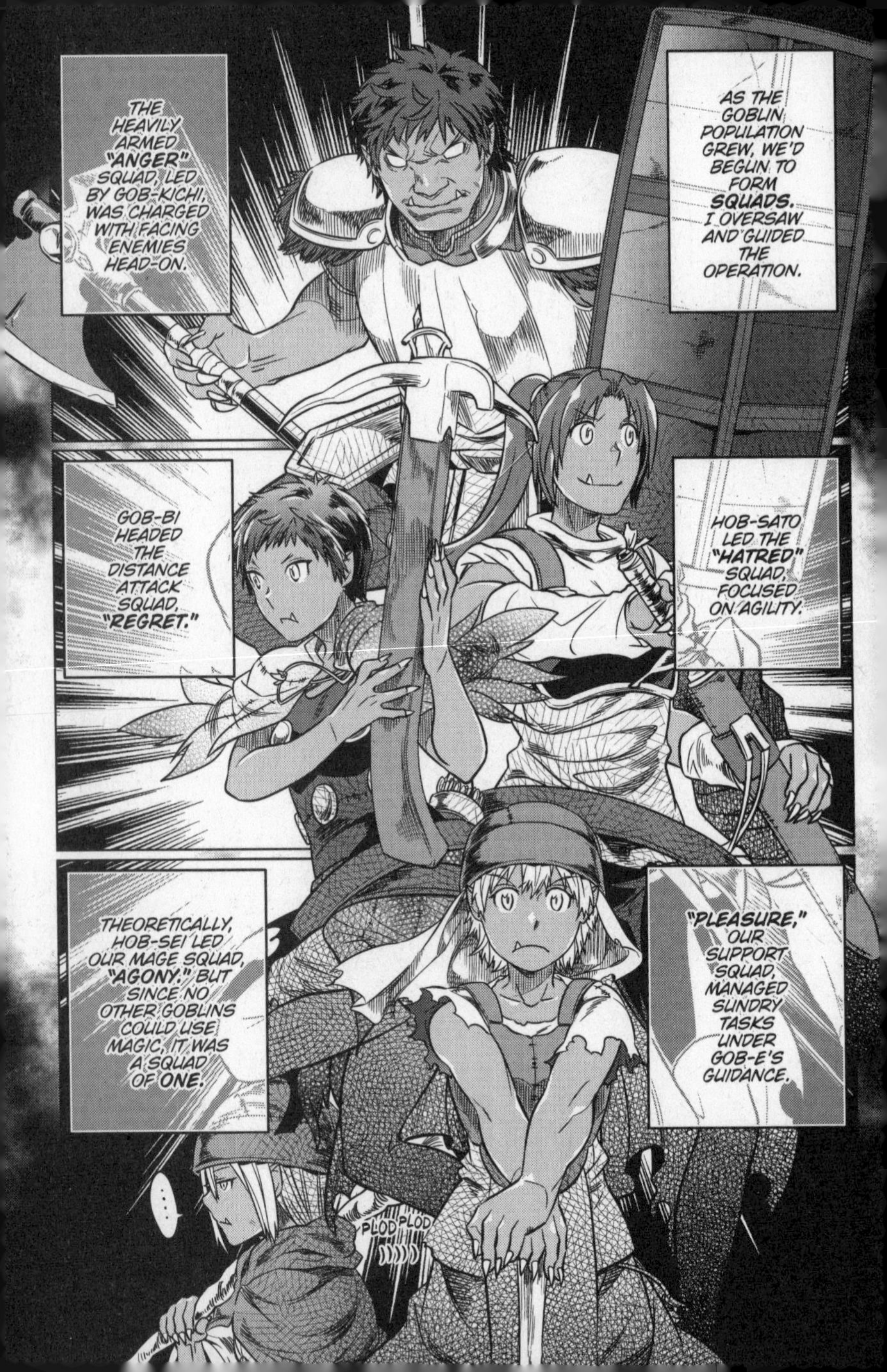
AS THE GOBLIN POPULATION GREW, WE'D BEGUN TO FORM SQUADS. I OVERSAW AND GUIDED THE OPERATION.
THE HEAVILY ARMED "ANGER" SQUAD, LED BY GOB-KICHI, WAS CHARGED WITH FACING ENEMIES HEAD-ON.
HOB-SATO LED THE "HATRED" SQUAD, FOCUSED ON AGILITY.
GOB-BI HEADED THE DISTANCE ATTACK SQUAD, "REGRET."
"PLEASURE," OUR SUPPORT SQUAD, MANAGED SUNDRY TASKS UNDER GOB-E'S GUIDANCE.
THEORETICALLY, HOB-SEI LED OUR MAGE SQUAD, "AGONY." BUT SINCE NO OTHER GOBLINS COULD USE MAGIC, IT WAS A SQUAD OF ONE.
....
PLOD PLOD

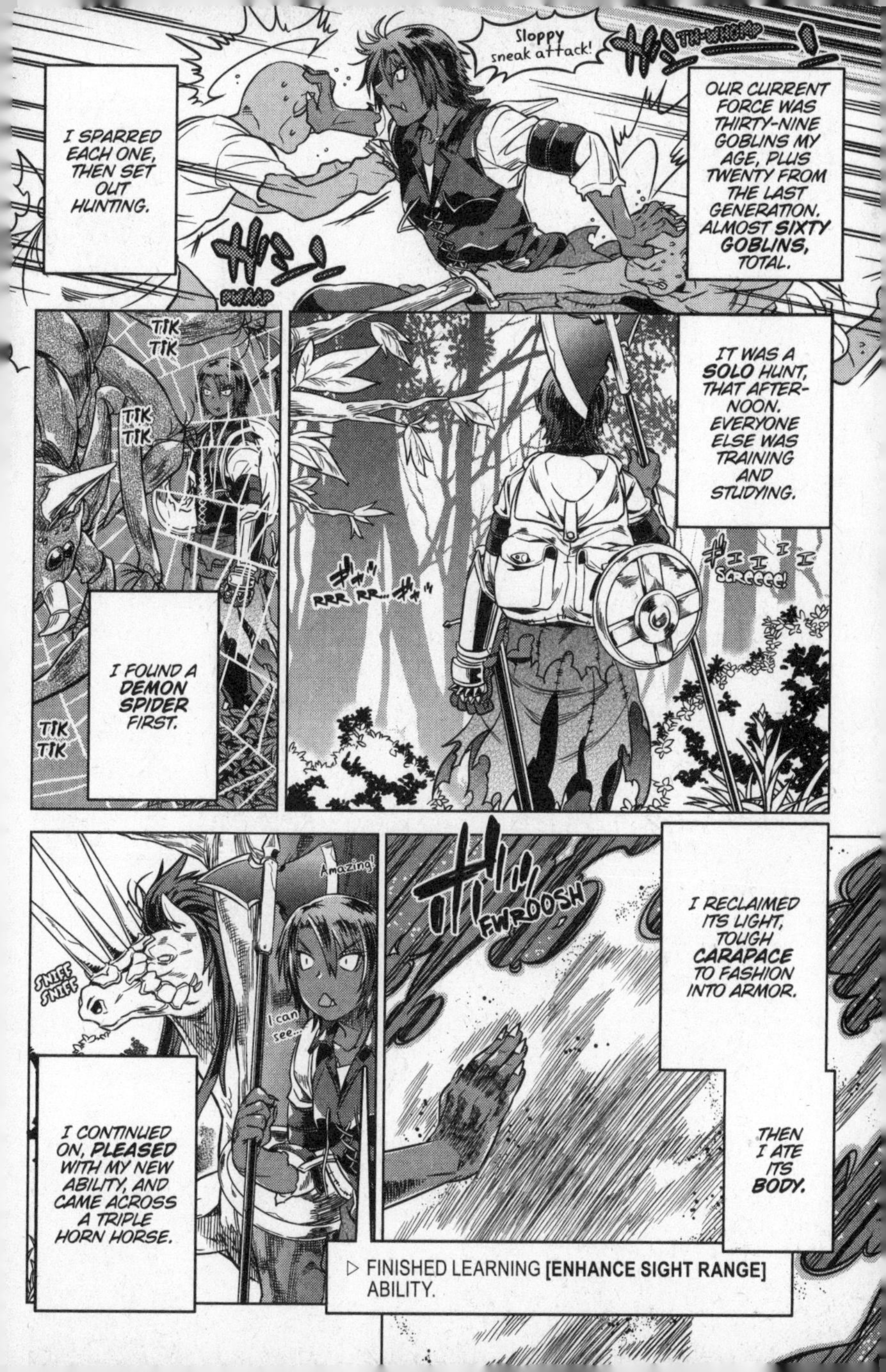
OUR CURRENT FORCE WAS THIRTY-NINE GOBLINS MY AGE, PLUS TWENTY FROM THE LAST GENERATION. ALMOST SIXTY GOBLINS, TOTAL.
TH-WHOMP
Sloppy sneak attack!
I SPARRED EACH ONE, THEN SET OUT HUNTING.
FWAAP
IT WAS A SOLO HUNT, THAT AFTERNOON. EVERYONE ELSE WAS TRAINING AND STUDYING.
SCREEEE!
RRR RR...
TIK TIK
TIK TIK
I FOUND A DEMON SPIDER FIRST.
TIK TIK
I RECLAIMED ITS LIGHT, TOUGH CARAPACE TO FASHION INTO ARMOR.
FWROOSH
THEN I ATE ITS BODY.
▷ FINISHED LEARNING [ENHANCE SIGHT RANGE] ABILITY.
Amazing!
I can see...
SNIFF SNIFF
I CONTINUED ON, PLEASED WITH MY NEW ABILITY, AND CAME ACROSS A TRIPLE HORN HORSE.

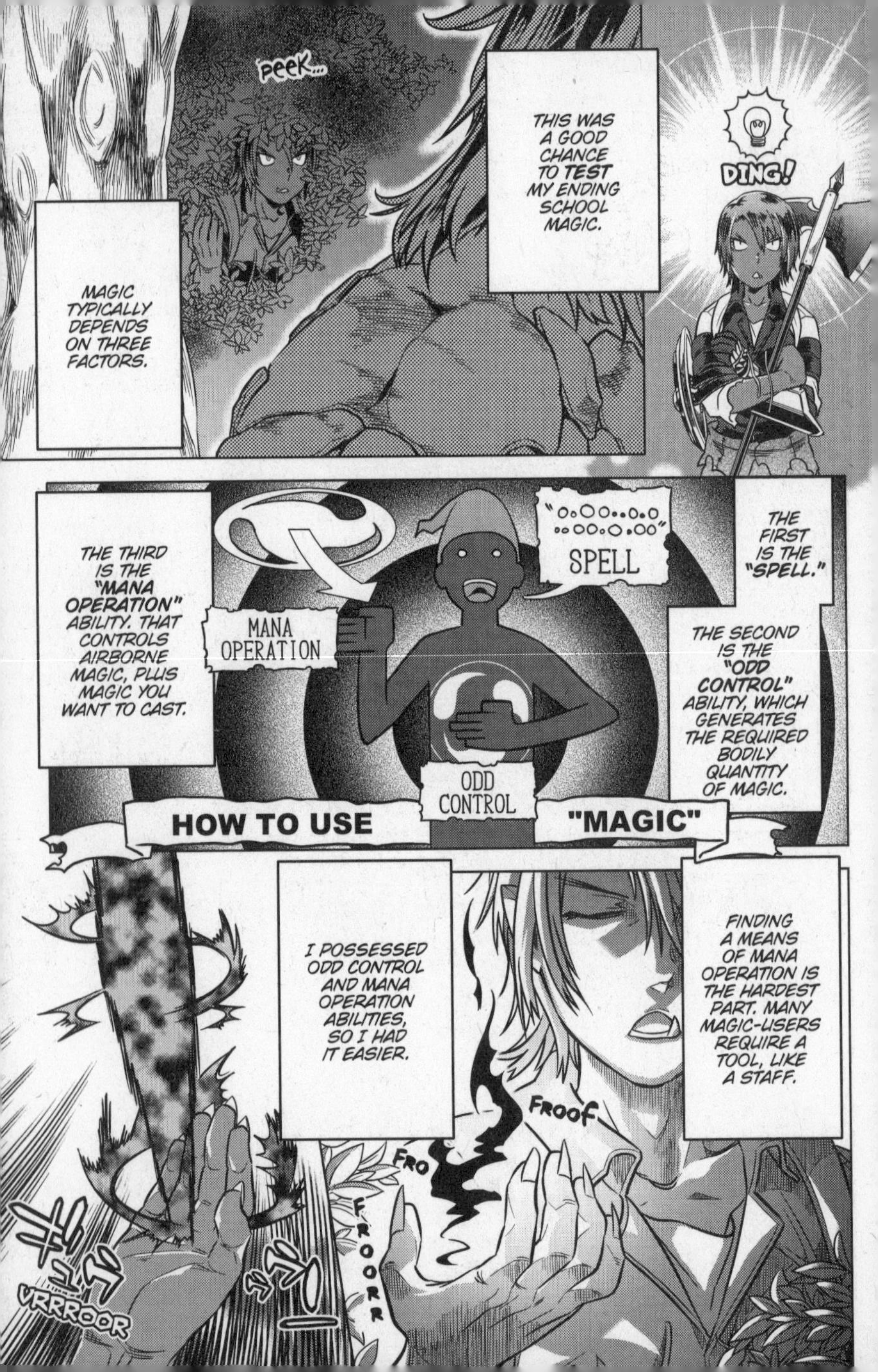
DING!
THIS WAS A GOOD CHANCE TO TEST MY ENDING SCHOOL MAGIC.
PEEK...
MAGIC TYPICALLY DEPENDS ON THREE FACTORS.
THE FIRST IS THE "SPELL."
"o.oOo..o.o.o oo.OOo.o.o.oo"
SPELL
THE SECOND IS THE "ODD CONTROL" ABILITY, WHICH GENERATES THE REQUIRED BODILY QUANTITY OF MAGIC.
ODD CONTROL
MANA OPERATION
THE THIRD IS THE "MANA OPERATION" ABILITY. THAT CONTROLS AIRBORNE MAGIC, PLUS MAGIC YOU WANT TO CAST.
HOW TO USE "MAGIC"
FINDING A MEANS OF MANA OPERATION IS THE HARDEST PART. MANY MAGIC-USERS REQUIRE A TOOL, LIKE A STAFF.
I POSSESSED ODD CONTROL AND MANA OPERATION ABILITIES, SO I HAD IT EASIER.
FROOF
FRO
FROORR
VRRROOR

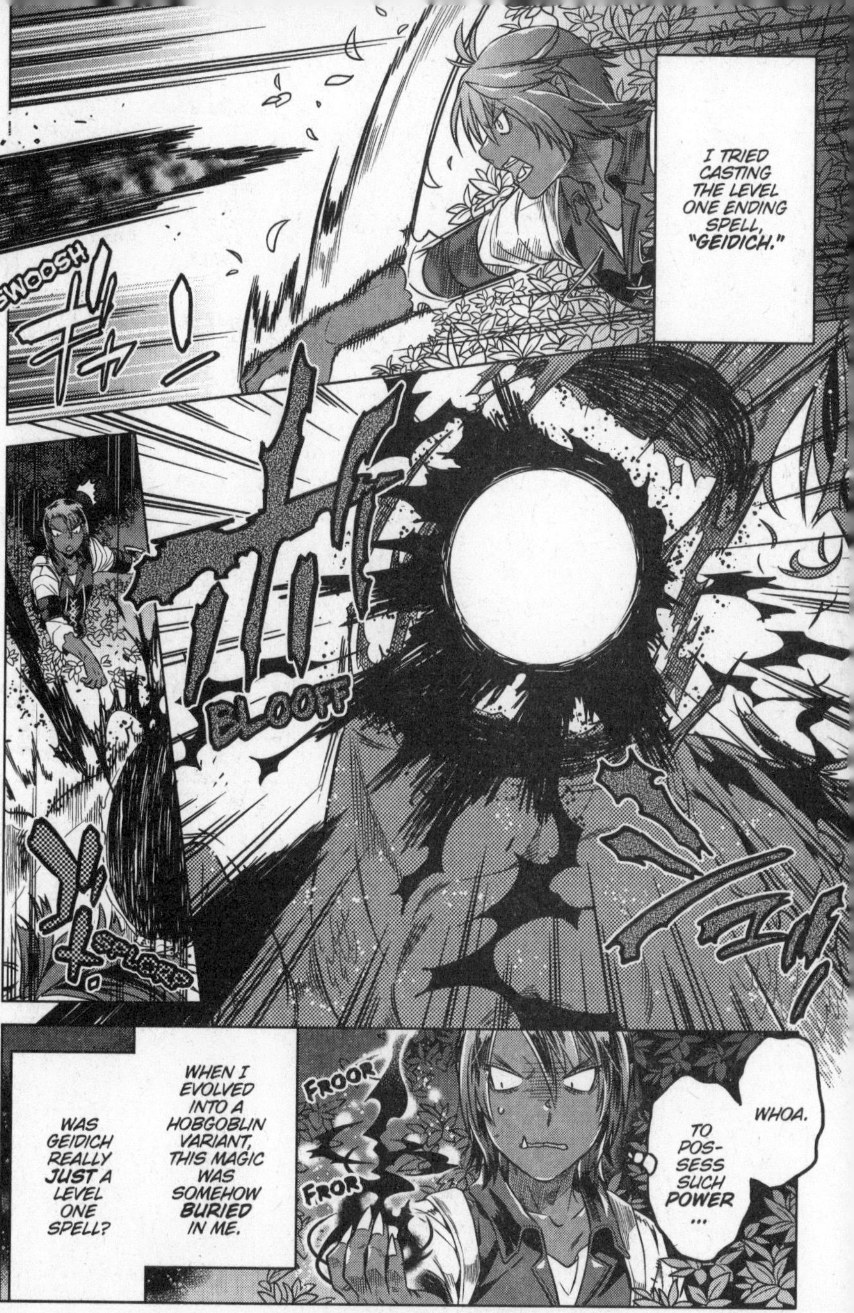
I TRIED CASTING THE LEVEL ONE ENDING SPELL, "GEIDICH."
GWOOSH
BLOOFF
SPLORP
WHOA.
TO POSSESS SUCH POWER ...
FROOR
FROR
WHEN I EVOLVED INTO A HOBGOBLIN VARIANT, THIS MAGIC WAS SOMEHOW BURIED IN ME.
WAS GEIDICH REALLY JUST A LEVEL ONE SPELL?

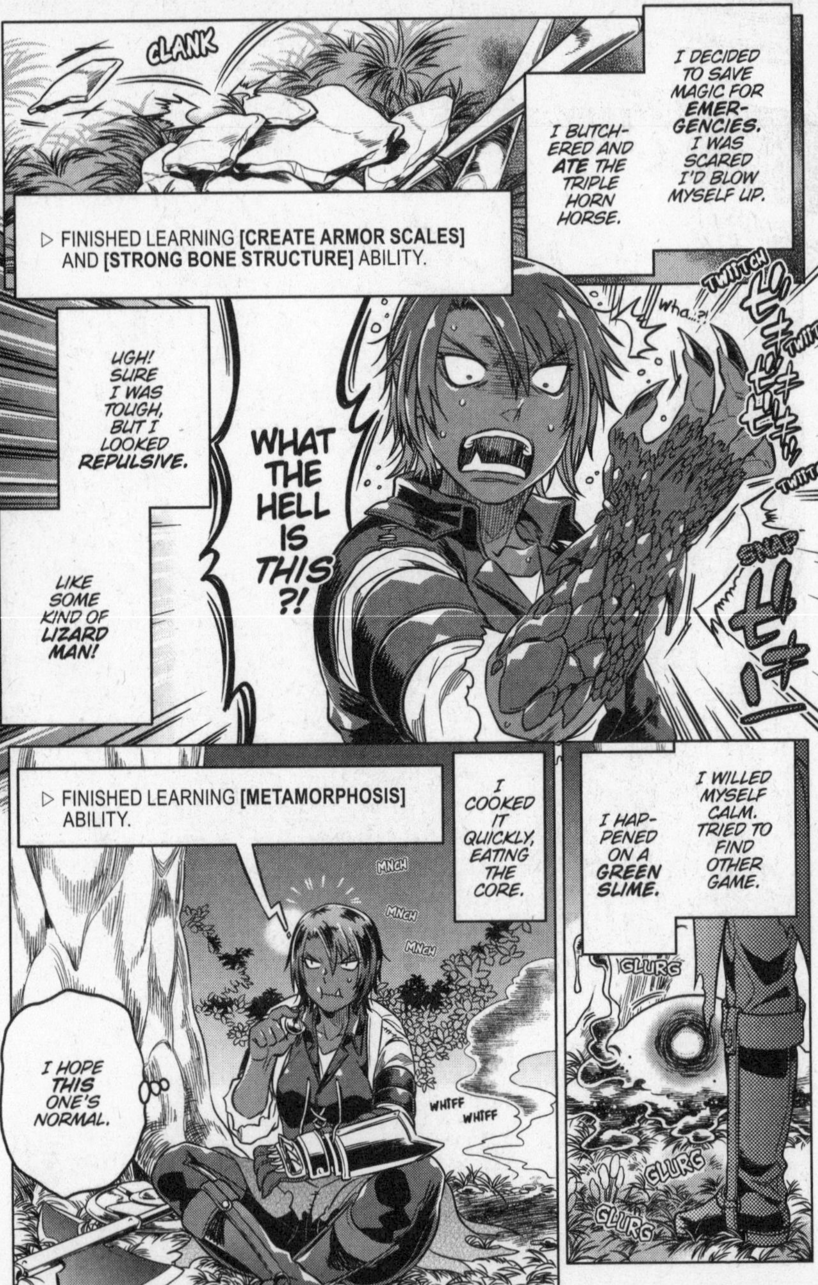
I DECIDED TO SAVE MAGIC FOR EMERGENCIES. I WAS SCARED I'D BLOW MYSELF UP.
I BUTCHERED AND ATE THE TRIPLE HORN HORSE.
CLANK
▷ FINISHED LEARNING [CREATE ARMOR SCALES] AND [STRONG BONE STRUCTURE] ABILITY.
TWITCH
TWITCH
TWITCH
Wha...?!
WHAT THE HELL IS THIS?!
SNAP
UGH! SURE I WAS TOUGH, BUT I LOOKED REPULSIVE.
LIKE SOME KIND OF LIZARD MAN!
I WILLED MYSELF CALM. TRIED TO FIND OTHER GAME.
I HAPPENED ON A GREEN SLIME.
GLURG
GLURG
GLURG
I COOKED IT QUICKLY, EATING THE CORE.
▷ FINISHED LEARNING [METAMORPHOSIS] ABILITY.
MNCH
MNCH
MNCH
WHIFF WHIFF
I HOPE THIS ONE'S NORMAL.

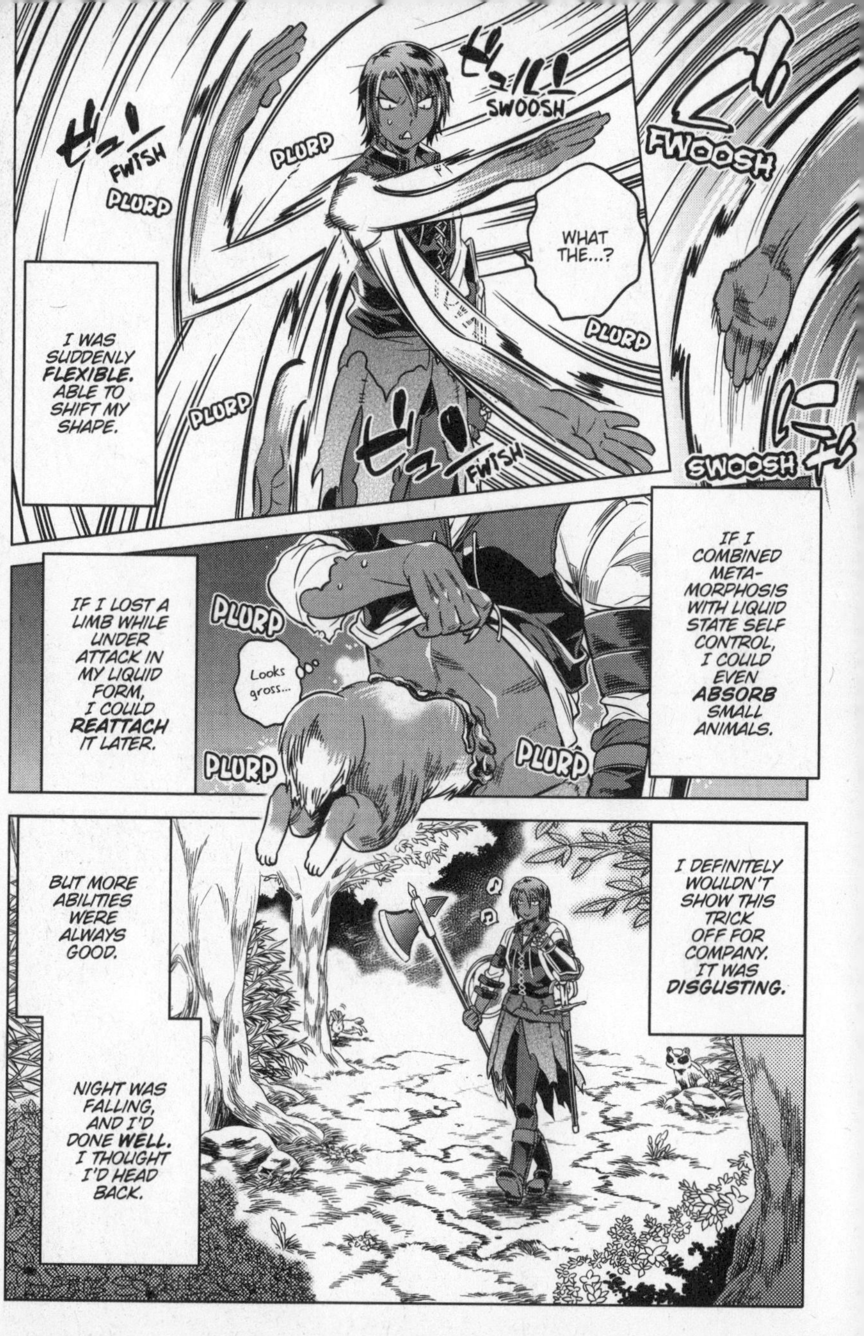
FWOOSH
SWOOSH
WHAT THE...?
PLURP
SWOOSH
PLURP
FWISH
PLURP
PLURP
FWISH
I WAS SUDDENLY **FLEXIBLE.** ABLE TO SHIFT MY SHAPE.
IF I COMBINED META-MORPHOSIS WITH LIQUID STATE SELF CONTROL, I COULD EVEN **ABSORB** SMALL ANIMALS.
PLURP
Looks gross...
PLURP
PLURP
IF I LOST A LIMB WHILE UNDER ATTACK IN MY LIQUID FORM, I COULD **REATTACH** IT LATER.
I DEFINITELY WOULDN'T SHOW THIS TRICK OFF FOR COMPANY. IT WAS **DISGUSTING.**
BUT MORE ABILITIES WERE ALWAYS GOOD.
NIGHT WAS FALLING, AND I'D DONE **WELL.** I THOUGHT I'D HEAD BACK.

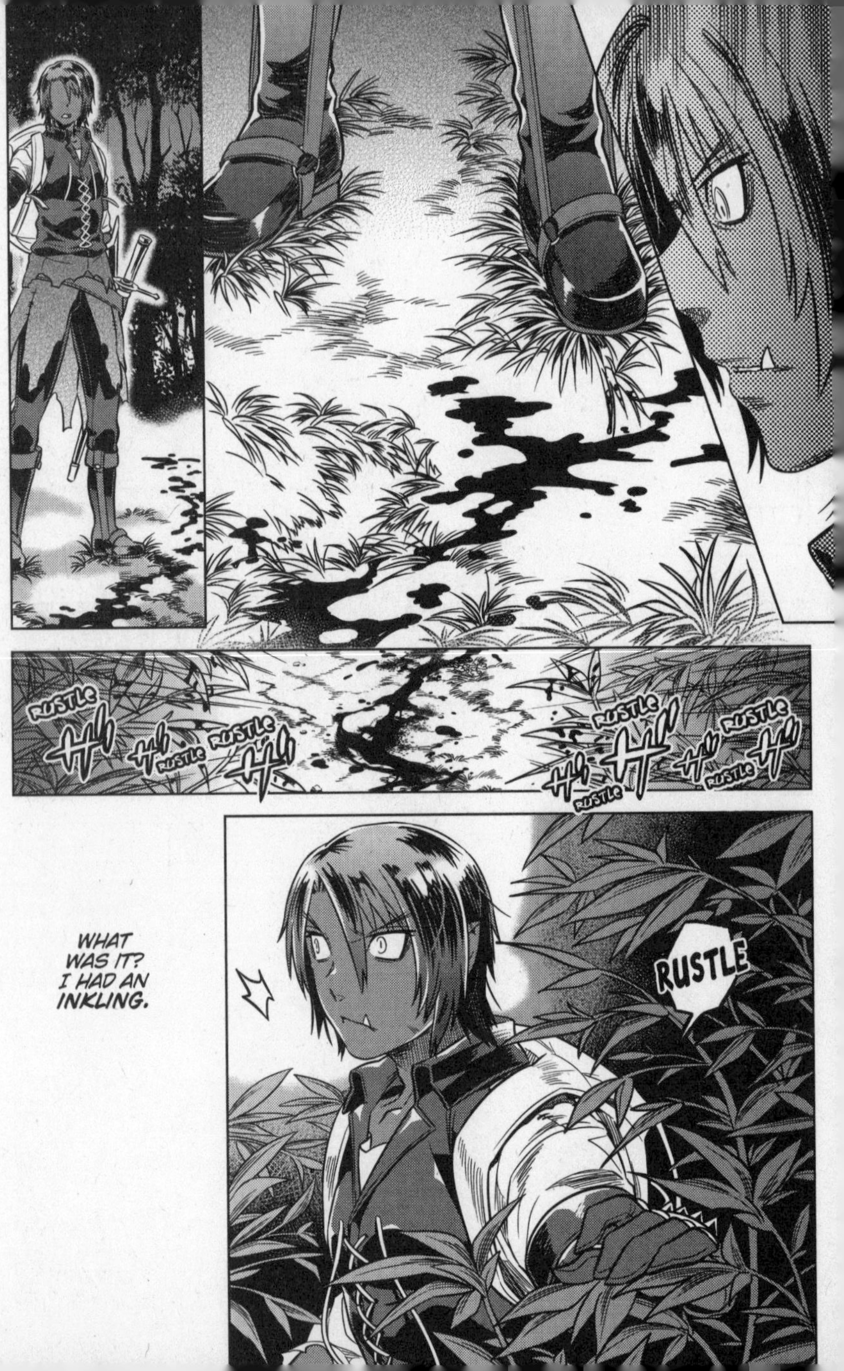
RUSTLE
RUSTLE
RUSTLE
RUSTLE
RUSTLE
RUSTLE
RUSTLE
WHAT WAS IT? I HAD AN INKLING.
RUSTLE

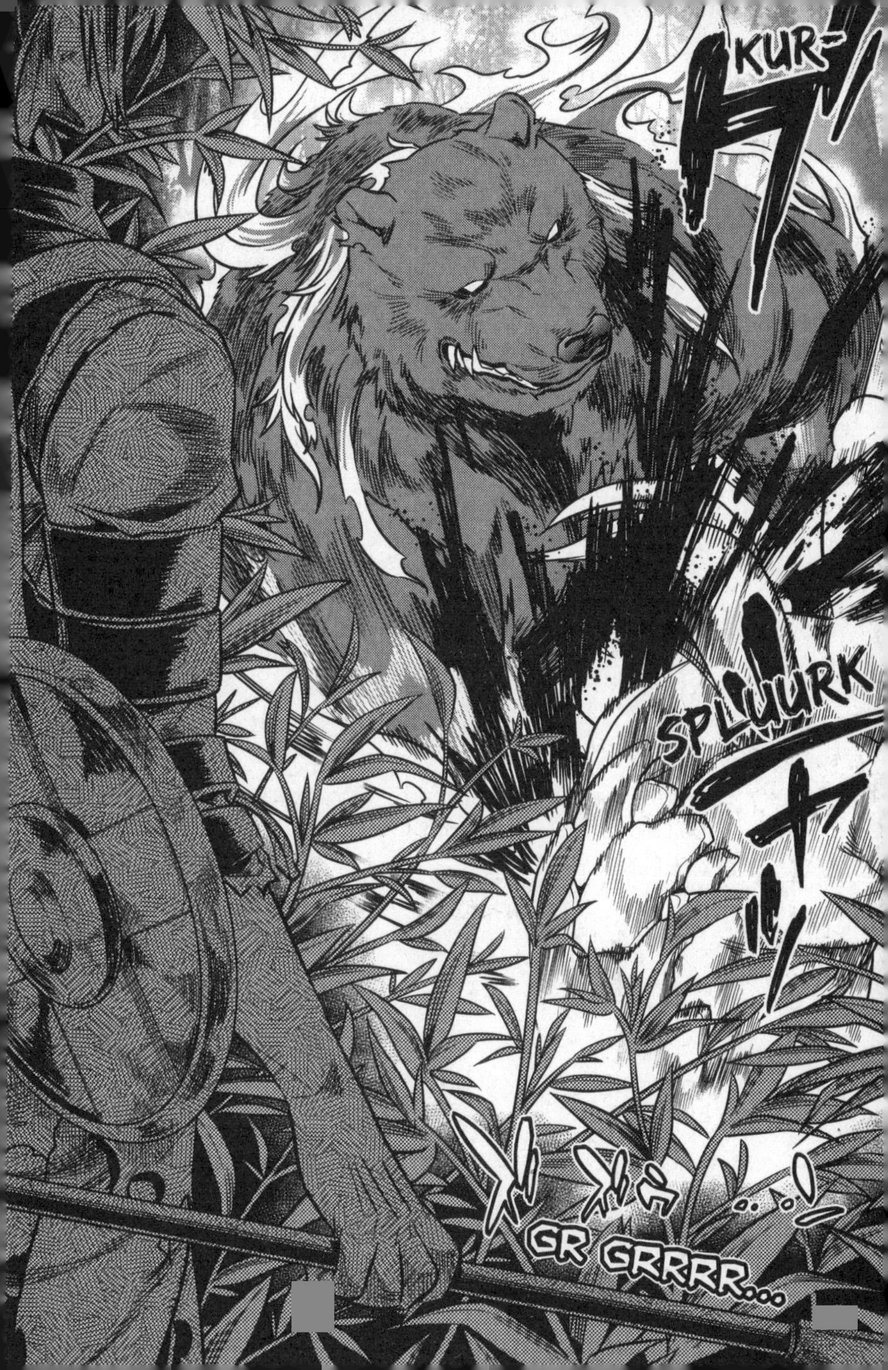
KUR-
SPLUUURK
GR GRRRR...

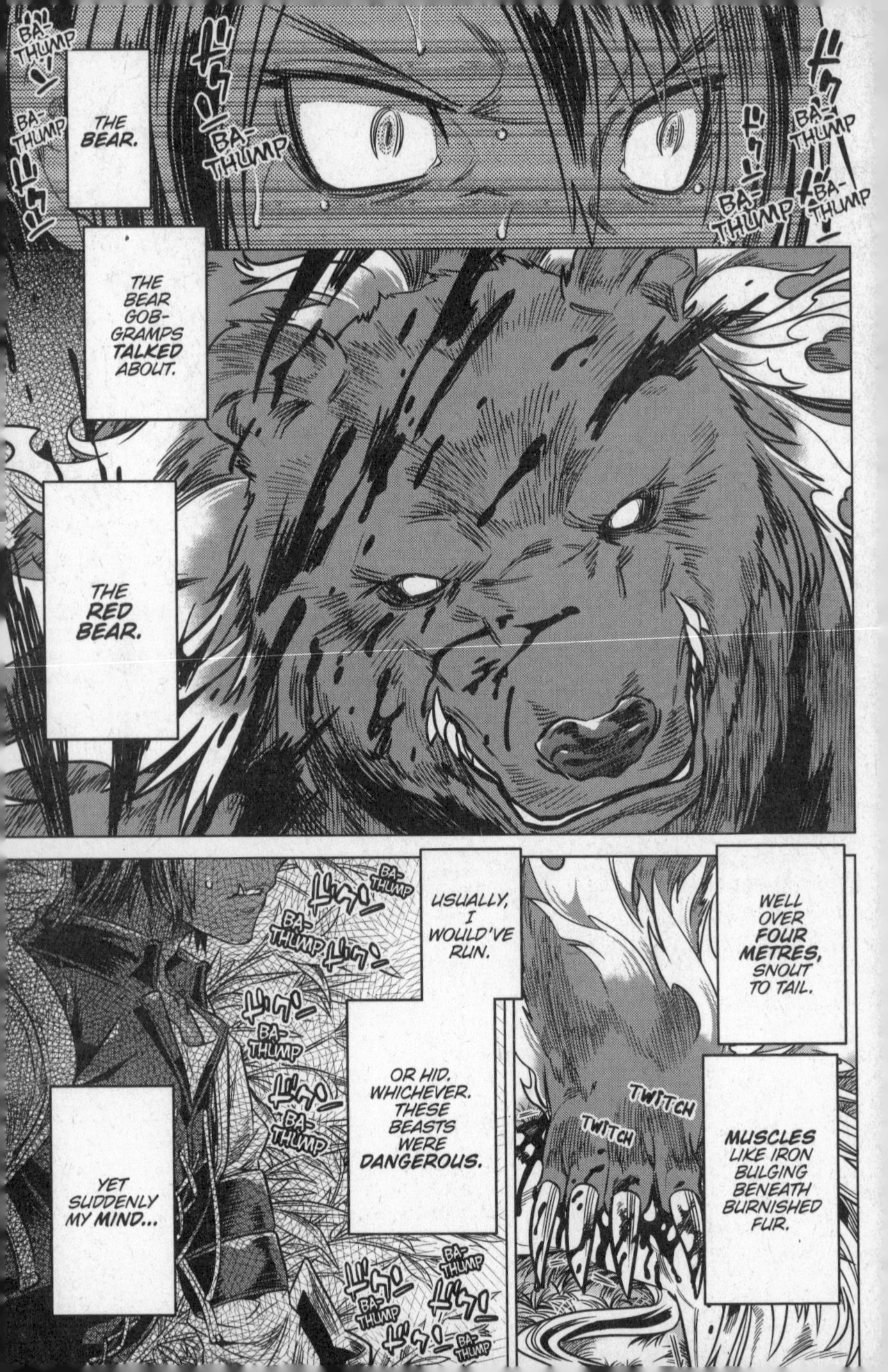
BA-THUMP
BA-THUMP
BA-THUMP
BA-THUMP
BA-THUMP
BA-THUMP
THE BEAR.
THE BEAR GOB-GRAMPS TALKED ABOUT.
THE RED BEAR.
WELL OVER FOUR METRES, SNOUT TO TAIL.
TWITCH
TWITCH
MUSCLES LIKE IRON BULGING BENEATH BURNISHED FUR.
USUALLY, I WOULD'VE RUN.
OR HID. WHICHEVER. THESE BEASTS WERE DANGEROUS.
BA-THUMP
BA-THUMP
BA-THUMP
BA-THUMP
YET SUDDENLY MY MIND...
BA-THUMP
BA-THUMP
BA-THUMP

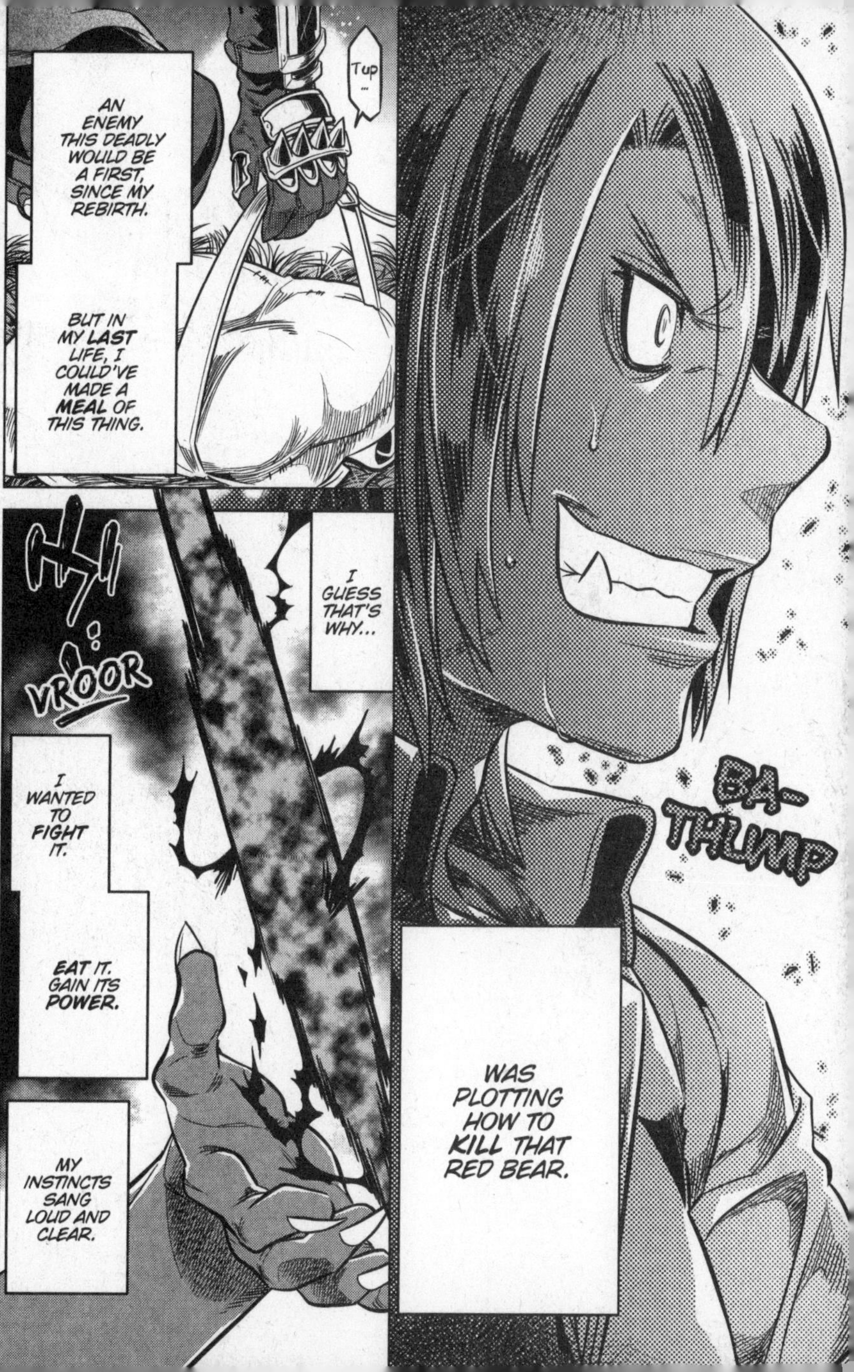
Tup...
AN ENEMY THIS DEADLY WOULD BE A FIRST, SINCE MY REBIRTH.
BUT IN MY LAST LIFE, I COULD'VE MADE A MEAL OF THIS THING.
I GUESS THAT'S WHY...
VROOR
I WANTED TO FIGHT IT.
EAT IT. GAIN ITS POWER.
MY INSTINCTS SANG LOUD AND CLEAR.
BA-THUMP
WAS PLOTTING HOW TO KILL THAT RED BEAR.

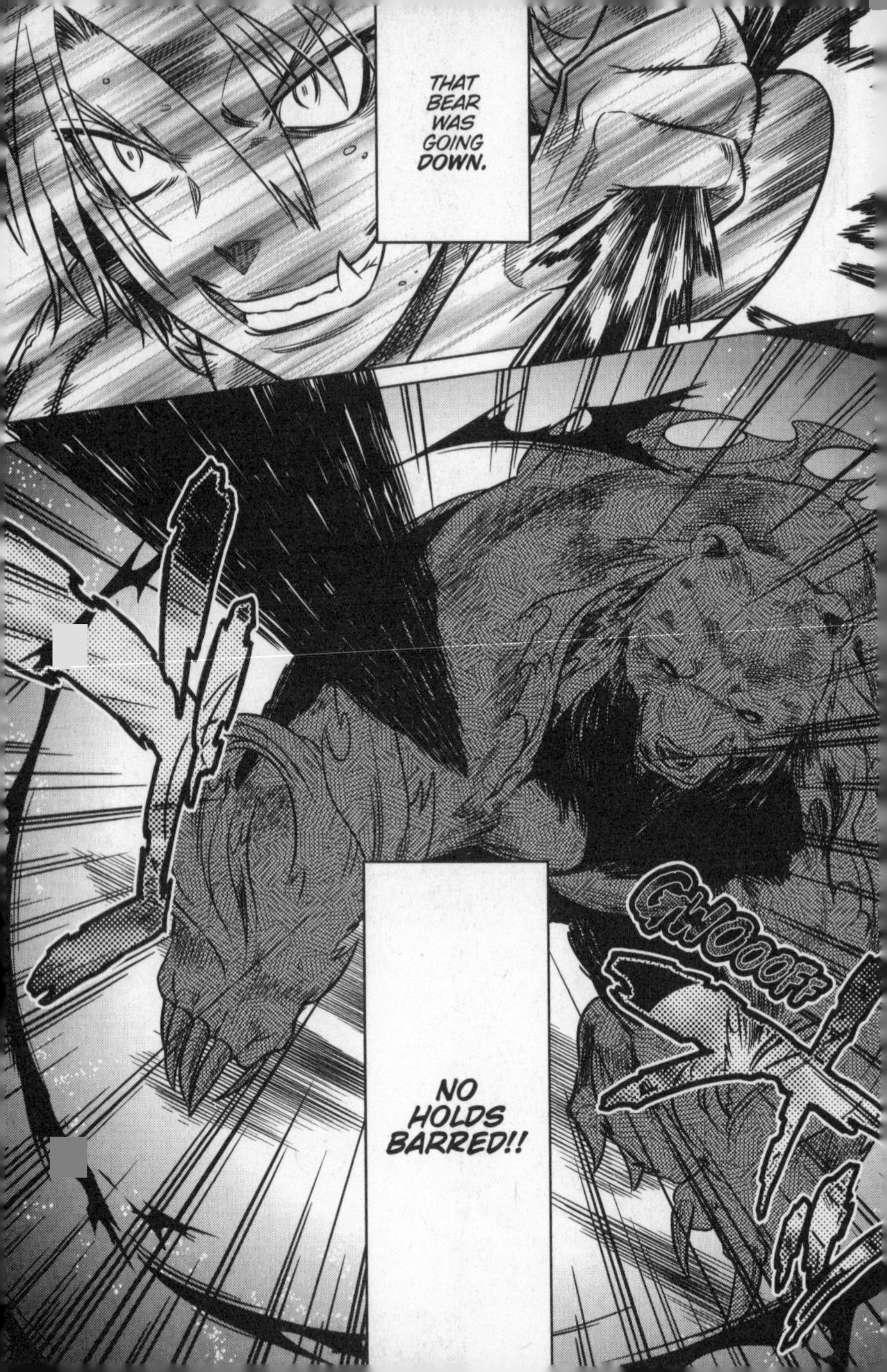
THAT BEAR WAS GOING DOWN.
NO HOLDS BARRED!!
GWOOOFF

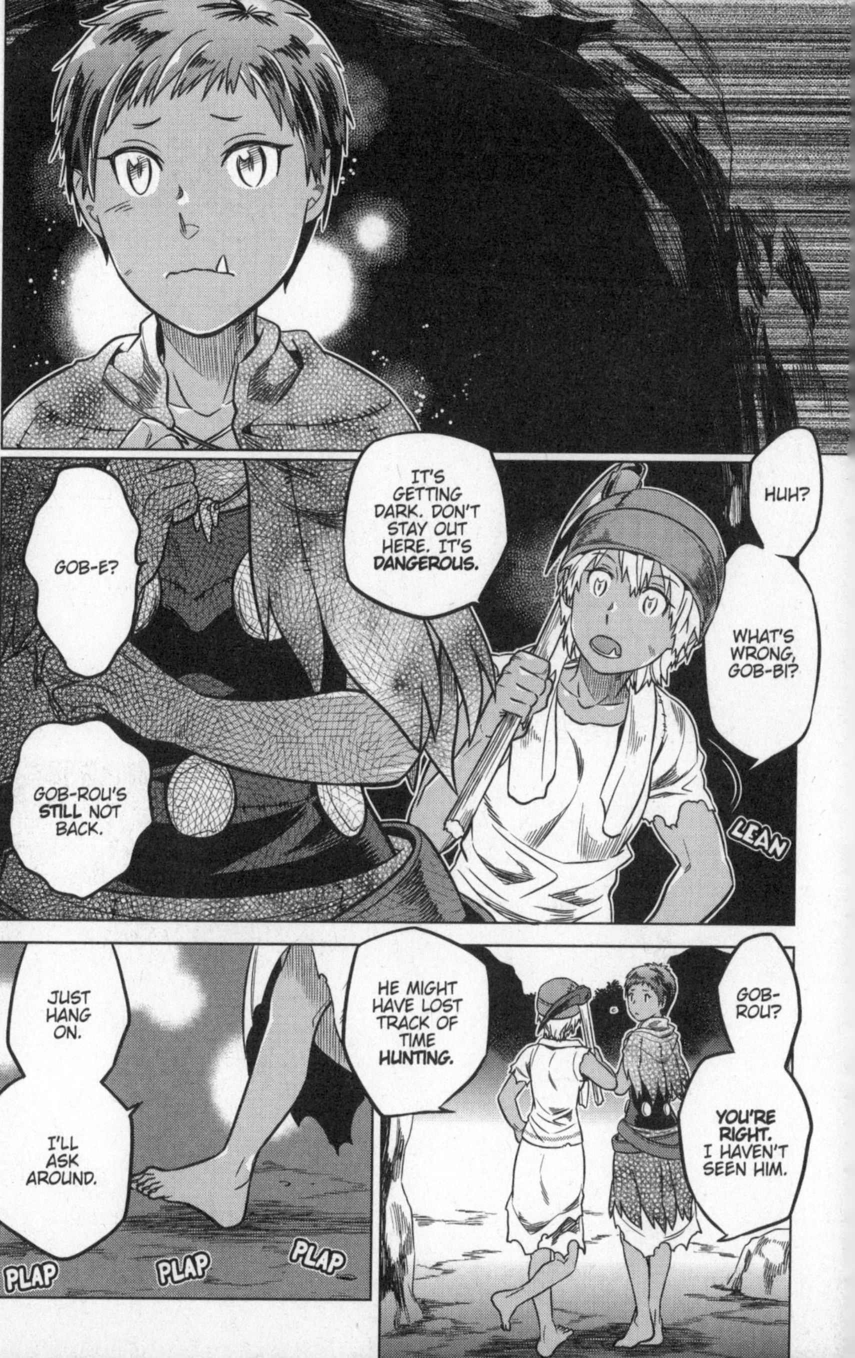
HUH?
WHAT'S WRONG, GOB-BI?
IT'S GETTING DARK. DON'T STAY OUT HERE. IT'S **DANGEROUS.**
LEAN
GOB-E?
GOB-ROU'S **STILL** NOT BACK.
GOB-ROU?
YOU'RE RIGHT. I HAVEN'T SEEN HIM.
HE MIGHT HAVE LOST TRACK OF TIME **HUNTING.**
JUST HANG ON.
I'LL ASK AROUND.
PLAP
PLAP
PLAP

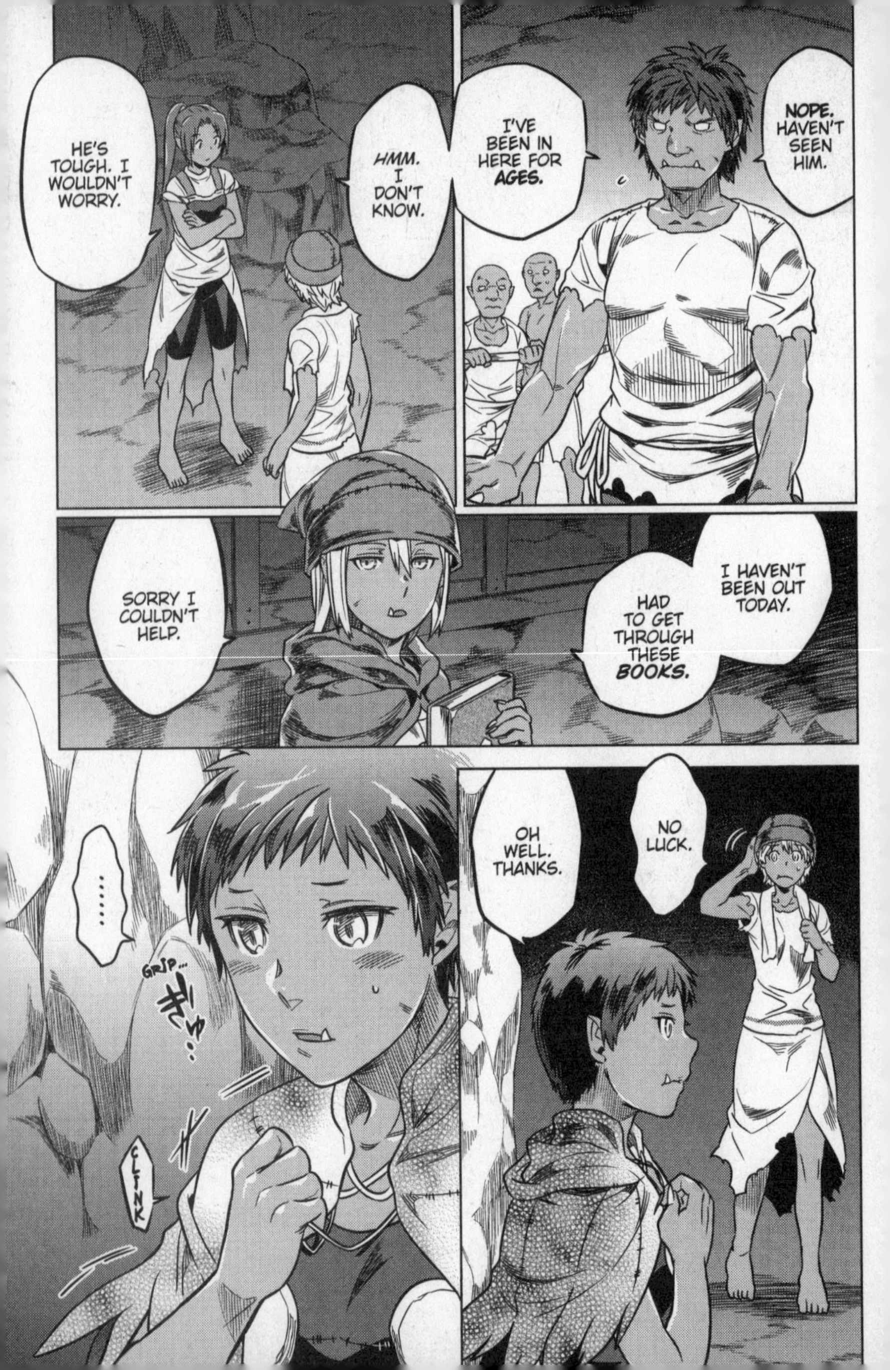
NOPE. HAVEN'T SEEN HIM.
I'VE BEEN IN HERE FOR AGES.
HMM. I DON'T KNOW.
HE'S TOUGH. I WOULDN'T WORRY.
I HAVEN'T BEEN OUT TODAY.
HAD TO GET THROUGH THESE BOOKS.
SORRY I COULDN'T HELP.
NO LUCK.
OH WELL. THANKS.
......
GRIP...
ぎゅ...
CLINK

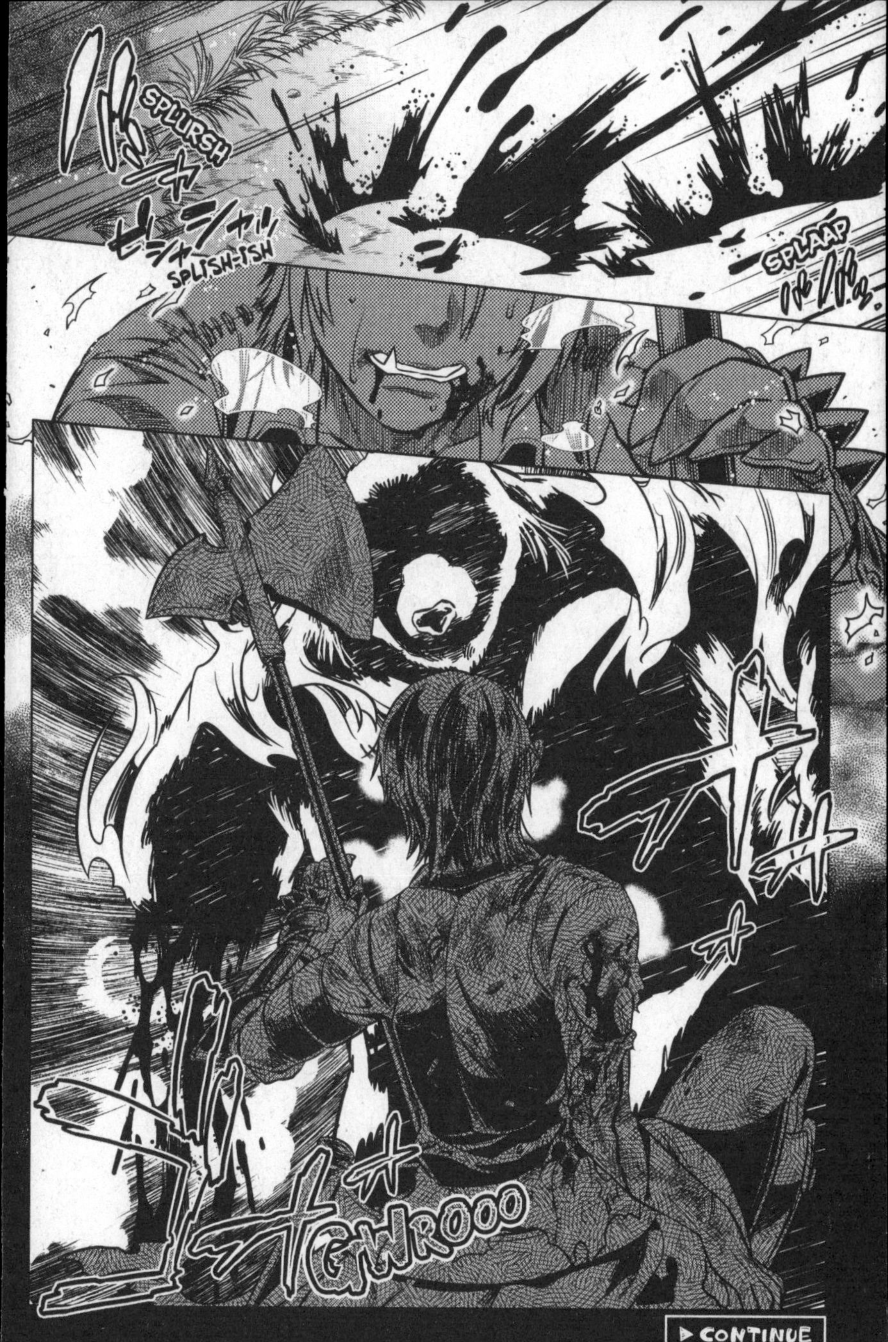
SPLAAP
SPLURSH
SPLISH-ISH
GWROOO

▶ CONTINUE

SEVEN SEAS ENTERTAINMENT PRESENTS

Re:Monster vol. 1

story by **KOGITSUNE KANEKIRU**   art by **HARUYOSHI KOBAYAKAWA**

TRANSLATION
Lu Huan

ADAPTATION
Rebecca Schneidereit

LETTERING AND RETOUCH
Meaghan Tucker

ENGLISH COVER DESIGN
Nicky Lim

PROOFREADER
Lee Otter

PRODUCTION MANAGER
Lissa Pattillo

EDITOR-IN-CHIEF
Adam Arnold

PUBLISHER
Jason DeAngelis

RE:MONSTER VOL. 1
© KOGITSUNE KANEKIRU, HARUYOSHI KOBAYAKAWA 2015.
First published in Japan in 2015 by KOGITSUNE KANEKIRU and
HARUYOSHI KOBAYAKAWA.
English translation rights arranged with AlphaPolis.
Book design by ansyyqdesign.

Seven Seas books may be purchased in bulk for promotional, educational, or
business use. Please contact your local bookseller or the Macmillan Corporate
and Premium Sales Department at 1-800-221-7945, extension 5442, or by
e-mail at MacmillanSpecialMarkets@macmillan.com.

Seven Seas and the Seven Seas logo are trademarks of
Seven Seas Entertainment, LLC. All rights reserved.

ISBN: 978-1-626924-12-3
Printed in Canada
First Printing: November 2016
10 9 8 7 6 5 4 3 2 1

FOLLOW US ONLINE: **www.gomanga.com**

READING DIRECTIONS

This book reads from *right to left*, Japanese style.
If this is your first time reading manga, you start
reading from the top right panel on each page and
take it from there. If you get lost, just follow the
numbered diagram here. It may seem backwards at
first, but you'll get the hang of it! Have fun!!

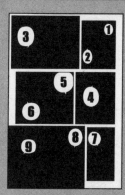

Re:Monster

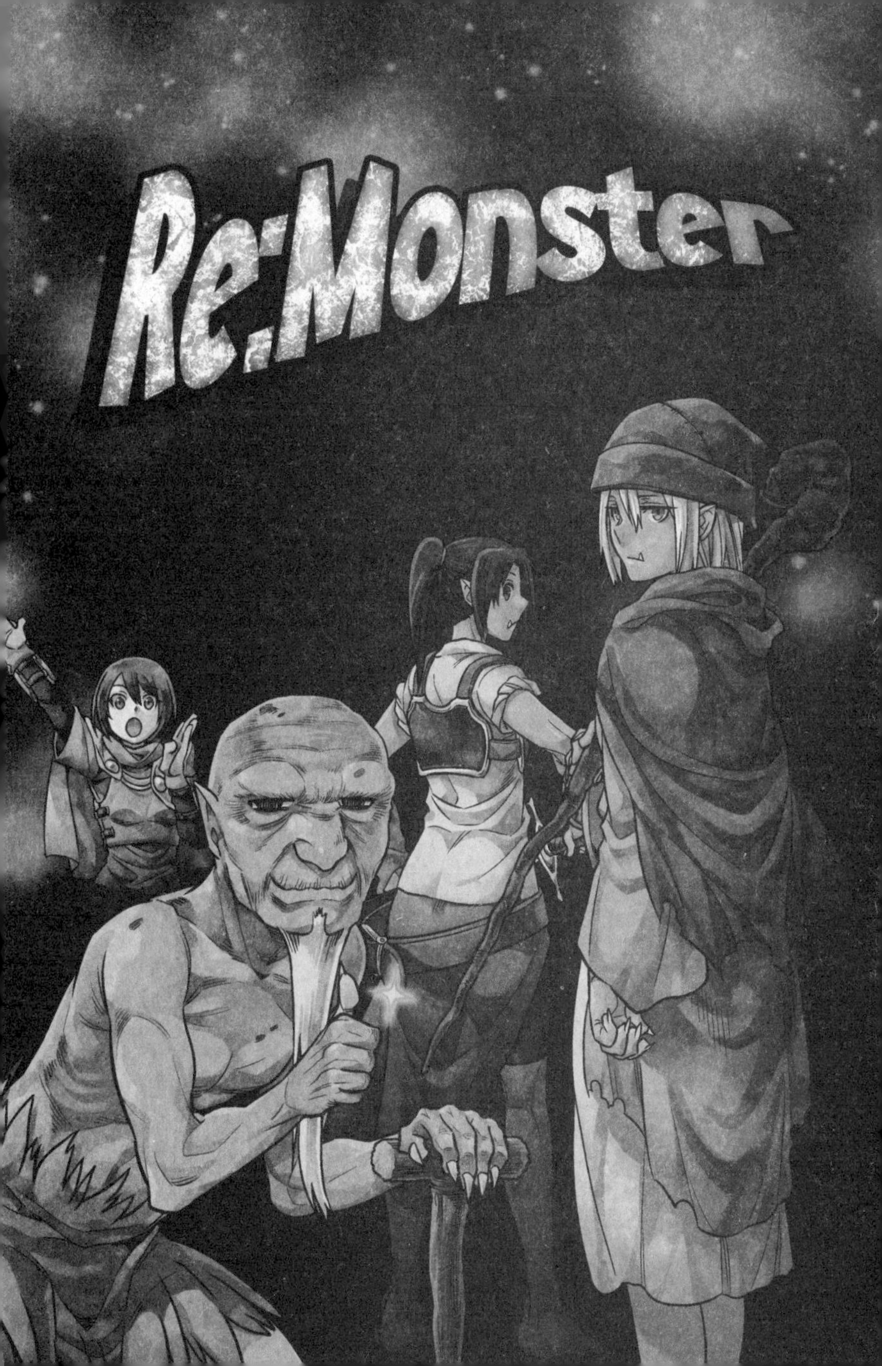
Re:Monster

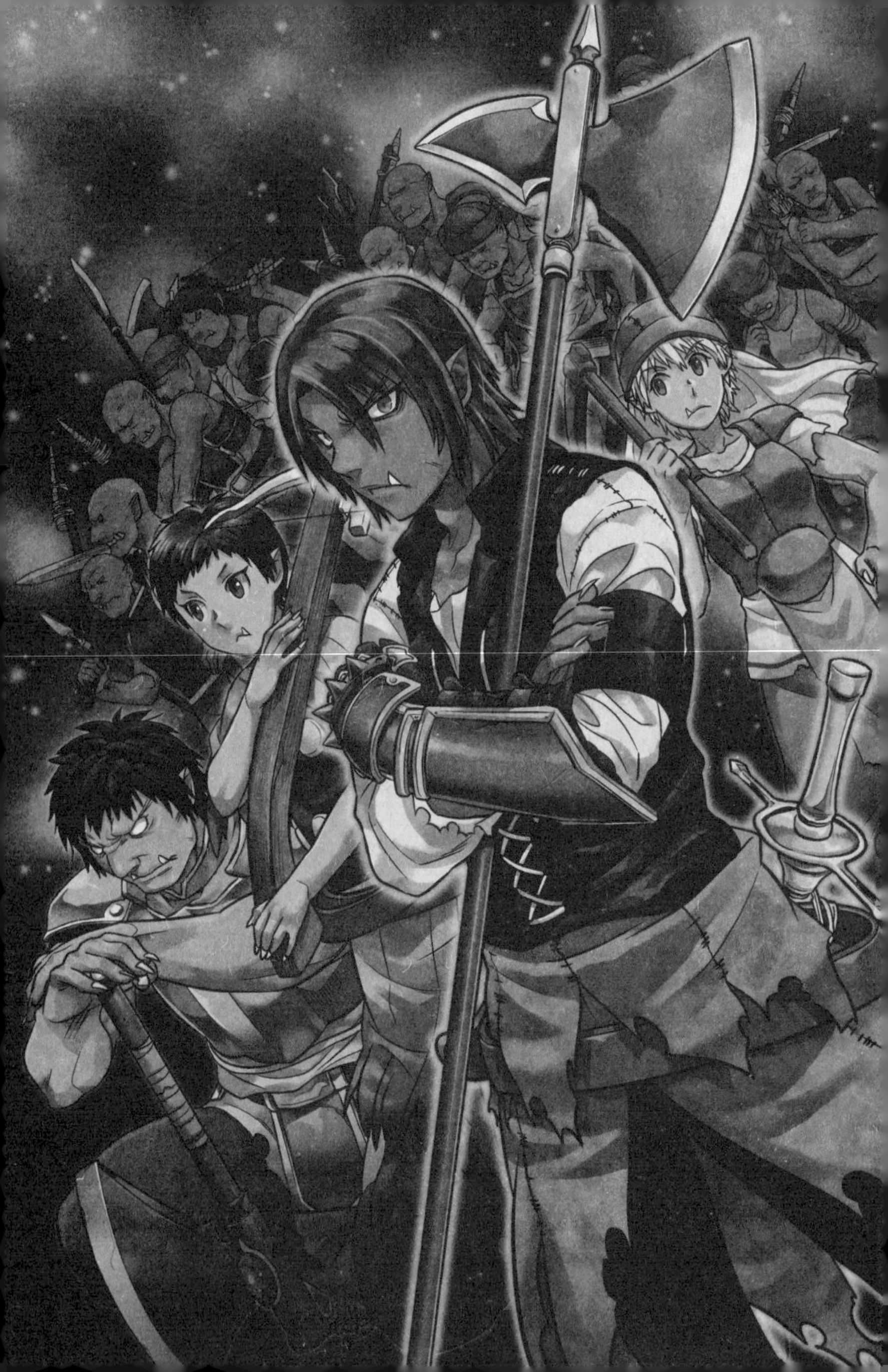

He's happy (honestly).